# THE ALL AMERICAN CHEESE AND WINE BOOK

## PAIRINGS, PROFILES & RECIPES

LAURA WERLIN

Photographs by Andy Ryan

STEWART, TABORI & CHANG

NEW YORK

TO MY MOTHER AND QUIET CO-AUTHOR, TO WHOM THIS
DEDICATION PALES IN COMPARISON TO HERS

Published in 2003 by
Stewart, Tabori & Chang
An imprint of Harry N. Abrams, Inc.

Library of Congress Cataloging-in-Publication Data
Werlin, Laura.
    All American cheese and wine book : pairings, profiles, and recipes / Laura Werlin ;
photographs by Andy Ryan.
        p. cm.
    Includes index.
    ISBN-13: 978-1-58479-124-9
    ISBN-10: 1-58479-124-1
1. Cheese—United States. 2. Cheese—Varieties—United States. 3. Wine and wine
    making—United States. 4. Cookery (Cheese) 5. Cookery (Wine) I. Title.
    SF274.U6W469 2003
    641.3'73—dc21

Printed and bound in China

10 9 8 7

HNA
harry n. abrams, inc.
a subsidiary of La Martinière Groupe
115 West 18th Street
New York, NY 10011
www.hnabooks.com

# CONTENTS

# ACKNOWLEDGMENTS

Over the past two years, I have had a world open up to me that I never could have imagined. My exploration of American cheese and American wine has meant the chance to meet people whose lives are often harried and difficult, and yet whose humanity dictates civility and patience. Their kindness and support have been essential to the writing of this book and, no less, to my well-being.

To my agent, Carole Bidnick, who knows no limits to helpfulness as a professional nor kindness as a friend. I can only shake my head in awe—and gratefulness. To my editor, Julie Stillman, who saw me through my first book and who had the stamina to do it again. She deserves an award. To Leslie Stoker, president and publisher at Stewart, Tabori & Chang, ditto. To the others at Stewart, Tabori & Chang: Caroline Enright, ace publicist and someone who maintains grace in the face of constant pressure and unreasonable author demands. To Jack Lamplough, director of publicity, whose incredulous reactions I can vividly recall when I now ponder having made those unreasonable demands. And to Beth Huseman, who turned odds and ends into a cohesive whole. I thank you all.

To my photographer, Andy Ryan, who delved into cheese and wine with curiosity and professionalism and emerged with a sensitivity that transformed his exquisite photos into beautiful stories. And to copy editor Maggie Carr, who was able to make order out of chaos more often than I care to admit.

A book about cheese and wine could not be written without the people who make these two products. When it came to exploring wine, I was a true neophyte. But the kindness of winemakers and wine organization administrators more than saw me through. First, my deepest appreciation to Jim Trezise of the New York Wine and Grape Foundation. He is that rare individual who will offer the shirt off his back and mean it. My visit to the Finger Lakes district of New York was made so very simple by him, and I will be forever grateful. My thanks also to the people at the Washington Wine Commission who helped guide me through the maze of emerging wineries in their state.

Equal thanks to winemakers Amy Wesselman of Westrey Winery in Oregon, who shuttled me over hill and dale in the Willamette Valley introducing me to some of the best vineyards in the state; Ken Wright of Ken Wright Cellars, who shared his passion for the land by carefully explaining the very basics of vineyard planting and management; Kay Mackey and Clay Simon of Chinook Winery in Prosser, Washington, who opened up their doors—and wine—to a stranger and invited me in for a home-cooked meal; Christophe Baron, who insisted I hobble over the stones that comprise his vineyards, and in so doing, learn why his Syrah is so darn good; Doug Fletcher, who generously gave me the crash course I needed in vine growth and management, leaving me to ponder why his wisdom has not been harnessed and standardized; and Bryan Babcock, whose patience with a fledgling wine journalist helped put me on the path toward writing this book.

The cheese world is at once so vast and yet so intimate, and thankfully, the people who comprise it are extraordinarily generous. To the people at Edelman Public Relations Worldwide in Chicago—Mia McWilliams, Stacey Duffy, Christy Dieckmann, Amanda Marcum, and the entire cheese team—who work tirelessly to give American cheese its deserved spotlight, I thank them for their help and for choosing me to be on their team. My thanks also to Dairy Management Incorporated and Kevin Burkham and Chris Moore for their help and support. And what would I do without the people at Context Marketing in Sausalito, California? Bob Kenney, Patricia Schneider, Lynne Devereux, Deneen Wohlford, and the entire Context group—there are no words. They are simply awesome. This is equally true for Nancy Fletcher of the California Milk Advisory Board. My thanks also to Serena Ball of the New England Dairy Promotion Board for her help with the Great Cheeses of New England. To Dee Harley of Harley Farms; Mariano Gonzales, Tom Butler, and John Fiscalini of Fiscalini Farms; and the Giacomini family at Point Reyes Farmstead Cheese Company—I will always remember their graciousness, hospitality, and willingness to show me the ropes.

To my dear friend, Lori Lyn Narlock, without whom neither my last book nor this book would have been possible. She endured countless hours of uninterrupted kvetching, and after all was said and done, still remained unwavering in her support and love. To Cheryl Gould, who once again proved to be an ace recipe tester and forever a friend, and to Cheryl Dobbins, who tested recipes with a dedication and expertise most cookbook authors merely dream of. To all my other friends, who once again tolerated my tendency to go underground for months at a time, surfacing long enough to apologize for not being around, and then burrowing once again. Their patience is limitless, and so too, is my gratitude.

And to my family: First, I must thank my father, whose vast email network has been more effective in author/daughter public relations than any hired firm could have been. To my sister, Andrea, whose diagnosis and struggle with breast cancer put my own struggles instantly in perspective, and whose courage has served as my model. She is my hero. To my mother, without whom this book could not have been written. Period. And to my husband, Artie, who is responsible for re-igniting my passion for cheese by exposing me to "real" cheese when we first met. Hopefully he isn't regretting that too much. I love you.

# INTRODUCTION

**WHAT MARVELOUS PRODUCTS FERMENTA-TION PROVIDES! THEY ARE STILL ALIVE WHEN THEY COME INTO THE KITCHEN AND FREE US FROM THE TYRANNY OF TIME.**
—Dominique Fournier, *The Magazine of the Slow Food Movement*

My earliest memories of uniting cheese with wine admittedly precede my legal drinking age. But a transfer from a southern California university to the University of California at Berkeley meant a sudden leap closer to the famed Napa Valley. Weekend jaunts to the wine country became de rigueur. The beauty of this extraordinary wine region was a needed aesthetic diversion from the usual fluorescent-lit environment in which we students dwelled. But most of all, after a short drive we entered a fantasy world where, at least for the day, we felt part of some privileged class.

Like all visitors to the wine country, my friends and I lounged in the shade of the oak trees and surrounded ourselves with fresh-baked bread, a bottle of chilled wine, a variety of splendid cheeses, and some seasonal fruit. It didn't take much to be contented by such fare, nor to be seduced by this glorious lifestyle, especially since even our meager student budgets could support it. But for me these visits were unquestionably more than escapes from academic toils. The marriage of cheese and wine instantly shook my world; from that time on, I knew that the twosome would forever play a major role in my life. And so they have.

At that time, some twenty years ago, the wines we selected for our wine country picnics were always local. A visit to Napa automatically meant purchasing Napa wines. Cheese, however, was a different matter. The choices were not extensive, and, with the exception of the cheeses made in nearby Sonoma by the Vella Cheese Company, Sonoma Cheese Factory, and a bit later, Laura Chenel, the cheeses one encountered at food stores were not made in this country. Although we were hardly deprived, we were limited.

Fast-forward to the 21st century, and a visit to the Oakville Grocery or Dean & Deluca—just a couple of the noteworthy food stores in the Napa Valley—reveals a spectacular selection of domestically-made cheeses. What a fantastic change! No longer do wine country visitors need to pair the local wines with imported cheese.

Today we are lucky to have a vast array of American-made artisan and specialty cheeses *and* wines available to us. As the crafts of cheesemaking and winemaking inch toward perfection, and as Americans sweep up these great domestic cheeses and wines, it seems appropriate to place these two American-made products within the covers of the same book. No question, Americans have an unadulterated passion for enjoying cheese and wine together. The combination is universal and ancient. It is the focus of still-life paintings and memorable meals. It is the stuff of great picnics.

Since I wrote *The New American Cheese* in 2000, a book that champions the wonderful cheeses being made in America and the people making them, I have been struck by the veritable flood of new domestic cheeses that are regularly introduced in this country. Where are these cheesemakers coming from, I've wondered? They are getting more skilled at their craft, more courageous in their difficult pursuit, and they are supplying the increasingly sophisticated American palate with fabulous-tasting cheese. One need only look at the trend in the membership of the American Cheese Society (ACS) for proof. In 1999 there were eighty-five cheesemaker members of the ACS; today there are over 150—an increase of nearly 100 percent. And certainly, there are many other cheesemakers who are not ACS members.

As for American wineries, they number in the thousands—about two thousand, last anybody counted. Wine is made in all fifty states, and almost every day a newcomer is added to the ranks of American winemakers. In New York alone, there are now 150 wineries. Compared to the paltry nineteen just twenty-five years ago, this is an extraordinary jump. Likewise, in Oregon there were five wineries in 1970; today the number has increased to about 180. Growth can also be seen in Washington, Texas, Virginia, Pennsylvania, Ohio, and several other states, including California, where one would think there could be no more wine growth. No question about it: An increase in the number of new wineries is a trend throughout the nation, even in states where winemaking might not seem to be such an obvious pursuit.

Places such as the Texas Hill Country, New York's Finger Lakes area, western Colorado, and Albuquerque, New Mexico, are just a few of the areas that are making wines that are all the more impressive because of the inherent difficulty in producing wines in those regional climates. After all, every year a Colorado winery takes a chance of losing its entire crop, because freezing comes all too easily to grapes grown at 5,800 feet. Humidity and hot temperatures can ruin a Texas grape crop in a New York minute. Nonetheless, winemakers in these states and every other state in America persevere and, in the process, contribute to the wide array of domestic wines that are available to American consumers.

In the states of Washington and Oregon, which are better known for their wines, winemakers are continuing to break new ground every day. They exhibit an infectious passion for their craft as well as pride in their region. Not only are the relatively new winemakers in these states working diligently to improve their own wines, they are looking toward the future

and working together to develop their areas as world-class wine-growing regions. There's no doubt that they have already made significant inroads. The Willamette Valley of Oregon—prime Pinot Noir–growing territory—and many parts of eastern Washington are, as one Washington winemaker proudly put it, "Grand Cru regions," referring to the finest of the French vineyards. The wines emerging from these places are proving that in spades. And it's all so new!

The practice of bringing cheese and wine together, as age-old and indisputably romantic as it is, is not quite as effortless as its long history might suggest. As two fermented agricultural products and as two distinctly different entities, cheese and wine can often bring out the worst in each other, rather than the intended best. In the course of writing this book I discovered, through numerous tastings, that many of the traditional ideas about pairing cheese and wine were simply outdated—and wrong. And then there were the extreme views.

During my research, I came upon a few wine professionals who were adamantly against the notion of combining cheese with wine—ever. Cheese ruins wine, they said. Period. While I disagree, this does underscore how subjective the notion of taste really is. What may taste syrupy to one person may taste merely sweet to another. What is bitter to someone may not be to someone else. And so it goes. Everyone perceives tastes and therefore flavors differently, proving there are no absolutes. In this book my goal is to guide you toward matches that are more likely to work than not; pairings that are proven more times than not; and, most important, toward building an understanding of both cheese and wine so that you can develop your own approach to pairing the two.

I bring to this book a deep understanding of and love for cheese as well as a passion for wine. Because I started this book project with a greater knowledge of cheese than of wine, I set out to close the gap, so that I could suggest helpful strategies for matching the two. I figured that many of the wine questions I had were ones that you might have too. So I have included chapters on the basics of wine, including how it is made, how to taste it, and varietal descriptions, among other things.

Then, instead of suggesting pairings centered on wine, I shifted the focus to cheese. So, in addition to learning all about the basics of cheese, you will be able to read about the seven principal styles of cheese, understand what they are and how they are made, and consequently be able to figure out the style(s) of wine that will go with different types of cheeses. This is a "cheese-centric" rather than wine-centric book, but it is equal parts cheese and wine education.

Equally important was the entire notion of pairing American-made cheeses exclusively with American wines. While it is nearly impossible to match regional cheeses with regional wines in this country—because most winemaking is concentrated in a few places, whereas cheesemaking is done all over—I was interested in drawing from the wide array of American-made wines to pair up with our American cheeses. The more fruit-forward yet amply acidic American wines are perfectly compatible with our cheeses.

Because we are talking about American wines, it is important to bear in mind the stylistic differences between American and European wines. For example, a Pinot Gris from Oregon is leaner and less floral than the same wine from Alsace. The Oregon wine is compatible with a fresh goat cheese, while the fruitier Alsatian wine is not. Another example of the many differences between American and European wines is American Dolcetto—it is often more full-bodied than its Italian counterpart. When it comes to pairing

cheese and wine, knowing the unique characteristics of American-made wines is helpful, which is why I provided descriptions of the most widely-grown varietals in America based on how those varietals are expressed in the vineyards and in the hands of American winemakers.

In addition to providing descriptions of so-called vinifera wines such as Chardonnay and Cabernet Sauvignon, I have also included a discussion of hybrid grapes. Here in the United States, we make wine in areas where the climate is inhospitable to vinifera. Hybrids, such as Vignoles and Seyval Blanc, have been developed to withstand these extreme conditions. While hybrids may not have the depth and complexity of vinifera—and because of that, are perceived as inferior to vinifera—they still make some very good wine. Best of all, they are wonderful companions to cheese.

Since pairing wine and cheese is hardly a science, I have explored various methods. First, I thought it might be important to taste the cheese first and then the wine. Then I realized that if I didn't know how the wine was supposed to taste, I couldn't possibly know how—or whether—the cheese affected the taste of the wine, and vice versa. So I opted to taste the wine, then the cheese, then the wine again. This method worked quite well.

My next challenge was to figure out how to go about tasting so many cheeses and so many wines. Should I try several cheeses with just one wine? Or should I try several wines with just one cheese? In the end, I tested pairings both ways, because I didn't find one method better than the other. Tasting Cabernet Sauvignon with seven different styles of cheese was just as enlightening as pairing a Brie with seven different styles of wine.

Although I sometimes did these pairings on my

own, I also enlisted the help of friends. I hosted cheese and wine gatherings in which I handed out worksheets and asked my friends to weigh in on the matches. What worked? what didn't? and why? This approach proved to be more enlightening than I might have imagined because it was in the course of gauging my friends' reactions that I saw that a cheese and wine combination that worked for one person might be unappealing to another. I wondered if I could make sense of this. In the end, the answer was a qualified yes, as you will see.

In attempting to understand more about food and wine compatibility I learned that it was important to pay attention to *all* the flavors in food—not just those in cheese and wine. Whenever I ate anything, no matter what it was, and especially when that food was accompanied by wine, I began to take mental notes about the flavors in the food I was eating. I also "listened" to the flavors I was detecting in the wine. I then tried to ascertain why the food and wine went together (or didn't). This may have been the most important exercise of all. The more I practiced, the more easily I could identify the various flavor components in the food and in the wine. In so doing I saw certain patterns emerge, which led to many of the suggested cheese and wine pairings that appear here.

The winemakers and cheesemakers whose stories I have told in this book appear here because they are, in various ways, contributing to the new profiles of American cheese and wine. In most cases, the winemakers are small producers, although their wines are usually available by mail order. There are some inherent complications related to shipping wine, and for that reason I have included information on wine shipping laws in the United States (see page 61). The cheesemakers, though also small, usually have regional distribution, and almost all of them are willing to mail their cheese directly anywhere in the country, weather permitting. (Some cheesemakers won't ship during the summer, when the heat can ruin their cheese.)

Finally, what would a cheese and wine book be without recipes? Since most of us think of cheese and wine as the twin gastronomic mainstays of home entertaining, I have provided recipes for just that purpose. What you will find to be different, though, is the section devoted to cheese plates. Here I have created simple but elegant recipes meant to go with a single cheese. The fennel currant marmalade goes beautifully with an Emmentaler; the cherry compote, with Gruyère. Each recipe is a lovely way to showcase just one cheese, to offer a cheese course that isn't too filling, and to celebrate cheese the way it is meant to be eaten: simple but exalted. Along with these recipes, I have suggested an appropriate wine or two as well. I have also included information on how to organize your own cheese and wine party.

Matching cheese with wine is neither science nor art. It is fun, and it is a great means of entertaining. Pick up a few cheeses, one or two wines, and you're on your way to a great party, picnic, or an intimate dinner for two. But if you want to take your experience to another level and really understand cheese and wine pairing, then the best way to do it is to taste, taste, taste.

Much has been written about cheese and wine created in other countries, but it is now time to shine the spotlight on American cheese and wine. They are exceptional, and the rest of the world is recognizing that too. So settle in, pour yourself a glass of wine, cut a slice or two of cheese, and enjoy the journey as you explore the magnificent cheeses and wines made in America.

# ALL ABOUT CHEESE

**HOW CHEESE IS MADE** It is nothing short of miraculous to watch an animal being milked, to then see that milk being whooshed into a vat, and to watch that milk become cheese. For milk to become cheese, it must be processed in a series of steps, each of which is painstakingly watched over by the cheesemaker. Decisions have to be made along the way. One wrong temperature, an incorrect amount of salt, an expired lot of rennet, not enough acidity, or innumerable other factors can ruin an entire batch of cheese. It is not surprising that fledgling cheesemakers usually throw away many more batches of cheeses than they sell. As intuitive as cheesemaking is, it is also a science that must be respected and understood.

## MINDING THE CURDS AND WHEY

After the milk has been obtained from the animal, the first of many decisions is made. Will the milk be pasteurized or not? If not, it goes immediately into the cheesemaking vat. If so, it will go into the pasteurizer first, where it is heated for fifteen seconds at 160°F and then immediately cooled. Following that step, the starter cultures are added to the milk. Not only do cultures add flavor, they also convert the enzyme lactase to lactic acid, thus raising the acidity of the milk. The acidity is crucial to the matting, or solidifying, of the curds.

Once the starter cultures have been added and the acidity of the milk reaches the desired level, the cheesemaker will then add the rennet, or coagulating enzyme. The type of rennet used is yet another decision the cheesemaker must make, as there are several choices: animal, vegetable, or microbial. The particular flavor and consistency the cheesemaker is looking for will usually determine which rennet is chosen. Other factors are weighed too. If the cheesemaker wishes to make a fully vegetarian product, then a vegetable-derived rennet is the usual choice. Some cheesemakers prefer the genetically engineered microbial rennet (technically vegetarian), because it acts like animal rennet, while others believe that animal-derived rennet confers the best flavor to their cheese.

After the rennet is added, the cheesemaker has to wait for the solids, or curds, to firm up. This can take anywhere from thirty minutes to an hour and a half—or longer. Then it is time to cut the curds. To do this, the cheesemaker uses a device, sometimes called a harp, that has very thin vertical wires and sometimes horizontal wires as well. This tool is deftly swept through the curds, causing them to break into small pieces and release the whey, or liquid. At this juncture, some of the whey might be released from the vat so that the curds can begin the process of drying out. Or, if a cheesemaker wants a high-moisture curd, all or part of the whey is retained, at least for a while.

Along the way, other decisions are made as well. Is it to be a cooked-curd cheese? a stirred curd cheese? a washed-curd cheese? Each of these styles necessitates different temperatures and procedures, and all will have different results. A cooked-curd cheese is one in which the curds are brought to a very high temperature. These high temperatures extract the greatest amount of whey, resulting in tighter and drier curds. The end results are semi-hard and hard cheeses.

A stirred-curd cheese entails a more gentle approach and is, as the phrase implies, a cheese that is made by the constant but gentle stirring of the curds. This action helps the development of curds while

**ABOVE:** Cheesemakers create goats' milk feta cheese at Lively Run Goat Dairy. **LEFT:** Harley Farms' fresh chèvre is decorated with edible flowers and aptly called Monet.

maintaining the proper acidity level. Many cheeses, from cheddar to certain blue cheeses, are made this way. A washed-curd cheese is one in which the acidity of the cheese is lower because the curds are literally washed with water. This rinsing action curtails the naturally rising acidity that happens as the curds form.

After the curds have been cut, the type of cheese being made will determine the ensuing steps. If it is a *pasta filata*, or stretched-curd cheese—such as mozzarella, Provolone, and the ultimate pasta filata, string cheese—the whey isn't drained right away. Instead,

These wheels of Parmesan cheese at Fiscalini Farms will be aged at least two years before they are sold.

the cheese is kept immersed in the hot whey and formed, often by hand, into the shape and size the cheesemaker wants. Otherwise, the whey is drained and either thrown out or fed to the animals on the farm. Sometimes the whey is used to make ricotta, which literally means "re-cooked." Ricotta originated as a natural by-product of mozzarella cheesemaking; it is considered re-cooked because the whey is heated again to a high temperature to form the new cheese. To make ricotta, vinegar (or citric acid) and salt are added to the whey, the mixture is heated to a very high temperature, and, ultimately, ricotta is created.

After the intended amount of whey has been drained and the curds are at the desired acidity level, the curds might be salted. Salting adds flavor and also stems the rising acidity. Again, whether or not the curds are salted at this point depends on the type of cheese being made. Some cheeses, such as Gouda, aren't salted until later, when they are immersed in a brine solution, while others, like Camembert, may be salted after they are formed.

Now it is time to form the cheeses. For this, the curds are scooped into hoops or molds for further drainage and shaping. That is, unless the cheese being made is cheddar. Cheddar, which is actually a verb referring to a type of cheesemaking process, is made differently. After the curds are cut, they are then left at the bottom of the vat, where they naturally mat together again, forming a sheet of curds. Those sheets are then stacked one on top of the other, resulting in further drainage of the whey, owing to the weight of the stacked sheets of curds. But this process also results in higher acidity, since the cheese's acidity level will continue to rise until it is stopped by the addition of salt.

After the proper acidity level has been reached, the cheesemaker will then take the sheets of curds, cut them into manageable blocks, and feed them through a mill that cuts the curds into tiny pieces. The curds are then salted and molded, and the cheesemaker follows the more standard cheesemaking procedures from there.

# BORDERS.

## Returns

Returns of merchandise purchased from a Borders, Borders Express or Waldenbooks retail store will be permitted only if presented in saleable condition accompanied by the original sales receipt or Borders gift receipt within the time periods specified below. Returns accompanied by the original sales receipt must be made within 30 days of purchase and the purchase price will be refunded in the same form as the original purchase. Returns accompanied by the original Borders gift receipt must be made within 60 days of purchase and the purchase price will be refunded in the form of a return gift card.

Exchanges of opened audio books, music, videos, video games, software and electronics will be permitted subject to the same time periods and receipt requirements as above and can be made for the same item only.

Periodicals, newspapers, comic books, food and drink, eBooks and other digital downloads, gift cards, return gift cards, items marked "non-returnable," "final sale" or the like and out-of-print, collectible or pre-owned items cannot be returned or exchanged.

Returns and exchanges to a Borders, Borders Express or Waldenbooks retail store of merchandise purchased from Borders.com may be permitted in certain circumstances. See Borders.com for details.

# BORDERS.

## Returns

Returns of merchandise purchased from a Borders, Borders Express or Waldenbooks retail store will be permitted only if presented in saleable condition accompanied by the original sales receipt or Borders gift receipt within the time periods specified below. Returns accompanied by the original sales receipt must be made within 30 days of purchase and the purchase price will be refunded in the same form as the original purchase. Returns accompanied by the original

**BORDERS.**

BORDERS
BOOKS AND MUSIC
34300 WOODWARD AVE
BIRMINGHAM MI 48009
248.203.0005

STORE: 0180    REG: 08/65  TRAN#: 0409
SALE          12/22/2010 EMP: 00175

GIFT RECEIPT

ALL AMER CHEESE & WINE BK
7132636   CL T           RKHB
                                 · RKHB

MICHIGAN 6%   TAX

12/22/2010 06:24PM

For returns within 60 days of
purchase accompanied by a Borders
Gift Receipt the purchase price
(after applicable discounts) will be
refunded via a gift card.

Once a cheese is scooped into molds, any number of things might happen. Cheese is always left to drain for some period of time, a longer period for a hard cheese and a shorter time for a soft or fresh cheese. The cheese is then turned and usually drained a while longer, maybe as much as a few days for a hard cheese. Next, in the case of fresh cheeses such as goat cheese, cottage cheese, fromage blanc, and mozzarella, the cheese is packaged and sold. Otherwise it might go into a saltwater brine for a few days before being aged, or it may go straight into the aging or ripening room.

## AGING CHEESE

It is at the ripening stage that a cheese can be elevated from a simple fermented milk product to a flavor and texture sensation. Indeed, in France only a few individuals have the exalted job of aging cheese. They are called *affineurs*, and they usually spend a lifetime perfecting their craft. A visit to one will usually reveal that he or she works in several different aging rooms—one for soft-ripening cheeses, one for washed-rind cheeses, one for harder mountain-style cheeses, and one for blue cheeses. In this country, we have not yet gotten to the point where we employ full-time affineurs, but that is just a matter of time. In the meantime, the cheesemaker is also the one who cares for the cheese during the aging process.

Aging a cheese requires a number of steps: For one, the cheese will almost always be turned regularly during the first few days of its being made, since it still has a good deal of whey in it and needs to drain. Turning the cheese helps distribute the whey evenly and expedites the evaporation process.

Perhaps the most crucial job in aging cheese, however, is tending to the rind. The rind is not a by-product of cheesemaking; it is the element that sets the stage for what the cheese will become. Take, for example, a Brie. This is a soft- or mold-ripened cheese (see page 27 for more on soft-ripened cheeses), which means that the mold contained in *and* on the cheese exists not only to flavor the cheese, but also to ripen or age it. Since the cheese softens from the outside in as it ages (think about the times you've seen a

Brie that has been creamy, almost translucent, just underneath the rind), it is called a soft-ripening cheese. In the case of these and all mold-ripened, natural-rind, or washed-rind cheeses, the cheesemaker must tend to the cheese, making sure the aging room has the proper temperature and humidity levels to foster the mold growth and therefore the proper aging of the cheese.

In the case of a washed-rind cheese (see page 28 for more on washed-rind cheeses), the cheesemaker (or affineur) will smear the cheese with a mixture of bacteria, water, and usually salt. These ingredients are what account for the aromatic and deeply flavorful components of a washed-rind cheese. If it is a natural-rind cheese, then the rind will develop naturally, just as the phrase implies. Natural rinds usually look a little crusty, possibly wrinkly, and sometimes hard. The air and natural bacteria in the cheese aging room as well as the bacteria and molds in the cheese come together to create this type of rind, although the cheesemaker still must turn the cheeses and check to

## CHEESEMAKING AT A GLANCE

1. Starter cultures are added to sour the milk. The cultures selected also determine some of the final flavors and texture of the cheese.
2. Rennet is added to curdle the milk and begin the process of separating the curds (solids) and the whey (liquid).
3. The curds are cut to expel the whey.
4. Some or most of the whey is drained off, depending on what type of cheese is being made.
5. The curds, which may or may not be salted at this point, are scooped into molds and left to drain further.
6. The handling of the cheese and the subsequent aging process proceeds, depending on the style of cheese being made. Fresh cheeses will be packaged and sent to market immediately; other types of cheese will be aged for varying amounts of time.

make sure they are not cracking. If there is surface cracking, the cheese might develop undesirable types of molds, including a blue mold. A cheesemaker can usually stave off cracking by applying oil, lard, or butter to the rind.

Another type of rind is the brushed rind. The cheesemaker will brush or wipe the rind on a regular basis to keep mold growth from occurring on the cheese. The end result is a smooth rind that may or may not be edible.

Cloth and wax, while very different, are two examples of inedible coverings that are used to age cheese. In the case of waxed-rind cheeses, the development of the cheese is purely anaerobic—that is to say, the aging process happens without air. Instead, the enzyme activity going on inside the cheese will ripen it. Many Goudas, cheddars, and several artisan cheeses have waxed rinds.

Cloth-bound cheeses, such as a few handcrafted cheddars now made in America, are not only beautiful, with their rustic, textural appearance; they also have unparalleled flavor. The cloth helps the cheese breathe, while at the same time protecting it throughout its extensive aging period. A cloth-wrapped cheese will often be aged for as long as two or three years. The end result is a cheese that doesn't have the typical "high notes" or sharp flavors that many American cheddars have; instead it is rounder, mellower, and more earthy. It's a marvel to behold and, even better, to taste.

The last form of "aging" is done with plastic. Again, some anaerobic activity will facilitate the aging of the cheese, but plastic will inhibit, if not stop, flavor development. Yet many fresh cheeses are packaged in plastic, as are many aged cheeses. Cheese is often wrapped in plastic to preserve it, although in the case of the aged cheeses, the plastic hampers the full development of flavor in the cheese.

Aged goats' milk cheeses are relatively rare in the United States, but these raw milk cheeses (Harvest Cheese from Hillman Farms), are aged for as long as seven months.

Wheels of newly made blue cheese at Point Reyes Farmstead Cheese Company in California begin the aging process in the curing room. This is where the distinctive blue veins begin to form.

Throughout the aging process, the cheesemaker is also mindful of how long he or she should age the cheese to bring it to its maximum flavor and texture. Remember that the more moisture that is left in the cheese, the softer it will be. A soft-ripened cheese may be aged for anywhere from ten days to two months, while a harder-style mountain cheese, such as Gruyère, might be aged for over a year. Semi-soft cheeses can be aged for a week or two, or they can be aged for six months. The longer a cheese is aged, the harder it will become. But also, with age comes flavor, which is why many small American cheesemakers find themselves in the difficult position of wanting to hold on to their cheeses for several months to optimize the flavor but at the same time needing to meet the demands of the market. Since cheese that is in the aging room is cheese that has not been paid for, it is all too tempting, not to mention understandable, for cheesemakers to end up selling the cheese before they would like to.

Once the cheese has aged for the desired time, it is wrapped and readied for market. What an amazing feat! Indeed, the next time you go to your local farmers' market or cheese shop, think about all the decisions, time, and hard work that went into creating the beautiful cheese you're buying. You will almost certainly have newfound respect for that piece of Emmentaler, that sliver of Camembert, or that crumble of blue cheese. What an irony it is that such tremendous effort has gone into something that brings all of us cheese aficionados such uncomplicated, simple pleasure. How lucky we are.

## TASTING CHEESE

I don't know about you, but I certainly did not grow up with an array of cheeses on the table. Any cheese I had was usually sandwiched between two slices of bread or on top of a hamburger, not a stand-alone food. Consequently, I did not learn to taste cheese on its own until I was old enough to seek out cheeses and enjoy them just as they were. But even then, the vocabulary of cheese was just as foreign to me as were most of the imported cheeses I was eating at the time.

Today we're eating American cheeses that are not only as good as or better than the imports, but their names are also easier to pronounce. And, as we begin to eat cheese all by itself, we are naturally becoming familiar with the language of cheese. No longer do we just ooh and ahh when we taste a cheese we like; we are now taking it a step further and attaching words like "creamy," "tangy," "earthy," "nutty," and the like, to describe our experience.

But to taste cheese properly, we need to know a little something about *how* to taste it. First, there is a difference between taste and flavor. Taste applies to the taste buds or receptors we have throughout our tongue, the back of our throat, and in our nose. We actually taste with the entire area, although sometimes we don't recognize just how important our sense of smell is to our sense of taste. Flavor is the end result of what our taste buds tell us. If our taste buds say "sour," we will say the food has a sour flavor. It is the same if the food we're tasting is bitter, salty, or sweet.

The best way to really taste cheese and therefore determine its flavor is to draw on as many sense receptors as we can, including those in the nasal cavity. You can do this very simply: Take a bite of cheese, hold your nose, swallow the cheese, and then un-pinch your nose and breathe out through your nostrils. You will find that the flavors of the cheese are much more pronounced because you've utilized *all* of your "taste" receptors rather than only those confined to your tongue. Not only that, you've maximized your enjoyment of the cheese by allowing it to literally fill your senses.

As for the vocabulary of cheese, it can be embraced or discarded, just as with that for wine. Sometimes, though, the words are useful because they help deepen your understanding of cheese. If you find a particular type of cheese chalky, for instance, and you decide you don't like the tactile sensation or mouthfeel of a chalky cheese, then you can more easily remember to avoid that type of cheese. If, on the other hand, you have discovered a buttery cheese and you enjoy it, you'll probably begin to look for other cheeses with that buttery flavor. By being able to attach the word "buttery" to that cheese, you can then ask your cheesemonger for other "buttery" cheeses.

The way you go about tasting cheese for evaluative purposes is simple. The main components to pay attention to are the aroma, texture, and appearance of the cheese. Of course, flavor is important too, but we'll get to that in a moment.

## AROMA

The way a cheese smells can be thoroughly enticing or utterly dreadful, depending on who is smelling the cheese (as well as on the condition of the cheese). Hopefully, you won't run across an offensive cheese too often, but if a cheese smells bad it could be because it has simply gone bad, or it might be that the strength of its aroma is downright repugnant to you. That's perfectly fine, especially since by judging the cheese by its smell, you are allowing your sense of smell to guide you.

Determining whether or not the aroma is appropriate for the particular type of cheese you're examining is a little more tricky. You've probably wondered whether a cheese is "stinky" because it is *supposed* to be that way or because it's a good cheese gone bad. Although there is no fail-safe method to make this determination, you can probably come close by doing one of two things: ask the cheese vendor or, if that is not possible, look at the other characteristics of the cheese, including the texture and appearance. If either or both of these seem compromised, then that strong aroma you're picking up from the cheese is probably there because the cheese has passed its prime.

## TEXTURE

Not only is texture the primary window into the style and health of the cheese; it also tells us how we will physically taste the cheese. If the cheese is semi-hard, then we will have to chew it a little longer and wait for the flavor components to emerge. A soft cheese, on the other hand, will likely coat the mouth and the flavors will be obvious a little sooner. In both cases, the mouthfeel is important because it will affect how you perceive the cheese and, ultimately, whether or not you like it.

## APPEARANCE

The way a cheese looks has a lot to do with how it tastes. Even though you don't literally eat with your eyes, your visual perception of a food definitely has an impact on your enjoyment of it. Therefore, if a cheese is uniform, fresh-looking, and in the style you were

## A RAW DEAL?

**Cheesemaking in America is at a crossroads.** It is developing faster and better than it has in our short history, but it is hitting a few roadblocks along the way. The most significant of these is a move by Codex Alimentarius, a division of the World Health Organization charged with setting standards for international food safety, to stop production of all raw, or unpasteurized milk, cheeses. This prohibition would affect not only domestic cheesemaking, but all imported cheeses. Why ban raw milk cheeses? The current law, which was enacted after World War II, states that a raw milk cheese must be aged a minimum of two months (sixty days) at a temperature of at least 35°F. It is believed that any or all harmful bacteria that are present in the raw milk will dissipate within that two-month period. So far, that theory has been borne out, although some studies have suggested that *E. coli* 0157:H7 could survive the sixty-day aging period, as could salmonella and listeriosis. Significantly, however, the majority of cheese-related illnesses in the United States have been traced to the mishandling of cheese—not the fact that raw milk was used.

The concern gets down to one big "what-if": What if there were a case of cheese contamination traced to raw milk? The natural follow-up question would be, "Could the problem have been avoided had the milk been pasteurized?" Answering the latter question is something the government is trying to avoid. If Codex Alimentarius is successful in stopping the production of raw milk cheese, consumers and cheesemakers will pay a great price.

Many cheesemakers could not afford the costs entailed in making the transition from raw to pasteurized milk cheeses. It isn't so much the cost of a pasteurizer that would be prohibitive as the time that the cheesemakers would have to spend trying to replicate the flavors lost through pasteurization. The natural bacteria found in raw milk would, by definition, be wiped out of the milk during pasteurization, and along with it would go much of the flavor the cheesemaker

had been at such pains to develop in the first place. Re-creating that flavor would be at best challenging, at worst impossible. Either way, the transition would mean losing several batches of cheese and, with an aged cheese, several months or even years. The lost time would spell economic disaster for many cheesemakers.

The consumer stands to lose because the diversity of cheeses we now enjoy would be seriously diminished were all cheeses required to be made with pasteurized milk. A raw milk cheddar and a pasteurized milk cheddar taste very different. Both are good, but we would no longer have a choice between the two should these regulations take effect. This ban would also affect all imported raw milk cheeses, such as Parmigiano-Reggiano and Gruyère, which have been made with raw milk since they were first developed.

Fortunately, we do have a safety model we can follow—many cheesemakers already do—which could be an excellent alternative to banning raw milk cheeses. It is called Hazard Analysis and Critical Control Point (HACCP), and it is a technique for monitoring the various points along the way in cheesemaking (and other food processing) where potential hazards exist. By closely documenting everything from milk temperatures to outside temperatures on the day the cheese is made, cheesemakers not only know exactly what's happening at each step of the process; they can also refer back to the data later, if need be.

The bottom line is why outlaw a food that, overall, has an impeccable health record? Unpastuerized milk is not dirty milk, but somehow those who are attempting to outlaw it are trying hard to make us think so. Responsible cheesemaking is the key, and since that's something that is already done (think of how many disease outbreaks there would be if cheesemaking were truly unsanitary or if raw milk was indeed the health hazard we've been led to believe?), a program like HACCP, although more work for the cheesemakers, seems like an excellent trade-off to the mostly unwarranted concern that is leading to the possible ban on raw milk cheese.

Sweet Grass Dairy's
Georgia Gouda.

expecting, the chances of it being the right cheese for you are obviously much greater. If it is slimy, moldy, or cracked and dried, then it's probably over the hill. You should always select a cheese based, at least partly, on how it looks. If it is wrapped in foil or obscured by a label, ask your cheesemonger to "unveil" it for you. That way you'll get the chance to look at the cheese and, no less important, smell it, to help you make your final decision. In addition, a cheese's appearance will tell you about its freshness. Don't compromise when buying cheese!

### FLAVOR

Flavor in cheese, of course, is ultimately what matters to all of us. But the way to learn to appreciate flavor, as well as the other components of tasting cheese, is by "listening" for them as you taste. You may find the following guidelines helpful:

◆ Always taste cheese at room temperature. If the cheese is too cold, its flavors will be muted and you will not be able to discern its nuances.

◆ If your only choice is to taste cold cheese, break off a small bit and rub it between your thumb and forefinger to warm it up.

◆ Try to avoid tasting the cut surface of a cheese that has been wrapped in plastic. If you're buying cheese, ask the cheesemonger to shave off the part that has been against the plastic and cut you a fresh piece, untouched by plastic.

◆ Once you put a piece of cheese in your mouth, chew carefully, breathe through your nose and mouth, and pay attention to the various sensations as the cheese passes through your mouth. It might taste salty; it might be creamy; it might be crumbly; it could taste strong; or it could be dry. How does it seem to you, and most important, do you like it? Either way, try to determine what it is you like (or don't like), and proceed from there.

◆ Since cheeses differ in texture, learn to pay attention to the types of texture you most enjoy. If you like super-hard cheeses, then taste a variety of them. With time you will see how, even within the same category, cheeses differ in flavor, especially when it comes to saltiness. Also, cheeses made with different milks will have distinct flavor characteristics.

◆ Pay particular attention to aroma. How a cheese smells influences how you will taste it. In addition, as you begin to notice the many aromas of cheese, you will begin to home in on your favorites.

- Taste cheeses within the same category to learn the nuances that differentiate similar cheeses. If you are tasting a variety of cheeses that come from different milk sources and are of varying textures, you might enjoy yourself, but you won't learn as much as if you take a more focused approach. Instead, stick to cheeses within the same category based on texture—semi-soft, semi-hard, hard, and so forth—or flavor—cheddar cheese, blue cheese, and so forth. The American Dairy Association calls this type of tasting a "cheese flight." This approach makes eminent sense when it comes to enjoying and learning about cheese.

- When you're really focusing on tasting cheese for educational purposes, drink regular or sparkling water alongside—nothing else. Of course, if you're having a cheese and wine tasting or some type of cheese-centered get-together, then serve what you like.

You may be saying that the very idea of "thinking" about what you're tasting takes away the fun of it. To some degree, that may be true, but concentrating on your experience can lead you to an even greater enjoyment too. Equally important, understanding cheese more thoroughly will definitely guide you toward some great wine accompaniments for that cheese. Here's how.

- As you taste cheeses, you'll see, for example, how the fresh cheeses share certain characteristics, such as acidity and slight sweetness, and from there you can begin to seek out similar wines.

- As your familiarity with different cheeses increases, your ability to choose accompanying wines will increase too. That semi-hard, nutty, and fruity Gruyère that you now know so well may remind you of that semi-dry Riesling you've been holding on to for a while. Now, you think, it's time to uncork it because you're pretty sure, with its apple and peach flavors balanced by fairly high acidity, that the wine will taste just fine alongside that wonderful Gruyère.

- The actual methods you use to taste cheese come in handy when it comes to tasting wine, too. See more on tasting wine on page 51.

Learning how to taste cheese is a useful technique for increasing your pleasure. Taking the time to pay attention to the taste of cheese, or any food or wine you're trying, heightens your enjoyment and your appreciation of it. The payoff of such "slow" tasting is a greater understanding of the food you're trying. If you would like to take cheese tasting a step further and have on hand a supply of descriptors to use when you've just eaten that perfect slice of cheese, you may want to draw upon the chart on page 82 and start naming your cheeses with complete and total abandon.

In the chart, you will note that certain words are repeated in different categories and that, in some cases, a word that appears in the "Not-So-Good" category will also appear in the list of favorable descriptors. In fact, a feature that may be good for one type of cheese may be a flaw in another. If, for example, a cheddar cheese has Swiss cheese–like holes, its so-called open texture is considered a flaw. On the other hand, if a Swiss cheese has holes, then that open texture is desirable and therefore considered favorable. These are basic guidelines. Feel free to create your own vocabulary, or none at all.

# TASTING CUES

## MOUTHFEEL TERMS

- Buttery
- Chalky
- Chewy
- Crumbly
- Dense
- Grainy
- Hard
- Pasty
- Silky
- Smooth
- Soft
- Toothsome
- Velvety
- Waxy

## NOT-SO-GOOD MOUTHFEEL TERMS

- Acidic
- Chalky
- Coarse
- Curdy
- Gummy
- Porous
- Rubbery
- Runny
- Supple

## TEXTURE AND/OR APPEARANCE

- Cloth-wrapped
- Cracked
- Crumbly
- Fresh-looking veiny
- Natural rind
- Open
- Plastic-wrapped
- Runny
- Smooth
- Solid
- Vacuum-sealed
- Veiny
- Wax or paraffin rind
- Well-shaped

## NOT-SO-GOOD TEXTURE AND/OR APPEARANCE

- Dried out
- Dull
- Huffed *(the cheese is swollen because of gas fermentation, and its shape has gone from flat to oval)*
- Ill-shaped
- Lopsided
- Moldy
- Mottled
- Off-color
- Oily
- Open
- Pale
- Rind rot
- Rust-colored *(soft-ripened cheeses)*
- Saggy
- Transparent
- Unnatural color
- Unappetizing

## FLAVORS

- Acidic
- Balanced
- Butterscotch
- Buttery
- Clean
- Citrusy
- Coconut
- Coffee
- Creamy
- Delicate
- Earthy
- Farmlike
- Fresh milk
- Fruity
- Grainy
- Grassy
- Herbacious
- Herb spice-flavored
- Lemony
- Musty
- Nutty
- Peppery
- Pungent
- Rich
- Robust
- Rustic
- Salty
- Savory (umami)
- Sharp
- Smoky
- Springlike
- Strong
- Sweet
- Wine-cured

## NOT-SO-GOOD FLAVORS

- Acidic
- Ammoniated
- Burning
- Bitter
- Cowy
- Fermented
- Flat
- Goaty
- Grainy
- Lanolin
- Muttonlike
- Oily
- One-dimensional
- Oniony
- Overpowering
- Overripe
- Plastic wrap
- Pungent
- Rancid
- Sharp
- Soapy
- Sour
- Sulfurous
- Vegetal
- Watery
- Weedy
- Yeasty

## AROMAS

- Coconut
- Earthy
- Floral
- Fresh
- Fresh milk
- Fruity
- Musty
- Pineapply
- Pungent
- Sweet

## NOT-SO-GOOD AROMAS

- Acrid
- Ammoniated
- Barnyardy
- Cowy
- Goaty
- Lanolin
- Overpowering
- Pungent
- Sour milk
- Subtle

## THE SEVEN STYLES
## OF CHEESE

Although we tend to describe cheese in terms of its flavor, the fact is we don't always know how it tastes until we sample it. But what if we're not in a place where we can taste the cheese before buying it? How can we know if we are going to like it? The texture of a cheese will tell you almost everything you need to know about most cheeses without even tasting them. If a cheese is hard, then you can bet it will be fairly salty; if it is a fresh cheese, then it will likely taste like the fresh milk from which it has been made; and so on. The one exception is blue cheese. You will at least have a clue, just by looking, as to the dominant flavors in a blue cheese because you can see the blue veins. That is a telltale sign of the cheese's flavor. However, understanding texture also helps provide clues to a blue cheese's flavor too.

Seven primary types of cheese are outlined in the following pages. Once you understand texture, you'll be way ahead when trying to determine the type of cheese you're in the mood for and the type of wine that will go best with it.

### FRESH OR SOFT CHEESES

The soft or fresh category is defined as cheeses that are unripened, or not aged. Instead of spending time on the aging shelves, these cheeses are sold within a couple of days when they are made. The shelf life of fresh cheeses is much shorter than that of other cheeses, and their texture is sometimes "soupy" owing to the higher amount of whey. Because of the cheesemaking process for this type of cheese, the whey, or liquid part, has not had time to evaporate, or it may be left in deliberately. Some cheeses in the fresh cheese category have a harder texture, but they are considered fresh cheeses because they are not allowed to ripen. Fresh cheeses include cottage cheese, goat cheese, fromage blanc, feta, ricotta, mozzarella, mascarpone, and many others.

While fresh cheeses have their freshness in common, they still differ tremendously. Mozzarella, for example, falls into the category of pasta filata, or stretched-curd cheeses. In addition to being more solid than, say, cottage cheese, pasta filata is made differently. The curds are literally stretched while they are warm, and ultimately they are formed into balls or other shapes. (Mexican-style Oaxaca cheese, for example, is braided.) Stretching the curds causes the cheese to be slightly stringy or layered, which is why, when you cut open a whole mozzarella, you will find it "peels" in strips.

Ricotta cheese, on the other hand, has a very soft, creamy texture. It is traditionally made from the whey that is left over from cheesemaking (often as a mozzarella by-product). When you see "whole milk ricotta," that means that some or all of the ricotta has been made with whole milk and is not the by-product of another cheese.

Fresh goat cheese, or chèvre, which is similar in texture to ricotta, is usually made over the course of three days. The first day, the milk is coagulated and then scooped into molds or cheesecloth to drain. The next day, the curds continue to drain and are salted. On the third day the cheese is packaged. The natural acidity of goats' milk is relatively high. When the milk is turned into a fresh cheese, its acidity makes for a tangy flavor.

Some great examples of fresh chèvres made in this country are ones made by Port Madison Farm in Washington and Lively Run Goat Dairy in New York. Both are snow-white, mild, and ever so creamy. The cows' milk feta made by Bel Fiore in California is noteworthy, as is Vermont Butter & Cheese's goats'

As its name, Acapella, implies, this beautiful soft-ripened goats' milk cheese, made by Andante Dairy, needs no accompaniment.

Feta cheese curds are relatively dry and crumbly.

milk feta. And some of the best ricotta in this country comes from Sweet Grass Dairy in Georgia and Bellwether Farms in California. Both cheesemakers use superior Jersey milk. Bellwether Farms also makes a wonderful sheep's milk ricotta.

Because of their mild and creamy nature, fresh cheeses are often used for cooking. Some of them make a nice addition to a cheese course. A dollop of fresh goat cheese is refreshing and has enough flavor that it needs little or no accompaniment, while mozzarella, though mild, can create the perfect starting point on a plate of cheeses.

## SEMI-SOFT CHEESES

If you've ever had to use a spoon to eat a cheese that, by all rights, should require a knife, then you know what a semi-soft cheese is. "Creamy," "liquidy," "milky," and "delectable" are adjectives that come to mind when describing semi-soft cheese, but so too do words like "fresh milk," "tangy," "floral," and even "nutty." The semi-soft category of cheeses includes a broad spectrum of cheeses, from the well-known runny California Teleme to a firmer-style high-moisture Monterey Jack or Colby cheese.

Semi-soft cheeses such as Teleme and Crescenza are made in such a way that the curds remain large and therefore retain a lot of the whey, or liquid. This creates a higher moisture cheese. Semi-soft cheeses are not made to age for a long time, and they're usually rindless. The starter cultures used by the cheesemaker also contribute to the creamier consistency of the cheese. This softer style of semi-soft cheese has a fairly short shelf life—about ten days to three weeks.

Other cheeses that qualify as semi-soft, such as certain styles of Monterey Jack and Colby, are made similarly, but the cheesemaker draws out more of the

whey in the process and the result is a slightly harder cheese. Either way, these cheeses have a fresh quality but maintain distinctive flavors based on the cultures, rennet, and cheesemaking method used. Their flavors can be described in varying ways, including sharp, nutty, fruity, salty, slightly bitter, creamy, pungent, and milky. In addition to Monterey Jack and Colby, other semi-soft cheeses are some forms of Gouda, Havarti, brick, Fontina, Provolone, American Muenster, Gorgonzola, and many others. Most of these cheeses can be made from all three types of milk.

Americans are probably most familiar with the semi-soft category of cheeses that are produced in factories at the rate of millions of pounds each year and predominate on supermarket shelves. Nevertheless, American artisan cheesemakers have created many of their own flavorful and distinctive versions of these cheeses. Among these is Vermont-made Crowley cheese. Crowley is similar to Colby although, according to its makers, it predates the invention of Wisconsin Colby by a few years, having been created in the 1880s. This raw milk cheese is aged from two months to over one year (and therefore crosses into different categories of cheese, from semi-soft to hard) and develops more and more flavor along the way.

There are, of course, many goats' and sheep's milk cheeses that fall under the semi-soft category as well. Virginia's Meadow Creek Dairy's Appalachian

Jack straddles the line between semi-soft and semi-hard, and Laura Chenel's goats' milk Tomme is smooth and semi-soft—a perfect vehicle for capturing the flavor of goats' milk.

## SOFT-RIPENED CHEESES

"Soft-ripened" means that the cheese gets softer and creamier as it ripens, and that the softness starts on the outside of the cheese and slowly makes its way inward. That's why soft-ripening, or so-called mold-ripened cheeses—the most famous being Brie and Camembert—begin to ooze just under the rind as they ripen. Eventually, that creaminess makes its way toward the interior, or paste, of the cheese.

Besides ripening from the outside in, a soft-ripening cheese is distinguished by its white, so-called "bloomy" rind. The rind is created either through the use of a special mold, usually *Penicillium candidum*, which is added to the milk used to make the cheese, or by spraying the mold onto the cheese after it's been formed; or sometimes the mold is incorporated in both ways. Once the mold and air interact, the rind turns into a fluffy, downy-like surface. There is a striking contrast between the white exterior and the golden interior of the cheese (that is, if it's a cows' milk cheese; the paste of goats' and sheep's milk soft-ripened cheeses is whiter in color). But the visual contrast is not the only noteworthy phenomenon; bloomy rinds also have distinct flavors all their own, owing to the bacteria used to create them.

The flavors of soft-ripened cheese, paste and rind combined, are often likened to mushrooms and sometimes to garlic. These accents are certainly an authentic Camembert's distinguishing features. Soft-ripened cheeses can also be buttery, fruity, salty, and even tangy—the flavor depends on the milk with which the cheese has been made. In America we're fortunate to have soft-ripened cheeses made from the milk of cows, goats, and sheep. Some of these cheeses

have cream added to the milk, turning them into a rich, buttery, decadent, and delightful indulgence. These cheeses are commonly known as double- or triple-crèmes, depending on how much cream has been added. If the butterfat content is between 60 and 70 percent the cheese is considered a double-crème; if

Andante Dairy specializes in soft-ripened cheese. This cheese, called Rondo, is enhanced by a sprinkling of herbes de Provence and pink peppercorns.

it is over 70 percent it is a triple-crème.

In the United States a variety of domestic soft-ripened cheeses is available, including Old Chatham Sheepherding Company's unparalleled Hudson Valley Camembert, made with a combination of cows' and sheep's milk; the same company's Shepherd's Wheel, which is made entirely from sheep's milk; Cypress Grove's classic Humboldt Fog, made with goats' milk; Marin French Cheese Company's soul-satisfying triple crème; and Andante Dairy's combination cows' and goats' milk cheese called Melange.

Soft-ripening cheeses are equally serviceable in the kitchen, on a cheese board, or served as part of a picnic. Think of trying them melted in polenta, or as the star ingredient in a fruit and cheese turnover, or sandwiched in between slices of a French roll with a slathering of honey-rhubarb compote.

## WASHED-RIND CHEESES

Washed-rind cheeses are unfortunately the most underrepresented category among cheeses made in America. Their aromatic and sometimes downright stinky nature has made them scary prospects for many American consumers. Given the pejorative manner in which they are described—smelling like "old socks" or a "barnyard floor"—it's no wonder that a lot of us haven't embraced these cheeses in quite the same way we have all the others. But, oh, are they good!

You may be familiar with some European washed-rind cheeses, such as Taleggio from Italy and Reblochon and Munster from France. *Munster*, which hails from the Alsace region, is entirely different from American *Muenster*, which is not only spelled differently but is as mild as a true Munster is strong. The European washed-rind cheeses sport a pinkish-orange or sometimes tan-colored rind and get increasingly runny—and flavorful—with age.

Washed-rind cheeses get their name from the process used to treat their rinds. The rinds are smeared or washed with a solution made up of *Brevibacterium linens* (or B. linens for short), salt, and water during the ripening process. The cheeses are aged in a humid environment, which facilitates the proliferation of the B. linens and keeps the cheeses moist so they don't crack as they ripen. The B. linens ripens the cheeses as well as facilitates the development of their characteristic aromas. Like soft-ripened cheese, washed-rind cheese ripens from the outside in, but instead of being mold-ripened it is bacteria-ripened.

Once a cheesemaker introduces B. linens into the aging room, he or she is instantly carving out a unique environment—and flavor—for the cheese. Every aging room develops its own microflora, which eventually imparts unique qualities to the cheese. To keep the cheese from becoming too aromatic, the rind is often washed with water after the B. linens has been introduced.

You may be wondering why anyone would intentionally seek out such smelly cheeses. One word: flavor. First of all, these cheeses are not usually as strong-tasting as they are aromatic, although they do have lots of flavor. The flavor can be like just-toasted hazelnuts combined with roasted mushrooms and a touch of fruit. These cheeses can also have gamy or barnyardy flavors, particularly the ones that are made with goats' milk. This is not an offensive quality—just a distinguishing characteristic. The usually soft nature of washed-rind cheeses adds a creamy component that makes them irresistible. That same creaminess also works well in cooking. Try a washed-rind cheese in a fondue—its flavor is strong and satisfying.

American washed-rind cheeses tend to be made in a somewhat harder style than the European ones, primarily because the softer varieties are extremely difficult to make. Cheesemakers here are just learning how to make washed-rind cheeses, although there are a few wonderful ones. Judy Schad of Capriole, in

A mixture of *Brevibacterium*, salt, and water smeared on the outside of a washed-rind cheese creates stronger aromas and flavors.

Indiana, makes a washed-rind goats' milk cheese called Mont St. Francis (it is an American Cheese Society blue ribbon–award winner). Another noteworthy washed-rind cheese now being made in America with goats' milk is called Gray's Chapel, by Goat Lady Dairy in Climax, North Carolina and Cowgirl Creamery in Point Reyes, California, makes a fantastic triple-crème washed-rind cheese called Red Hawk. Bingham Hill Cheese Company in Fort Collins, Colorado, makes two incredible washed-rind cheeses called Harvest Moon and Angel Feat. The latter is made with sheep's milk and is a blue ribbon award winner.

## SEMI-HARD CHEESES

Talking about semi-hard cheeses in relation to semi-soft ones may seem like more a question of attitude rather than fact. Is the cheese half-hard or half-soft? The distinction comes down to the amount of moisture in the cheese. A semi-soft cheese has more moisture than does a semi-hard one, owing to the way each type of cheese is made. As a result semi-hard cheese, as the name would imply, is harder than its semi-soft cousin because, given the process used to create it, the cheese is more solid than liquid and it is aged longer.

The curds of these cheeses are cooked, washed, or cheddared—all processes that leach out the liquid (whey); the curds are generally cut much smaller, again a method that serves to expel more whey; the curds are pressed; then, once they are scooped into their molds, they are drained for a longer period of time. The longer aging time translates to more moisture loss, which creates a harder consistency. Cheeses that fall into the semi-hard category include Gruyère, many cheddars, Swiss, some Colbys, Crowley cheese (from Vermont), Major Farm's Vermont Shepherd, Upland Cheese Company's Pleasant Ridge Reserve, and many other wonderful American artisan cheeses. Semi-hard cheeses might have natural rinds, brushed rinds, cloth rinds, or no rind, if they are waxed. Their texture is, of course, firm but not solid; semi-hard cheese bends but does not break.

This class of cheeses is quite diverse and often wonderfully complex. It is hard to find a boring cheese in the semi-hard family because of the time these cheeses spend in the aging room, the starter cultures that are used to ensure the slow development of flavor, and the usually high temperatures at which the curds are cooked, among other things. Adjectives such as "nutty," "earthy," "sharp," and "fruity" are often conjured up by semi-hard cheeses. Sometimes semi-hard cheeses are downright meaty or chewy, or they might gravitate toward dessert, with distinct caramel flavors. These cheeses range from mild to strong and are positively magnificent on their own and equally good cooked. The classic cheese fondue is made with

Cheesemaker Mariano Gonzalez of Fiscalini Farms in Modesto, California, holds a wheel of his award-winning bandage-wrapped cheddar. The sixty-pound wheel is aged a minimum of eighteen months.

this category of cheeses (Gruyère or Emmentaler), and a cheese soufflé might have cheddar or baby Swiss as its main ingredient.

Noteworthy semi-hard cheeses made in America are the Pleasant Ridge Reserve from Uplands Cheese Company in Wisconsin, Virginia's Meadow Creek Dairy Mountaineer, Vermont's Lazy Lady Capridose, and California's Fiscalini San Joaquin Gold and Pedrozo Cheese Company's Northern Gold.

A few blue cheeses fall into the semi-hard category, such as Cayuga Blue, a goats' milk blue made by Lively Run Goat Dairy in New York.

## HARD CHEESES

While hard cheeses may be so named because they are the hardest in texture, they are some of the easiest cheeses to love. Think about the nuttiness of a long-aged Asiago or the caramel flavors in a super-aged Gouda. The fact that they are aged for a long time— sometimes years—creates complexity and with it, full-flavored, assertive, and memorable qualities.

Hard cheese is so called because it has a minimal amount of moisture and as a result is quite hard in texture. A cheesemaker creating a hard cheese does a few things during the cheesemaking process to ensure the development of the cheese's texture, longevity, and flavor. For one, the curds are heated and/or cooked at a high temperature in order to concentrate the curds and facilitate the releasing of the whey, or liquid portion of the cheese. Heating caramelizes the milk sugars, or lactose, creating a slightly sweet flavor in the final cheese. Also, the curds are cut into tiny pieces, which helps toughen them further as well as expel more whey.

Another distinguishing feature of many hard cheeses is the presence of an enzyme called lipase. It is responsible for the astringency that is detectable in many hard cheeses and is in fact the hallmark of this style of cheese. Anyone who has eaten a true Parmigiano-Reggiano from Italy is familiar with the astringent, somewhat tart flavor that is imparted by the lipase. The long aging process of Parmigiano-

Reggiano (and other cheeses with lipase) intensifies the sharp flavors.

Hard cheeses are also made with a fair amount of salt, which contributes to moisture reduction, helps preserve the cheese, and, quite on purpose, creates a salty cheese. As the cheese ages, the solids, including

The tags on these wheels of cheddar help the cheesemaker keep the cheeses organized once they are aging on the shelves.

the salt, become concentrated. The salt also preserves the cheese, so that it can age for months and, in many cases, years, without going bad. It is the salt that makes hard cheeses go far in the kitchen and on the table because a little goes a long way. A fine sprinkling of a grated hard cheese can be used to season an entire pot of risotto. The flavor of hard cheese is so pronounced that when serving it as a cheese course item, one need indulge in only the smallest amount to satisfy the longing for cheese after a meal. The saltiness of hard cheeses is an added bonus when it comes to pairing them with wine. A sweet wine and a salty, aged cheese is a textural symphony and a classic flavor combination.

But salt is not the only distinguishing characteristic of hard cheeses. They are usually nutty; they have hints of caramel and/or butterscotch; and their flavor may even be reminiscent of pineapple. They're often a little gritty, and their aroma may range from mild to extremely pungent. They also will finish a bit sweet, as if the journey from the salty, gritty consistency has its own reward.

Many American cheesemakers have begun to experiment with hard cheeses. Notable results include cheeses made by Three Sisters Farmstead Cheese and Fiscalini Cheese Company in California as well as the hard goat cheese called Capricious made by MyTime Ranch, also in California. Bel Gioioso, in Wisconsin, makes a beautiful Parmesan, as does Antigo Cheese Company, also in Wisconsin; Washington state's Quillisascut Cheese Company's Curado is an aged goats' milk cheese; Austin, Texas, producer Pure Luck Grade A Goat Dairy makes a Parmesan-style goats' milk cheese; New Mexico's Sweetwoods Dairy produces The Black Sheep, a lovely sheep's milk cheese; and Colorado's Haystack Mountain Goat Dairy makes Grateful Chèvre. The granddaddy of hard cheeses in America, though, is the dry Jack made by Vella Cheese Company. As it ages beyond a year, it develops beautiful flavor and texture, becoming nutty and honeylike.

## BLUE CHEESES

There is one thing that can almost always be said about blue cheese: People either love its assertive flavor or they hate it. For those in the blue cheese camp, it is not just a cheese they like—it's often their hands-down favorite.

Blue cheese is somewhat of a misnomer, since the cheese usually isn't blue. Calling it blue-veined cheese would be much more accurate—although depending on how much veining exists and the type of milk used to make the cheese, it can take on various hues from gray to golden to white. Even the vein colors may vary, depending on what types of molds are used. The veins can range from the proverbial blue to green to blue-green to purple and even black.

What makes a blue cheese "blue"? Basically, when air interacts with certain types of molds in the cheese, usually the *Penicillium roqueforti* mold, blue veining will form wherever the air is allowed to circulate. The veining is often encouraged when the cheesemaker punctures or skewers the cheese with a special device, allowing air to rush in and work with the molds to create the veining. If a cheese has not been punctured but blue veining is present, as in many Gorgonzolas, the blue veining occurs because the curds are kept rather large and are loosely packed. As the cheese matures, air is still able to find its way into the cheese and create the distinctive veining.

As for flavor, blue cheeses have a variety of characteristics. In addition to being salty, they can be buttery, musty, and yeasty; they can have hints of caramel, chocolate, hazelnuts, almonds, and anise; and they can be tangy or somewhat sweet.

Sometimes a cheese that tastes like a blue cheese doesn't have any veins. In this case, the cheesemaker

A cheese plug is used to extract a small portion of cheese from the center of a wheel of Cayuga Blue made by Lively Run Dairy.

Point Reyes Farmstead Cheese Company cheesemaker Monte McIntyre scoops the cheese curds into their molds by hand. The cheeses will become seven-pound wheels of Original Blue.

has used the same molds as for a blue cheese, and has thus imparted the same distinctive flavor to the cheese, but the curds are packed in such a way that no air can get into the cheese. What happens instead is that a blue "skin" forms on the outside of the cheese—the only place where the cheese is exposed to air. A prime example is a cheese made by Bob and Debby Stetson of Westfield Farms in Westfield, Massachusetts. Their cows' milk Hubbardston Blue and their goats' milk Classic Blue Log are both made this way. The end result is a grayish-blue skin and a creamy-textured interior.

Although we talk about blue cheese as if it were one cheese, in fact it is really a family of cheeses. Blue cheeses range from soft and creamy to hard and crumbly; they can be made from cows', sheep's, or goats' milk, and they can have all kinds of different veining.

Gorgonzola is a creamier-style blue cheese that can range from relatively mild to pungent, depending on its age. Roquefort-style cheese is usually a little more assertive, yellowish or white in color (depending on the source of the milk), and has a medium amount of veining. Stilton-style cheese is harder and crumbly and often has an almost toasty, butterscotch-like flavor. Many American producers are beginning to make this harder style of blue cheese, including the blue ribbon award–winning Bingham Hill Cheese Company in Colorado, White Oak Farm in Washington, and Meadow Creek Dairy in Virginia.

Each cheese is distinctive, but Bingham Hill Cheese Company's blue cheese is the only one that has a rind, albeit usually inedible. The others either have no rind at all, or sometimes they have a thin "skin."

Many American cheesemakers are developing their own distinct styles. Some noteworthy examples include the Vermont Blue made by Green Mountain Blue Cheese in Highgate Center, Vermont, a study in veining and texture; Point Reyes Farmstead Cheese Company's Original Blue which is a silky, tangy cheese; and South Mountain Products' Berkshire Blue which is creamy and slightly sweet.

## NAVIGATING THE CHEESE COUNTER

If you've ever wandered into a popular cheese shop on a Saturday afternoon, you have likely witnessed cheese buying at fever pitch. The activity is part entertainment, part intimidation, for while it's usually fun to listen to the cheesemongers attempt to wade through their customers, for the customers, wading through all that cheese can be intimidating. It can be hard for cheese buyers to make a decision when they are confronting two or three hundred cheeses. What to do?

First, if that customer is you, calm down. There's no need to panic. After all, the worst that can happen is that you will end up with a cheese you don't much like. Second, realize that although there are many,

many different cheeses, each one falls into one of the seven main categories we have been discussing: fresh, semi-soft, soft-ripened, semi-hard, hard, washed-rind, and blue. If you just think about the characteristics of each category of cheese, you will be able to navigate the cheese counter without knowing a single thing about specific cheeses.

For example, if you are told that a cheese is a washed-rind variety, you know that it is likely to be a strong, aromatic cheese. Sometimes we refer to washed-rind cheeses as "stinky," and for many that's exactly what they're looking for in a cheese. For others, of course, stinky cheese is not at the top of their wish list. But the point is that if you know the basics about washed-rind cheeses, you will know the style in which that cheese has been made and therefore what general flavors to expect from it. Other sections in this book will help you select the best cheese for your purposes.

Some retailers organize their cheese counters by region, others do it by texture, and still others arrange their cheeses according to the milk source. Because the arrangement differs from place to place, knowing what category cheeses fall into makes it much easier to decide which ones you want. Equally important, though, is knowing what type of milk the cheese has been made with. If you're not a sheep's milk fan, then you'll obviously want to stay away from sheep's milk cheeses. If you don't know what milk a particular cheese is made from (and really, why would you unless you're a cheese scholar or a die-hard cheese fanatic?), then by all means ask!

In the following pages are lists of the primary cheeses made in America, organized by texture since that is the easiest way to understand cheeses. Bear in mind, though, that sometimes the same cheese will be

made in both an aged and a less-aged form. For example, Monterey Jack can be a semi-soft cheese, aged for just a short while, or it can be aged from six months to a few years, achieving varying degrees of firmness. Therefore Monterey Jack will be found under the semi-soft, semi-hard, and hard categories. Asiago is another cheese that is made in both semi-hard and hard forms, as are many others. Also, since many American cheesemakers make their own unique cheeses, I have listed specialty one-of-a-kind cheeses at the end of each category. If you're confused, you can always ask the cheesemonger for guidance, although

Harley Farms' fresh chèvre is packed into a mold lined with edible flowers, which creates a beautiful and distinct design on the top of the cheese.

perhaps you'll want to consider visiting the cheese counter at midweek—at least to start.

## FRESH CHEESES
- Bakers cheese
- Chèvre (*fresh goat cheese*)
- Cottage cheese
- Farmer cheese
- Feta (*some*)
- Fromage blanc
- Mascarpone
- Mozzarella
- Oaxaca
- Panela (*Mexican cheese*)
- Pot cheese
- Quark
- Queso blanco fresco (*also called queso para freir*)
- Queso fresco (*Mexican cheese*)
- Requeson (*Mexican cheese similar to ricotta*)
- Ricotta
- Scamorza

### WHAT TO LOOK FOR
Because fresh cheeses have such a short shelf life, selecting one is quite easy. Ricotta, fromage blanc, and fresh goat cheese should all smell fresh with no sour notes. Ideally, mozzarella that is packaged in water or whey should be purchased within a couple of days of when it was made. If you are buying mozzarella at the grocery store, look in the specialty cheese section for a cheese that is made from whole milk, packaged in liquid rather than vacuum-sealed, and if possible made fairly close to where you live. Or simply ask a store manager or your cheesemonger for the freshest mozzarella available.

## SEMI-SOFT CHEESES
- Asadero (*Hispanic cheese*)
- Beer Käse (*also spelled beerkaese and bergkaese*)
- Brick
- Butter Käse (*also spelled butterkaese*)
- Colby (*some*)
- Crescenza

- Crottin (*some*)
- Crowley (*some*)
- Edam
- Fontina (*some*)
- Gorgonzola
- Gouda (*some*)
- Havarti
- Limburger
- Monterey Jack (*some*)
- Muenster
- Provolone (*some*)
- Teleme
- Tilsit (*some*)
- Various specialty sheep's, cows', and goats' milk cheeses

### WHAT TO LOOK FOR
As we have already learned, semi-soft cheeses range in texture, which has a bearing on the shelf life of these cheeses. Those that are soft and creamy, such as Crescenza, will last only about ten days from when they were made. Try to buy this type of cheese as soon as possible after it arrives at the store. Teleme, on the other hand, has a longer shelf life, but if it is already at the "oozing" stage when you buy it, it probably has only another week or so of life.

Harder-style semi-soft cheeses, such as Gouda, Monterey Jack, and Colby, have a surprisingly long shelf life. Since most of these types of cheeses have waxed rinds or no rinds, you can inspect their condition before buying them. If a cheese is smooth, has a nice fresh milk aroma, and looks fresh, then it is the one to buy. If, on the other hand, it looks dried, cracked, or there is mold starting to grow on it, then you can assume that it is past its prime. Some cheeses from other categories that fit this description may be perfectly fine. That's why it's important to understand the style of cheese you're looking at.

**Well over three hundred cheeses vie for shelf space at Dean & Deluca in the Napa Valley.**

## SOFT-RIPENED CHEESES

◆ Brie

◆ Camembert

◆ Various specialty sheep's, cows', and goats' milk cheeses

### WHAT TO LOOK FOR

Soft-ripened cheeses should give a little in the center when you gently press them. If they are quite hard, then they are not ripe. Some will ripen over time, but unfortunately, many Bries and Camemberts made for the mass market are not made in such a way that they will ever fully ripen. Your safest bet is to buy soft-ripened cheeses from smaller specialty cheese shops, in the specialty cheese section of the supermarket, or ideally directly from the cheesemaker.

The rind of a soft-ripened cheese should look white—not pink—and the aroma should be fresh. If the cheese has a pinkish hue and smells like ammonia, don't buy it; it's over the hill.

## WASHED-RIND CHEESES

◆ Specialty sheep's, cows', and goats' milk cheeses

### WHAT TO LOOK FOR

Because of the special bacteria that are used to create washed-rind cheeses, the rinds will often be pink, orange, and sometimes tan-colored, depending on how old the cheese is. The rind should be uniform and should not be cracked. Be sure to smell the cheese. Although the aroma will be quite strong, the cheese should not smell ammoniated. You'll definitely be able to tell the difference between a strong aroma and a cheese gone bad. In terms of texture, a washed-rind cheese should give to the touch. Sometimes it will be extremely runny, which is a good sign. Be aware that when it gets to the runny stage, its shelf life will be shorter. In other words, eat it soon after you bring it home.

Since there is no washed-rind cheese tradition in this country, all of the washed-rind cheeses made in the United States are unique to the cheesemaker. By way of comparison, a few of the well-known European washed-rind cheeses are Taleggio from Italy and Reblochon, Pont-l'Evêque, and Livarot from France.

A small wheel of Legato (Camembert) made by Andante Dairy is ripe and ready to eat.

A selection of cheeses made by Andante Dairy shows the diversity of cheeses now made in America. Clockwise from top: Musette, Legato (Camembert), Figaro, and Nocturne.

## SEMI-HARD CHEESES

- Asiago (*some*)
- Baby Swiss
- Blue cheese (*some*)
- Cheddar (*some*)
- Chontaleño
- Colby (*some*)
- Crowley (*some*)
- Emmentaler
- Fontina (*some*)
- Gouda (*some*)
- Gruyère
- Kasseri
- Menonita (*Mexican cheese*)
- Monterey Jack
- Queso blanco
- Swiss
- Tilsit (*some*)
- Various specialty sheep's, cows', and goats' milk cheeses

### WHAT TO LOOK FOR

Semi-hard cheeses are among the easiest to find in excellent shape because they generally last quite a long time. Their rate of spoilage is slower and their shelf life is longer. When buying these cheeses, look for ones that have smooth, solid textures and don't appear grainy. As opposed to semi-soft cheeses, which have a somewhat slick and creamy appearance, semi-hard cheeses should look relatively dry—though not dried out. If the cheese has a rind, make sure it doesn't have lots of cracks, dry spots, or mold on it, and try to buy a piece cut to order rather than one that has already been cut and wrapped.

The aroma of semi-hard cheeses will vary, but these cheeses rarely smell very strong. Their relative lack of moisture tends to produce comparatively mild aromas. Also, many of these cheeses are wrapped in wax or plastic, which masks aromas until the cheese is unwrapped. Even then, the cheese you buy may or may not be particularly aromatic. Naturally, there are exceptions. Semi-hard cheeses that have been washed with so-called *Brevibacterium linens*, such as the Pleasant Ridge Reserve, made by the Uplands Cheese Company, have a somewhat stronger aroma—and the flavor to match. And, of course, blue cheeses are quite spirited too.

## HARD CHEESES
- Asiago (*some*)
- Cotija
- Dry Jack
- Enchilado (*chili- or paprika-coated Mexican cheese*)
- Parmesan
- Ricotta Salata
- Romano
- Various specialty sheep's, cows', and goats' milk cheeses

## WHAT TO LOOK FOR

Buying a hard cheese can be a bit tricky. You want it hard, but you don't want it dried out. Generally speaking a hard cheese should look pretty solid with a minimum amount of cracking. It really shouldn't have any visible mold (although there are a few exceptions), and it should either be well wrapped (most retailers wrap hard cheeses in plastic) or a whole wheel. Since a hard cheese has already lost most of its moisture, exposure to air will only dry it out more quickly, creating a rock-hard cheese. That's why you want to be sure that the cheese has been protected while on the shelves.

## BLUE CHEESES
### Semi-Soft
- Gorgonzola
- Maytag Blue
- Various specialty sheep's, cows', and goats' milk cheeses

### Semi-Hard (Stilton-style)
- Various specialty sheep's, cows', and goats' milk cheeses

## WHAT TO LOOK FOR

Just as there is a range of textures in blue cheese, there is also a range in longevity. The creamier, younger cheeses, such as some Gorgonzolas, should have a nice, soft texture and no ammonia aroma. They should not be mushy or watery. Generally this style of cheese will last two to four weeks.

Roquefort-style blue cheeses have a much longer shelf life. Look for cheese that is holding its shape (this style of blue cheese is almost always made in at least a five-pound wheel) or, if it has been cut from the wheel, has a clean-looking paste, distinctive blue veins and/or sometimes blue "speckles." The aroma should be clean, with no ammonia-like overtones.

A Stilton-like blue cheese has the longest shelf life. When buying this style of blue cheese, avoid ones that are too hard, since they may have been on the shelves a little too long. A little bit of visible cracking is fine, though. Look for cheese that has a paste that is solid and firm, much like a cheddar in consistency, only with veining. The paste will also most likely be a darker yellow or tan color, regardless of the type of milk used to make it. A goats' milk blue made in this style will probably look grayish; a cows' milk will look tan, gray, or light gold. These harder-style blue cheeses usually have lots of veining as well.

## MAKING CHEESE LAST

When storing cheese at home, remember that it wants to breathe but it also wants to be protected from excessive exposure to air. The optimum wrapping for most types of cheese is waxed or parchment paper. Since proper storage can help ensure longer-lasting, good tasting cheese, let's look at the best techniques for storing each category.

## FRESH CHEESES

Fresh cheeses—goat cheese, ricotta, cottage cheese, fromage blanc, mozzarella, feta, and others—are almost always best left in their original containers. Usually, these types of cheeses are packaged in plastic containers or, in the case of fresh goat cheese, sometimes vacuum-sealed. If a cheese is vacuum-sealed, then you have two choices: open the top portion of the plastic, scoop out the amount of cheese you need with a spoon, fold up the packaging leaving the remainder of the cheese undisturbed, and then put the cheese in a larger plastic bag. Although plastic is usually a cheese's foe, keeping the cheese in its original container or wrapping can actually help preserve the cheese a little longer. Your other option is to scoop out the remaining cheese and transfer it to an airtight plastic container, where it will keep for about a week.

Mozzarella and feta are often packaged in water or brine, or they may be vacuum-packed. The same rule holds true: leave the cheese in its original packaging. If the cheese comes in water or brine, you may want to change the liquid every couple of days. To replenish the brine, simply add a little bit of salt to some water, mix, pour the liquid over the cheese, and reseal the container.

Dark green or black spots that may look a little furry are a tell-tale sign that a fresh cheese has gone bad. The signs are less obvious on fresh cheese such as goats' milk or feta, which starts to turn a little yellow on the edges as it goes bad. These cheeses will also become slimy. Both symptoms are indications that the cheese should be thrown away.

### SEMI-SOFT AND WASHED-RIND CHEESES
These types of cheeses include Colby, Monterey Jack, Teleme, and many specialty cheeses. Although semi-soft and washed-rind cheeses differ, they should be stored the same way. Unless the cheese is runny, as Teleme can be, it should be wrapped in parchment or waxed paper. It is important to change the wrap every other day, or each time you use the cheese—whichever comes first. Wrapping the cheese in waxed or parchment paper is the best way to preserve it and keep it free from the off flavor that plastic wrap imparts.

If your cheese is runny, then about the only way to store it is in a bowl or on a plate with a loose layer of plastic draped over it. It is best if the plastic does not touch the cheese directly but instead is simply anchored over the edges of the plate. One way to prevent the plastic from making contact with the cheese is to place a piece of waxed paper over the cheese, followed by a sheet of plastic wrap. If the cheese is particularly aromatic, as some washed-rind cheeses are, and you'd rather not have the cheese imparting its aromas to other foods in your refrigerator, then be sure to place the cheese, plate and all, in a separate drawer.

Point Reyes Original Blue is made on a California ranch where the cows are able to graze throughout the year.

## SOFT-RIPENED CHEESES

Cheeses that fall into the soft-ripening category are easily identified by their white, bloomy rind. Among the most well known are Brie and Camembert, but many American cheesemakers make their own version of soft-ripened cheeses. No matter who makes them, all soft-ripened cheeses require the same method of storage.

A soft-ripened cheese will continue to develop its white downy mold if given the chance. There is nothing wrong with this, but it is something to be aware of. When storing a soft-ripened cheese, you first need to assess how ripe it is. If you have a creamy, runny cheese, then you need to do the same thing you did for your runny semi-soft cheese: Place the cheese on a plate, cover it with waxed or parchment paper, and then drape it with plastic wrap on top. Although soft-ripened cheeses normally like to breathe, which means they should not be stored in plastic wrap, you should properly cover super-runny cheeses, because they are likely to dry out if they are not kept well guarded from the air.

If your soft-ripened cheese is still on the firm side, then wrap it in waxed or parchment paper and be sure to keep it in a drawer of your refrigerator to prevent it from drying out. If, for some reason, you cannot use one of your refrigerator drawers for storing cheese, place your soft-ripened cheese in an airtight plastic container. It can be wrapped or not—whichever you like—but bear in mind that if it is not wrapped, the white bloomy rind will probably continue to develop. The rind is harmless, but you may or may not like its appearance.

If, after a few days or longer, you notice that your cheese is turning a light pink or orange color, you will need to smell it. This discoloration indicates the cheese is turning and is probably no longer good. Your nose will be the final arbiter. If the cheese has a faint (or strong) ammonia aroma, it is time to buy a new piece and get rid of the old one. You can try leaving your cheese on the counter for a couple of hours to see if the smell dissipates. If it does, then take a nibble and see how it tastes. It may still be okay to eat. The development of an ammonia-like scent, however, is usually a sign that a soft-ripened cheese is going bad (and this is so with washed-rind cheeses as well).

## SEMI-HARD CHEESES

Once you get into the semi-hard cheese category, which includes Swiss, cheddar, Gruyère, and a whole host of other cheeses, your concern is retaining some moisture in the cheese. Doing so requires storing the cheese in a material that will allow it to breathe yet keep it sufficiently sheltered from the air, which will draw out its moisture. Your best bet, once again, is to use waxed or parchment paper. Regardless of whether there is a natural rind, wax, or cloth, be sure to keep the rind on the cheese; it is there for protection. Indeed, it may even be best to wrap your cheese in such a way that the rind remains exposed, but this is often impractical, as invariably the cut surface of the cheese will be exposed too. Leaving the inner part of the cheese open to air will hasten the cheese's demise.

One of the nice features of a semi-hard cheese is that it seems almost indestructible. If the cheese starts to develop mold, then all you need to do is cut the mold off, replace the wrapping, and refrigerate the cheese. Or consume what's left. It is important, when cutting off mold, that you wipe your knife after each cut so as to keep mold spores from spreading onto the remaining cheese.

## HARD CHEESES

Cheeses that fall into this category—Parmesan, Asiago, extra-aged Gouda, and the like—are hard because their moisture has been drawn out in the cheesemaking and aging process. You don't want to lose any more moisture. To avoid a jaw breaker, you'll need to double-wrap hard cheeses, just as you did with the runny and washed-rind cheeses: First wrap the cheese in waxed or parchment paper, then follow with a tight layer of plastic wrap.

## BLUE CHEESES

Blue cheeses are made in varying styles and should therefore be stored according to their texture. In other words, if it's a semi-soft blue cheese wrap it in waxed or parchment paper; if it is semi-hard do the same, and if it's quite hard follow the guidelines for hard cheeses. If, however, your blue cheese is creamy yet firm with a tendency to crumble, you can hold it together with thin—not heavy-duty—foil. Since foil is pliable and impermeable, it will work best for this type of cheese. Otherwise, treat blue cheese like a hard cheese and wrap it first in parchment or waxed paper, followed by plastic wrap. Once again, you do not want plastic in direct contact with the cheese.

## THE WRAP ON CHEESE

You may wonder, if plastic is such an enemy of cheese, why do you see it used for packaging cheese in grocery stores and cheese shops? The reason is that it is the most efficient way to display the cheese and keep it from losing its moisture. Remember that cheese shops often keep their cheeses in an open refrigerated case where they are exposed to a lot of air. This exposure accelerates the aging process and therefore creates high costs for the vendor, unless the cheese is sold as soon as it's cut.

In addition, cheese sellers realize that it is important that customers be able to see the cheese in order to evaluate whether or not they want to buy it. If they can't see it, they won't buy it. Good cheese shops, of course, will try to cut as little cheese from the wheel as possible, preferring to work on a cut-to-order basis, but that isn't always practical.

Although it may seem laborious, once you bring your cheese home, you absolutely must change the

A selection of marvelous goats' milk cheeses made by Lively Run Goat Dairy. From left to right: Cayuga Blue, Caper, Bluebird, and Chèvre.

wrapping on it frequently. This means that every time you cut a piece, rewrap the remaining cheese in a clean piece of wrapping. If you haven't eaten your cheese for a while, try to remember to change the paper anyway, preferably every other day.

Since most home refrigerators are quite cold, and since cheese prefers a medium-cold and relatively humid environment, it is best to store cheese in one of the drawers marked for produce or in the designated "cheese" drawer, if your refrigerator has one, as long as the compartment isn't on the refrigerator door. With each swing of the door, your refrigerator experiences a brief but ultimately detrimental temperature swing. Cheese does not like that and will deteriorate faster than if it's in a cozy, stable environment.

## CHEESE COURSE GUIDELINES

Because of its diversity, cheese often shows up in a number of settings. It might be an ingredient in a finished dish or, increasingly, it is the center of attention, served just as it is—unadorned. Sometimes it is served as an appetizer, but more often it will finish a meal. Although there are myriad ways to serve cheese, it is often best in its most basic form. Following are a few guidelines—and, I hope, a few new ideas—to help get you started entertaining with cheese.

◆ Always serve cheese at room temperature. Take cheese out of the refrigerator about 1½ hours before serving.

◆ If you are serving several different cheeses, offer a knife for each kind of cheese.

◆ If you are serving a particularly pungent or flavorful cheese, such as a blue cheese or a runny washed-rind cheese, put that cheese on its own separate plate.

◆ When you are tasting a variety of cheeses, start with the mildest and end with the strongest. And start with the softest cheese and move toward the hardest. The only exception is if you have a very pungent soft cheese. In that case, save it for last.

The occasion on which cheese is being served determines the quantity as well as what, if any, accompaniments might be served along with it.

◆ If you're having an informal get-together where cheese (and wine) is the main focus, then select four or five cheeses and allow for about four to six ounces per person. The accompaniments should be varied, including both savory items (olives and nuts) and sweet items (dried and fresh fruit) and one or two kinds of bread. For variation, cut one of the breads thin and toast the slices.

◆ When cheese is served as an appetizer, select two or three varieties and plan on about two to three ounces per person.

◆ When cheese is served following a meal, plan on offering one to three selections and allow for about two ounces per person.

◆ Select cheeses based on a theme:

**Cheese flights.** In a cheese flight, the cheeses served are from the same family based on flavor or texture. An example would be a blue cheese flight, in which two or three different styles of blue cheese comprise the cheese course. Serving a cheese flight is a great way to learn about similar, yet different, cheeses.

**One milk.** Choose cheeses from one milk source only, either cows', goats', or sheep's milk.

**Three milks.** Choose one cheese from each milk source—cow, goat, and sheep.

**Three textures.** Choose cheeses that represent different textures—for example, soft, semi-hard, and hard.

**One cheese.** Choose just one exemplary cheese and showcase it. (See recipes in the Cheese Plates section, page 152.)

Harvest Cheese made
by Hillman Farms.

# ALL ABOUT WINE

**HOW WINE IS MADE** On the surface, the making of wine seems rather straightforward. Grapes are grown and harvested; they're crushed and placed in tanks or barrels; natural or commercial yeast goes to work on the juice, turning the grape sugar to alcohol; the juice is then drained or perhaps it's left in contact with the stems, seeds, and skins for a while; the juice may or may not be filtered; it then goes into barrels or stays in the tanks; and eventually the wine is bottled.

Below the surface, however, the art of winemaking is quietly at play, so that every bottle of wine bears the stamp of its maker. Each wine is as distinct from that of other winemakers as are two people's fingerprints. Like cheesemaking, winemaking is a blend of art and science with nature inextricably involved as well.

## THE GRAPES

As every winemaker will tell you, winemaking begins in the vineyard. How the grapes are grown and tended and what the year's weather provides will determine what ends up in the bottle. Winemakers differ in their judgments of how grapes are best grown; how much of a crop should be "dropped," or literally cut off the vine and thrown away in order to send the plant's energy to the remaining grape clusters; and when the grapes should be picked. Many winemakers get involved in the growing of the grapes, but many others leave that work to the crucial vineyard manager, whose fundamental job is to oversee the vineyard and make sure he or she is growing the best grapes possible. Innumerable decisions go into growing grapes, including how much water the vines should get, how large the vines should be allowed to grow, how much exposure to sun a variety of grape should get, how the vines should be pruned in the winter—a true art— how or whether the shoots should be trellised, what type of cover crop to grow between rows of vines for maximum water and pest management, and so on. Although the role of a vineyard manager is often overlooked, conscientious stewardship of the growing vines is critical to producing quality grapes, and thus quality wine.

Once the grapes are ripe, winemakers, often along with their vineyard managers, determine when they think it is best to pick the grapes. A device called a refractometer measures the sugar level, or Brix, in the grapes, and often the decision to pick is based on this measurement. Some winemakers, though, choose to use their own taste buds to determine whether the grape is ripe for picking. Some red wine makers, in particular, are less dependent on the Brix level and,

instead, are concerned about the discernible tannins in the grape. Tannins, which come from the skin, seeds, and stems of the grape, are the astringent and/or bitter compounds found mostly in red wines. Some winemakers choose to manage the tannins in the course of the winemaking process, after the grapes have been picked, while others believe they can control how much tannin ends up in the wine by managing the grapes while they are still on the vine, thereby reducing or eliminating the need to manage the tannins later. This latter method requires waiting a little longer to pick the grapes, when the grapes are more physiologically mature, as the tannins will actually begin to mellow by then. But choosing the right time isn't easy, given the capricious nature of fall weather. If

**LEFT:** A rainbow casts an arch over the golden vines that creep down to Cayuga Lake, one of New York's famed Finger Lakes.

Harvesting the grapes
in the vineyard of
Anthony Road Winery.

the grapes are ripe, and a freeze or severe rainstorm descends, then the possibility of ruining the grapes is greatly increased. Either way, the grapes are eventually picked. From that point onward, how the grapes become wine is a matter that is up to the individual winemaker.

Winemaking begins when the grapes are put in either a crusher-destemmer or in a press (or sometimes both, depending on the individual winemaking method). In the case of some wineries, the grape or berry clusters are hand-sorted before they are placed into the crusher, so that only the best clusters make it into the wine. Once in the crusher-destemmer, the grapes, as the name of the machine implies, are crushed and destemmed and, in the case of white wine, the juice is separated from the solids (skins and seeds), and the latter are discarded. In red wine making, the grapes are left in contact with the solids until after fermentation.

Sometimes grapes are gently pressed after they are crushed. This extracts more of the juice and the flavor that comes from the seeds and skins. Winemakers have to be cautious not to press for too long, or they run the risk of making the juice bitter.

Another type of juice, called free-run juice, comes from grapes that have been crushed and then transferred to a holding tank or sometimes a fermentation vessel. The free-run juice is considered much better than juice that comes from pressing.

## FERMENTATION

At this point the juice is ready to be fermented into wine. Fermentation is simply the conversion of natural grape sugar into alcohol and carbon dioxide. The vessel in which the juice is fermented—a steel tank, a wooden tank, or a wooden barrel—is another decision that is up to the individual winemaker. If a winemaker does not want a wood or oak flavor imparted in the wine, then the wine will be fermented in steel or neutral oak. Neutral oak can be either oak that has not been toasted or oak barrels that have been used many times—in both cases the oak has no strong flavor imparting components. The reason for choosing neutral oak is that it breathes but it doesn't impart oak flavors to the wine. The wine will mature in a rounder fashion in neutral oak versus steel because wood, by nature, is breathable and soft. Otherwise, depending on the quantity and the desired end result, the wine will be fermented in wood tanks or barrels.

Fermentation time varies, depending on a variety of factors. If the wine is white, then some winemakers attempt to do long, cool fermentations, which they believe will produce a more full-textured wine. Long, cool fermentations for red wines will result in the extraction of more color and more tannins, which can extend the life of a wine but also run the risk of making it bitter. Fermentation might start in a tank, with the still-fermenting juice moved to barrels for completion, or it may begin and end in the original vessel.

In red wine making, another process takes place usually before fermentation ends: maceration. The juice is allowed to remain in contact with seeds, stems, and grape skins to allow for further extraction of color and tannin. The color, tannins, and flavor come from phenolics, chemical compounds that are present in the solid matter of the grape—the seeds, stems, and skins. Maceration is a process that needs the winemaker's help. Since the seeds, skins, and stems float to the surface of the wine to form what is called a cap, the winemaker must literally punch down the cap to ensure that it remains in contact with the juice. This process is sometimes done by hand with a wooden "punch," although it's extremely hard work, and sometimes it is done mechanically. In the case of bigger wine operations, the wine is mechanically pulled up from the bottom of the tank and literally pumped over the cap to keep it submerged. If maceration is allowed to go on for too long, however, the phenolics can cause bitterness and astringency.

Although maceration usually takes place when the juice is fermenting and therefore the temperature is fairly high (another natural by-product of fermentation is heat), cold maceration is another option. This takes place prior to fermentation and is done because the winemakers believe they can get better extraction *before* the sugar converts to alcohol.

Another by-product of fermentation is dead yeast cells, or lees, as they're called. The notion of dead yeast cells may not sound very appetizing but, in fact, they add a lot to a wine's texture. When the wine is left in contact with the lees (called *sur lie*), the net effect is

creamier and more complex wine as well. The lees also serve to soften the tannins that come from the oak barrel and/or the phenolics. The lees also encourage malolactic fermentation, the conversion of the tart malic acid to lactic acid.

Malolactic fermentation, sometimes called secondary fermentation owing to the fact it takes place after the first or primary fermentation, is done with almost all red wines and some white wines. Often

Red Newt Cellars owner and winemaker, Dave Whiting, punches down the cap or the accumulation of skins and seeds.

referred to simply as "ML," malolactic fermentation brings forth a creamy and buttery quality in the wine, lessening any sour or harsh flavors due to excessive acidity. Although some acidity is desirable in wine, too much acidity is not. ML can happen on its own owing to the presence of natural bacteria in wineries, and because of that, the winemaker must control when (or if) it happens and for how long. Otherwise, it can happen spontaneously, perhaps after the wine has been bottled, creating an undesirable fizziness in the wine. ML can be stopped by the introduction of sulfur dioxide to the wine.

### AGING

After fermentation, the wine is ready to be aged. Some white wines will remain in fermentation tanks until they are ready to be bottled, while others, both red and white, might be "racked off" into barrels. Racking is the process by which the juice is separated from the sediment (skins and seeds, mostly) and put into barrels. White wines will almost always first undergo some type of clarification or filtering process to help facilitate the separation of the sediment from the liquid. Filtering is done because most people do not like solids floating around in their white wines! Red wines may or may not be filtered. Many winemakers believe that filtering will deprive the wine of its complexity, and

usually the wine is separated sufficiently from the solids during the racking and aging process anyway. Still other winemakers prefer to filter their wine to rid it not only of any sediment but also of any harmful yeast or bacteria, a process called sterile filtration.

Another process that might take place at this time is called fining. This is a method used to clarify the wine. It also serves to reduce bitterness from excessive tannins. Many winemakers are loathe to fine their wine and are indeed proud to say that they neither fine nor filter their wines. Other winemakers have no objection to softening their wines through this process. Whether or not filtration and fining are done, the wines are next aged in the barrels for anywhere from a few months to a few years, although during that time the barrels will occasionally have to be topped up because of evaporation.

### BLENDING

Before bottling a wine, a winemaker may often carry out one more crucial step: blending. For example, a maker of Sauvignon Blanc may want to produce a

Cabernet Sauvignon and Merlot at Chimney Rock Winery are kept at a constant cool temperature in barrels as they age.

Fermentation tanks at
Anthony Road Winery.

wine that is fermented and aged mostly in stainless-steel tanks, but with a little bit of oak-aged Sauvignon Blanc mixed in too. Before bottling, therefore, the winemaker will blend the wines using various lots to achieve the flavor profile he or she is looking for. Likewise, winemakers may want to combine vineyards or even different grapes, again depending on the desired final product. The choices for blending are practically endless, and because of that, a blended wine will, by definition, bear the signature of the winemaker.

## TASTING WINE

Few gastronomic experiences are as intimidating as tasting wine. After all, wine has hundreds of flavor compounds in it, so how can we possibly master it? As a wine aficionado and decidedly not a wine expert, I am here to tell you that you can have your wine and describe it too. The most important thing to remember is not to let words get in the way. Instead, take a sip and determine only one thing: Do you like it? If the answer is yes and you find yourself whirled into a fit of descriptors, so much the better. If you like it and still no particular words come to mind, then that's fine

too. If you don't like it, then it's useful only to note what you don't like about it so that you can try to avoid a similar wine down the road.

If, however, you are someone who wants to know more about wine and its flavor components, read on. Understanding wine's flavor is extremely helpful to understanding what cheeses (and other foods, for that matter) to pair with it. But to understand wine's flavor and its appropriate vocabulary, it is important to understand flavor in general.

Flavor is different from taste. Taste has to do with the way a food hits our tongue—the place where our taste buds reside. From our taste buds we can sense if something is sour, bitter, salty, or sweet. Flavor, on the other hand, is a combination of a large number of sensory inputs that are derived from what we eat or, in this case, drink. All our senses—smell, taste, texture, sight, and even hearing (in some cases)—are involved with how we taste. It is the sense of smell, however, that is most important to how and what we taste.

The reason is that the orthonasal pathway, the pathway through the nose, is the first point of entry for smell. Lift a glass of wine, swirl it, and breathe deeply through your nose, and you're smelling that wine from the outside in. Swallow that wine and pay attention to what you smell—not what you taste—as the wine goes down and you're smelling from the inside out, using the retronasal passage. This is the internal passage that extends from the back of the tongue up through the nose, and it is critical to how we smell *and* taste. This is why a cold hampers your ability to taste—it's because you can't *smell* the food.

To test how this works, swirl a glass of wine and smell it. Then take a sip, hold it in your mouth, pinch your nose to prevent air (or aromas) from coming in, and swallow the wine at the same time that you un-pinch your nose and breathe out. The flavor of the wine will be decidedly enhanced because the retronasal passage is at work.

An important "fifth taste" now getting wide recognition is known as umami. Discovered by a Japanese researcher, umami has been defined as the naturally occurring form of monosodium glutamate, or MSG. In short, it is the savory or protein taste unde-tected by any of the other taste buds. Umami is impor-tant because it helps us understand how cheese and wine interact. If a food is high in umami, as cheddar, Parmesan, shrimp, mushrooms, anchovies, and many other foods are, then the wine consumed with these foods will generally taste more astringent or bitter. That is, umami makes wine stronger. With this in mind, we know to look for wines that are more fruity and medium-bodied rather than those that are high in tannins and alcohol to go with cheeses that are partic-ularly high in umami. All cheese has some degree of umami, but those that are high in acid and salt con-tent, such as Parmesan and cheddar, contain the most. This knowledge provides an important clue about which wines to pair with them.

When it comes to tasting wine, there are two main elements to bear in mind: first, the wine's basic components—alcohol, acidity, tannins, and sugar. These are extremely helpful to your understanding of wine itself and ultimately of how to pair it with cheese. Second, the sensory experience—taste, aroma, visual appearance, and texture, as well as the circum-stances surrounding the drinking of the wine. An off-shoot of tasting wine is the vocabulary used to describe it. This may or may not be important. For some, it is helpful; for others it is a hindrance.

## WHAT'S IN A GLASS?

Let's start with the primary components of wine. First, there is acidity. Does the wine remind you of a green apple or an overripe peach? If you detect the green apple, then you're keying in on the acidity. Many wine aficionados are self-avowed "acid freaks," which means they love the tart high notes of an acidic wine. Not coincidentally, high-acid wines are very often good food wines, because the acid either mirrors or balances many other flavors found in food.

Acid occurs naturally in grapes, and the level of acidity that is present varies according to the grape, the winemaking methods, and the region in which the grape is grown. Generally, warm-region grapes or grapes grown during a warmer growing season have lower acidity because the heat develops the sugars in the fruit. In California, where the climate and growing season are generally warm, acid may legally be added to wine to bring it into balance. Sugar, however, may not be added to California wines because it is pre-sumed that the grapes will have sufficient sugars when they are made into wine. Conversely, grapes grown in cooler regions, such as New York, retain acidity—sometimes too much. For that reason, sugar may be added legally to such wines.

This brings us to the next component: sugar. Is the wine sweet or is it fruity? Sometimes people mistakenly use the word "sweet" to describe what is actually a fruity component in the wine. Sweetness technically refers to the amount of residual or added sugar in the wine, while "fruity" simply describes a fruitlike characteristic in the wine. If a wine is sweet, either sugar has been added or the grape juice has not fermented completely—that is, the yeast has not con-verted all the sugar into alcohol. This phenomenon is called residual sugar. When you taste a sweet wine, the sugar is immediately apparent. The sweetness of a wine has a great deal to do with your enjoyment of it. As long as there is sufficient acidity, wines that have a strong fruity component—whether they are dry wines or dessert wines—are quite enjoyable and make good food companions. It is when acidity is low that a wine will taste "flabby," or lacking in acidity or structure.

The alcohol in wine is yet another important component for evaluating it. The percentage of alcohol is listed on the bottle, and for most table wines, falls

## WINE PRICES

**One of the most intimidating factors about wine can be its price.** It is not unusual to find bottles priced at $100 or more in fine wine shops. But in those same shops there might also be bottles priced at $10. Can most people tell the difference? Probably not. What matters more than the price of the wine is the style and flavor of the wine itself. If it is the varietal you're looking for; if it falls within your price range; and, ideally, if someone at the wine store recommends it, then be confident about buying it.

Just like the wines at your local shop, the wines mentioned in this book vary in price. In general, the wines mentioned here range from $9 to about $60. A few will be less, a few will be more.

As a point of reference, Chardonnay is usually the most expensive American white wine, and Cabernet Sauvignon is usually the most expensive American red. In both cases, the price is based largely on the popularity of these varieties—they command a high price because people will pay it. In the case of Cabernet, the price also reflects time spent in the barrel and bottle before it is released, as well as its longevity. There are myriad other factors that determine the price of a wine, such as the availability of the grapes, the particular vineyards from which the grapes come, the quality of the vintage, the reputation of the winemaker, and the quantity of available wine.

The bottom line is that there are good and even great wines at almost every price point. Wines between $12 and $20 will satisfy most people. Wines between $20 and $50 may offer more complexity, while wines over $50 offer subtleties that require tasting experience to appreciate.

between 11 and 14 percent. If a wine is particularly high in alcohol, it may be referred to as "hot"—it is almost like a blast of heat when you taste it. On the other hand, if the wine is in balance—that is, no single component significantly outweighs the others—then a high-alcohol wine can be appealing. Also, a high-alcohol wine is generally perceived to be sweeter. In the case of fortified wines, such as port and sweet styles of sherry, the wine *is* sweeter—and higher in alcohol.

The fourth component of wine is tannin. While most white wines have almost no perceptible tannins, many red wines do. Cabernet Sauvignon, Syrah, and Petite Sirah, among others, are red wines with particularly high tannins. Tannins, which come from the so-called phenolics, lend a wine an astringent and sometimes bitter quality (see How Wine Is Made for more on phenolics, page 32). They are key to a wine's ageability, although contrary to popular belief they do not inherently make an age-worthy wine. There are many additional factors that contribute to creating a wine that is worth cellaring. For some people, strong tannins in wine can be off-putting, and for others the tannins can be the main draw. Either way, the presence of tannins makes a significant contribution to the wine and your perception of it.

### THE SENSORY EXPERIENCE

Your experience of a wine begins with the circumstances in which you are drinking it. Strange as that may sound, many of our taste memories are based on the environment in which the tasting occurs. If we are sitting on a veranda at sunset overlooking the Pacific Ocean and sipping wine, we will almost assuredly have a good memory of that wine—not only what the wine is but also how it tastes. The next time we try it, if we are in a more ordinary setting, we might very well wonder why it doesn't taste as good as we remembered. It's because we had an emotional attachment to that wine that changed when the environment around it changed.

Like many wineries throughout the United States, Chimney Rock Winery offers consumers the chance to taste wines before buying them.

The next sensory input comes from the way a wine looks. The instant a wine is poured into a glass we automatically start to evaluate it, whether or not we're aware of doing so. If it's a white wine, we look at whether it's a pale yellow or a golden color. We will probably then predict that the wine that is paler in color will be lighter in flavor. This may or may not be true, but that's probably what we will think.

When the wine is poured into the glass, we will then smell it. Smelling the wine not only prepares our taste buds for the wine; it also tells our brain what to expect. Is it floral? toasty? vegetal? These traits are usually pretty easy to detect with our nose.

Finally, we taste the wine. The first taste is not always the most accurate because our mouth has to assimilate the flavors that are being introduced. With the second taste we will begin to get a sense of what the wine is about, and it is at this point that vocabulary really comes into play. The lexicon in and of itself is not terribly important, but the fact is that if you can describe a wine, your chances of remembering its salient qualities are far better. Not only is a taste memory important for future reference (do you want to buy that wine again?); it is also important for knowing what cheese to match with it. If you remember that the

Sauvignon Blanc you drank reminded you of fresh grass, then chances are that just-made goat cheese will also come to mind as a soulmate for that wine.

Next we get to mouthfeel. How does the wine literally feel in your mouth? Is it creamy? light? full-bodied? chewy? The "weight" of a wine has a lot to do with our overall enjoyment of it. If you're looking for a light, crisp white wine and the one you've selected turns out to be full-bodied and almost "thick," then you're probably not going to enjoy drinking it. Wine may fundamentally be a liquid, but each type of wine has a different weight.

Developing your own vocabulary of wine is a lifelong discovery process, and it comes with experience and experiments. Next time you drink a wine, pay attention to its components, identify them if you can, and then do so again and again. Soon you'll be able to evaluate with greater clarity what you like, what you don't like, whether a wine seems balanced to you, and eventually even factors such as what climate the wine grapes were likely grown in and how the grapes might have been grown. We will talk more about how knowing these sorts of things helps when pairing cheeses and wines. In the meantime, just enjoy the journey.

## WINE VARIETALS

For the most part, what a wine tastes like isn't nearly as important as whether or not you like it. When it comes to pairing cheese with wine, though, it can sometimes be helpful to have an idea of the common characteristics and weight of the wine you're serving. That way you can more easily anticipate what cheese will go with that wine, and vice versa.

What follows is a list of the most common varietals and hybrids in the United States and a few flavor descriptors to help further your understanding of the varietal characteristics. This listing is by no means comprehensive, but it is meant to increase your understanding of wine and ultimately help you to pair it with cheese.

### WHITE WINES

- **Arneis**—almonds, anise, mineral, peach, pear; light- to medium-bodied
- **Cayuga White** (*hybrid*)—apple, grapefruit, peach, pear, spice; light- to medium-bodied
- **Chardonnay**—apple, apricot, butter, butterscotch, citrus, cream, lemon, melon, peach, pear, pineapple; medium- to full-bodied
- **Chenin Blanc**—citrus, grass, green apple, honey, melon, mineral; light- to medium-bodied
- **Gewürztraminer**—cloves, diesel, lychee, mango, nutmeg, peach, perfume, spice; medium- to full-bodied
- **Muscat**—apple, jasmine, orange blossom, peach, perfume, spice; light- to medium-bodied
- **Pinot Blanc**—almond, apple; medium- to full-bodied
- **Pinot Gris**—almond, apple, citrus, mineral, pear; light- to medium-bodied
- **Riesling**—apricot, banana, citrus, diesel, mango, peach, pear, steel, tangerine; light- to medium-bodied

- **Sauvignon Blanc**—apple, grapefruit, grass, honeydew, lime, melon, oak, pineapple; light- to full-bodied
- **Sémillon**—citrus, fig, grass, honey, lemon, pear; light- to medium-bodied
- **Seyval** (*hybrid*)—citrus, honeydew, mineral, pineapple; light- to medium-bodied
- **Vidal Blanc** (*hybrid*)—apple, apricot, lemon, peach; light- to medium-bodied
- **Vignoles** (*hybrid*)—apricot, honey, lemon, melon, pineapple; light- to medium-bodied
- **Viognier**—apricot, honey, mango, orange blossom, peach, pineapple; medium- to full-bodied

### SPARKLING WINES

Apricot, cherry, green apple, honey, lemon, plum, raspberry, toast, toasted nut, yeast

### RED WINES

- **Baco Noir** (*hybrid*)—blackberry, earth, herb, raspberry; light- to medium-bodied
- **Barbera**—allspice, berry, dried cherry, plum; light to medium-bodied
- **Cabernet Franc**—cherry, chocolate, earth, plum, raspberry, toast; medium- to full-bodied
- **Cabernet Sauvignon**—bell pepper, blackberry, black cherry, black pepper, cassis, cedar, chocolate, eucalyptus, green olive, licorice, mint, red currant, tobacco; medium- to full-bodied
- **Carignane**—anise, blueberry, blackberry, cherry, smoke, raspberry, strawberry; light- to medium-bodied
- **Dolcetto**—almond, blackberry, cherry, licorice, plum; light- to medium-bodied
- **Grenache**—black currant, blackberry, black pepper, raspberry, spice, strawberry; medium- to full-bodied

Sparkling wine can contain hints of green apple, honey, or toasted nuts.

- **Merlot**—blackberry, cherry, currant, earth, licorice, olive, plum; medium- to full-bodied
- **Petite Sirah**—blackberry, black pepper, boysenberry, chocolate, earth, mocha; full-bodied
- **Pinot Noir**—blackberry, cassis, cherry, clove, currant, earth, mushroom, raspberry, spice; light- to full-bodied
- **Sangiovese**—blackberry, black cherry, dried herbs, earth, plum, raspberry, spice, strawberry; light- to full-bodied

- **Syrah**—black pepper, cherry, chocolate, pepper, raspberry, strawberry; medium- to full-bodied
- **Zinfandel**—blackberry, black pepper, boysenberry, cherry, clove, earth, mint, plum, raspberry; medium- to full-bodied

### FORTIFIED WINES

- **Port**—chocolate, plum, raisin, strawberry, tobacco, vanilla
- **Sherry**—almond, honey, orange

## WHAT IS AN AVA?

In France, the term for a designated growing area is *Appellation d'Origine Contrôlée* (AOC). If a wine has AOC on the label, it means that the wine in the bottle comes from a precise place where only a specific variety of grape or grapes is allowed to be grown, and the wine is made in a particular style required of that specific AOC-designated area.

In the United States, we have a different system, although the word "appellation" is usually used to denote it. Technically, we use the phrase American Viticultural Area, or AVA. An AVA designates a particular geographic region, but unlike in France and other parts of Europe, it does not tell us what grape or grapes are grown in that area. For example, if a white wine from the Chablis region of France has AOC on the label, you can be sure the wine was made with Chardonnay grapes. That is what is required of an AOC Chablis, among other things. In the United States, however, anyone can grow any grape he or she wants within an AVA. An AVA label is simply a means of designating a geographical area.

AVAs do usually have particular distinguishing characteristics, and growers will try to plant the varieties that are best suited for that AVA. But the only way you can tell the variety or varieties of grapes in an American bottle of wine is by reading the label. (Even then, you may not know, because winemakers are increasingly using phrases such as "Red Table Wine," and they may or may not choose to list the grape varieties on the label.) If a label lists an AVA, then 85 percent of the grapes used to make that wine came from that AVA. In addition, there are many sub-AVAs such as Stag's Leap District in the Napa Valley, which is a sub-AVA of the Napa Valley AVA.

The Alcohol and Tobacco Tax and Trade Bureau is the agency that approves AVAs. Today, there are approximately 150 AVAs.

## STORING AND SERVING WINE

No matter how good the wine you buy might be, if the retailer hasn't stored it properly or if you don't store it properly, it will quickly lose its value and most important, its flavor. Learning to store and serve wine at its optimum point is not all that difficult, but it does take some attention.

### STORING WINE

Because wide temperature swings will ruin a wine faster than you can pop a cork, it is best to store any wine that you do not intend to drink within a week or two in a temperature-controlled environment. Even if you don't have a cellar, there are ways to do that.

Here are a few facts about wine storage:
◆ Wine should be kept free from wide temperature swings.

◆ Wine should not be exposed to extreme heat. It is the bane of many California winemakers to see their newly purchased wine being hurled into the backseat of someone's convertible, knowing that its occupants will likely be tooling around under the summer sun for several hours.

◆ Wine should always be stored on its side. When wine stands upright for a long time, there is no contact between the wine and the cork, significantly increasing the likelihood of the cork drying out and cracking, allowing air to get into the wine. Oxidized wine is compromised at best and usually undrinkable.

◆ The ideal temperature for wine is between 55°F and 65°F. Some may quibble with the higher temperature in this range, but some wine purveyors believe a slightly higher temperature is a better way to coax a wine along. If wine is kept too cold, they say, it will stay stagnant, or progress at a much slower rate. This matter is surely up for debate, but the point is that wine definitely likes relatively cool, constant temperatures.

◆ Do not store wine in the refrigerator for more than about a week. Just as extreme heat is a wine's enemy, so too is extreme cold. Unless your refrigerator is warmer than 50F (most hover between 38F and 45F), you will compromise the flavors in the wine. Also, when wine is in the refrigerator, it is subject to constant vibration. That type of movement is never good for wine.

◆ Place white wine in the refrigerator about one hour before serving and sparkling wine three to four hours before serving. The thickness of the bottles used for sparkling wine necessitates the longer cooling time.

◆ To chill a bottle quickly, fill a container, such as an ice bucket or pitcher, with ice and water and immerse the bottle for ten to fifteen minutes. Do not place wine in the freezer.

This vineyard, planted on the property of Chimney Rock Winery, is part of the highly prized sub-appellation in the Napa Valley called the Stags Leap District.

So how do you achieve optimum storage conditions? First, many people are able to create makeshift cellars by squaring off a small area of the basement and installing shelves or ready-made wine racks. This will work fine, as long as the area retains a constant temperature that is below 65°F, does not get sunlight, and is not next to your water heater, air conditioner, or the like.

If you do not have the luxury of space, there are many small wine refrigerators on the market these days. These are helpful because they control the temperature for you. In some cases these refrigerators have two different temperature-controlled areas, one for white wine and one for red.

Or you may simply buy only as much wine as you have appropriate space to store it in. It will do no good to buy a really terrific bottle of wine if you cannot keep it properly. By the time you go to drink it, you will have run the risk that it has already gone bad, or at least been diminished in quality.

## SERVING WINE

Just as with cheese, the flavors in anything too cold—including wine—are muted. To bring out the subtleties of your wines, remember to serve white wine warmer than refrigerator temperature and red wine warmer than cellar temperature.

To serve a white wine, remove it from the refrigerator about twenty minutes before serving, depending on how hot the weather is. Needless to say, if it's quite hot, then just let the wine warm up slightly to enhance its flavor.

While you do not want a warm red wine, it is best to bring it out of its temperature-controlled environment about thirty minutes before serving it. The bottle should still feel cool, but not ice-cold. The wine will also warm up in the glass, but, again, you do not want a chilly red wine, or your reaction to it is likely to be the same.

## SHIPPING WINE

When Prohibition was followed by Repeal, states and counties were effectively given the right to establish their own liquor sales policies. What the framers of the 21st Amendment chose to ignore was how that legislation might affect interstate commerce for wine, beer, and liquor. Moreover, they never could have imagined the advent of the Internet. Because they didn't have a crystal ball, there are still a few tricky and, some say, antiquated laws that inhibit the public's access to good wine and winemakers' ability to ship it to certain destinations.

There are many permutations of wine shipping laws, ranging from reciprocity to a felony. When states have reciprocity with each other—and thirteen states do at this time—that means that wine can be shipped freely and directly between those states. This means that individuals can have wine shipped to them without having to go through an intermediary, such as a wholesale retailer.

At the opposite extreme, a number of states, including Florida, Indiana, and Kentucky, have deemed wine shipping illegal, except when it involves a licensed distributor or wholesaler. Direct shipping constitutes a felony in those states. This does not mean that wine may not be sold in such states; it just means that wine cannot be directly shipped to individuals in those states. So, for example, if a Florida resident is visiting the California wine country, he cannot have any wine he has purchased shipped to him. He is, however, allowed to carry it back with him. Otherwise, he must purchase wine from a Florida retailer.

The way it works in most states right now, wine is shipped through a wholesaler/distributor, and sold to a retailer, who then sells it to the consumer. The problem with this system is that only the larger wineries have the opportunity to develop a national buyership for their wine, because the smaller wineries often fall below the radar of large distributors, or the large distributors simply don't want to deal in the limited quantities that many small wineries offer. Small wineries are therefore dependent on direct sales. Since many states don't allow consumers to buy wine direct, the small wineries' opportunities for sales and growth are curtailed.

With the advent of the Internet two new wrinkles have arisen: How does the seller know whether a wine shipment is going to someone who is actually of legal drinking age? And how can states cash in on alcohol taxes when the Internet is mostly a tax-free avenue of commerce? To combat this, Senator Orrin Hatch, R-Utah, created the 21st Amendment Enforcement Act. This legislation enables the state attorneys general to prosecute anyone who is suspected of breaking a state's alcohol shipping laws. Those who opposed this act claim there are available safeguards that would prevent alcohol from being sold to minors. And, they say, wineries have volunteered to pay taxes in states where their wine is shipped to compensate for the potential loss of tax money through Internet commerce.

Those who were in favor of the act, however, claim that the age safeguards are not adequate. They also say that the issue of tax revenues is thorny because it would place the burden on either the wineries or the consumers to report their shipments and/or purchases so that the proper taxes could be collected. They're skeptical this would happen.

These are just a few of the issues surrounding wine shipping. What is certain is that with the existing barriers, small winemakers have limited means by which to bring attention to their wines, and wine consumers do not have access to the vast majority of wines being produced in America.

Many organizations are now working to change wine shipping laws. Among them is the consumer group called Free the Grapes. See the Resources section in the Appendix for details on this group and other wine organizations.

# BRINGING CHEESE AND WINE TOGETHER

**BRINGING CHEESE AND WINE TOGETHER** Now that you know a little about cheese and a little about wine, it is time to bring these two ethereal pleasures together. Before we get started though, bear in mind that there will be no use of the word "rules" in this chapter nor in this book. Rules, by definition, imply restrictions, and the idea here is to have fun and hopefully learn a few things along the way. That said, perfect cheese and wine pairings *are* hard to come by. For this reason, I have come up with ten basic guidelines that should help get you closer to finding satisfying cheese and wine companions.

# Ten Basic Guidelines

1. Pair textures of cheese and wine.

2. Pair light cheeses with light wines.

3. Pair white wines with cheese.

4. Pair fruitier-style wines with cheese.

5. Pair sparkling wines with blue, creamy, and salty cheeses.

6. Pair red wines with (almost) anything.

7. Pair cheeses and wines with comparable flavors.

8. Pair cheeses and wines with "opposite" flavors.

9. Pair dessert wines with cheese.

10. Pair aged, mild cheeses with older, milder wines.

## 1. PAIR TEXTURES OF CHEESE AND WINE

The texture of a cheese—be it soft, hard, or something in between—is probably the most important characteristic to gauge when you are looking for a compatible wine. When you know the texture of a cheese, you are also getting a window into its flavor. For example, if the cheese is a washed-rind cheese, you know its texture is probably creamy and its flavor generally strong. If it is a soft-ripened cheese, you know it will have a slightly musty yet clean bloomy rind flavor, while the paste, or interior, of the cheese will have a creamy mouthfeel and usually a relatively mild flavor. Or, if a cheese is super-aged, you can be fairly certain that it will be somewhat granular in the mouth and probably salty, likewise with fresh, semi-soft, semi-hard, and to some degree, blue cheeses.

In addition, knowing the texture of a cheese will help you match it up with a wine with a similar weight. If, for example, a cheese is quite creamy, almost viscous, then a wine should share similar textural characteristics. Conversely, you can be fairly certain that a full-bodied "heavy" wine will pounce all over a lighter-style cheese.

Some people in the food and wine pairing business scoff at the notion of matching textures. Instead they contend that as long as the food is balanced—that is, it has proper acidity, salt, and sweetness—the wine will find its place just fine. To some degree that is true. Here, though, we are not talking about generic food; we are talking specifically about cheese, which cannot be "balanced" or altered as, say, coq au vin, can. Cheese is, however, very much about texture and flavor. So, too, is wine.

Think about the last time you drank a "thin" glass of wine. It somehow slipped right down your throat essentially without your noticing it. This may have had more to do with what you were eating than with the wine itself. Perhaps that meaty swordfish didn't go with the light white wine you were drinking. While some of your perception of the wine could have to do with how the fish was prepared (was it grilled? sautéed? bathed in a sauce?), at least some of the reason lies in the texture of the fish. Swordfish is dense, and while the idea of the light wine seemed appropriate, you probably needed a meatier white or red wine. The same is true with cheese.

If you are going to eat a "meaty" cheese, such as a washed-rind cheese, which is very flavorful and creamy, then pick a "meaty" wine. In other words, find a full-bodied (higher alcohol) wine. This could be a Gewürztraminer, perhaps a Zinfandel, or certain Cabernet Francs.

Perhaps you're in the mood for a semi-hard cheese, say a cheddar or a Gruyère. Those two cheeses are completely different, but they share a medium-

**LEFT:** A wide selection of cheeses includes: (clockwise from top left) Sweet Grass Dairy's Georgia Gouda, Bingham Hill Cheese Company's Rustic Blue, and Three Sisters Farmstead Cheese's Serena.

firm texture. This is your cue for the style of wine to choose. In this case a Washington Chardonnay might make a nice match for the Gruyère, while a medium-bodied Sonoma County Zinfandel might be just the thing for the cheddar.

Blue cheeses are a bit of an exception to the texture rule, but not entirely, for two reasons. First, most people perceive the flavor of blue cheese as generic. Though it is true that blue cheeses share their characteristic "blue" flavor, they are made in many different styles and as a result develop many different flavors. Second, blue cheese, regardless of its texture, will almost always be compatible with some type of sparkling wine. In this case, it is because of opposing textures. The bubbles in the sparkling wine provide a light texture that offsets the more solid cheese. This is a case of two different but well-matched textures.

As for still wine (non-sparkling) matches, again think texture. A young, creamy Gorgonzola-like blue cheese might go nicely with a creamier- and perhaps fruitier-style wine, such as a late-harvest Muscat or a semi-dry Riesling, while an aged, harder-style blue cheese, having developed more earthy, rustic tones and a more solid texture, would likely match up nicely with a heavier-style wine, such as a late-harvest Zinfandel, a port, or an older, mellow Cabernet Sauvignon.

Repeating for the sake of emphasis: Texture is your big window into the flavor of the cheese. This, in turn, is your key aid in finding a great wine match for the cheese.

Following are some examples of cheese and wine matches based on texture:

- Cheddar (semi-hard) and medium-bodied Zinfandel, Merlot, ruby port

- Gruyère and Chardonnay, Gewürztraminer, Riesling, or medium- to full-bodied Syrah

- Monterey Jack (semi-soft) and Chenin Blanc, light- to medium-bodied Sangiovese, light to medium-bodied Merlot

- Ricotta and Pinot Gris

- Gorgonzola and late-harvest Muscat or Riesling

- Washed-rind cheese and Cabernet Franc, Cabernet Sauvignon (older), Gewürztraminer, Pinot Noir (fruity) or Zinfandel

## 2. PAIR LIGHT CHEESES WITH LIGHT WINES

This may be the most obvious of the approaches, but "obvious" is good. It makes things easier. Again, this harks back to matching textures. A light cheese is usually one that falls in the fresh or semi-soft category. Because cheeses in these categories are not aged for very long, if at all, they don't have the complex flavor profiles that older cheeses do.

Not coincidentally, the likely wine companions for light cheeses are produced rather similarly. That is, they have little to no oak aging or fermentation, they have good acidity, and they are generally of a low to medium alcohol level (10 to 12 percent). That lack of oak usually translates to a lighter-style wine, one that does not have the typical toasty and vanillin flavors that come from oak. The wine is likely to be more crisp in style. A higher acid wine creates that perception of crispness and provides a backbone not only for the fruit in the wine, but also for any accompanying cheeses. The alcohol content is your key to the extent of body in the wine. The higher the alcohol, the greater the body and the less likely it is to go with light cheeses. Knowing a wine's alcohol level helps you determine the wine's texture and therefore the style of cheese to match with it.

If you don't know whether or not the wine has been exposed to oak, or if you don't know about the acid in the wine, simply ask. If, by chance, you are buying your wine in a place where there are no knowledgeable people on hand, you can sometimes tell by the descriptions printed on the back labels. If the label includes words like "citrus" or "green apple," you'll have a clue that the wine has good acid, at least according to the person who wrote the notes. If you see words like "vanilla" or "toasty," you'll know that that wine has met with some oak.

Following are some examples of pairing light cheeses and light wines:

- Fresh goat cheese (often called chèvre) and Sauvignon Blanc, Chenin Blanc, Pinot Gris, rosé

- Fromage blanc and Pinot Gris

- Mozzarella and Dolcetto or a light Sangiovese

- Fontina and Gewürztraminer or low-alcohol dessert wine (for example, Muscat)

- Crottin and Arneis, Sauvignon Blanc

## 3. PAIR WHITE WINES WITH CHEESE

To many, the idea of matching white wines with cheeses seems like blasphemy. We've been drinking red wine with our cheeses throughout the ages, and now we're supposed to drink *white* wine? The reason is that white wines, with their less assertive (though not necessarily less complex) nature, are simply more cheese friendly. Specifically, many white wines have more pronounced acidity. This quality makes them more compatible with high-acid cheeses, including fresh and slightly aged goat cheese. In addition, white wines are often characterized by butteriness and fruit. A buttery quality in wine makes for a natural affinity with many cheeses, particularly soft-ripened cheeses. (Think once again about texture: buttery, rich wine— buttery, rich cheese.) That buttery quality will also hold its own with more aged cheeses too.

The fruit often found in white wine also makes white wine a great candidate for cheese. The saltiness of most cheeses enhances the fruit character of the wine. If the wine lacks fruit, it is simply harder to find a compatible cheese.

Naturally, not all white wines go with all cheeses. Some white wines, such as the super-oaked Chardonnays, are no more food- or cheese-friendly than the most tannic red wines. The reason is the same: They are fundamentally bitter, tasting of wood more than of fruit. Also, a super-acidic wine with little discernible fruit is best left to be enjoyed with

highly acidic foods—not cheese. But a well-balanced white wine—one that has good acid and fruit—is very likely to go well with many cheeses, since cheese shares these same basic components and has the added components of salt and fat.

For some, the notion of having a cheese course along with white wine makes no sense, especially after having just drunk a red wine with the main course. Although it may seem awkward, if you want your cheeses to go well with the wine, you should probably make that switch. If the idea of doing so makes you uncomfortable, then switch to a fruity white wine or dessert wine. As you will see in the next guideline, that style of wine is a near certain match for most cheeses.

Following are some examples of pairing white wines and cheeses:

- Brie (regular, double- or triple-crème) and lightly oaked Chardonnay or Sauvignon Blanc

- Cheddar and Gewürztraminer

- Crottin (slightly aged disk-shaped goat cheese) and Chenin Blanc

- Gouda and Pinot Blanc

- Gruyère and Riesling

- Washed-rind cheese (goats' milk or cows' milk) and Riesling or Gewürztraminer

- Asiago and Muscat

## 4. PAIR FRUITIER-STYLE WINES WITH CHEESE

This is true for both white and red wines. The best example lies in one grape alone: Riesling. Riesling is an inherently fruity grape, but it is also high in acid. Few grapes strike this balance. What this means for cheese is that Riesling effectively extends the flavors of the cheese by tacking on a fruit note that otherwise isn't there. You may think you don't want your cheese to taste like fruit. It won't; the experience is far more subtle than that. Riesling simply gives most cheeses an

A view from Spring Mountain Road in the heart of the Napa Valley.

added dimension that isn't too assertive. The effect is understated and sublime; the flavors are a little bit sweet, a little bit salty, a little bit rich, and altogether balanced.

Gewürztraminer is another grape that rides beautifully side by side with many cheeses. The prefix "gewürz" basically means "spice" in German, and that spicy quality in the grape makes it exciting with cheese. "Gewürz" is also sometimes interpreted as "perfumed," so you can begin to see the character of this intriguing grape emerge—it is spicy and perfumy. The Gewürztraminers that are being made in some of the cooler climates in the United States—New York's Finger Lakes area, Mendocino County in California, and parts of Oregon and Washington—are utterly fantastic, owing to their peach, mango, and lychee-like flavors. The same grape grown in hot climates often ends up being too perfumy, cloying, and bitter. A well-balanced Gewürztraminer, though, works wonderfully with many cheeses.

The concept of matching fruity wines and cheese has less to do with the *grape* from which the wine has been made and more to do with the grape's ripeness the *style* of the wine (with the possible exception of Riesling). If the wine, either white or red, has been made in a fruity style, it is automatically a better candidate for most cheeses because the salty and lactic flavors in the cheese can knock a super-dry wine off balance quite easily. But if it is a fruity wine, it will usually stand on its own and provide a yang to the cheese's yin.

To test this, try putting a bone-dry wine together with a variety of cheeses. You'll likely find far less compatibility across the board than you will with a fruity wine. Some or perhaps all of the cheeses may make the dry wine taste bitter. Try the same set of cheeses with a fruitier-style wine and see what happens. Both the cheese and the wine will hold their own much better, and the wine is not likely to taste bitter. For this reason even a light, fresh cheese such as

mozzarella will go nicely with a red wine if that wine is made in a light, fruity style. Normally, such a light cheese would find compatibility only with a light white wine, because the cheese is so easily overwhelmed. A lighter-style fruity red wine, though, gives a faint hint of sweetness and has just enough lightness to play off the lactose (sweetness) in the cheese.

To be clear, when we talk about fruity wines, we are not talking about fruit wines—those that are made from fruit such as blueberries, strawberries and the like. Nor are we talking about sweet wines. Sweet wines are ones to which sugar has been added, or ones that haven't been entirely fermented. Although sweet wines are wonderful with cheese (we'll get to that later), the idea here is that you choose wines where fruit flavors such as melon, peach, apricot, ripe plum, and so forth, are dominant. It is ideal if that same fruit-forward wine has good acid structure too, so that the wine isn't cloying and so that it is more likely to be compatible with cheese, not to mention more enjoyable overall.

Following are some examples of pairing fruitier-style wines with cheeses:

- Goats' milk cheese (aged) and Chenin Blanc or Riesling

- Sheep's milk cheese (aged) and Riesling, Gewürztraminer, or fruity Zinfandel

- Asiago (aged) and fruity Syrah

- Cheddar and Gewürztraminer, fruity Syrah, or fruity Zinfandel

- Fontina (semi-soft) and Chenin Blanc or Riesling

- Gruyère and Gewürztraminer, Riesling, or fruity Merlot

- Washed-rind cheese and Gewürztraminer (dry or sweet)

# 5. PAIR SPARKLING WINES WITH BLUE, CREAMY, AND SALTY CHEESES

As noted earlier, sparkling wine goes well with blue cheese. The textural qualities of both the cheese and the wine work nicely when the two are matched together. But sparkling wines also go well with blue cheese because of the compatibility of the flavors. Indeed, the yeasty, toasty qualities found in many sparkling wines make them prime candidates for enjoying with blue cheeses. The bubbles also make sparkling wines equally good companions with creamy and salty cheeses. Sparkling wine, in fact, is probably second to Riesling as an overall cheese match.

Blue cheeses, although they differ significantly from one another, share the blue mold flavor in common. If the cheese is particularly aged and harder in style, with some caramel notes, such as Bingham Hill Cheese Company's Rustic Blue, then an older, vintage sparkler will work beautifully. If, on the other hand, the blue cheese is creamier and more tangy, like the one made by Point Reyes Farmstead Cheese Company, then a fruitier style sparkling wine is in order. Either way, the bubbles and the yeasty quality usually provide a nice backdrop for the pungent cheese.

Creamy cheeses, especially double- or triple-crèmes, linger in the mouth long after the bulk of the cheese has made its way down. The cream gives real definition to the term "mouthfeel." What could be better than bubbles to lap up what's left? Not only is the combination refreshing; the earthy flavors in the wine are favorably accentuated by the sweet, fruity cheese.

Salty cheeses are also aided by the bubbles in sparkling wine. If you've ever had a chunk of Parmesan with an older vintage sparkler, you'll understand. The bubbles help diffuse the salt, and in this case the aged cheese has taken on some nutty and possibly caramel characteristics that become a heavenly match with the caramel-like and toasty wine.

The same is true with other salty cheeses, too. Even a fresh cheese like feta, because of its high salt content, finds a nice match in sparkling wine. Feta often has a creamy mouthfeel, even though it's usually crumbly, so this makes it doubly good with sparkling wine.

Although different from sparkling wine, certain dessert wines have a similar agreeable effervescence. These are, of course, sweet rather than dry, but the effervescence works the same way with blue and creamy cheeses as do the sparkling wines. Dessert wines also work with the salty cheeses, but more because they are sweet. We'll get into that a little later.

Following are some examples of pairing sparkling wine with blue, creamy, and salty cheeses:

- Aged (harder-style) blue cheese with an older vintage brut

- Creamy, tangy-style blue cheese with a non-vintage blanc de noirs

- Sweeter-style blue cheese, such as Gorgonzola, with sweet-style sparkling wine or effervescent dessert wine

- Double- or triple-crème with vintage brut or blanc de blancs

- Hard goats', sheep's, or cows' milk cheese and older vintage brut

# 6. PAIR RED WINES WITH (ALMOST) ANYTHING

As we have discovered, white wines find their way with cheese more effortlessly than do red wines. That is not to say that you should not drink red wine with cheese. But red wine will often seem bitter when sipped with many cheeses, because the tannins in red wine are exacerbated by salt and umami. Many cheeses have a good amount of discernible salt, which brings the tannins to the fore.

Generally speaking, the lighter and fruitier the red wine, the easier it is to find the right cheese matches. Such wines have more perceptible acidity and fewer assertive components for the cheese to butt up against. As an example, a light-bodied fruity Sangiovese is quite nice with mozzarella. The flip side, of course, is that a wine that is too light may simply get lost with a cheese that is substantially more flavorful than the wine. Beyond that, we can draw on the notion of texture as well as flavor and come to a few conclusions.

The lighter and generally milder nature of semi-soft cheeses will dictate a similar wine, be it red or white. Semi-hard cheeses, despite the fact that they are often more flavorful and complex, paradoxically are often the easiest to pair with wine, both white and red, due to their natural balance of salt, acidity, and umami. A fruit-forward, jammy wine will go just as well as a red wine with more pronounced acidity. Semi-hard cheeses also go well with older wines.

If you're looking to uncork that fabulous twenty-year-old Cabernet Sauvignon you've been saving, then try to select cheeses that are a little "older" as well. That is, a more aged cheese will often share some of the same qualities embodied in your older wine: earthiness, perhaps some nuttiness, and coffee or caramel flavors. An aged Gouda is a good choice in this case as long as it isn't too sharp. Other bigger red wines, such as Zinfandel, Syrah, and some Merlots, will find companionship with many semi-hard cheeses such as Emmentaler, Gruyère, and cheddar, with one caveat: If the wines are particularly tannic, then they will probably taste bitter with those cheeses.

Hard cheeses with their salty yet sweet flavors go surprisingly well with many red wines. Keeping in mind that big tannins will be exacerbated by excess salt, the type of red wine to match with hard cheeses should again be an older vintage and/or be fruit-forward.

Soft-ripened cheeses present a few more challenges when it comes to finding good red wine matches, owing to the different flavors in the rind versus the paste (the interior) and also to the distinct textures inherent in this type of cheese. The rind of Camembert, for example, can be a little strong and slightly chewy. The paste, on the other hand, might be creamy and buttery, perhaps with hints of mushroom. These contradictions make finding the right wine pretty tough, not only because of the disparate flavors within the cheese but also because of the fact that creaminess usually flattens any existing tannins. In effect, the creaminess demolishes the wine. Thus the people of Normandy probably have it correct when they pair their native soft-ripened cheeses with the region's famous hard cider. But since we're talking about red wine here, choose one that is light- to medium-bodied and that has some earthy *and* fruity characteristics, such as Pinot Noir, Sangiovese, or even some not-too-tannic Cabernet Francs, such as the ones made by S. Rhodes Vineyards in Colorado or a medium-bodied, fruity Syrah. Washed-rind cheeses, which have the same creamy texture as a ripe soft-ripened cheese, are almost always disastrous with big red wines. The strong earthy, often gamy, and toasted nut flavors in washed-rind cheeses require a more delicate, fruity, or sweet wine companion. Most red wines are simply too bold. (Don't tell this to the Burgundians, who swear by their pairing of Epoisses—a very aromatic regional washed-rind cheese—with the famous Pinot Noir of that region!)

When it comes to pairing blue cheeses and red wine, in general this combination simply does not

**Aged cheddar pairs nicely with an older vintage Syrah.**

work because of the strong, pungent nature of the mold flavor. In addition, the high salt content in blue cheese often makes a red wine taste more tannic. As with other cheeses, though, a fruity wine will improve your chances of creating a good match. If you're dying to match a red wine with a blue cheese, then select an older wine in which the tannins have mellowed and an older, harder-style blue cheese. A light- to medium-bodied Cabernet Sauvignon or Merlot will work with more aged blue cheeses; a younger, creamier-style blue cheese, although hard to match with red wine, will find some affinity with a mild, light- to medium-bodied Zinfandel, and surprisingly, a fruit-forward Pinot Noir.

Following are some examples of pairing red wines and cheeses:

- Blue cheese (semi-soft and sweet) and fruity, light- to medium-bodied Zinfandel or Pinot Noir

- Blue cheese (semi-hard) and older or light- to medium-bodied Cabernet Sauvignon or Merlot

- Camembert and Pinot Noir, Sangiovese, or Cabernet Franc

- Cheddar (semi-hard, earthy—not sharp) and Zinfandel (full-bodied)

- Colby and Barbera or Carignane

- Fontina (semi-soft) and Dolcetto

- Gouda (aged) and older vintage Cabernet Sauvignon or Merlot

- Mozzarella and Sangiovese

## 7. PAIR CHEESES AND WINES WITH COMPARABLE FLAVORS

This is common advice about food and wine pairing, and it works for chese and wine too. Identify the dominant flavors in the cheese you're eating and seek out a wine or wines that share a similar flavor profile. You can begin by looking at the varietal descriptors on pages 56 and 57 to become familiar with the primary characteristics in each type of grape. From there, you can begin to draw some conclusions about the cheeses to choose.

We have already talked about choosing cheeses and wines that have a textural likeness. We have also discussed the notion of selecting light wines for light cheeses. Now let's make a few choices based on the specific flavors in the cheeses and the wines. A fresh goat cheese, for example is usually lemony, citrusy, acidic, tangy, and salty. What wines share some, or most, of those characteristics? An Oregon Pinot Gris or Sauvignon Blanc. Let's take another example: a double- or triple-crème cheese, such as Marin French Cheese Company's Le Petit Crème. It is a rich, buttery, creamy cheese. What better to pair with it than a rich, buttery (but not excessively oaky) Chardonnay?

Another example centers on a fortified wine— sherry. While there aren't a lot of sherries made in the United States yet, there are a few notable ones, including one made by Hunt Country Winery in New York's Finger Lakes district. With its distinctive nuttiness and slight fruitiness, sherry is one of cheese's greatest companions. A nutty sheep's milk cheese and a glass of sherry is an unbeatable combination. And so it goes. Find like characteristics in the cheese and in the wine, taking into account texture too, and you're on your way to a great match.

Following are some examples of pairing cheeses and wines with comparable flavors:

- Brie or Camembert (triple-crème) and Chardonnay

- Dry Jack and sherry or tawny port

- Emmentaler and Riesling or medium-bodied Merlot

- Goat cheese (fresh) and Sauvignon Blanc or Pinot Gris

- Goat cheese (aged) and Syrah

- Sheep's milk cheese (aged) and Gewürztraminer or sherry

# 8. PAIR CHEESES AND WINES WITH "OPPOSITE" FLAVORS

The notion of opposites attracting isn't a far-flung theory when applied to cheese and wine pairing. Much of the way we put food and wine together is based on this idea, whether or not we're aware of it. For example, you might slather a pork tenderloin with a sweet apricot compote, or coat some salty popcorn with caramel sauce to create caramel corn. Enjoying sweet and salty or sweet and savory flavors together is a fundamental physiological pleasure, which is why cheese and wine make such fine bedfellows.

An advantage to choosing opposing flavors in cheese and wine is that such pairs are simply more obvious. If you have a particularly salty cheese, then it is fairly easy to figure out that a dessert wine will provide the opposing sweet flavors. This type of pairing works more times than not, as long as the saltiness and the sweetness are in balance. If you have a marginally salty cheese and a very sweet wine, this theory goes out the window.

There are many classic "opposite" cheese and wine pairings, including Roquefort and Sauternes and Stilton and Port, but those are all European combinations. In this country, where many of the dry wines (those in which all of the sugar has been fermented into alcohol) still taste fairly fruity because of the warm climates in which the grapes have been grown, finding opposite or contrasting pairings is relatively easy. A Dry Creek Zinfandel from Sonoma County will usually have dominant fruit and alcohol, so a salty, aged cheese like Sonoma's aged dry Jack will work as its attractive opposite. A Texas Viognier will have pretty dominant fruit characteristics, so a more subdued yet salty cheese like a semi-hard Asiago will usually go alongside pretty well. A semi-dry Riesling from the Finger Lakes will go beautifully with a New York cheddar, while a Washington Merlot will have an affinity with a salty sheep's milk feta.

Following are some examples of pairing cheeses and wines with "opposite" flavors:

- Asiago (semi-hard) and (fruity) Viognier
- Blue cheese (semi-soft, crumbly) and late-harvest Sauvignon Blanc, Muscat, or ruby port
- Blue cheese (semi-hard) and late-harvest Gewürztraminer, Riesling, cream sherry, or tawny port
- Dry Jack and (full-bodied) Zinfandel
- Cheddar and semi-dry Riesling
- Feta and (fruity) Merlot

# 9. PAIR DESSERT WINES WITH CHEESE

When it comes to the term "dessert wine," there can be a wide variety of meanings. It always means sweet, but the degree of sweetness varies. One way to gauge the sweetness of a dessert wine is to look at the percentage of residual sugar in the wine, which is often listed on the label. (Residual sugar is not indicated on dry wine labels because there is usually no measurable amount. Residual sugar is, however, often listed on off-dry wine labels and usually hovers around 1 percent). The higher the percentage, the sweeter the wine.

In addition, the words "late harvest" and "fortified" are telltale indicators that the wine is sweet. "Late harvest" means that the grapes for the wine were picked after the normal harvest period. The longer period on the vine means that the grapes have developed more sugar. You can find almost every type of white grape in a late-harvest form, though Riesling, Sauvignon Blanc, and Gewürztraminer are probably the most common in this country. As for red wine, you will occasionally find a late harvest Zinfandel, but most red grapes are picked earlier and made into dry wine or fortified wine, such as port. Fortified means that a high-alcohol liquid, such as brandy, has been added to the wine to stop fermentation and maintain the remaining sugars in the juice. (Fermentation yeasts die when subjected to high levels of alcohol.) The addition of the brandy significantly boosts the alcohol level of the wine and also ensures a sweet wine.

In the United States, we are blessed with innumerable marvelous dessert wines—the Finger Lakes' Anthony Road Vignoles (a French-American hybrid grape), Mendocino County's Navarro Late-Harvest Gewürztraminer, Oregon's Andrew Rich Late Harvest Gewürztraminer, Robert Mondavi's Moscato d'Oro, Bonny Doon's Vin de Glaciere, and ice wines from Washington, to name just a few. This means that not only do we have great wines to choose from, but we also have great wines to match with cheese. Cheese together with dessert wine is a fantastic combination, whether the combination is served before, during, after, or instead of a meal.

The concept of matching dessert wines with cheese is akin to the notion of pairing contrasting cheeses and wines, but it is different in that the sweetness of dessert wines makes them compatible with all kinds of cheeses, regardless of whether they have contrasting or similar flavors. Robert Mondavi's Moscato d'Oro has slight effervescence, low alcohol, and sweet but not cloying flavors. Put together with, say, Fontina cheese, it isn't exactly a study in opposites but rather one of distinct flavors that meld together. The creamy and sometimes pungent cheese comes full circle with the refreshingly sweet wine, helping to accentuate the fruit even further. A late-harvest Sauvignon Blanc, while it may range from sweet to very sweet, will find a companion in aged goat cheese because the cheese has earthy and salty qualities which, again, will elevate the fruit in the wine.

The point is that dessert wine—depending on just how sweet it is and how much alcohol it contains—can be wonderful at all times, not just for dessert. Try sipping a not-too-sweet "dessert" wine with a cheese or two before dinner; or use cheese as the primary ingredient in your first course, and instead of matching it with a dry wine, seek out an appropriate sweet wine. For the same reasons cheese and fruity wines often make successful pairs, cheese and dessert wines find successful companionship, too.

As a guide, the primary flavor characteristics of various dessert wines include: dried fruit (raisin, apricot, fig, prune), chocolate, coffee, honey, mineral, caramel, orange, toffee, and nuts.

Following are some examples of pairing cheeses and dessert wines:

- Brie or Camembert and late-harvest Muscat

- Cheddar and late-harvest Gewürztraminer

- Fontina and late-harvest Muscat

- Goat cheese (aged) and late-harvest Sauvignon Blanc

- Gouda (aged) and cream sherry or late-harvest Zinfandel

- Parmesan and late-harvest Riesling or cream sherry

# 10. PAIR AGED, MILD CHEESES WITH OLDER, MILDER WINES

The idea of an "aged, mild cheese" may sound like an oxymoron, since we tend to think of cheese getting stronger as it gets older. How a cheese ages depends on the type of cheese. For example, a washed-rind cheese gets undeniably stronger with time and therefore does not fall into the category of cheeses we're talking about here. Gruyère, on the other hand, might be aged a year or more, yet it will never become particularly strong. It will be flavorful but not strong. An older wine acts similarly: It no longer has bright fruit or tannic characteristics but, instead, in the case of bigger red wines such as Cabernet Sauvignon and Merlot, is more mellow and earthy. Older white wines will likely have taken on caramel and butterscotch characteristics. An aged cheese like Gouda also has caramel and butterscotch flavors and can therefore be linked with an older white wine. Gruyère, with its nutty yet sweet components, matches nicely with an older Chardonnay. A super-aged cheddar takes on almost haunting characteristics, including a deep earthiness with a rounded sharpness, sort of like the tip of a butter knife. An older, mellow red wine with this type of cheese is a good match.

The concept of "older" wine might mean anything from about five years and beyond, depending on the grape. In the case of red wines, certain wines like Zinfandel and (American) Pinot Noir should probably be drunk within eight to ten years. After that, age will start to diminish instead of enhance the wine. An older white wine is one that is about four or five years old. A grape such as Chardonnay can hold for this long—and longer—but in this country we tend not to like the flavors that older Chardonnays and other white wines deliver. Also, we don't really make these wines in a style that is meant to age. Chenin Blanc, however, is worth some attention as it has proven to be a wine that has the ability to hold up for years—even decades—although at this point in time, this is more true for European than American Chenin Blanc.

As cheese and wine mellow, they assume identities different from those they had when they were younger. Their vibrant youth is supplanted by tranquility; forward fruit retreats into the background; a once-astringent wine is now suave. With certain cheeses, extended time in the aging room allows them to become sweet, mellow, and sometimes a little grainy. Together, these older cheeses and wines find companionship because neither is interested in wrestling the other for attention. Instead, they are respectful of one another and find companionship side by side.

Following are some examples of pairing aged, mild cheeses with older, milder wines:

- Cheddar and Cabernet Sauvignon

- Dry Jack and Syrah

- Gouda and Chardonnay or Chenin Blanc

- Gruyère and Chardonnay

# Clues for Perfect Pairs

Now that we've gone through the basic guidelines for pairing cheese and wine, it's time to get specific. In the following section, each of the seven styles of cheese is listed, followed by wine pairing suggestions for those cheeses.

## F R E S H   C H E E S E S

The unaged character of fresh cheeses often equates to mild, fresh milk flavors. With fresh cows' milk cheeses, the flavor sometimes makes them a little tougher to match with wine, but if you consider mild wines with a little bit of butteriness and/or sweetness, you'll be on track. A light-bodied Chardonnay will work; so, too, will Chenin Blanc or even a higher-acid red wine such as Sangiovese. Another white wine, Sémillon, is a great match for fresh cheeses, and winemakers in the state of Washington are making some noteworthy Sémillons. A more challenging wine match is fromage blanc, which is very tangy, almost sour. Although it's unlikely you would be eating fromage blanc by itself, if you did you would be well advised to choose a simple, tart wine to match. Pinot Gris would be a good choice.

Goats' and sheep's milk cheeses also have that fresh milk flavor, but because the milk from goats and sheep has more pronounced flavors, these cheeses might taste a little stronger, sometimes even gamy. In almost all cases, the acidity level of such fresh cheese is relatively high, and this equates to citrusy, tangy qualities, especially in goat cheese. That is why the classic match for fresh goat cheese is Sauvignon Blanc. It too has these citrusy qualities.

Although high in acid, sheep's milk ricotta is also buttery. For that reason, a medium-bodied Chardonnay or a light-bodied Sangiovese is a good wine choice for this type of cheese.

KEYWORDS: Acidity, Citrusy, Fresh milk, Mild, Tangy

| PERFECT PAIRS | |
|---|---|
| Fresh goat cheese | Sauvignon Blanc, Sémillon, or Pinot Gris |
| Ricotta (cows' milk) | Sauvignon Blanc, Chenin Blanc, or Chardonnay |
| Ricotta (goats' milk) | Sauvignon Blanc |
| Ricotta (sheep's milk) | Chardonnay or Sangiovese |
| Mozzarella | Chenin Blanc or Sangiovese |
| Fromage blanc (cows' milk) | Pinot Gris |

# SEMI-SOFT CHEESES

The less creamy but still mild cheeses, such as Monterey Jack, Gouda, and Fontina, also pair well with these same white wines, but because of their firmer texture, occasional saltiness, and in some cases more assertive flavors, these types of semi-soft cheeses interplay wonderfully with some high-acid and lighter-style red wines too. These would include a light-bodied Pinot Noir and, if you can find it, Dolcetto. More and more American winemakers are experimenting with Dolcetto, which is a good thing for all cheese and wine lovers! A light-bodied, fruity Zinfandel will also work with these cheeses.

Because semi-soft cheeses vary dramatically in both flavor and texture, so too do compatible wine choices. When choosing a wine, remember once again that texture should also be taken into account. Both cheese *and* wine have texture and are often best matched accordingly. As for flavor, the runny-style semi-soft cheeses tend to be mild, although certainly not lacking in flavor. Teleme and Crescenza, for example (the latter made by Bellwether Farms in California), have a silken texture and are a combination of fruity and faintly sharp flavors. These factors make these cheeses good candidates for light- to medium-bodied, fruity white wines. Chenin Blanc, Viognier, and Riesling are all good choices. Although hard to find in this country, lighter, fruitier-style Chardonnays are lovely with this style of cheese too, while a light dessert wine, such as a low-alcohol Muscat (also known as Moscato), makes another excellent match.

KEYWORDS: Creamy, Silken, Sharp, Fruity, Salty, Bitter, Assertive

| PERFECT PAIRS | |
|---|---|
| **SILKEN CHEESES** | |
| Teleme | Chardonnay (light-bodied; no oak), Chenin Blanc, late-harvest Muscat, Riesling, Viognier |
| Crescenza | Chardonnay (light-bodied; no oak), Chenin Blanc, late-harvest Moscato (Muscat), Riesling, Viognier |
| **SLIGHTLY FIRMER CHEESES** | |
| Brick | Riesling |
| Colby | Riesling, Barbera, Dolcetto, Pinot Noir |
| Crowley | Chenin Blanc, Riesling, Dolcetto, Pinot Noir, Zinfandel (light- to medium-bodied; fruity) |
| Gouda | Chardonnay, Chenin Blanc, Riesling, Dolcetto, Zinfandel (light- to medium-bodied; fruity) |
| Fontina, Havarti, and Muenster | Riesling, Barbera, Dolcetto |
| Monterey Jack | Chardonnay, Riesling, Zinfandel (light- to medium-bodied; fruity) |
| Provolone | Chenin Blanc, Riesling, Dolcetto |

As we know, soft-ripened cheeses can be made from each of the three types of milk. While this gives us a wonderful variety of soft-ripened cheeses to choose from, it also makes it a little more difficult to assign these cheeses to one particular wine category. They're also more challenging to pair with wine because the rind and the paste taste distinctly different. Remove the rind and you're left with a creamy consistency and usually sweeter flavors; eat the rind along with the paste and you have two different textures—one that is slightly chewy (the rind) and one that is creamy (the paste)—and two different flavors (buttery, mushroomy, and sometimes even a slight ammonia taste and aroma). One thing is always true about these cheeses: They are rarely one-dimensional, owing to the different flavors of the rind versus the paste. If made right, these cheeses are almost always creamy or at least have a creamy mouthfeel.

## COWS' MILK CHEESES

Knowing that the words "buttery" and "creamy" are usually used in the same sentence as "soft-ripened cheese" should be a broad hint as to the types of wine that will pair nicely with these cheeses. A buttery, though not excessively oaky, Chardonnay is astoundingly good with many cows' milk soft-ripened cheeses. Pinot Noir might also be good, with its soft tannins and nice jammy yet earthy flavors, which complement the floral and earthy qualities in the cheese. But Pinot Noir is finicky, and unfortunately it can often be a cheese *mis*match rather than a good match. The only way to really know is to try it, although if you can ask your retailer to pick out a Pinot Noir in which red fruits such as raspberries are accentuated, then you'll probably have a good chance that it will go well with your soft-ripened cheese.

Another surprising wine companion features bubbles: sparkling wine. If the cheese is salty, the bubbles in a sparkling wine tend to play off that saltiness and bring out the creaminess of the cheese. The creamy quality of the wine further enhances that quality in the cheese, as does the toastiness inherent in sparkling wine. Choose a sparkling wine with a hint of fruit, such as a blanc de noirs or rosé.

## GOATS' MILK CHEESES

Since goats' milk cheeses are not as buttery as cows' milk cheeses and retain some tartness, Chardonnay, with its tropical, buttery, and often oaky flavors, is *not* a good choice. Instead, Sauvignon Blanc, with its relatively high acidity, is a better choice. Also, a goats' milk soft-ripened cheese often has herbal flavors, bolstering the case for pairing it with an herbal wine such as Sauvignon Blanc. Once again, Pinot Noir often works. Either a fruity or earthy style works, primarily because this style of cheese is usually fairly complex. It can withstand the power of the wine and will, in fact, bring out the best in the wine.

If the cheese is quite ripe, as distinguished by a faint ammoniated aroma and a very creamy texture, then think about choosing light- to medium-bodied red wines that strike a balance between acidity and fruitiness. Believe it or not, certain Merlots and Cabernet Sauvignons can work surprisingly well if they are youthful and relatively light in style. No high-alcohol Napa blockbusters here, though! Another wine to consider is a California Sangiovese, which has just enough fruit to counterbalance the tanginess and saltiness of the cheese, yet a good amount of acidity to marry well with the relatively sharp-flavored rind.

## SHEEP'S MILK CHEESES

Finally, while we have only a few 100-percent sheep's milk soft-ripening cheeses in this country (so far), Old Chatham Sheepherding Company's Shepherd's Wheel is noteworthy. Sheep's milk is not tangy, but in this case neither is it as buttery as cows' milk. The rind of the sheep's milk cheese is somewhat tart or even pleasantly bitter, and the paste is ivory-colored. The texture is creamy, and its flavor is a bit grassy, with hints of butter. As a result, red wines with earthy overtones, such as Pinot Noir or Sangiovese, make nice companions. A dry sparkling wine, or brut, also works well.

KEYWORDS: Creamy, Buttery, Fruity, Garlicky, Herbal, Milky, Mushroomy, Salty, Tart

| PERFECT PAIRS | |
|---|---|
| **COWS' MILK CHEESES** | |
| Brie | Sparkling wine, Chardonnay, Pinot Noir |
| Camembert | Sparkling wine, Chardonnay, Pinot Noir |
| Triple Crème | Sparkling wine, Chardonnay, Pinot Noir |
| **GOATS' MILK CHEESES** | |
| Camembert | Sauvignon Blanc (some oak is okay), sparkling wine, Pinot Noir |
| (Slightly) aged soft-ripened goat cheeses | Sauvignon Blanc, Sangiovese, Pinot Noir, light-bodied Merlot, light- to medium-bodied Cabernet Sauvignon |
| **SHEEP'S MILK CHEESE** | |
| Camembert | Sparkling wine, Pinot Noir, Sangiovese |

# WASHED-RIND CHEESES

Washed-rind cheeses are downright pungent. Because of this, they require a light and fruity wine. In the Alsace region of France, where Munster is from, the cheese is traditionally paired with the fruitier Alsatian wines, particularly Gewürztraminer. The strong, earthy cheese needs a fruity counterpart. Riesling and the hybrid grape Vignoles will make nice matches, as will several styles of dessert wine, including Muscat and cream sherry. Just be sure that the wine isn't overwhelmingly sweet, since the strong flavors in the cheese will automatically accentuate that sweetness. Acidic wines won't work with washed-rind cheeses because of the creamy nature of these cheeses (even when they're not extremely creamy, they're still rather rich), and oaky wines will simply introduce unwanted flavors. Red wines, as usual, are tough to match up with this style of cheese. Some people enjoy meritage wines (a blend of Cabernet Sauvignon, Cabernet Franc, Merlot, and sometimes Malbec and Petite Verdot) with washed-rind cheeses, but keep in mind that the wine and cheese both have very pronounced flavors, and the chances are that the cheese will accentuate the tannins and quash the fruit in the wine. A loud faction of cheese and wine lovers swears by Pinot Noir with washed-rind cheeses. Again, there are more flavors to clash than to meld, but it's worth a try. You might try a medium-bodied Zinfandel, but be sure it has plenty of forward fruit flavors.

KEYWORDS: Barnyardy, Creamy, Fruity, Gamy, Meaty, Toasted hazelnut, Roasted mushrooms

| PERFECT PAIRS | |
|---|---|
| All washed-rind cheeses | Gewürztraminer, late-harvest Gewürztraminer, Muscat, Pinot Noir, Riesling, Vignoles, Zinfandel (medium-bodied, fruity), cream sherry |

# SEMI-HARD CHEESES

The diversity within the semi-hard cheese category makes discovering wine companions a particularly exciting journey. Because many of these cheeses are made in large wheels, the part of the cheese closest to the rind might taste decidedly different from and have a somewhat different mouthfeel than the paste or interior of the cheese. That is because the flavors and texture in the area nearest the outside of the cheese will begin to change sooner than will the interior portion, becoming a little musty and slightly harder. The rind, too, might impart flavor. Nonetheless, a wine that goes well with this style of cheese will usually match just fine with both the inner and outer portions of the cheese.

## COWS' MILK CHEESES

Many semi-hard cows' milk cheeses have a decidedly nutty character. They are also often sweet and sometimes buttery too. The exceptions are higher-acid cheeses like Swiss and sharp cheddars. So choose your wines based on the style of semi-hard cheeses you're eating. For less pungent cheeses like Gruyère and mellow cheddars, the sweet and nutty elements are distinct clues. In this case, think sherry. Or, if you're not a sherry fan, Gewürztraminer also fits the bill. The relative mellowness of cows' milk semi-hard cheeses also makes them nice companions for an older Chardonnay. "Older" is the key, as it will have mellowed, just like the cheese, and become a bit caramel-like—also like many semi-hard cheeses. One more lovely choice is Viognier.

The peach and apricot flavors, along with the hint of oak that is in some American Viogniers, go nicely with the fruity qualities of many semi-hard cheeses.

Many people enjoy red wines with this style of cheese, and for good reason. The complexity and rich qualities of theese cheeses often find those same qualities in red wine. Select a red wine that has good fruit and body such as Cabernet Sauvignon, Grenache, Merlot or Zinfandels. You have another option with this style of cheese, and that is dessert wine. Choose one that isn't overly sweet or alcoholic, such as a Muscat or a late-harvest Riesling.

If you would like to finish off that pungent cheddar or Emmentaler you've had in the fridge, then think in terms of fruity, semi-dry, or dessert wines. Dry wines will invariably taste bitter with these sharper cheeses, although a lighter red, such as Cabernet Franc, will work alongside an Emmentaler, as will Riesling. Choose a ruby port, late-harvest Zinfandel, late-harvest orange Muscat, or late-harvest Gewürztraminer.

## GOATS' MILK CHEESES

Semi-hard goats' milk cheese is among the most exciting of all goat cheeses. This is partly because it is an artisan cheese; there are no mass-produced ones. Producers such as Cypress Grove in California, which makes a semi-hard cheese called Mt. McKinley, and White Oak Farm in Washington, whose Golden Rose is as lovely as its name, have really contributed to the ever-increasing array of goats' milk cheese.

Semi-hard goats' milk cheese tends to be flavorful, often earthy, and sometimes gamy. It can also become faintly sweet as it ages, as compared with fresher-style goats' milk cheese, which is usually more tart. The result is cheese that walks the line between earthiness and fruitiness. The wine for this type of cheese, therefore, should do the same thing. Earthy and fruity can mean a Gewürztraminer, which has both of those flavors. On the red side choose a Pinot Noir, medium-bodied Merlot, or a medium-bodied or older vintage Cabernet Sauvignon.

## SHEEP'S MILK CHEESES

Semi-hard sheep's milk cheeses are a breed in and of themselves. The high-butterfat milk lends a richness and complexity to the cheese that is beyond compare. In some countries, semi-hard sheep's milk cheeses taste downright barnyardy, but for the most part, that does not seem to happen to American-made cheeses. Instead, the cheese will often be quite earthy, but never unfavorably strong or tasting of lanolin (the distinctive "lamb" aroma and flavor). The cheese is usually yellowish gold in color and, with a few exceptions, has a natural rind. For this group of cheeses, Gewürztraminer is once again an excellent choice as is a dry or medium-dry sherry. On the red wine front, Sangiovese can match up nicely.

KEYWORDS: Caramel, Chewy, Earthy, Fruity, Gamy, Meaty, Mineral, Nutty, Sharp

| PERFECT PAIRS | |
|---|---|
| COWS' MILK CHEESES | |
| Cheddar (not sharp) | Gewürztraminer, late-harvest Riesling, Viognier, Zinfandel, Cabernet Sauvignon (light- to- medium-bodied), sherry |
| Cheddar (sharp) | Grenache, Merlot, Zinfandel, late-harvest Gewürztraminer |
| Emmentaler | Riesling, Grenache, Zinfandel, late-harvest Gewürztraminer |
| Gruyère | Gewürztraminer, late-harvest Riesling, Viognier, Zinfandel, sherry |
| GOATS' MILK CHEESES | |
| Aged farmhouse | Gewürztraminer, Merlot, Cabernet Sauvignon (older vintage), Pinot Noir |
| SHEEP'S MILK CHEESES | |
| Aged farmhouse | Gewürztraminer, Sangiovese, or sherry |

# H A R D   C H E E S E S

Despite their name, hard cheeses are relatively easy to pair with wine because, as a family, they simply don't differ from one another quite as much as other cheeses do. This makes wine pairing a little more intuitive. When it comes to selecting suitable wines, hard cheeses are also more versatile than one might think.

First, let's consider the salt in hard cheeses. A cheese high in salt, such as Parmesan, automatically calls for a wine that will do something to tame that salt. This brings to mind three elements of taste and/or texture to look for in a wine: sweetness, dryness, and bubbles. On the sweet front, a dessert wine or a fruity wine provides a natural balance with the saltiness in the cheese. If the cheese is moderately salty, you might choose a Riesling or a Gewürztraminer in either their dry or sweet (dessert) forms, or a tawny port. These wines will work well because of their fruit overtones, which are pronounced enough to counter the salt in the cheese but not so excessive that they taste cloying compared to the moderately salty cheese. It is very important that the degree of saltiness in the cheese be taken into account when you decide how sweet your wine should be.

A dry wine can of course come in many forms. A nice benefit of pairing a hard cheese with a dry wine is that the fruit that *does* exist in the wine is brought forward by the salt in the cheese. That salt serves to emphasize the fruit. Conversely, hard cheeses sometimes have pineapple or other fruitlike flavors, which can make the wine taste bitter, because the fruit in the wine will be diminished by the fruitlike flavors in the cheese. But if the wine is not bone dry, it will find companionship with salty hard cheeses. If the wine is particularly tannic, a very salty cheese will unfortunately often do its part to raise the profile of those tannins. A white wine (once again) will usually save the day. Or, if you prefer red wine, choose ones that are rich and jammy in style.

One "compromise" wine is sherry. This fortified beverage, especially in its dry form, has nuttiness *and* sweetness. As such, it is not a contrasting wine but one that parallels the nuttiness in the cheese and "one-ups" the cheese only slightly on the fruity front. Even in its driest form, a sherry is quite nice with most hard cheeses.

On the bubble front, a sparkling wine will affect a hard cheese much as it does a blue cheese. The bubbles serve to diminish the salty flavors in your mouth, almost giving the impression that the salt is being lifted from your tongue. Both blanc de noirs and brut will work with these cheeses.

KEYWORDS: Butterscotch, Caramel, Grainy, Gritty, Lipase, Nutty, Pineapple, Pungent, Salty

| PERFECT PAIRS | |
|---|---|
| Asiago, Parmesan, and many artisan cows', sheep's, and goats' milk cheeses | Carignane, Gewürztraminer, Riesling, Sangiovese, sherry, sparkling wine |

# BLUE CHEESES

There are a couple of qualities common to all blue cheeses: They are usually salty, and they range from mildly assertive to very assertive. If a cheese is particularly salty, it's almost always safest to look for a wine that offers contrasting flavors. In other words, think sweet. A fruity wine, like a Riesling or a Gewürztraminer, which has a sweet flavor (although no sugar has been added), or a sweet dessert wine, will go wonderfully with most blue cheeses.

Do all sweet or fruity wines go with all blue cheeses? The answer is yes *and* no. The reason is that the degree of saltiness in the cheese and the degree of fruitiness or sweetness in the wine varies. The best rule of thumb is if you are choosing a milder, creamy blue cheese, select a dry or almost dry wine rather than a dessert wine. This means a young Gorgonzola is best with a light Muscat or perhaps a semi-dry Riesling. The next category of blue cheeses—the Roquefort-like ones—can handle sweeter wines, and thus almost any late-harvest dessert wine will work beautifully. As for the hard blue cheeses, the words "butterscotch," "hazelnut," "chocolate," and "caramel" come to mind. The classic match for this type of cheese, therefore, is port, since it shares many of these same qualities, with one important addition: sugar. Thus you get contrasting *and* complementary flavors in one wine.

Sweet and fruity wines are not the only blue cheese–friendly wines. In fact, blue cheese probably has more wine companions than does any other type of cheese. Three other categories of wine—sparkling, older red wine, and sherry—also go well with blue cheese.

Sparkling wines have many complementary flavors that are found in blue cheese: musty, yeasty, and toasty, to name a few. These wines also offer the perfect counterpart to blue cheese: bubbles. The salt in blue cheese is diffused by these bubbles and, together, wine and cheese become a symphony in the mouth. Add to that a hint of fruit in the wine, and you've got a remarkable pair. A brut or a blanc de noirs will be great.

Red wines are a lot trickier, but some can work. An older red wine is almost always a better choice than a recent vintage for pairing with blue cheese because of the tannins. Harsh tannins and blue cheese add up to a cacophony of flavors in the mouth. A symphony is preferable. For this to happen, choose an older vintage Cabernet Sauvignon or Merlot.

There are different types of sherry, but one element they all share is nuttiness. They also have some amount of sweetness. This combination makes for a lovely blue cheese companion. Choose a drier-style sherry to accompany a younger blue cheese and a sweeter-style sherry for older and firmer blue cheese.

KEYWORDS: Almond, Anise, Buttery, Caramel, Chocolate, Creamy, Hazelnut, Musty, Tangy, Toasty, Salty, Sweet

| PERFECT PAIRS | |
|---|---|
| Soft, creamy, and young blue cheese, such as Gorgonzola | Riesling, Gewürztraminer, sherry (dry) |
| Firmer, more pungent blue cheese | Riesling, Gewürztraminer, late-harvest Riesling, late-harvest Orange Muscat or Muscat Canelli, sparkling wine (brut, blanc de noirs, or brut rosé) |
| Semi-hard blue cheese | Cabernet Sauvignon (older), Merlot (older), sherry (medium-dry or cream), late-harvest Riesling, late-harvest Orange Muscat or Muscat Canelli, sparkling wine (brut, blanc denoirs, or brut rosé) |

## CHEESE

| Cheese | Arneis | Cayuga White (hybrid) | Chardonnay | Chenin Blanc | Gewürztraminer | Muscat (late-harvest) | Pinot Blanc | Pinot Gris | Riesling | Sauvignon Blanc | Sémillon | Seyval (hybrid) | Sparkling Wine | Vidal Blanc (hybrid) | Vignoles (hybrid) | Viognier | Dessert Wines (medium sweet) | Dessert Wines (very sweet) |
|---|---|---|---|---|---|---|---|---|---|---|---|---|---|---|---|---|---|---|
| Asiago |  |  |  | ◆ |  |  |  |  | ◆ |  |  | ◆ | ◆ |  |  | ◆ |  |  |
| Baby Swiss |  | ◆ | ◆ |  | ◆ |  |  |  |  |  |  |  |  |  |  |  |  |  |
| Blue Cheese (semi-soft) |  | ◆ |  | ◆ |  |  |  |  | ◆ |  |  |  | ◆ | ◆ | ◆ |  |  |  |
| Blue Cheese (semi-hard and/or salty) |  |  |  | ◆ |  |  |  |  | ◆ |  |  |  | ◆ |  | ◆ | ◆ |  |  |
| Brie and Camembert (cows' milk) |  | ◆ | ◆ |  |  | ◆ |  |  |  |  |  |  | ◆ |  |  |  |  |  |
| Camembert (goats' milk) | ◆ | ◆ |  | ◆ |  |  | ◆ |  | ◆ | ◆ | ◆ |  |  |  |  |  |  |  |
| Cheddar (semi-soft, not sharp) |  | ◆ |  |  |  |  | ◆ | ◆ |  |  |  |  |  | ◆ |  |  |  |  |
| Cheddar (semi-hard, earthy) |  |  | ◆ |  |  |  |  |  |  |  |  |  | ◆ | ◆ |  |  |  |  |
| Cheddar (sharp) |  | ◆ |  | ◆ |  |  |  |  | ◆ |  |  |  |  | ◆ |  |  |  |  |
| Colby |  | ◆ |  |  |  |  | ◆ |  | ◆ |  |  |  |  | ◆ | ◆ |  |  |  |
| Crescenza |  | ◆ |  | ◆ |  | ◆ |  |  |  |  |  |  |  | ◆ | ◆ |  |  |  |
| Crottin | ◆ |  |  |  |  |  |  |  | ◆ | ◆ | ◆ | ◆ |  |  |  |  |  |  |
| Crowley (semi-soft) |  |  | ◆ | ◆ |  |  |  |  | ◆ |  |  |  |  |  |  |  |  |  |
| Crowley (semi-hard) |  |  |  | ◆ |  |  |  |  | ◆ |  |  |  |  | ◆ |  |  |  |  |
| Dry Jack |  | ◆ | ◆ | ◆ | ◆ | ◆ | ◆ |  | ◆ |  |  | ◆ |  | ◆ |  |  |  |  |
| Edam |  | ◆ | ◆ |  |  |  |  |  | ◆ | ◆ |  |  |  |  |  | ◆ |  |  |
| Emmentaler |  | ◆ |  | ◆ |  |  |  |  | ◆ |  |  |  | ◆ | ◆ |  | ◆ |  |  |
| Feta (cows' milk) |  | ◆ |  |  | ◆ |  |  |  |  | ◆ |  |  |  | ◆ |  |  |  |  |
| Feta (goats' and sheep's milk) | ◆ |  |  | ◆ |  |  | ◆ |  | ◆ | ◆ |  |  |  | ◆ |  | ◆ |  |  |
| Fontina (semi-soft) |  |  |  | ◆ |  |  |  |  | ◆ |  |  |  |  |  |  |  |  |  |
| Fontina (semi-hard) |  | ◆ |  | ◆ |  |  |  |  | ◆ |  |  |  |  | ◆ |  |  |  |  |
| Fromage Blanc |  |  |  |  |  |  | ◆ |  |  | ◆ | ◆ |  |  |  |  |  |  |  |
| Goats' Milk Cheeses (fresh) | ◆ | ◆ |  | ◆ |  |  | ◆ |  | ◆ | ◆ | ◆ |  | ◆ |  |  |  |  |  |
| Goats' Milk Cheeses (semi-hard) |  |  |  | ◆ |  |  |  |  | ◆ |  |  |  |  | ◆ | ◆ |  |  |  |
| Gorgonzola |  | ◆ |  | ◆ |  |  |  |  | ◆ |  |  |  | ◆ | ◆ |  | ◆ |  |  |
| Gouda (semi-soft) |  | ◆ |  | ◆ |  |  |  |  | ◆ | ◆ |  |  |  | ◆ |  |  |  |  |
| Gouda (semi-hard) |  |  | ◆ |  | ◆ |  | ◆ |  | ◆ |  |  | ◆ |  | ◆ |  |  |  |  |
| Gruyère |  |  | ◆ | ◆ |  |  |  |  | ◆ |  |  |  | ◆ | ◆ | ◆ |  |  |  |
| Havarti |  | ◆ | ◆ |  |  |  |  |  | ◆ |  |  |  |  |  |  |  |  |  |
| Liederkranz and Limburger |  |  |  | ◆ |  |  |  |  |  |  |  |  |  |  |  |  |  |  |
| Monterey Jack (semi-soft) |  | ◆ | ◆ | ◆ |  | ◆ |  |  | ◆ |  |  |  |  |  |  | ◆ |  |  |
| Monterey Jack (semi-hard and hard) |  | ◆ | ◆ | ◆ |  | ◆ |  |  | ◆ |  |  |  | ◆ | ◆ |  |  |  |  |
| Mozzarella |  |  | ◆ |  |  |  |  |  |  |  |  |  |  |  |  |  |  |  |
| Muenster (American—not Alsatian Munster) |  |  | ◆ |  |  |  |  |  |  | ◆ |  | ◆ |  | ◆ |  |  |  |  |
| Oaxaca |  |  | ◆ |  |  |  |  |  |  |  |  |  |  |  |  |  |  |  |
| Parmesan |  |  |  | ◆ |  |  |  |  | ◆ |  |  |  | ◆ |  |  |  |  | ◆ |
| Provolone (semi-soft) |  |  | ◆ |  |  |  |  |  | ◆ |  |  |  |  |  |  |  |  |  |
| Provolone (semi-hard to hard) |  |  |  | ◆ |  |  |  |  | ◆ |  |  |  | ◆ |  | ◆ |  |  |  |
| Ricotta (cows' and sheep's milk) | ◆ |  | ◆ | ◆ |  | ◆ |  |  |  | ◆ |  |  |  |  |  |  |  |  |
| Ricotta (goats' milk) | ◆ |  |  | ◆ |  |  |  | ◆ |  | ◆ | ◆ | ◆ |  |  |  |  |  |  |
| Sheep's Milk Cheeses (semi-soft) |  |  |  | ◆ |  |  |  |  | ◆ | ◆ |  |  |  |  |  |  |  |  |
| Sheep's Milk Cheeses (semi-hard and hard) |  | ◆ | ◆ |  |  |  |  |  | ◆ |  |  |  | ◆ | ◆ |  | ◆ |  |  |
| Swiss |  | ◆ |  | ◆ |  |  |  |  | ◆ |  |  | ◆ | ◆ |  |  | ◆ |  |  |
| Teleme |  | ◆ | ◆ |  |  | ◆ |  |  |  |  |  |  |  | ◆ | ◆ |  |  |  |
| Washed-Rind Cheeses |  | ◆ |  | ◆ |  |  |  |  | ◆ |  |  |  |  | ◆ |  | ◆ |  | ◆ |

RED WINE

CHEESE

| Cheese | Port | Sherry | Zinfandel (light- to medium-bodied) | Zinfandel (full-bodied) | Sangiovese | Syrah | Pinot Noir (medium-bodied) | Pinot Noir (full-bodied) | Petite Sirah | Grenache | Merlot | Dolcetto | Carignane | Cabernet Sauvignon | Cabernet Franc | Barbera | Baco Noir (hybrid) |
|---|---|---|---|---|---|---|---|---|---|---|---|---|---|---|---|---|---|
| Asiago | ◆ | ◆ | ◆ |  |  |  | ◆ |  |  |  |  |  | ◆ | ◆ |  |  | ◆ |
| Baby Swiss |  |  |  |  |  |  |  |  |  |  |  |  |  | ◆ |  |  |  |
| Blue Cheese (Gorgonzola and semi-soft) |  | ◆ | ◆ | ◆ |  |  |  |  |  |  |  |  |  | ◆ |  |  |  |
| Blue Cheese (semi-hard and/or salty) | ◆ | ◆ |  |  |  |  |  |  |  | ◆ |  |  |  |  | ◆ |  |  |
| Brie and Camembert (cows' milk) |  |  |  |  |  |  | ◆ | ◆ | ◆ |  |  |  |  | ◆ |  |  |  |
| Camembert (goats' milk) |  |  |  |  |  |  |  |  | ◆ |  |  |  |  | ◆ | ◆ | ◆ | ◆ |
| Cheddar (semi-soft, not sharp) |  |  |  | ◆ |  |  |  |  | ◆ |  |  |  |  |  |  |  |  |
| Cheddar (semi-hard, earthy) |  |  |  | ◆ |  | ◆ |  |  |  | ◆ | ◆ | ◆ |  |  | ◆ |  |  |
| Cheddar (sharp) |  |  |  |  |  |  |  |  |  |  |  |  |  |  |  |  |  |
| Colby |  |  |  |  |  |  |  |  |  |  |  | ◆ |  |  |  |  |  |
| Crescenza |  |  |  |  |  |  |  |  |  |  |  |  |  |  |  |  |  |
| Crottin |  |  |  |  |  |  |  | ◆ | ◆ |  |  |  | ◆ |  | ◆ | ◆ |  |
| Crowley (semi-soft) |  |  |  |  | ◆ |  |  |  |  |  |  |  |  | ◆ |  |  |  |
| Crowley (semi-hard) |  |  |  |  | ◆ |  |  |  |  |  |  |  |  |  |  |  |  |
| Dry Jack |  | ◆ |  |  | ◆ | ◆ | ◆ | ◆ | ◆ |  |  |  |  | ◆ | ◆ |  | ◆ |
| Edam |  |  |  |  |  |  |  |  |  |  |  |  |  | ◆ |  | ◆ |  |
| Emmentaler | ◆ | ◆ |  |  |  |  |  |  |  |  |  |  | ◆ | ◆ |  |  |  |
| Feta (cows' milk) |  |  |  |  |  |  |  |  |  |  |  |  |  |  |  |  |  |
| Feta (goats' and sheep's milk) |  |  |  |  |  |  |  |  |  |  |  |  |  |  |  |  |  |
| Fontina (semi-soft) |  |  |  |  |  |  |  |  |  |  |  |  |  | ◆ | ◆ |  | ◆ |
| Fontina (semi-hard) |  | ◆ |  |  |  |  | ◆ |  |  | ◆ |  |  |  |  | ◆ |  |  |
| Fromage Blanc |  |  |  |  |  |  |  |  |  |  |  |  |  |  |  |  |  |
| Goats' Milk Cheeses (fresh) |  |  |  |  |  |  |  | ◆ |  |  |  |  |  | ◆ | ◆ | ◆ | ◆ |
| Goats' Milk Cheeses (semi-hard) |  |  |  |  |  | ◆ |  | ◆ |  |  |  | ◆ |  |  |  |  |  |
| Gorgonzola | ◆ |  |  |  |  |  |  |  |  |  |  |  |  |  |  |  |  |
| Gouda (semi-soft) |  |  |  |  |  |  |  |  |  |  |  |  |  | ◆ |  |  |  |
| Gouda (semi-hard) |  | ◆ |  |  |  |  |  |  |  | ◆ |  |  |  | ◆ |  | ◆ |  |
| Gruyère |  | ◆ |  |  | ◆ |  |  |  | ◆ | ◆ |  |  |  |  | ◆ |  |  |
| Havarti |  |  |  |  |  |  |  |  |  |  |  |  |  |  |  | ◆ | ◆ |
| Liederkranz and Limburger |  |  |  |  |  |  |  |  |  |  |  |  |  |  |  |  |  |
| Monterey Jack (semi-soft) |  |  |  |  |  |  |  |  |  |  |  |  |  |  |  | ◆ |  |
| Monterey Jack (semi-hard and hard) |  | ◆ |  |  | ◆ | ◆ | ◆ | ◆ | ◆ |  |  |  | ◆ | ◆ |  | ◆ |  |
| Mozzarella |  |  |  |  |  |  | ◆ |  |  |  |  |  |  | ◆ |  |  |  |
| Muenster (American—not Alsatian Munster) |  |  |  |  |  |  |  |  |  |  |  |  |  |  |  |  |  |
| Oaxaca |  |  |  |  |  |  | ◆ |  |  |  |  |  |  | ◆ |  |  |  |
| Parmesan | ◆ | ◆ |  |  | ◆ |  | ◆ |  |  |  |  |  |  |  | ◆ | ◆ |  |
| Provolone (semi-soft) |  |  |  |  |  |  |  |  |  |  |  |  |  | ◆ |  |  | ◆ |
| Provolone (semi-hard to hard) |  |  |  |  |  |  |  |  |  |  |  |  |  |  |  | ◆ |  |
| Ricotta (cows' and sheep's milk) |  |  |  |  |  |  | ◆ |  |  |  |  |  |  |  |  |  |  |
| Ricotta (goats' milk) |  |  |  |  |  |  |  |  |  |  |  |  |  |  |  |  |  |
| Sheep's Milk Cheeses (semi-soft) |  |  |  |  |  |  |  |  |  |  |  | ◆ |  |  | ◆ | ◆ |  |
| Sheep's Milk Cheeses (semi-hard and hard) |  | ◆ |  |  | ◆ |  | ◆ |  |  | ◆ | ◆ | ◆ |  | ◆ |  | ◆ |  |
| Swiss | ◆ | ◆ |  |  |  |  |  |  |  |  |  |  | ◆ |  | ◆ |  |  |
| Teleme |  |  |  |  |  |  |  |  |  |  |  |  |  |  |  |  |  |
| Washed-Rind Cheeses |  |  |  | ◆ |  |  |  |  | ◆ |  |  |  |  | ◆ |  |  |  |

# HORS d'OEUVRES

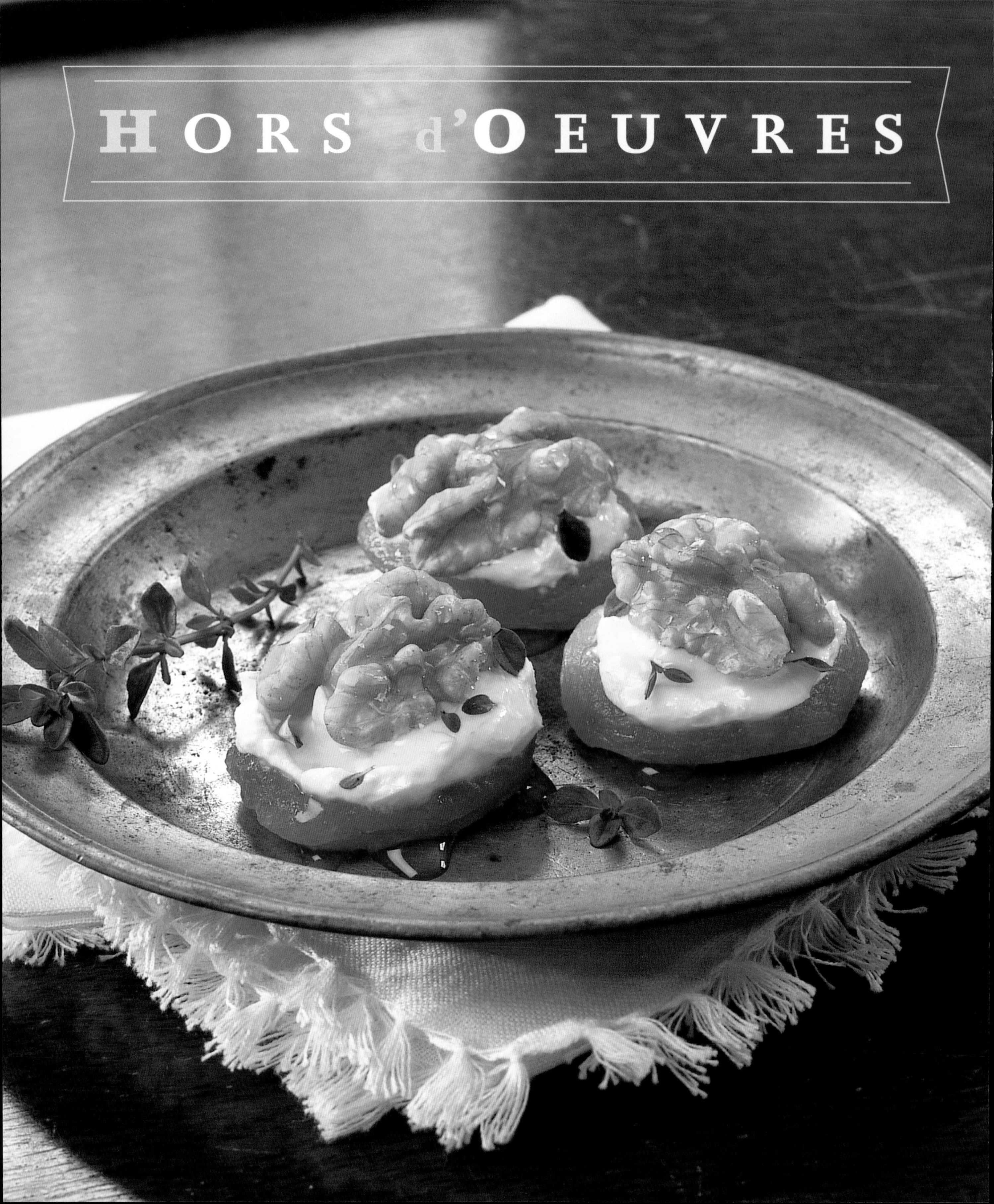

Becker Vineyards

SPRING PEA, RICOTTA, AND BASIL CROSTINI

Harley Farms

APRICOT COINS

Mason Cellars

CHERRY TOMATOES WITH
HERBED GOAT CHEESE AND SHRIMP

Point Reyes Farmstead Cheese Company

BLUE CHEESE–STUFFED DATES

Anthony Road Winery

CAESAR FINGERS WITH CHEESE CRISPS

Hillman Farms

FENNEL WITH AGED CHEESE AND FENNEL SEED OIL

Ken Wright Cellars

CARAMELIZED ONION, BACON, AND GRUYÈRE FONDUE

MONTEREY JACK–EMMENTALER FONDUE
WITH FENNEL AND TOMATOES

Gruet Winery

CHEDDAR-PARMESAN CRACKERS

FROMAGE BLANC CRACKERS WITH
CRISPY PROSCIUTTO AND FROMAGE BLANC

Sweet Grass Dairy

ARTICHOKE LEAVES WITH SPINACH-RICOTTA FILLING

White Oak Farm

BEETS AND GOAT CHEESE ON BUTTERED BRIOCHE

Lively Run Goat Dairy

SPICED EGGPLANT WITH BAKED FETA

Cayuse Vineyards

BRIE-MANGO QUESADILLAS WITH LIME CREAM

Apricot Coins, recipe on page 92

# Becker Vineyards

**ABOUT AN HOUR'S DRIVE WEST OF AUSTIN, TEXAS, LIES THE SPRAWLING TEXAS HILL** Country. In a state better known for its long stretches of flat, dusty plains, the phrase "Hill Country" as a description of a swath of central Texas comes as a surprise to the uninitiated. For those in the know, the Texas Hill Country is not only a familiar area, it is a popular destination. The verdant land, the iridescent Indian paintbrush plants that line the roads in springtime, the picturesque farmland, and now, the wineries, draw people from throughout Texas and beyond.

In the heart of the Hill Country is the storybook town of Fredericksburg. A cross between Main Street, USA, and Rodeo Drive, this town, originally settled by Germans, attracts antique shoppers and anyone looking for a weekend getaway. The Fredericksburg area alone is home to an impressive three hundred bed-and-breakfast inns.

Just a few miles east of this tourist mecca is the town of Stonewall. There, on Jenscheke Lane, is the home of Becker Vineyards, one of the Longhorn state's forty wineries. Founded by Richard and Bunny Becker, this winery produces some of the state's best wines, and it is bringing well-deserved attention to the growing wine industry in Texas.

Richard Becker, an endocrinologist in San Antonio, and his wife, Bunny, often visited the Fredericksburg area, particularly because of their affinity for antiques. They were also fascinated with wine and winemaking, which they dabbled with at home. Those interests, combined with a love for gardening, sent them on a search for a log cabin and some land in the Fredericksburg area. They eventually found the right place in Stonewall in 1992.

On their parcel of land stood a log cabin that had been built in the 1880s and a 19th-century German stone barn. Along with the land came a history of grape growing, although the particular grapes that had been grown there—Mustang—were not the sort the Beckers were looking to plant. Nonetheless, the 1,500-foot elevation and the rich soils were enough to convince them that vinifera could grow there.

In 1992 the Beckers planted sixteen different varieties of grapes, including Viognier, Chardonnay, Mouvedre, Syrah, and Merlot, on thirty-six acres. In 1995 they produced their first Becker Vineyards wine, and by the next year the Beckers had transformed part of the German barn into a tasting room, complete with an antique bar from the Green Tree Saloon, a 19th-century fixture in San Antonio. The rest of the barn houses the winery.

The beautiful limestone building makes for a lovely visual surprise after one makes the turn off Highway 290. Depending on the time of year, the barn might be framed by the purple stalks of the hundreds of lavender plants the Beckers have planted, and it stands sentry above acres of billowy vines. It seems more Provençal than Texan. The antique furnishings make theirs one of the more unusual tasting rooms in the nation, and in the heart of this history-rich area, it is an inviting place to linger and sip wine.

For many, the origins of the phrase "Texas wine" harks back to the state's native grape—sweet but not "real" wine. Becker Vineyards wine has done a lot to change that impression. The early harvest—late July and August—speaks to the extreme heat in the region, but for the most part the grapes in this area get adequate hang time to produce the necessary sugars and flavor. White wines do particularly well in this case, although the Beckers have shown tremendous skill with red wines too. They have numerous awards to prove it. Their Claret, a blend of Cabernet Franc, Cabernet Sauvignon, Merlot, Malbec, and Petit Verdot, is a remarkable wine with hints of berries and cassis, and one that tastes richer than its Texas roots might suggest.

The Becker Vineyards Viognier is always popular, selling out every year, but the Reserve Chardonnay is a real standout. The wine is aged in new French oak and aged sur lie for six months. It is a particularly well-balanced wine with some honey and floral tones and a resonance of oak. The slightly sweet Riesling speaks to the area's German roots, even though this particular grape was probably not grown until relatively recently in this region. It has a wonderfully perfumy nose and hints of peach and honeyed apricot. From Cabernet Sauvignon, the Beckers also make an award-winning vintage port, which they age for two years in new French and American oak.

Although the Beckers have employed an on-site winemaker, Richard Becker does all the blending of the wines. He is no absentee owner and clearly takes great pride in his product—and in its future. Although the Texas wine industry dates back over two hundred years, it didn't pick up again until the 1970s. Richard and Bunny Becker seem to be making up for lost time and helping to propel the "new" Texas wine industry well into the 21st century.

## WHAT THEY MAKE

**White wines**
Chardonnay
Chardonnay Reserve
Fumé Blanc
Riesling
Viognier

**Red and Rosé wines**
Cabernet Sauvignon
Cabernet-Syrah
Claret
Merlot
Provence

**Dessert/Sweet wines**
Muscat Canelli Amabile
Riesling
Vintage Port

## HOW TO REACH THEM

Stonewall, Texas
830-644-2681 (phone)
830-644-2689 (fax)
www.beckervineyards.com

# SPRING PEA, RICOTTA, AND BASIL CROSTINI

**THE BRIGHT GREEN COLOR OF THIS SPRING-THEMED SPREAD PROVIDES THE VISUAL CUE FOR ITS FRESH, CLEAN TASTE.** The lively flavors of fresh peas and basil are bridged by the sweet, creamy ricotta. When smoothed all together onto a slice of hearty bread, this spread enters the realm of ethereal. Although this recipe makes about sixteen crostini, the mixture can easily be doubled or even quadrupled if you're planning to have a big party. Even simpler, the spread can be made a day ahead and refrigerated. Bring it to room temperature before spreading on the bread and serving.

1 cup water

1 teaspoon salt

1½ cups shelling peas, preferably English (about 1¼ pounds, or use large-size frozen peas)

¼ cup plus 1 tablespoon coarsely chopped fresh basil (about 30 leaves)

2 tablespoons olive oil plus extra for brushing

2 tablespoons ricotta cheese

Salt and freshly ground pepper

1 sourdough baguette

Preheat the broiler.

In a small pot, bring the water and salt to a boil. Add the peas and cook for 4 minutes. Drain and rinse under cold water to stop the cooking process. Pat dry.

In a food processor, combine the peas, the ¼ cup basil, oil, cheese, and salt and pepper. Process until creamy. Taste and add more salt or pepper as needed.

Cut the baguette into sixteen ¼-inch-wide slices. Place the bread slices on a baking sheet and spray or brush them on both sides with olive oil. Broil until the bread is a light golden-brown color, 1 to 2 minutes. Turn slices and repeat. (Watch carefully, as bread can burn easily.) Remove from broiler and let cool.

To assemble, spread about 1 tablespoon of the pea mixture on each slice of bread. Sprinkle with remaining chopped basil. Serve immediately.

Makes 16 crostini; serves 4

## PERFECT PAIRS

**SINCE THERE'S NOTHING** acidic in this dish, and spring peas at the height of the season are creamy and sweet, you might try a Viognier or a buttery (but not too oaky) Chardonnay. If the peas are not super-sweet, choose a white wine that has some fruit with a touch of acidity, such as a Chenin Blanc or a Sauvignon Blanc, which will marry with the herbaceousness in the spread.

# Harley Farms

DEE HARLEY MIGHT HAVE GUESSED THAT FARMING WOULD BE IN HER FUTURE. When she was fifteen, a standard school personality test revealed that the outdoor profession was a perfect fit. The results were surprising, given that she lived far from any farm in a small town in northern England. Nevertheless, Harley's adventurous spirit sent her on a path that would eventually lead her to a life that would prove the prescience of that test.

About ten years ago, Dee Harley left England to visit the United States. The visit turned into full-time residence when she landed in California in the small seaside town of Pescadero, about thirty miles south of San Francisco. There isn't much going on in this former fishing village, but Harley managed to find Duarte's Tavern, a local institution started three generations ago by the Duarte family and now run by Tim Duarte. There Harley found Tim, and eventually the two were married and took up residence on nearby property owned by Tim's family.

**Harley Farms**

**Goat Dairy**
*Pescadero, California*

Harley's as yet unmanifested destiny became a glimmer with her first job as a salesperson for a start-up produce company in the area. Among the products she sold were sun-dried tomatoes to Santa Cruz-based Sea Stars goat cheese maker Nancy Gaffney, who flavored some of her cheese with the tomatoes. As it happened, Gaffney was in need of more goats' milk. On a visit to Harley's farm, she suggested that Harley get a few goats and sell the milk. Never one to shy away from adventure, Harley happily complied and promptly acquired six goats.

Always a hands-on, energetic sort, Harley, to her own surprise, became interested in the goats and the land on which she—and they—lived. She slowly grew her herd as well as the pasture area and maintained a constant, excellent milk source for Gaffney. In 1998 Harley began to learn the art of cheesemaking from Nancy, and when Gaffney decided to focus on her lavender business and leave cheesemaking behind, Harley bought the cheesemaking business from her.

Now with three hundred goats and room to grow, Harley is continuing Gaffney's Sea Stars tradition under the name Harley Farms, and is making Gaffney's signature fresh goat cheese with edible flowers. Harley has also added many cheeses of her own, including a rare goats' milk ricotta, which she makes from whole milk. It is a rich, dense cheese and is unusually good all by itself, although Harley is especially proud of the goat cheese ricotta ravioli that is served at Duarte's Tavern.

Home for Dee, Tim, their son, Ben, and their herd of goats is amidst rolling green hills and occasional fields of sweet peas, cultivated flowers, strawberries, artichokes, and other agricultural bounty. This part of California is cool and frequently blanketed with fog. The mild, damp climate ensures a verdant landscape and, because of this, contented goats. The goats are usually confined to one quadrant of the pasture on one day, and moved to another the next. They are milked twice daily, and Harley is proud to show off her clever milking parlor with trap doors on either end—one to usher the goats in and the other to let them out. While they are being milked, the goats feed from a trough that lies behind a series of vertical wooden slats that are angled to keep the goats in place. The wooden device, like much of the metal and other woodwork on the farm, was handmade by a friend of Harley's.

Although Harley's cheese is magnificent, her hands-on devotion to the operation and to the people who help her is perhaps most striking. The bachelor's buttons, pansies, borage, calendula, johnny jump-ups, pineapple sage, and other edible flowers that she grows are painstakingly placed, one by one, at the bottom of the muffin tins used to form the cheese. On any given day, three women in the cheesemaking

room will have piles of the brilliantly colored flowers in front of them, and, alongside, a bucket of the fresh chèvre. Depending on which cheese they're making (all the cheeses have different flowers and patterns), the women lay a piece of plastic wrap in the bottom of a muffin tin. They then delicately place the flowers upside down and fill the tin with goat cheese. The plastic wrap is then sealed. When they flip the cheese over, the flowers are right side up, creating a beautiful pattern. These cheeses have appropriately been christened Monet and Van Goght. (The latter, a goat-themed play on the artist's name, has sunflower seeds among other additions, an ode to the artist's most famous painting.)

Harley Farms produces about two hundred pounds of cheese seven days a week, and, for now, the cheeses made by the operation will remain fresh cheeses. Eventually Harley plans to make aged cheeses as well. Although an excellent palate is important for making good cheese, Harley insists the quality of the milk is key to the flavors in her cheese. Indeed, the goats live a leisurely life, eating pasture year-round except when it's raining (they don't wander out during inclement weather), and their feed is supplemented by specially formulated grain prescribed by an animal nutritionist who visits the farm four times a year.

Harley, for whom conversation usually comes easily, becomes practically speechless when she attempts to convey the joy she derives from her life on the farm. The blue ribbons on her walls are objective confirmation of the quality of her cheese, but her dedication to her animals, the flowers, and the life she has created is much more subtle. She puts it simply, "I just love the hands-on life." And it shows.

WHAT THEY MAKE

Fresh chèvre
Flavored chèvre (*chive, dill, herb, pepper*)
Tortes (*with flowers: Van Goght— sunflower seeds and basil; Monet— herbes de Provence; flavored: tomato-* *basil, apricot-pistachio, cranberry-walnut, salmon-dill*)
Feta
Fromage Blanc
Ricotta

HOW TO REACH THEM

Pescadero, California
650-879-0480 (*phone*)
650-879-9161 (*fax*)
www.harleyfarms.com

# APRICOT COINS

**THIS HORS D'OEUVRE NOT ONLY LOOKS FESTIVE AND TASTES TERRIFIC, IT ALSO COULD NOT BE EASIER TO MAKE.** The goat cheese can be whipped in advance and refrigerated for up to 2 days. Be sure to bring it to room temperature and give it a good stir before using it.

4 ounces fresh goat cheese

2 teaspoons milk more if needed

40 dried apricots, (about 6 ounces),
    preferably Turkish

2 teaspoons honey

1 tablespoon finely chopped fresh thyme
    leaves (or 1½ teaspoons dried thyme)

40 candied walnut halves (see page 157)

In the bowl of a stand mixer place the cheese and milk. (Or use a medium-sized bowl and a wooden spoon.) Using the paddle attachment, whip the cheese (or stir it vigorously) for at least 5 minutes, or until it is very smooth and creamy. If the cheese is still crumbly, add more milk ½ teaspoon at a time.

To assemble, spread about ⅛ teaspoon of cheese on each apricot. (If using California apricots, put the goat cheese on the shiny side.) Drizzle a little honey over the cheese and top with a light sprinkling of thyme. Place a walnut half on top, arrange the apricots on a platter, and serve.

Makes 40; serves 10 to 12

## PERFECT PAIRS

**THE COMBINED FLAVORS** of the sweet-tart apricots and fresh goat cheese call for an un-oaked Viognier, Sauvignon Blanc, or dry Riesling.

# Mason Cellars

TO MANY, WINE IS A DAUNTING SUBJECT. ITS TERMINOLOGY, ITS VARYING FLAVORS, the pomp and circumstance that often surround it often repel rather than attract. But if winemaker Randy Mason came along with every bottle sold, wine would quickly lose any pretentiousness associated with it and become an immediately likable, accessible, and thoroughly enjoyable beverage. That is because behind his immense knowledge and unquestionable winemaking skills, Mason embodies these qualities.

As the former winemaker and chief executive officer of the Napa Wine Company (which not only makes wine under its own name but is also a custom crush facility), Mason has probably made more styles of wine than just about anyone. A custom crush facility is one where winemakers bring their grapes and use the facility to make and store their wine. Many small producers choose this alternative because it is cheaper and more convenient than building their own winery. About eighty wineries make their wines at the Napa Wine Company, including several well-known producers such as Staglin and Pahlmeyer. Mason's role at the facility, where he makes his Mason Cellars wine, was to make the wine under the Napa Wine Company's own label, spirit seven thousand tons of grapes through the facility every harvest, and oversee the production of the one million cases of wine that were made there annually. He also lent his winemaking expertise to many of the winemakers who passed through.

All this hands-on experience naturally led Mason to create his own label. Born in Marin County, California, Mason studied veterinary science at the University of California at Davis. But after four years of undergraduate studies, he could not get into graduate school. Instead, he stayed an extra year at Davis and studied animal science and fermentation science. This

MASON

1999
NAPA VALLEY
CABERNET
SAUVIGNON

ALCOHOL 13.9% BY VOLUME

latter subject captured his fancy, and in the early 1970s he went to work for Chappellet Winery in Napa as a vineyard manager. He also learned winemaking and ultimately became the winemaker and general manager at the now-defunct Lakespring Winery, also in Napa. (Lakespring is now home to the highly regarded Havens Winery.) In 1993, some twenty years after he began, Mason landed at the Napa Wine Company, helping kick off the operation with owner Andy Hoxsey. There Mason made a name for himself with his Sauvignon Blanc.

Mason's lighthearted demeanor turns unmistakably serious when he starts discussing his wine. "I just love Sauvignon Blanc," he says. He always has, even though when he first began making it he said the grape was considered the "Rodney Dangerfield of grapes"—it got no respect. All that has changed, in part owing to winemakers like Mason who have elevated the grape beyond its former status as a Chardonnay wanna-be. Because winemakers were making Sauvignon Blanc in the same oaky style in which Chardonnay is made, the line between the two distinct grapes was mercilessly blurred. Now, winemakers like Mason are no longer trying to suppress the citrus and sometimes herbal qualities inherent in the Sauvignon Blanc grape by over-oaking it and/or putting it through 100 percent malolactic fermentation.

As a strong believer that the wine is made in the vineyard, Mason is hands-on when it comes to managing the growing of the grapes. "If you get in the field and taste the berries, you get a feel where flavor is. If you taste every week, you can taste when it's ready. You can't do that when you get in the lab," he says.

Mason's real passion is blending, although that does not necessarily mean blending different varieties.

Instead, it might mean that he'll strive for an interplay of green and gold fruit; all the grapes are Sauvignon Blanc, but some of them might have ripened later and developed a higher sugar content, while others that will also go into the wine are picked a little earlier and have higher acids. "I like grapes that are green enough so that you get that Sauvignon Blanc herbaceous quality," he says, which primarily comes from the grapes grown on the morning or cooler side of the vine. But, he says, he likes the citrus and lemon-lime, peachy and fig character that comes from the sunny or afternoon side of the vine. He describes it as a 7-Up and fig flavor. By putting together grapes from both sides of the vine, he has created a wine with great acid structure and lovely fruit. It is a near-perfect food (and cheese) wine.

In addition to Sauvignon Blanc, Mason makes two red wines. His Merlot is positively luscious, with its black cherry and somewhat floral flavors underlined with pleasant oak and very soft tannins. The fruit comes from the Yountville area toward the southern end of the Napa Valley. Although the days are very warm there, the summer nights are relatively cool—conditions Mason believes are ideal for Merlot. He also now makes a Cabernet Sauvignon, with grapes from the reputable Rutherford area of Napa. By far his biggest production is Sauvignon Blanc, of which about twenty thousand cases are made annually. By comparison, Mason makes only about three thousand cases of Merlot and less still of Cabernet Sauvignon.

Mason, along with his wife, Megan, began the Mason Cellars label in 1993, and his Sauvignon Blanc has experienced a meteoric rise ever since. It is truly exemplary, if not quintessential, in its class evidence that devotion to one grape can yield a superior product.

WHAT THEY MAKE

**White wines**
Sauvignon Blanc

**Red wines**
Cabernet Sauvignon
Merlot

HOW TO REACH THEM

Napa, California
707-944-9159 (phone)
707-944-1293 (fax)
www.masoncellars.com

# CHERRY TOMATOES WITH HERBED GOAT CHEESE AND SHRIMP

**STUFFED CHERRY TOMATOES ARE A TRADITIONAL HORS D'OEUVRE ITEM, BUT WHEN TOPPED WITH HERBED GOAT CHEESE, THEY BECOME A CONTEMPORARY TREAT.** The shrimp brings it all together, especially because of its companion herb, tarragon. The whipped cream in this recipe serves to lighten the texture of the filling, but if you don't want to use it, it is not essential. Just know that the filling will be a little stiffer.

48 cherry tomatoes (about 1½ pints), stems removed
3 ounces fresh goat cheese
1 teaspoon finely chopped fresh tarragon
½ teaspoon minced shallot
Kosher salt
2 tablespoons heavy cream
¼ pound cooked bay shrimp
Freshly ground pepper

Cut a very thin slice off the stem end of each tomato and place the tomato, cut side down, on a serving platter. Set aside.

In a medium bowl, mix together the cheese, tarragon, shallot, and salt to taste. In a small bowl, whip the cream until stiff peaks form. Fold the whipped cream into the cheese mixture. Taste and add more salt, if necessary. (The filling can be made up to 1 day in advance and refrigerated. Bring to room temperature and mix well before using.)

Using a spoon or a pastry bag fitted with a star tip, spoon or pipe about ¼ teaspoon filling over the rounded top of each tomato. Top with 1 shrimp. Repeat with remaining tomatoes and filling. Sprinkle tomatoes with a little pepper and serve.

Makes 48; serves 10 to 12

## PERFECT PAIRS

**ALTHOUGH GOAT CHEESE** plays a prominent role in this hors d'oeuvre, the tarragon, shrimp, and tomatoes add plenty of their own flavor. In addition, the heavy cream cuts some of the tartness of the cheese. For that reason, a Viognier or Chardonnay will work with this, but so will the more acidic wines, such as Sauvignon Blanc. If you'd like to have a red wine, then choose one with plenty of acidity, such as Dolcetto or a light-bodied Sangiovese.

# Point Reyes Farmstead Cheese Company

IT'S 5 A.M. AND EXCEPT FOR THE DIS-TINCT BARITONE HUM COMING FROM SOME predawn cattle conversation, the Giacomini ranch in Point Reyes, on the northern California coast, lies still under the full moon.

Inside one of the outbuildings, the whir of machinery provides a startling contrast to the serenity outdoors, a signal that part of the ranch is in full operation. The cows' fresh milk is about to make "its leap into immortality," as writer and former *New Yorker* book editor Clifton Fadiman once wrote. Over the next few months, that milk will become cheese.

This outbuilding is the hub for the Point Reyes Farmstead Cheese Company and its cheese, Original Blue—California's first commercial blue-veined cheese. The Giacomini family, which is behind this venture, is one of eleven relatively small dairy farming families in California that are making the transition from selling milk to making and selling cheese. Cheese has become the means by which some California dairy farms have been able to remain small yet maintain a viable business. As Americans clamor for specialty cheese, families like the Giacominis are happily answering the call, especially because the business appears to be instilling in the offspring of farmers an interest in staying on the farm.

The Giacomini dairy farm is perched above a windy stretch of Highway 1, a stone's throw from Tomales Bay in northern California. Here, the black and white Holsteins wander the vast green hillsides before they are summoned, twice daily, to relinquish their milk. Milk cows have been the farm's livelihood throughout its forty-one-year history, but two years ago ranch owner Bob Giacomini and three of his daughters got the idea to transform the milk into more valuable cheese. It was a decision that would allow Bob Giacomini to "do less and less," he says impishly, and

POINT REYES

*original blue*™

FARMSTEAD
CHEESE COMPANY
www.pointreyescheese.com

he says, "It got the kids back on the farm."

Until the notion of making cheese surfaced, none of Giacomini's daughters had expressed interest in carrying on the dairy operation. But cheese appealed to the gourmand in each of them, and the business proposition it presented ignited a fire under these heirs to great milk. They appointed themselves cheesemakers and immediately turned their vision into action.

Daughters Karen, Lynn, and Jill dispatched themselves to various parts of the country, interviewing cheesemakers, restaurateurs, scientists, and retailers to determine what type of cheese they should make. "Unanimously, every food lover, cheese lover, expert, and chef thought about that question, and everyone said 'blue,'" says Jill Giacomini Basch. That's because relatively little good blue cheese is made in this country, yet it's a popular cheese with a healthy dose of romance associated with it. Making this style of cheese would fill a niche in the American cheese market and particularly in California, where no blue cheese was being made at the time.

When most dairy farmers start to think of turning their milk into cheese, they usually surround themselves with cheesemaking manuals. How-to business primers are left behind, and the nascent cheesemakers are often left scrambling to learn about sales and marketing *after* they've got a product to sell. In the case of the Giacominis, each of the daughters already had extensive sales and marketing experience. But even so, they were anxious. "I remember looking at ourselves and I thought, 'what are we doing?'" says Karen Giacomini Howard.

To begin, they transformed an old horse barn into the cheesemaking facility. Bob Giacomini says there was some old equipment in the building that indicated it may have been used for cheesemaking sometime in the past—a viable theory since, prior to

the advent of refrigeration, most dairies in the area converted their milk into butter and cheese. Once their cheesemaking facility was completed, the Giacominis immediately knew it was too small. But serendipity would make the first of many appearances in this enterprise: the family learned of a 1,500-gallon cheesemaking vat sitting empty at the nearby Sonoma Cheese Factory, where new vats had just been installed. Bob Giacomini convinced owner David Viviani to sell.

Along with this acquisition came word that the former cheesemaker from Maytag Dairy Farm in Newton, Iowa—the country's preeminent blue cheese producer—was looking to make cheese again. Monte McIntyre, who had been with Maytag for ten years, had precisely the expertise the Giacominis were looking for. The Giacomini daughters could then remove "cheesemaker" from their titles, which was a great relief to all of them.

On a typical day, McIntyre wanders in about the time the first round of milking has concluded. The milk is pumped directly into a holding tank in the cheese room, and from there the cheesemaking gets under way. While the basic process of turning milk into cheese is fairly standard—a starter culture is added to the milk, followed by the addition of rennet to curdle the milk, and ultimately the processing of the curds—the creation of a specific cheese, such as a blue cheese, is always unique to the cheesemaker. Think chocolate cake: all bakers have their own recipe for a chocolate cake, the one they think is the best, even though the basic ingredients are pretty much the same.

After the curds are formed into wheels, salted, and cured, the cheese is then punctured in several places with a thin metal skewer that allows air to penetrate the cheese. This provides a perfect host for the mold to proliferate and eventually form the distinctive blue veins. In the case of Original Blue, the approximately seven-pound wheels are then sealed in plastic bags and aged for the legal minimum of two months.

Original Blue's best flavor comes at around six months. By then, the cheese is tangy and creamy, and the blue mold flavor has really begun to take hold. The cheese itself is whitish ivory in color, with light blue spots of color and occasional veining throughout. In a way, the color of the cheese mirrors the cheesemaker's bayside setting. As for the flavor, patriarch Bob Giacomini says, "I don't know what it is, but I think there's something about that salt air that makes our cheese taste the way it does."

These luscious wheels recall an earlier time in Point Reyes, when butter and cheese were made throughout the entire area. Now cheeses like Original Blue are helping to keep the area tied to its roots while satisfying the modern-day appetite for great cheese. And, no less important to Bob Giacomini, cheese has brought his kids back to the farm.

WHAT THEY MAKE

Original Blue
Point Reyes Original Blue Dip & Dressing

HOW TO REACH THEM

Point Reyes Station, California
800-591-6878 (toll-free)
415-663-8881 (fax)
www.pointreyescheese.com

# BLUE CHEESE–STUFFED DATES

**IT'S ALWAYS NICE WHEN AT LEAST ONE PART OF A MEAL IS SIMPLE TO PREPARE.**
This hors d'oeuvre, which works equally well as a pre-dessert cheese course, could not be easier. Just whip the cheese and spread it right onto a date. For a variation, you can also use pitted dried plums (prunes) or dried figs.

2 ounces creamy blue cheese, such as
   Original Blue, at room temperature
12 dried dates, preferably Medjool dates, or
   some other type of large, fleshy date (about
   8 ounces), pitted and cut in half lengthwise
24 blanched almonds (see page 158), toasted
Cayenne pepper

Using a hand mixer, in a small bowl mix the cheese until creamy. You may need to add a few drops of milk if the cheese is crumbly. Set aside.

Place the dates on a serving platter. Using a knife, spread about 1 teaspoon cheese on the cut side of each date. Top with 1 almond. Sprinkle the stuffed dates with a dash of cayenne pepper and serve.

## PERFECT PAIRS

**ALTHOUGH IT MAY SEEM**
strange to serve a dessert wine with hors d'oeuvres, a wine such as a Muscat Canelli, preferably one with some effervescence, would be a terrific match for the sweetness of the dates and an equally good contrasting match for the blue cheese. Otherwise, a young, fruity-style sparkling wine, such as blanc de noirs, would make a fine choice as well. Finally, a Gewürztraminer would also work because of the subtle yet present dusting of cayenne pepper.

# Anthony Road Winery

DRIVING ACROSS THE ROLLING HILLS OF UPSTATE NEW YORK'S FINGER LAKES region, one is gently transported to another place and time. The long dresses of the girls riding their bicycles, the women in black with their horses and buggies, the golden green stretches of luminescent farmland, and the occasional road sign—all say that this is a place like no other. The Menonnites and Amish make up some of the population and provide part of the area's story, and so too do the vast, billowy rows of grapevines making their way toward the sun. Here nature takes precedence, and those driving through are but brief intruders. Technology, though everywhere, seems hushed here.

About forty wineries make their home in this storybook setting. Here, the crystal lakes reflect the verdant land that surrounds them and generously contribute to the taste of the wines that are made within their reach.

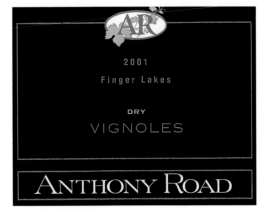

One of those wineries whose vineyards creep toward Seneca Lake is Anthony Road. Owned by John and Ann Martini, two people whose kindness is reminiscent of another, gentler time, this winery is quietly but steadily raising the bar for winemaking in this fledgling wine country. They are aided in this effort by their German winemaker, Johannes Reinhardt, whose passion mirrors the region's summer thunderstorms—dramatic and intense. Born into a family of winemakers, Reinhardt learned the craft by virtue of his exposure to it. He began practicing it, first in Germany, and later at Dr. Konstantin Frank's Vinifera Wine Cellars on nearby Keuka Lake. He joined the Martinis in 2000.

Although he has proven his talents in winemaking, Reinhardt is quick to dismiss his skill and defer to the vineyards as the real source for good wines. "People have to realize that what is most important is what happens in the vineyard," he says, and in the course of a conversation, he reiterates this point repeatedly. The Martinis' son, Peter, is the vineyard manager and, together with Reinhardt, he works intently on growing the best grapes he can. In 2001, this attention to the grapes and to the vineyards caught the attention of esteemed vineyard owner Robert Young, whose California vineyards have produced some of that state's most prestigious wines. The octogenarian purchased 105 acres next door to the Anthony Road Winery because of his belief in the potential of Finger Lakes wines. The Martinis are now charged with developing and managing Young's vineyard.

The Martinis founded their winery in 1989 after working as grape growers for many years. Like many winery owners in the area, they were growing grapes for the huge Taylor Wine Company in the 1970s. But when that company was bought by Coca-Cola, the new owners no longer sourced their grapes locally. Grape growers were faced with the choice of finding a new line of work or creating their own wines. The Martinis took the bold step of choosing the latter. They were aided by New York's Farm Winery Act of 1976, which made it easier for small wineries to enter the business.

Anthony Road wines are now produced at the rate of about ten thousand cases a year, but the Martinis' goal is to grow to thirty thousand cases. The lovely wines and the family's significant emphasis on value are likely to get them there, although they understand that getting the finest quality in the bottle may take some time in such a new winegrowing region. Since vines don't really start producing grapes for three years, and growing good quality grapes takes a few more years, Martini recognizes that today's beliefs about what grapes will grow best in the area may change as time goes on.

Members of the Anthony Road Winery team. Bottom row, from left to right, Ann Martini and Elizabeth Castner. Top row, left to right, Peter Martini, Matt Scutt, John Martini and Johannes Reinhardt.

Winemaker Reinhardt, however, is not taking a wait-and-see attitude. "It is definitely possible to make wines in the Finger Lakes. Not just average, but really, really great [wines]," he says. But, he says, it is imperative to respect the material coming in and work with it.

Right now, his "material" mostly takes the form of Riesling, Vignoles, Chardonnay, and Cabernet Franc. Riesling is among the most commonly made wines in the Finger Lakes area, and for good reason. The cool growing conditions lend themselves to this fruity, high acid grape. Reinhardt makes his in two styles—dry and semi-dry. The dry Riesling has nice, crisp acidity with some apricot tones, while the semi-dry Riesling, with about 1 percent residual sugar, retains that important acidity but brings in more noticeable sweetness.

Reinhardt shows amazing restraint and grace with his wines. His Chardonnay is a good example.

He does only 25 percent malolactic fermentation (many Chardonnay producers do full ML), and only 30 percent of the wine is aged in oak. Moreover, that oak is old—not new. Using these methods, Reinhardt manages to coax out as much of the fruit as possible rather than mask it. It's a very nice wine.

A taste of the semi-dry Vignoles instantly conjures up images of a tropical island. The wine is spicy and floral, and because of that, it goes particularly well with similar flavors. It also accompanies cheese very well because of the balance of fruit and acidity. Although not vinifera, this hybrid grape is impressive, and all the more so in Reinhardt's hands.

With a new tasting room, an expanded winery, and an eye toward innovation, the Martinis are in the process of creating a blueprint not only for the Anthony Road wines, but for the wines that will be made in the Finger Lakes for generations to come.

## WHAT THEY MAKE

**Red wines**
Cabernet Franc
Cabernet Sauvignon
Lemberger
Merlot

**White wines**
Chardonnay
Pinot Gris
Riesling
Vignoles

## HOW TO REACH THEM

Penn Yan, New York
315-356-2182 (*phone*)
800-559-2182 (*toll-free*)
315-536-5851 (*fax*)
www.anthonyroadwine.com

# CAESAR FINGERS WITH CHEESE CRISPS

**ONE OF THE MOST POPULAR SALADS IN AMERICA IS THE CAESAR.** But why wait until the salad course when you can enjoy the same thing as an hors d'oeuvre? You can top the lettuce leaves with the dressing about an hour before serving, keeping them refrigerated, but don't add the cheese crisps until you're ready to serve, otherwise they will get soggy. If you wish to make a traditional Caesar salad, simply double the recipe for the dressing. This recipe will make enough for one bunch of romaine.

Preheat the oven to 375°F.

To make the dressing: In the bowl of a food processor, combine the anchovies, garlic, lemon juice, mayonnaise, vinegars, Worcestershire sauce, and pepper to taste. Process for 10 seconds. Add the olive oil through the feed tube and process until the mixture thickens. With the machine still running, add ⅓ cup of the cheese and pulse off and on until it is incorporated. The mixture will not be smooth. Pour the dressing into a bowl or jar and set aside. (The dressing can be refrigerated for up to 3 days.) Makes about ⅓ cup.

To make the cheese crisps: Grease a baking sheet or preferably use a silicone baking mat, such as Silpat. (You may need two baking sheets, or you can bake the cheese crisps in two batches.) Spread 1 teaspoon of the cheese in a strip about 3 inches long. Repeat with the remaining cheese. Bake for 8 to 10 minutes, or until the cheese is golden brown. Remove from the oven and immediately slide the cheese strips onto a flat plate to cool. Repeat with the remaining cheese. You should have 24 crisps.

To assemble, separate the lettuce leaves. Cut the stems to make uniform-size 4-inch leaves. (You will be cutting the leaves in half. Save the cut stems to toss in a mixed green salad or discard.) Place the leaves in a spoke-like pattern on a serving platter with the stem ends toward the middle. Starting at the stem end, drizzle about 1 teaspoon of the dressing down the length of each leaf. Top with a cheese crisp. Repeat with the remaining leaves and cheese. Sprinkle a little pepper over the "fingers" and serve immediately.

Makes about 24 leaves; serves 6 to 8

2 anchovies in oil or Spanish white anchovies, finely chopped

2 cloves garlic, peeled and minced

2 tablespoons fresh lemon juice

1 tablespoon mayonnaise

¾ teaspoon balsamic vinegar

½ teaspoon red wine vinegar

Dash of Worcestershire sauce

Freshly ground pepper

2 tablespoons olive oil

3 ounces (about ¾ cup) finely grated salty aged cheese, such as Parmesan, Asiago, or dry Jack

2 hearts of romaine lettuce, washed and dried thoroughly, leaves left whole (or buy whole bunches of romaine and use only the tender, lighter green leaves on the inside)

Freshly ground pepper

## PERFECT PAIRS

**YEARS AGO, THE THEN-**sommelier of the Little Nell restaurant (now called Montagna) in Aspen, Colorado, showed my husband and me the virtues of Riesling with Caesar salad. That sommelier, Robert Stuckey, is now at the Napa Valley's famed French Laundry restaurant and, I would imagine, still touting this unbeatable combination. An off-dry Riesling works particularly well.

# Hillman Farms

PART OF THE MAGIC OF CHEESEMAKING IN AMERICA IS THE SMALL OPERATION THAT goes about its work in a quiet, unassuming manner, making cheese, tending to animals, and eking out a living only from what the land provides. Hillman Farms is one such place. Nestled in the rolling hills of the Berkshires in northwest Massachusetts, Carolyn and Joe Hillman have carved out a life that harks back to their ancestral farm roots, sharing the land with oxen, pigs, goats, and enough pasture to feed the animals until, well, the cows come home. It should come as no surprise, then, that the food products from such a place would be as grounded as the people who have created them. The Hillman Harvest cheese is resolutely true to its origins.

Carolyn Hillman, who makes the cheese, was not always a farm dweller. She went the city route, attending art school in Boston and then living there for many years. But she found she was inexorably drawn to the country and to animals, so she decided to move out of the city. She rented a cabin on the edge of the state forest, about a mile from the town of Colrain. There she met Joe Hillman, who was born in Colrain and was living on a farm there.

Before she moved to the country, Carolyn had developed a real love for goats' milk, buying it regularly from Westfield Farm in Hubbardston, Massachusetts. (Westfield Farm is well known for its excellent goats' and cows' milk cheeses.) Once Joe and Carolyn got together, she moved to his farm, and they acquired a few goats.

Carolyn began her cheese endeavor with a goat cheddar because that was the type of cheese Joe liked. Eventually she came up with another type of aged cheese. Harvest Cheese, as it is called, is so named because of the time of year that the cheese is released.

HARVEST CHEESE

A Traditional Goats Milk Cheese
HILLMAN FARM
COLRAIN, MA. 01340

Ingredients: Unpasteurized Grade A Goats Milk, Cultures, Enzymes, Salt.
Aged over 60 Days   Plant# 25-113

The process gets under way a few months earlier, in the spring, when the goats are having their kids and milk production begins. By the time the cheese is ready, it is fall or harvest time, and thus the natural name for this extraordinary cheese.

Harvest Cheese is made with the milk from the Hillmans' thirty goats. Other than the actual milking, which, by Massachusetts law, must be done by machine, the cheese is entirely handmade. First, the raw milk is hand-stirred. When it has curdled, the curds are hand-cut and then hand-ladled into the molds. The cheese is then placed in a brine solution for thirty-six hours and is turned constantly, by hand—of course. Finally, the cheese is ready to go into the Hillmans' new aging cellar, where it will remain for at least four months and usually five to six months.

The wheels of cheese start out weighing somewhere between eight and ten pounds. When they have aged for a few months, their weight will have dropped to between five and eight pounds. As the cheese loses its moisture, it naturally loses weight. While it ages, it is placed on wooden boards, whose porous surface helps foster the growth of good bacteria and lend flavor to the cheese. Hillman also occasionally washes the rind with a brine solution, which also enhances the flavor.

The cheese that emerges from the aging cellar displays a true tapestry of flavor. The goats, which are on a rotational grazing system, enjoy a steady diet of rye, clover, timothy, wild herbs, raspberry, thistle, and burdock. Their flavor-rich food translates to the cheese, which carries some of the same herbaceousness, floral qualities, and grassiness. The cheese is also a bit buttery, and its texture is smooth but ever so slightly granular. Harvest Cheese is very sophisticated because of the Hillmans' understanding and apprecia-

# Ken Wright Cellars

**"THE HARDEST THING TO LEARN IS HOW NOT TO GET IN THE WAY," SAYS KEN WRIGHT,** owner and winemaker of the eponymous Ken Wright Cellars, in Carlton, Oregon, about fifty miles southwest of Portland. He is talking about his role as a winemaker. "Experimentation should be based on the grape, to help that fruit to express the qualities that fruit already has," says Wright. This kind of restraint and modesty is precisely why Ken Wright is considered one of the state's preeminent Pinot Noir producers. He might be said to be a "deconstructor," a winemaker who is intent on learning how not to be a wrong influence.

Wright's approach to winemaking is very deliberate, and, like most winemakers, he knows his product has everything to do with what happens in the vineyard. That's why he produces several Pinot Noirs, most from single vineyards. To him, there is no question that the same grape, in this case Pinot Noir, tastes decidely different depending on where it is grown.

Press Wright on the topic of vineyard location, and you'll get a thoughtful, articulate explanation of the geology and topography of the Willamette Valley, the area where the state's best Pinot Noir is grown. He is an eloquent and knowledgeable teacher.

As he tells it, the Willamette Valley is made up of different types of soils, owing to the way the area developed geologically. It wasn't until the Pacific Plate in the west met up with the Continental Plate in the east that the Willamette Valley, and much of Oregon and Washington as we know them, were formed. The end result today is a combination of the sedimentary soils of the Willamette Valley, which used to lie under a body of water, and the volcanic soils that pushed up from beneath the sediment. That soil mixture has an enormous effect on grape growing. While the deep volcanic soils of the Dundee Hills to the northeast might develop wines with concentrations of red fruit flavors (strawberry, cherry, and raspberry), the Eola Hills further south, with their shallower volcanic soil, will produce dark fruit flavors in the wine, such as blueberry, black cherry, plum, and others. The Yamhill Foothills consist primarily of sedimentary soils, which drain well, and produce wines that have both dark and red fruit components with the addition of fresh earth notes as well. And the Coastal Range, with its sandy soils, produces dark, almost brooding wines with good structure.

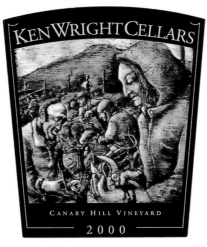

Wright grows grapes in all of these areas because he appreciates the varying expression of Pinot Noir in the different soils. "I became more and more impressed with the ability of Pinot Noir to convey characteristics of site and amazed at the diversity of the qualities this grape could show," he says. To learn about the Willamette Valley and its geological mix, he kept the grapes from each location separate. This practice set the stage for his predominantly single-vineyard production today.

Wright's wines are so popular that people line up during the Thanksgiving weekend—one of two long weekends when Willamette Valley wine producers open their doors for special tastings—to taste samples from the barrels and buy his wine. At this point the wine is a long way from being bottled, yet most all of it is spoken for by the end of the weekend. This phenomenon perplexes but pleases Wright.

The affable winemaker first developed an interest in wine when he was earning money waiting tables during college. The restaurant where he worked in Lexington, Kentucky, had a tremendous wine list, but because none of the staff knew much about wine, the owner gave wine seminars to teach them. When the lesson turned to Burgundy, the region in France where Pinot Noir is produced, Wright got hooked. He toiled in a friend's ill-fated Kentucky vineyard and eventually went to UC Davis for a formal winemaking education. He arrived in Oregon by way of the Napa Valley in 1986 in pursuit of his beloved Pinot Noir.

Today he produces about 10,000 cases, which makes his operation a medium-sized winery by Oregon standards.

Although Wright makes a Willamette Valley Pinot Noir, which means that the grapes come from different vineyards throughout the valley, he makes no fewer than twelve single-vineyard Pinot Noirs. Among them, the wines from his Carter Vineyard and Canary Vineyard, both in the Eola Hills, are particularly popular. While the Carter Vineyard is haunting with its black fruit characteristics and earthy overtones, the Canary Vineyard exemplifies the term "black cherry." The McCrone Vineyard Pinot Noir, made from grapes grown in the Yamhill Foothills, is a shy but intense, black fruit wine. The McCrone Vineyard

is located near Wright's home, with its 360-degree view of the valley. The Shea Vineyard produces one of the most integrated Pinot Noirs with brighter fruits and firm, earthy foundation. Although the vineyard is owned by Dick Shea, Wright helped develop it, and now several other Willamette Valley producers buy their fruit from this vineyard too. In addition, Dick Shea has his own label called Shea Wine Cellars.

To hear Ken Wright talk about Pinot Noir is like listening to a poet recite verse. Indeed, the Pinot Noir grape has been known to inspire poetry because of the mysterious yet nearly atavistic pleasure it provides. For Wright, Pinot Noir is the representation of the particular area that captivates him the most. "There is nothing like the expression of Pinot Noir from a great place; the array of aroma, flavor, and texture is amazing," he says. "It's magical. It's not about winemaking and marketing; it comes from nurturing." And Wright is unquestionably nurturing an entire industry by guiding what nature provides and gently capturing it in a bottle.

WHAT THEY MAKE

**White wines**
Chardonnay (*Washington: Celilo Vineyard*)
Pinot Blanc

**Red wines**
Pinot Noir (*Dundee Hills: Nysa Vineyard; Eola Hills: Canary Hill Vineyard, Carter Vineyard, Elton Vineyard; Yamhill-Carlton: Abbott Claim, Guadalupe Vineyard, McCrone Vineyard, Savoya Vineyard, Shea Vineyard, Wahle Vineyard; Coastal Range: Freedom Hill Vineyard*)

HOW TO REACH THEM

503-852-7070 (phone)
800-571-6825 (toll-free)
503-852-7111 (fax)
www.kenwrightcellars.com

# CARAMELIZED ONION, BACON, AND GRUYÈRE FONDUE

GRUYÈRE, ALONG WITH EMMENTALER AND APPENZELLER, IS ONE OF THE TRADITIONAL CHEESES USED IN CHEESE FONDUE. Here, the nutty cheese gets a boost from the sweet onions and the smoky bacon, and transforms into satisfying, rustic fare. As with all fondues, this really is best when a traditional fondue pot is used. However, you can serve it in a heavy-bottomed pot as long as you are prepared to reheat the fondue occasionally—if you don't, you'll end up with an unappetizing rubbery mess.

In a large sauté pan, warm the oil over low heat. Place the onions, thyme, salt, and pepper to taste in the pan and cook, stirring occasionally, for about 45 minutes. The onions should turn a golden color but should not brown. Be patient! If they stick, add a little bit of water. Keep warm over a very low heat. (You can make the onions up to 2 hours in advance. After they're cooked, remove them from the heat. Warm slightly before using.)

Cook the bacon until crisp. Drain on paper towels and set aside.

In a medium bowl, toss together the cheese and flour. Set aside.

Warm a fondue pot by filling it with hot water. Pour out the water and wipe the pot dry.

In a medium-sized, heavy-bottomed pot, heat the wine slowly over medium heat. Once the wine is hot but not boiling, add a handful of the cheese. Stir until melted before adding more. Continue with the remaining cheese (if the mixture is stiff, add a little more wine 1 teaspoon at a time). When all of the cheese has been added, stir in the bacon and all but about ½ cup of the onions.

Transfer the fondue to the fondue pot and top with the remaining onions. Serve immediately, with the bread cubes and potatoes.

Serves 4 to 6

¼ cup olive oil

2 medium yellow onions (about ¾ pound), thinly sliced

1 teaspoon finely chopped fresh thyme

¼ teaspoon salt

Freshly ground pepper

6 slices bacon, coarsely chopped

1 pound Gruyère cheese, coarsely grated

1½ tablespoons flour

¾ cup good quality, slightly fruity white wine such as a Riesling

Hearty country-style or sourdough bread with crust (about 1½–2 pounds), cut into 1-inch cubes, for serving

6 fingerling potatoes, boiled and cut in half lengthwise, for serving

## PERFECT PAIRS

THE RIESLING CALLED FOR in this fondue tastes wonderful accompanying the fondue as well. However, the addition of the sweet onions and smoky bacon means that red wine would also go nicely. A Syrah would be a nice choice, as would an earthy Pinot Noir or Grenache.

# MONTEREY JACK–EMMENTALER FONDUE WITH FENNEL AND TOMATOES

ONE OF THE BEST THINGS ABOUT FONDUE IS THAT YOU CAN ADD JUST ABOUT ANYTHING YOU LIKE TO THE BASIC CHEESE MIXTURE AND COME UP WITH YOUR OWN UNIQUE CREATION. In this recipe, the use of fennel not only adds nice flavor, it also makes a great textural addition. And using springy focaccia to scoop up the cheesy mixture creates yet another welcome textural element. For a fresh, zippy flavor, you can mix in some fresh chopped basil just before serving the fondue.

1 tablespoon olive oil

2 small fennel bulbs (about 1¼ pounds), cut into
    ¼-inch dice

3 medium plum tomatoes (about ¾ pound),
    seeded and cut into ¼-inch dice

Salt and freshly ground pepper

9 ounces Emmentaler cheese, coarsely grated

6 ounces Monterey Jack cheese, coarsely grated

2 tablespoons flour

¼ teaspoon cayenne pepper

¾ cup good quality, slightly fruity white wine
    such as Riesling

Focaccia or rustic Italian bread
    (about 1½–2 pounds), cubed

In a medium sauté pan, warm the oil over medium heat. Add the fennel and cook until translucent but still slightly crunchy, 8 to 10 minutes. Add the tomatoes and salt and pepper to taste, and cook, stirring occasionally, until the tomatoes have released their juices and most of the liquid has evaporated, about 7 minutes (it is important that you cook away most of the liquid or you'll end up with a watery fondue).

In a medium bowl, toss together the cheeses, flour, and cayenne. Set aside.

Warm a fondue pot by filling it with hot water. Pour out the water and wipe the pot dry.

In a medium-sized, heavy-bottomed pot, heat the wine over medium heat. Once the wine is hot but not boiling, add a handful of the cheese mixture. Stir until melted before adding more. Continue with the remaining cheese (if the mixture is stiff, add more wine 1 teaspoon at a time). When all of the cheese has melted, stir in the fennel mixture.

Transfer the fondue to the fondue pot. Serve immediately, with cubed focaccia bread and/or breadsticks.

Serves 4 to 6

## PERFECT PAIRS

AS ALWAYS WHEN COOKING with wine, it is wise to drink the same wine you used to make your dish. This fondue calls for a fruity wine, such as Riesling, and that should be the wine you serve alongside the fondue as well. If you're interested in a red wine, then a fruity Sangiovese or even a medium-bodied, fruity Zinfandel would be nice.

# Gruet Winery

THE IDEA THAT FINE CHAMPAGNE COULD BE MADE IN NEW MEXICO IS ABOUT AS foreign as the wine itself. But, in fact, fine Champagne, or sparkling wine as it is called in this country, spills out of the French-owned Gruet winery at the rate of about 45,000 cases a year.

The Gruet winery and tasting room are located in the heart of the city of Albuquerque. The estate-grown grapes, though, come from an area about 150 miles south, near the auspiciously named city of Truth or Consequences. Owner Laurent Gruet and his Champagne-making family in France took a chance when they decided to extend their sparkling wine business to the United States. Fortunately, there have been no adverse consequences—only success.

The Gruet family has been making sparkling wine in an area south of Epernay, in the Champagne region of France, since 1952. Laurent learned winemaking at his father's side, and after he worked as a winemaker and went to wine school, he and his family decided to expand their enterprise. Initially, they looked at the more obvious places in America, such as California and Texas. But they happened to meet some people who were planting vineyards in New Mexico, and the Gruets were quickly convinced that the soil, climate, and weather in the region were just what they were looking for.

At an elevation of 4,300 feet, it would seem unlikely that successful grape growing on any large scale would be possible, but the arid New Mexico climate means warm days, cool nights, and, most beneficial, a dearth of pests and no rot problems. The weather is just too dry for rot and other diseases that are common to more humid areas. Occasional frosts pose potential problems, but Gruet says they have experienced a detrimental frost only once. On that occasion, though, they lost almost 40 percent of their crop.

In normal years, their Chardonnay, Pinot Noir, and a tiny amount of Pinot Meunier, used in a very small percent of Champagne making, flourishes on the Gruets' hundred-acre plot. Gruet grew up learning the strict rules in Champagne making, and he continues that tradition with a fierce dedication here.

All of the grapes are hand-harvested, the grape clusters are pressed but not crushed, and the juice is then naturally fermented in vats for two to three weeks. After that, the wine is aged for six months. At this point, Gruet will blend the wines, depending on what he is making—blanc de noirs, brut, or blanc de blancs. Next, the wine is bottled, at which point Gruet adds what is called a *tirage*, or a mixture of yeast and sugar. The purpose of the tirage is to provoke a secondary fermentation in the bottle, which, in turn, transforms the still wine into sparkling wine. The dead yeast cells that result from this process are also responsible for giving sparkling wine much of its flavor. The wine will spend two years in the bottle in contact with the yeast sediments, or lees as they are known, or, in the case of the blanc de blancs, four years. (Gruet says he does not make blanc de blancs every year—only when the grapes used to make that particular wine are superior.) Next, the bottles are shaken to dislodge the resulting sediments, and then they are turned upside

down so that the lees gather in the neck of the bottle. The necks are then frozen, the bottles opened, and the sediment literally flies out as one big ice cube. Gruet then adds a *dosage*, which is a mixture of sugar and wine, to provide a little bit of sweetness in what is otherwise a bone-dry liquid. (The Gruet wines all hover at about 1 percent residual sugar.) Finally, the wines are corked, labeled, and sold.

And what fantastic wines they are. Sometimes a sparkling wine can taste bitter or too dry, but Gruet, who takes tremendous pride in the quality of his grapes, instills great flavor in each bottle. The brut is toasty and a little bit yeasty, with lots of small, flittering bubbles. The golden color is almost as enticing as the flavor. Blanc de blancs is drier and almost steely, but it still has good fruit character and is a fantastic food wine. Gruet also makes a rosé with mostly Chardonnay and a bit of Pinot Noir still wine added in. Unfortunately for rosé fans, he makes a woefully small amount.

The Gruet Winery is a family affair, with Laurent serving as the winemaker and co-owner and his brother-in-law, Farid Himeur, who is in charge of the office and some of the marketing. In addition to sparkling wine, Gruet is now making still wines, including Chardonnay, Pinot Noir (a natural outgrowth since these are the same grapes that go into his sparkling wine), and, lately, Syrah. He says he loves making still wines because of the challenge, and he particularly enjoys making the always difficult Pinot Noir. "I love to drink Pinot Noir. I know the vineyards, and I know the grapes," he says.

Although Gruet is French and he grew up around fine wine, he does not fit one important stereotype of a person in his position: He does not eat cheese. He admits it is strange, but he says he simply doesn't like it. He does, however, make an exception: "I like Swiss cheese," he says. He is referring to Emmentaler, Gruyère, and the like. Despite this apparent lapse in his gastronomic development, he more than makes up for it with his wine, which, incidentally, goes wonderfully with cheese.

WHAT THEY MAKE

**Sparkling wines**
Blanc de Blancs
Blanc de Noirs
Brut

**Still wines**
Chardonnay
Pinot Noir
Syrah

HOW TO REACH THEM

Albuquerque, New Mexico
505-821-0055 (*phone*)
505-857-0066 (*fax*)
www.gruetwines.com

# CHEDDAR-PARMESAN CRACKERS

**THESE CHEESY, BUTTERY GEMS WILL LIKELY BECOME A MAINSTAY IN YOUR REPERTOIRE.** Not only are they crispy, rich, and, well, addictive, they can be partially made up to a month in advance. That's because once the dough is made, it can be frozen and simply "cut to order" as you need it. Just be sure to freeze it in small portions so that you don't have to defrost it all at once. Although these crackers are great plain, you can draw on the age-old "apples and cheddar" theme by topping them with a dollop of Apple-Pear Butter (see page 174).

4 ounces cheddar cheese, coarsely grated

2 ounces Parmesan cheese, finely grated

¾ cup flour

¼ teaspoon dry mustard

¼ teaspoon kosher salt

⅛ teaspoon cayenne pepper

4 tablespoons (½ stick) unsalted butter, softened and cut into small pieces

2 tablespoons water, plus more if needed

In the bowl of a food processor, place all the ingredients except the butter and water. Pulse 5 times. Add the butter and pulse again until the butter pieces are the size of BBs. Add the water, 1 tablespoon at a time, and pulse just until the dough holds together. If the dough is still crumbly, add more water 1 teaspoon at a time until it reaches the right consistency.

Turn the dough out onto a large piece of waxed paper. Roll the dough into a log, 9 to 10 inches long, and square off the ends. Refrigerate, well wrapped, for at least 2 hours and up to 2 days. Or freeze it for up to 1 month. (You may want to cut the log in half or in thirds to freeze if you think you will want to defrost a smaller amount at a time.)

Preheat the oven to 375°F.

To make the crackers, cut the log into ¼-inch-thick slices. Arrange the slices on a baking sheet 1 inch apart. Bake for 8 to 10 minutes, or until the crackers are a light golden color. Turn the crackers and bake for 3 to 5 more minutes, or until they are golden around the edges. Cool on a rack. Serve at room temperature.

Makes about 3 dozen crackers; serves 8 to 10

## PERFECT PAIRS

**SPARKLING WINE IS TERRIFIC** with these crackers, as is Riesling. Another great option to go with is a rosé. All of these work nicely with the pungent Parmesan and rich cheddar.

# FROMAGE BLANC CRACKERS WITH CRISPY PROSCIUTTO AND FROMAGE BLANC

**THE TITLE OF THIS RECIPE MIGHT SEEM REDUNDANT, UNTIL YOU SEE THAT FROMAGE BLANC IS PUT TO USE IN TWO WAYS.** First it's used as one of the main ingredients in the shortbread-like crackers, and second it's piled on top of the cracker in its pure, unadorned form. The crispy prosciutto chips are the crowning glory. Like the Cheddar-Parmesan Crackers (see page 111), these, too, can be partially made and frozen before they are baked. Just slice, bake, and serve when ready. Also you may note that the crackers include rosemary. If you prefer another herb, or no herb at all, the choice is yours. The crackers are good no matter what.

8 tablespoons (1 stick) butter, at room
    temperature
12 ounces fromage blanc, at room temperature
    (or use cream cheese or fresh goat cheese)
1 cup flour
1½ teaspoons dried rosemary, finely chopped
½ teaspoon kosher salt
2 ounces prosciutto, sliced paper-thin

In the bowl of a stand mixer or using a hand mixer, cream the butter and 8 ounces of the cheese together. Add the flour, rosemary, and salt, and mix until the dough holds together and becomes smooth. This will take 2 or 3 minutes.

Turn the dough out onto a sheet of waxed paper. Roll the dough into a log, 9 to 10 inches long, and square off the ends. Refrigerate, well wrapped, for at least 2 hours and up to 2 days. Or freeze it for up to 1 month. (You may want to cut the log in half or in thirds to freeze if you think you will want to defrost a smaller amount at a time.)

Preheat the oven to 400°F.

Place the prosciutto slices on a baking sheet. Bake for 15 minutes. Turn the slices and bake for 5 to 7 minutes more, or until the prosciutto is crisp and very light brown around the edges. Remove from the oven and let cool completely. The prosciutto will continue to crisp as it cools. Reduce the oven temperature to 375°F.

Slice the cracker dough into ⅛-inch-thick slices. Arrange the slices on a baking sheet 1 inch apart. Bake for 8 to 10 minutes, or until they are a light golden color. Turn the crackers and bake for 6 to 8 more minutes, or until they are golden around the edges. Let cool completely.

To serve, place a small dollop of the remaining cheese on each cracker. Gently break off a small strip of prosciutto (the shape doesn't matter, just as long as it isn't larger than the cracker) and lay it over the cheese. Repeat with the remaining crackers, cheese, and prosciutto. Serve immediately.

Makes about 6 dozen crackers; serves 8 to 10

## PERFECT PAIRS

**FROMAGE BLANC IS** inherently tart, and, because of that, it finds a great wine companion in Pinot Gris. A crisp Sauvignon Blanc or Rosé will work too.

# Sweet Grass Dairy

**EVERY SO OFTEN, CHEESEMAKERS COME ALONG WHO, THROUGH THEIR PRODUCTS,** make it clear that their chosen profession was undeniably meant to be. While Desiree Wehner may not see it that way, especially since she decidedly did *not* like cheese when she was growing up, the cheese she produces is eloquent proof.

Wehner and her husband, Al, who grew up on a dairy farm in western New York State, began their married lives as dairy farmers in Florida. They worked for a large Holstein dairy where they were recognized for their exceptional milking and dairy practices. In the mid-1980s, they went to Italy to learn how to make a special whole milk yogurt, which they, along with a business partner, intended to produce in the United States. When their business partnership went sour, they moved over the border to Georgia to start their own dairy.

In 1993, disillusioned by the dairy business as they knew it, they sold all their Holsteins, trading them in for Jersey cows, and began a rotational grazing system. In their southeastern location, they were able to offer their cows year-round pasture. Like several American dairy people and cheesemakers who do rotational grazing, the Wehners recognized that their milk quality was exceptional as a result of this practice. They began to market it as such.

Once their dairy operation got underway, the Wehners hired Al's sister and brother-in-law to run the dairy, which left the rarely idle Desiree without much

to do. On a trip to California many years before, she had been introduced to goat cheese, which she had become instantly passionate about. A subsequent trip to Europe, where she tasted many great cheeses, convinced her to try her hand at making cheese.

In 1999, although she had no experience with goats, she acquired a dozen of them and began making cheese in her kitchen. She says she set out to evaluate whether she liked making cheese and whether she was capable of making good cheese. The answer to both was an emphatic yes. Another trip to France in 2000 convinced her of the need to show people at home the connection between foods and their producers—a link that is emphasized in Europe—and with that, her commercial cheesemaking got underway.

One of her finest cheeses was made by accident. Wehner had set out to make a goats' milk mozzarella, but when the curds became too acidic, she simply cut them up, put them into molds, and salted them. She left the cheese in a cooler for a few months, and when she tried it, she discovered she'd made a fine cheese. This cheese was made with spring milk, in which Wehner could taste the herbs, grass, and flowery flavor of the new growth, so she christened it Botana— a kind of derivative of "botanical." Although the original "mistake" was made with pasteurized milk, Wehner has since changed the Botana to an unpasteurized milk cheese, which she ages for four to six months. Just as Wehner says, the cheese is full of grassy and herbal flavors, but it is also a bit sweet, buttery, and nutty. The texture is semi-hard and smooth. Botana is a great cheese, with real sophistication and complexity.

Wehner also makes several wonderful cows' milk cheeses. In particular, she produces a cheese called Green Hill. If every American were to try this rich, creamy, buttery, cylindrical soft-ripening cheese, there would likely be a stampede to Georgia. It is positively mind-boggling that when Wehner created this and most of her excellent cheeses, she had been making cheese for all of a few months. Another of her cows' milk cheeses, called Greenwood, Wehner likens to a Colby, although that may be selling it short. The nine-month-old raw-milk cheese has depth and character that most Colbys do not have, and its golden color is derived from the milk itself; there is no dye added.

As is often the case with good cheese, the demand for Sweet Grass Dairy cheeses has increased dramatically. To keep up with demand Wehner has enlisted the help of her family. Her son-in-law, Jeremy Little, is now the cheesemaker, while her daughter, Jessica Little, handles the marketing. Not wanting to stray too far from the action, Wehner still makes her creamy, runny cheese called Velvet Rose, and she constantly experiments with new cheeses.

Although Wehner did not originally set out to make cheese, she has established a firm foothold in the world of artisan cheese. Her son-in-law has garnered several awards already, and the family's ambition and love of good food seems to know no bounds. Rare in the deep south, cheeses like those from Sweet Grass Dairy are unquestionably ones that set the standards for artisan cheese across America.

WHAT THEY MAKE

**Cows' milk cheeses**
Clayburne
Georgia Gouda
Green Hill
The Jake
Jessanne
Myrtlewood
Thomasville Tomme
Velvet Rose

**Goats' milk cheeses**
Botana
Chèvre (fresh, pecan-crusted)
Holly Springs
Lucille
Lumiere

HOW TO REACH THEM

Thomasville, Georgia
229-227-0752 (phone)
229-227-1403 (fax)
www.sweetgrassdairy.com

# ARTICHOKE LEAVES WITH SPINACH-RICOTTA FILLING

**THIS ALL-VEGETABLE HORS D'OEUVRE OFFERS LOADS OF FLEXIBILITY WITH INGREDIENTS.** Instead of ricotta, you can use fromage blanc or fresh goat cheese. And for a heartier rendition, you can add a little bit of pancetta to the cheese mixture. Cut two ¼-inch slices into ¼-inch dice and sauté until crisp. Let the pancetta drain on paper towels and then add it back into the mixture with the cheese and remaining ingredients. You can make the filling up to one day in advance and refrigerate it. Bring the filling to room temperature and mix well before assembling the hors d'oeuvre.

1 gallon water

1 teaspoon kosher salt

1 large globe artichoke (top trimmed ½ inch and sharp ends of leaves cut off)

1½ tablespoons olive oil

½ cup finely diced yellow onion

1 clove garlic, minced

5-ounces (½ package) chopped, frozen spinach, thawed and drained

2 ounces (¼ cup) ricotta cheese

2 teaspoons fresh lemon juice

2 tablespoons pine nuts, toasted

Salt and freshly ground pepper

In a medium pot, bring the water and salt to a boil. Add the artichoke, cover, and cook for about 40 minutes, or until the artichoke leaves can be pulled away with only slight resistance. Remove from the water and let cool.

Meanwhile, prepare the filling. In a medium-sized sauté pan, warm the oil over medium heat. Add the onion and cook for 5 minutes. Add the garlic and continue cooking until both are limp but not brown. Next add the spinach and cook until heated through, about 5 minutes. Turn off the heat and add the cheese, lemon juice, pine nuts, and salt and pepper to taste. Adjust the seasoning and let cool. (Makes a scant 1 cup filling.)

To assemble, remove the first two layers of leaves from the cooked artichoke. (Reserve the remaining leaves and heart for another use.) Arrange on a serving platter. Place about 1 teaspoon of spinach mixture onto the edible end of each leaf. Serve within an hour.

Note: The exposed surfaces of the artichoke leaves tend to darken slightly as the leaves sit. This does not change the flavor.

Yields about 30 leaves; serves 6 to 8

## PERFECT PAIRS

**CHOOSE A MILD WINE,** such as a Chenin Blanc, Arneis, or Sauvignon Blanc. You can also choose a sparkling wine to head off the difficult-to-match components in the artichoke and spinach.

# White Oak Farmstead

JEFF BROWN IS A QUINTESSENTIAL EXAMPLE OF THE AMERICAN CHEESEMAKER who settled on his profession because of an aching desire to return to the land. A software technician with Hewlett Packard, Brown took a voluntary severance package the company offered when it was downsizing, and he headed straight for the hills. Well, actually, he went to Arizona, where his brother had a herd of goats he was looking to sell. The "hell trip" from Arizona back to his home state of Washington in the middle of summer with twenty goats in tow is one that Brown says he will never repeat. Nonetheless, it was a necessary step toward becoming a cheesemaker. He was fortunate to come upon some dairy equipment from winemaker friends in Oregon who had entertained thoughts of making goat cheese. (They now make highly regarded wine under the Belle Pente label.) Brown got a pasteurizer and bulk tank from them and was on his way—sort of.

First he had to learn how to make cheese. To learn the basics, he enrolled in the renowned short course at Washington State University. He also had to complete his cheesemaking room. His five-acre parcel of land was a natural home for his herd of Alpines. The herd now numbers thirty goats (twenty of which are currently milked), and they are on pasture much of the year, where they eat grass, thistle, and blackberries. "I watch them eat those things, and my throat hurts at the thought," Brown says when observing the animals eating the sharp plants. In the winter, they are fed hay.

A humble man, Brown seems incredulous when asked about the universal enthusiasm for his cheese. His "gee whiz" attitude could be, in part, owing to the joy he gets in being able to do the type of work he has longed to do. He certainly hasn't taken on an easy life. His day begins at five A.M., when he does the first round of milking. After that, he decides which cheese he is going to make based on how much milk he has.

As it is, he makes only about forty pounds a week. The small size of the White Oak Farm operation is underscored when Brown explains how he is able to make two cheeses in one day. To do so, he plugs up one of his draining tables, fills it with water, and places two- and three-gallon steam table pans in the water. He then places the milk in these pans, just as he would a regular vat, and makes the cheese in these. This allows him to use the vat for making a separate cheese, and therefore to make two cheeses at one time. This no-frills method gives "table cheese" a whole new meaning.

The end result is, indeed, some very fine cheese. His White Oak Rustic Peppercorn table cheese looks like a reverse night sky, with a bright white background and peppercorn constellations. Because he adds lipase—the enzyme that provides the piquant flavor in Italian Parmigiano-Reggiano and other similar cheeses—his cheese has a tinge of sharpness that complements the spice. It is a magical combination because the cheese really holds its own against the pepper. Also, unlike most whole peppercorn cheeses, which are usually made with cows' or sheep's milk and are golden, his goat cheese is whitish, making it still more distinctive.

Brown's Pacific Blue is one of the more unusual American cheeses. It is a Stilton-like goat cheese, meaning it is drier and more crumbly than most other blue cheeses. It is made in four-pound wheels and aged for about three months, or for as long as he can keep it before his customers beg him to relinquish it. The demand is understandable, since the cheese has a nutty flavor and a pleasant grainy texture. It has lots of blue veining, and although it reaches a few high notes in sharpness, it is by no means astringent. Brown says Pacific Blue is his most popular cheese, although his Golden Rose is not far behind.

Also an aged cheese, Golden Rose falls somewhere between a cheddar and a Jack cheese. It is semi-hard and has a faint orange hue from the few drops of annatto dye Brown adds to the milk. (Annatto is the natural dye used by cheesemakers to turn their cheese orange.) This cheese is made in three-pound wheels, but Brown is currently experimenting with producing twelve-pound wheels. Golden Rose is one of the most well-balanced cheeses made in America, with its creamy texture and buttery, distinctive, though not strong, flavors. Because of demand, Brown does not age the cheese the several months he would like, but he says he is working toward that goal.

As an illustration of Brown's newcomer spirit, he recalls the time when a batch of his Golden Rose managed to pick up some of the blue mold that was floating around his aging room. This turned it into a slightly blue cheese, as will frequently happen. Rather than throwing the batch away, Brown tasted the cheese, liked it, and christened it "Blue and Gold." His customers loved it. He laments the fact he hasn't been able to duplicate it since.

Battle Ground, Washington, is just north of Vancouver, Washington, and is about seventy miles from Portland. Already, top chefs in Portland are clamoring for White Oak Farm cheese, but because of his small output, Brown says he can't meet demand—yet. As a one-man operation, growth comes slowly, but given that he just got his license in the fall of 2000, Brown has already tackled the tough job of building an excellent reputation. Now all he has to do is somehow make more cheese.

WHAT THEY MAKE

Black Peppercorn Table Cheese
Cascade Camembert
Chèvre (plain and herbes de Provence)
Feta

Golden Rose
Pacific Blue
St. Helens

HOW TO REACH THEM

Battle Ground, Washington
360-576-7688 (phone and fax)
www.white-oak.com

# BEETS AND GOAT CHEESE
# ON BUTTERED BRIOCHE

**SLIGHTLY SWEET BRIOCHE BRUSHED WITH MELTED BUTTER IS ADDICTIVE ALL ON ITS OWN.** But when tangy goat cheese and lemon-coated beets are placed on top, it becomes a symphony for the sweet, sour, and salty taste buds. The goat cheese and red beets on the yellow bread look lovely too. It is important that the bread slices stay crisp, so do not make them too far in advance. Once they are assembled, serve them right away. Also, if you cannot find brioche, use egg bread or challah.

¼ pound red beets (about 3 small beets), stems and greens removed

4 slices brioche or egg bread, crust removed

1 tablespoon plus 1 teaspoon unsalted butter, melted

1½ tablespoons fresh lemon juice

2 teaspoons extra-virgin olive oil

Salt

2 ounces goat cheese

Preheat the oven to 400°F.

Wrap the beets in foil and roast for 45 to 50 minutes, or until they are tender when pricked with a fork. Remove from the oven and let sit until cool enough to handle. Turn the oven to broil.

Cut the bread slices into 1½-inch squares. Place on a baking sheet and broil for 1 to 1½ minutes, or until the slices are lightly browned. Turn the slices and brush with butter. Broil about another 30 seconds, or until the butter is bubbling and the bread is lightly brown. Let cool completely.

When the beets are cool, peel and dice them into ¼-inch cubes. Place them in a small bowl and gently mix with the lemon juice and olive oil. Add a pinch of salt to taste.

To assemble, place about ¼ teaspoon of the cheese on each slice of bread. Top with about ½ teaspoon of the beet mixture. Serve immediately.

Makes about 24 pieces; serves 6 to 8

## PERFECT PAIRS

**THE LEMON JUICE AND** goat cheese in this dish suggest a Sauvignon Blanc or Pinot Gris. Or, if you prefer red wine, then a medium-bodied Pinot Noir will make a nice match for the earthy beets.

# Lively Run Goat Dairy

AN AREA ONCE KNOWN FOR ITS VAST DAIRY FARMS, THE NEW YORK FINGER LAKES district is now quickly making its reputation for fine wine. But Susanne and Steve Messmer are doing their part to maintain the area's dairy roots, with one slight difference: They're raising goats instead of cows. From those goats comes the milk used to make some of the finest goat cheese in the nation.

A native of Germany, Susanne was exposed to good cheese as she grew up, especially because her parents had a vacation home in France, northwest of Alsace. When Steve was stationed overseas in the military, not only did he meet with Susanne, but he also got to enjoy the local cheeses made near the family's vacation home.

After marrying, the Messmers came to Interlaken, New York, Steve Messmer's hometown, and began to search for a dairy business. They settled on goats simply because they were more affordable than cows. Their goal in pursuing agriculture was twofold: to make a living, and to create a farm-based business to which they could bring impoverished or persecuted refugees from other countries and teach them skills that they could take back to their homeland.

Interlaken, on the west side of Cayuga Lake—one of the largest Finger Lakes—happened to have a little goat cheese history of its own. In the 1970s an operation called Goat Folks had earned the area a reputation for making goat cheese. Lively Run Goat Dairy was started by Beth and Dick Feldman, who, coincidentally, had the same dream as the Messmers of helping Third World people. Their idea, though, was to do their work in Africa, so as luck would have it, the Messmers were able to run the Feldmans' goat dairy

LIVELY RUN
CHÈVRE
**Goat Milk Cheese**
Made from cultured pasteurized goat milk, salt, vegetable rennet.
Interlaken, NY 14847
(607)532-4647
**Net Wt. 4 oz.**

business when the Feldmans headed to Africa. This arrangement allowed the Messmers to learn about goat dairying and cheesemaking before making a capital investment of their own. Within a month, the business was in place, and the Feldmans were off.

Although the Feldmans later returned to Interlaken, by then, they were interested in selling the farm, and the Messmers were firmly entrenched in farm life. They decided to buy the farm and build their business. In 1999 they finally moved to the upgraded farm. Although they began their operation with 30 goats, they now have about 120 Nubians, Alpines, and a crossbreed of the two. They milk about 95 of their animals, which are fed with the alfalfa grown on the property.

Like most cheesemakers, Susanne Messmer had no formal training. She uses intuition as her guide, and the result is cheeses like Cayuga Blue, Bluebird, Feta, Fresh Chèvre, and Caper. The latter name shows a sense of humor, the name meaning "to jump or kick like a goat." The only kick in this cheese, though, is the one it gives its eater because of its absolutely luscious, buttery flavor and creamy yet firm texture. Caper is made in a Gouda style, but it doesn't really taste like a Gouda. Instead, it has very clean yet rich flavors, nothing sharp, and a light yellow color, despite its goats' milk origins. (Goats' milk is white, primarily owing to the lack of carotene in it.)

To make the Caper, Susanne cooks and washes the curd to create a smooth consistency. She knows the curds are at their optimum when they literally squeak when she bites down on them. She molds the curds in cylinders fashioned from some cement molds Steve cut to size. The molds are then put in the homemade oak press made from some old wood scraps that were left on the Messmers' property by a previous owner, who ran a sawmill. The cheeses are left in the press for half an hour, turned, left for a while again, and turned again. The pasteurized, natural-rind cheese is then placed in a brine overnight, patted dry, and aged for at least three months. Susanne says it's best at seven months, but her customers aren't content to wait that long.

The Cayuga Blue is as capricious as are the Messmers' animals—but it is always excellent. It has a thin rustic-looking skin and a round, rich, full-bodied flavor that ranks among the top blue cheeses in the nation, and is perhaps the finest goats' milk blue.

Messmer also makes two types of fresh chèvre. One is for her restaurant customers, and it is much creamier and milder than the other. That second one is made over the course of five days and becomes slightly drier and more flavorful. She explains that the chefs like a more pliable product, while her other customers enjoy the firmer, more complex version.

The Messmers have not yet realized their dream of housing refugees, but it remains their goal. They do welcome interns, though, from a program run by a special school in France. Their operation is a family effort, with their two sons being responsible for much of the milking, Steve running the business, and Susanne making the cheese. They don't distribute their cheeses far and wide, although their willingness to do mail order mitigates this limitation.

# SPICED EGGPLANT WITH BAKED FETA

**THIS CORIANDER-SPICED EGGPLANT MIXTURE HAS A VARIETY OF USES, ALTHOUGH IT'S TRULY FANTASTIC WITH THE BAKED FETA.** The sweet-sour combination comes together with the salty, bubbly cheese. Conveniently, the eggplant mixture can be made up to 2 days in advance and refrigerated.

As you will see, this recipe calls for pita chips or other thin crackers. To make your own pita chips, simply separate the two halves of the pita pocket bread by sawing around the edge with a knife. Cut each half into 10 wedges, spray or brush them with olive oil, sprinkle with salt, and broil for about 2 minutes. Once they're cooled, you can store the chips in an airtight container for up to 2 days. You should plan on 4 to 5 wedges per person, so you will probably need 4 to 5 pita breads.

1 medium eggplant (about 1¼ pounds),
   cut into ¼-inch dice
Salt
1 tablespoon plus 1 teaspoon whole
   coriander seeds
2 tablespoons plus 2 teaspoons olive oil
1 medium yellow onion (about ½ pound), cut
   into ¼-inch dice
1 large clove garlic, crushed
4 firm, ripe tomatoes (about 1½ pounds),
   peeled, seeded, and coarsely chopped with
   juices (about 1½ cups)
1 ear corn, kernels removed from cob,
   to make about 1 cup (or use 1 cup frozen
   corn, thawed)
⅓ cup red wine vinegar
2 tablespoons balsamic vinegar, or to taste
2 tablespoons sugar, or to taste
½ cup pitted green olives, thinly sliced
½ teaspoon salt
Freshly ground pepper
6 ounces feta cheese (not crumbled)
Pita chips or other thin crackers

Preheat the oven to 425°F.

Place the eggplant in a colander in the sink. Salt generously and let sit for about 30 minutes. Rinse and pat dry.

In a small skillet toast the coriander seeds over high heat, shaking constantly, until a few seeds begin to pop, 2 to 3 minutes. Remove from the heat and let cool. Grind with a mortar and pestle or in a spice grinder.

In a large sauté pan, warm the 2 tablespoons olive oil over low heat. Add the onion and cook, stirring frequently, until soft but not brown, about 10 minutes. Add the garlic and eggplant and sauté for 10 more minutes. Stir in the tomatoes, corn, vinegars, sugar, and olives. Cover and cook, stirring occasionally, until the eggplant is soft, about 20 minutes. Remove the cover and continue cooking until most of the liquid is absorbed, 15 to 20 minutes. Add the coriander, salt, and pepper to taste. Let cool to room temperature. You may need to adjust the vinegar and/or sugar, depending on your own taste.

Put the cheese in a ramekin or other ovenproof dish just large enough to hold the cheese. Drizzle with 2 teaspoons olive oil. Bake for 20 minutes or until the cheese is light brown and bubbly. Let cool for 5 minutes.

To serve, put the eggplant in a small serving bowl next to the cheese. Guests should spoon some eggplant onto a pita wedge, top it with a little cheese, and enjoy!

Serves 8 to 10

## PERFECT PAIRS

**THIS IS A VERSATILE WINE** dish. Sherry is a wonderful complement, or for dry wines choose Sauvignon Blanc, Rosé, Grenache, or a fruity Zinfandel.

# Cayuse Vineyards

"L'ENFANT TERRIBLE" IS NOT USUALLY A FAVORABLE DESCRIPTION OF A PERSON, but for Christophe Baron, winemaker and owner of Cayuse Vineyards in Walla Walla, Washington, the self-proclaimed "bad boy" description is a point of pride. The energetic young Frenchman has single-handedly brought out new dimensions in the Syrah grape by virtue of his restlessness and unwillingness to accept the status quo.

"The reason I came to Washington was the notion of freedom and liberty that you don't have in France," he says. "There, you have to play by the rules, and sometimes the rules don't make any sense," he adds.

Baron comes from a family that has been making Champagne since the 17th century. He remembers running through the vineyards as barely more than a toddler and being taught by his father and grandfather to have respect for the land.

Baron began his career by enrolling in viticulture school in Champagne. He later continued his wine education at two other viticulture schools in Burgundy. It was there, he says, where he became fascinated with the English language because of the large number of British who visited the area. In 1993, interested in learning English and furthering his wine education, he took his first trip to the United States, having secured an internship at Waterbrook Winery in Walla Walla (see page 147). That was the beginning of his career as a self-described "flying winemaker."

Baron traversed the globe, stopping first in nearby Oregon, and then going on to Australia, New Zealand, and Romania to learn about the different wine regions and potential wine-growing areas. (He says Romania had ideal growing conditions but a less than ideal political climate.) He returned to France in 1996 with the intention of growing grapes, and he got permission to plant exactly one acre. This frustrated him no end, so he made the decision to head back across the Atlantic. His destination was Oregon, but first he stopped in Walla Walla, Washington, to see friends. It was a visit that would change the course of Baron's life and the reputation of winemaking in Washington state.

During the visit, Baron recalls driving around the area and spotting a piece of land full of stones the size of baseballs. He told his friend, "Stop there!" Knowing what Baron was thinking, his friend gently reminded Baron that he would ruin his tractor on such rocky terrain. Undaunted, Baron declared his desire to plant Syrah in that spot. To the uninitiated, it would appear that nothing could grow in such a place, let alone grapevines. But Baron was familiar with the extremely rocky growing conditions of the Rhône, so he instantly recognized the land's potential.

In 1997 he planted the ten-acre Cailloux Vineyard on this ostensibly inhospitable parcel of land. Over the years, the soil, the deliberately low yield Baron insists upon, and the organic farming techniques he employs have all come together to produce his highly lauded Cayuse wines—named after the local Native American tribe. Baron keeps this praise in perspective, railing against the penchant these days for making winemaking into a cult. "There's not a guru winemaker, but there is a guru winegrower," he says, emphasizing his belief that the land on which the grapes are grown is crucial to the final product. Although he is not a certified organic grower, Baron believes that employing organic techniques is absolutely essential. Using pesticides means ridding the soil of its microbial life and, in so doing, diminishing the final flavor in the wine, he explains. Also, he says, it is imperative to create a synergy between the environment and the vineyards, and the only way to do that is to maintain as natural a growing process as possible.

Baron's wines are informed by his background because he has been drinking French wines since he was a child. One example is his Cailloux Syrah, which shows outstanding complexity, finesse, and elegance. "I'm not for the 'Mike Tyson' one wineglass and it knocks you out. I like it when it lingers," he says. As a result his wine is not only lovely on its own, but equally delicious with food. His Syrah is rich with anise, cassis, and black cherry flavors, and color to match. And, true to form, it is restrained and elegant, with structure that suggests it will be just as impressive in the future—although somewhat different.

The Cayuse tasting room is located in the heart of downtown Walla Walla. Designed by Baron and his father, it makes a bold statement, with its brilliant yellow façade and elegant, tasteful interior, complete with French antiques. Because the Cayuse wines are made in such small quantities, visitors sometimes are disappointed to find that the wines they want are sold out. Nonetheless, Baron says he doesn't want to grow much beyond three thousand cases because of concerns he will lose control over the quality of his wines.

For now, he continues to create wines such as the single-vineyard Cailloux Syrah as well as Viognier under the Cayuse label, a Cabernet-Merlot blend under a label he calls Camaspelo ("that's a Cayuse word for 'very expensive red,'" he jokes), and his newest label, Bullfight, to be released in 2004; it will feature Tempranillo (the most famous Spanish grape) and a Rhône-style blend.

Baron's approach, though seemingly laid-back, is deliberate and skilled, but his ebullience never wanes. The dawn of the first day of harvest in 2001, Baron was as excited as a child on Christmas morning. But unlike most winemakers, who are focused on getting the grapes to the winery to begin the winemaking process, Baron was in the field uncorking bottles of wine to share with his crew. As far as he was concerned, it was a day of celebration. L'enfant terrible was once again at play—although any doubt about the end product is laid to rest in one elegant drop.

WHAT THEY MAKE

**White wines**
Viognier

**Red wines**
Camaspelo
Syrah (Cailloux, Walla Walla Valley)

HOW TO REACH THEM

Walla Walla, Washington
509-526-0686 (phone)
509-526-4686 (fax)
www.cayusevineyards.com

# BRIE-MANGO QUESADILLAS WITH LIME CREAM

**THERE'S NOTHING LIKE MELTED BRIE.** Wrapped in puff pastry, it was the ultimate hors d'oeuvre in the 1980s, and it's making a comeback now. In the recipe that follows, though, the Brie oozes between layers of tortilla instead of puff pastry, and instead of the fruit jam often used in the 1980s version, this hors d'oeuvre gets a tropical treatment with the mango. These are best served right out of the stove, as Brie can turn a bit rubbery as it cools.

Preheat the oven to 300°F.

To make the lime cream: In a small bowl, mix together the crème fraîche and lime juice. Refrigerate until ready to use. (The lime cream can be made up to 1 day in advance and refrigerated.)

To make the quesadillas: In a large sauté pan, warm 1 tablespoon of the oil over medium heat. Place a tortilla in the oil, and working quickly, place one-third of the cheese slices followed by one-third of the mangoes and one-third of the chile on top of the tortilla. Lay a second tortilla on top, increase the heat to medium-high, and cook until the tortilla is golden-brown on the bottom, about 3 minutes. Flip the quesadilla and cook the other side, pressing gently so that the surface of the tortilla cooks evenly. When the tortilla is golden and the cheese has melted, remove and keep warm in the oven. Repeat with the remaining oil, tortillas, and fillings. Cut each quesadilla into 12 wedges, drizzle with a little lime cream, and serve immediately.

Makes about 36 wedges; serves 9 to 12

### FOR THE LIME CREAM
- ¼ cup plus 1 tablespoon crème fraîche or sour cream
- 1 teaspoon fresh lime juice

### FOR THE QUESADILLAS
- 3 tablespoons vegetable oil
- 6 large (11-inch) flour tortillas
- 8 ounces Brie cheese, rind removed, cut into ¼-inch-thick slices
- 2 mangoes, peeled, pitted, and cut into slices about ¼ inch thick
- 1 jalapeño chile, seeded and finely diced

## PERFECT PAIRS

**THIS DISH FEATURES** many flavors and textures, but an either slightly-oaked Viognier, with its tropical flavors and its companionship with the cheese, or a Gewürztraminer, with its spicy components, will make a wonderful—though different—accompaniment.

# PIZZAS

# PROFILES | RECIPES

Bacon, Tomato and Mozarella Pizza, recipe on page 148

# Garretson Wine Company

**THE T-SHIRTS SOLD BY GARRETSON WINE COMPANY ARE MORE REVEALING THAN MOST.**
No, the material isn't thinner. Rather, it's the silk-screened message emblazoned on the back of the shirt that reads WELL, WE NEVER HEARD OF YOU, EITHER. It's not a hostile message—just a self-effacing way of acknowledging the small size of the winery and the usual customer reaction before sampling the wine. After a sip or two of owner Mat Garretson's wine, such unfamiliarity is replaced by an indelible memory.

For Garretson, Rhône varietals are the holy grail. So devoted is he to grapes like Syrah and Viognier that he has created an entire international event around them. The annual Hospice du Rhône is held in the central California city of Paso Robles. It anoints the Rhône-style wines of the region and around the world and simultaneously raises money for the local Hospice of San Luis Obispo County. The fund-raiser takes its name from the famous Hospice de Beaune, a similar event that is held every year in the Burgundy region of France.

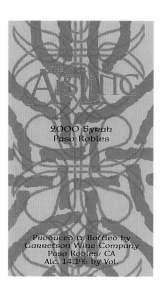

2000 Syrah
Paso Robles

Produced & Bottled by
Garretson Wine Company
Paso Robles/ CA
Alc. 14.1% by Vol.

Garretson is a wordsmith-cum-winemaker. His Gaelic background informs the names of his wines, like The Ceilidh ("celebration"), The Aisling ("dream" or "vision"), The Corcairghorm ("violet"), and so on, and, as noted, Hospice du Rhône borrows a phrase as well. What Garretson doesn't borrow is talent, although he is quick to credit others, especially his friend and fellow winemaker John Alban, for teaching him his craft.

The self-styled "Rhôn-e-gade" entered the wine business after many years of indulging a wine-drinking hobby. He had been in the aerosol manufacturing business in Georgia, but his passion soon became a pursuit. "I had an epiphany," says Garretson. "This is what makes me happy, and I don't want to be ninety years old and wish I'd been a winemaker." He followed his passion for Rhône wines, not to France, but to San Luis Obispo and Paso Robles, California, where he believed some of the best Rhône varietals were being grown.

Garretson worked for wineries such as Wild Horse, where owner and winemaker Ken Volk soon asked him to make the Rhône-style wines for that winery. He also worked for Eberle, and he met John Alban, whom he says is his single greatest influence. "He not only taught me a lot about winemaking, but he also taught me about the mind-set of winemaking: Keep it simple," says Garretson. To Alban, it's about having as "direct a route as possible through your cellar and into the bottle."

For that reason Garretson is meticulous about where he sources fruit. Not surprisingly, one of his most prized wines is his Alban Vineyards Syrah, which he calls The Finné, or "best man" in Gaelic. The name refers to the role John Alban had in Mat Garretson's wedding. But the wine has more than just a name—it has structure and finesse and lots of dark fruit flavors. Unfortunately, it is scarce because there is precious little fruit for sale from this respected vineyard.

About Syrah, Garretson says that he believes it is one of the most adaptable grapes of all. He talks about the "the variety of expression" of the grape. That is, it expresses the flavor and personality of the particular region in which it is grown—more so, he thinks, than do other varieties. An Australian Syrah, or Shiraz as it is known, has very bright, forward fruit, whereas a French Syrah is more brooding and dark; a California Syrah will be different from either of those, depending on where it is grown.

Garretson makes three different Syrahs, each exhibiting unique characteristics. The Aisling is a so-called late-bottled wine. Not to be confused with a late-harvest wine, this one is made from grapes harvested at the same time as those of the other wines, but the Aisling is simply held in the barrel longer before it is bottled. The Fralich Vineyard Syrah, whose Gaelic name means "violet," is so named because of its violet-like characteristics and its decided lack of tannins.

Garretson also makes a popular red table wine called Glimigrim (the word for "wine" in Jonathan Swift's *Gulliver's Travels*), a dry rosé from Syrah grapes (called The Ceilidh—"celebration"—in honor of the Garretsons' first son, Jack), and two white wines: a Viognier and a late-harvest fortified Rousanne. The latter, called The Berwyn, is Old English for "the harvest's son." It is an ode to Mat and Amie Garretson's second son, Thomas, who was born during the 2000 harvest. These wines are barrel-fermented in old or neutral oak to develop the mouthfeel. The Syrahs are aged in new French oak. In all, the Garretson Wine Company, or GWC for short, produces just three thousand cases per year. "I don't see us

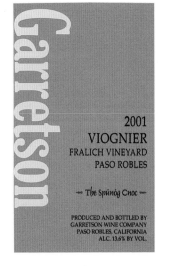

growing unless we have fruit that justifies the growth," says Garretson.

While there's no doubt that Garretson is making some great wine, equally impressive is his absolute passion for Rhône grapes and especially for exposing more people to them. He is adamantly against wine snobbery and works to foster camaraderie and education through such events as a "Rhône and Bowl" and the annual Hospice du Rhône gathering. The springtime event features two hundred wineries and attracts five hundred people to Paso Robles. Attendees have the opportunity to sip Rhône-style wines, meet the winemakers, attend seminars and lunches, and bid at a barrel auction, the proceeds of which go to the hospice.

By their very nature, passions are almost impossible to explain. But Garretson's passion for Rhône wines is owing to the wines being "so lush of fruit—aromatically and on the palate. They're beautiful and easy to drink, and they're unpretentious." This latter quality is probably the most likely explanation of all, since the man behind the wines happens to share this characteristic equally with his wine.

WHAT THEY MAKE

**Red table wine**
Glimigrim

**Dry Rosé**
The Ceilidh

**Late-Harvest Rousanne**
The Berwyn

**Syrah**
Alban Vineyards
Fralich Vineyards
Paso Robles

**Viognier**
The Spúnóg Cnoc

HOW TO REACH THEM

Paso Robles, California
805-239-2074 (*phone*)
805-239-2057 (*fax*)
www.mrviognier.com

# PIZZA DOUGH

**THIS IS ONE OF THE EASIEST, MOST FOOLPROOF, AND FLAVORFUL PIZZA DOUGHS I'VE MADE.** I guess it should be, since it's inspired by the master of pizzas, Wolfgang Puck. Although this recipe makes enough for two 14-inch pizzas, you may also divide the dough into fourths to make four 7-inch pizzas instead. Since you may not want to make two (or four) pizzas at one time, you can refrigerate the dough for up to twenty-four hours or freeze it for up to 3 months. Simply freeze the dough after the first rising period and thaw it in the refrigerator overnight before using.

1 envelope (¼ ounce) dry yeast

¼ cup warm water (110°F)

¾ cup water, at room temperature

2 tablespoons olive oil

1 tablespoon honey

1 teaspoon salt (use fine sea salt or table salt; if using kosher salt, increase amount to 1½ teaspoons)

3 cups all-purpose flour, plus a little extra for kneading

In a liquid measuring cup, dissolve the yeast in the warm water. Let the mixture sit for about 10 minutes, until it becomes foamy.

In a small bowl, mix together the ¾ cup water, olive oil, honey, and salt.

In the bowl of a food processor fitted with a steel blade, or in the large bowl of a stand mixer fitted with a dough hook, place the flour. Slowly add the honey mixture and process or mix just until the flour is coated with the liquid, about 10 seconds in the food processor. Add the yeast mixture and pulse until the mixture forms a ball, 8 to 12 seconds. You may need to add a very small amount of flour if the mixture is sticky.

If you are using a food processor, remove the dough and place it on a lightly floured board. Knead for about 5 minutes, or until the dough is smooth. If you are using a stand mixer, continue mixing the dough on low speed for about 5 minutes, or until the dough is smooth and slightly elastic.

Place the dough in a large oiled bowl, cover with a thin towel, and let it rest for 1 hour. The dough will rise, but it probably will not double in bulk. This is okay.

Divide the dough in half and place it on a baking sheet. Cover it with plastic wrap and then with a thin towel and place in the refrigerator until ready to use. (You can do this up to 24 hours in advance. To make the pizza, take the dough out of the refrigerator and let it rest at room temperature for 10 minutes.) Or, if you are using it right away, divide the dough, form each piece into a ball, and let it rest for about 15 minutes. Proceed according to the individual recipe.

Makes two 14-inch or four 7-inch pizzas

### PREPARING THE DOUGH

Remove the dough from the refrigerator and let it rest at room temperature for 10 minutes. On a lightly floured surface, slightly flatten the dough. Start stretching the dough by holding the side closest to you with one hand while gently pulling on the edge opposite you. Turn the dough a quarter-turn and repeat the process. You should be able to stretch it into an 8- or 9-inch circle. Now lift the dough and drape it over your knuckles. Gently stretch the dough from underneath with your knuckles, being careful not to break through. If you keep your knuckles under the thickest part of the dough, it shouldn't break.

When you're done, the dough should measure 14 inches in diameter. The edges will be slightly thicker than the center, which should be almost translucent. Place the dough on the pizza pan, peel, or baking sheet.

# GARLIC, GREEN OLIVE, AND SHEEP'S MILK CHEESE PIZZA

THIS PIZZA IS A GREAT EXAMPLE OF HOW JUST A FEW INGREDIENTS CAN ADD UP TO AN EXPLOSION OF FLAVOR. The toasted garlic flavor in the oil, the buttery cheese, and the rich olives make for a truly unforgettable taste sensation. If you can't find aged sheep's milk cheese, then the more commonly found cheeses such as Parmesan or aged Asiago will work just fine.

Cornmeal
¼ cup oil
1 large clove garlic, minced
Dough for one 14-inch pizza (see page 130)
6 ounces aged sheep's milk cheese, finely grated (about 2 cups) or use any dry, aged cheese
½ cup sliced green olives

Preheat the oven to 500°F. If you are using a pizza stone, place it in the oven.

Sprinkle a 14-inch pizza pan with cornmeal. Or, if using a pizza stone, sprinkle cornmeal on a wooden peel (paddle) or a rimless baking sheet. Set aside.

In a small pan, heat the oil over medium-high heat. Once the oil is very hot but not smoking, turn off the heat and add the garlic. Swirl the oil constantly until the garlic takes on a slightly caramel color. Remove from the heat and let cool to room temperature. Strain the oil and discard the garlic. (The oil can be made up to 3 days in advance and refrigerated. The oil will solidify, so bring it to room temperature before using it.)

Prepare the dough (see page 130).

Brush the dough liberally with the garlic oil. Distribute the cheese over the dough, then the olives, leaving about a 2-inch rim. Drizzle a little extra garlic oil over the cheese and olives. Slide the pizza onto the stone, if using. Bake for 8 to 10 minutes, or until the edges of the crust are golden-brown. Remove the pizza from the oven, let sit for 5 minutes, and serve.

Serves 6 to 8 as an appetizer.

Note: The pizza will cook more quickly with a pizza stone. Allow an extra 5 minutes' baking time if you're not using a stone.

## PERFECT PAIRS

ALTHOUGH YOU COULD get away with serving a white wine with this pizza, a red wine is a better bet. Fortunately, you have many choices, including Sangiovese, or Carignane on the lighter side, and Grenache, Syrah, or Merlot on the weightier side. No matter what, try to find a wine that is slightly fruity but has a good bit of acidity too.

# Red Newt Cellars

says David Whiting, owner and winemaker at Red Newt Cellars in Hector, New York. While this may seem like a statement of the obvious, it is surprisingly not always the case. Sometimes winemakers are forced to make wines that fulfill marketing needs but don't necessarily reflect their personal passion. Not so with Whiting, who, with his wife, Debra, purchased the former Wickham Winery in 1997.

Today the Whitings' ski lodge–like facility overlooking Seneca Lake houses the winemaking operation, but it is also the site of a popular bistro. Debra Whiting, a caterer (and former biochemist), has created a restaurant where the focus is local ingredients. Debra is the chef and originator of the constantly changing menu. The quality of the cuisine and the philosophy behind it have made the bistro a draw for people near and far.

Located on the southeast side of Seneca Lake, one of upstate New York's famous Finger Lakes, Red Newt Cellars makes some of New York's most acclaimed wines. In fact, Whiting's 2000 Riesling won the Governor's Cup—the equivalent of "Best of Show"—at the 2001 New York Wine and Food Classic. Not bad for a guy who began his affair with wine with little to his name except a sleeping bag and a few other basic necessities.

After college, Whiting took a trip from New York to California in the early 1980s to look for a job. He found himself buying wines from the Russian River Valley and tasting them at night while sitting beside his constant companion—a campfire. This singular experience convinced him to pursue winemaking as a profession.

In 1988 Whiting took a job as a "cellar rat" (essentially a grunt) at McGregor Vineyards on neighbor-

ing Keuka Lake. Soon after, many of the winemaking responsibilities began to fall to him, and Whiting called on many local winemakers for their help. "The winemakers of the Finger Lakes are a very helpful, sharing group," he says. With their aid, he slowly learned his craft.

Whiting says that when they were conjuring up a name for their winery, he and Debra were searching for something that was *connected* to a place but was not, itself, an actual place. They went through thousands of names, he says, but eventually they homed in on the object of their affection: the Eastern red-spotted newt, which lives happily in the pond on their property, as well as throughout the Northeast. The red-spotted critter would become permanently memorialized on their wine label.

The first vintage for Red Newt Cellars was in 1997. The Whitings now make about five thousand cases per year and a fairly wide variety of wines. Among the white wines are Chardonnay, Riesling, Gewürztraminer, and a white table wine, Red Newt White, which comes in a beautiful etched bottle and is a blend of the hybrid grapes known as Vidal Blanc and Cayuga. It is floral and refreshing, and has a surprising stream of acidity running through it to keep it from being too sweet.

Whiting says that among his whites, he enjoys making Gewürztraminer the most because of the inherent challenges in crafting it. He says the balance between fruit, sugar, alcohol, phenolics, and acid is more complex with Gewürztraminer than with any other white variety. Unlike most producers of this elusive wine, Whiting recommends holding his Gewürztraminer for at least six months, and preferably for two or three years. His careful attention to balance with this notoriously finicky grape results in a wine

that is devoid of bitterness, nicely spiced, not too per-fumy—and thoroughly enjoyable.

Red Newt's award-winning Riesling is a study in restraint. It is neither fruity nor acidic; it captures flavors typical of the variety—apricot and melon—and it also carries lovely mineral flavors along with it. The Chardonnay follows suit in that it too is restrained although still lively and floral. It isn't over-oaked, as so many are. When asked how he makes a particular wine, Whiting will tell you how he made that particular vintage, but he's quick to caution one not to assume that other vintages are made identically. "I don't make anything the same way two years in a row because the grapes are always different."

Unlike reliably hot climates, such as those in the Napa Valley and eastern Washington, which lend themselves to varieties like Cabernet Sauvignon and Merlot, the relatively cool and humid climate in the Finger Lakes area makes growing red varietals a challenging proposition. Yet Whiting's red wines manage to meet and exceed that challenge. His 1999 meritage, a blend of Cabernet Sauvignon, Merlot, and Cabernet Franc, is as good and complex as any you'll find in the traditionally warm areas. It is smooth, with well-managed tannins, not a lot of oak, and it has a surprising amount of fruit, given the growing conditions. Indeed, it is one of the best-integrated wines in all of the Finger Lakes. It is christened Viridescens, which is part of the Latin name for the Eastern newt.

Although the Whitings' winery is only about five years old, their wines show remarkable maturity and elegance. For anyone who thinks that New York wines cannot compare to those further east (in the Old World) or those on the West Coast, do not hesitate to seek out these wines. They are likely to change the minds of even the most ardent cynics.

## WHAT THEY MAKE

**Red wines**
Cabernet Franc
Cabernet Sauvignon
Merlot
Red Eft
Syrah-Cabernet Franc
Viridescens

**White wines**
Chardonnay
Gewürztraminer
Pinot Gris
Red Newt White
Riesling (dry and semi-dry)

## HOW TO REACH THEM

Hector, New York
607-546-4100 (phone)
607-546-4101 (fax)
www.rednewt.com

# GOUDA AND RED ONION PIZZA

**ALTHOUGH THIS RECIPE CALLS FOR RED ONION, WHICH CAN BE FOUND ANY TIME OF THE YEAR, YOU MIGHT THINK ABOUT USING SPRING ONIONS AS A NICE ALTERNATIVE.** These are usually found in late April and May, and although their flavor isn't significantly different when they are cooked, they are certainly a harbinger of spring and consequently a festive way to adorn a pizza.

Cornmeal

2 tablespoons olive oil, plus extra for brushing

1 large red onion (about ½ pound), thinly sliced
   (or use ½ pound spring onions, red or white,
   bulbs only, thinly sliced)

1½ tablespoons fresh thyme (or ¾ teaspoon dried)

Salt and freshly ground pepper

Dough for one 14-inch pizza (see page 130)

8 ounces medium-aged Gouda cheese,
   coarsely grated

Preheat the oven to 500°F. If you are using a pizza stone, place it in the oven.

Sprinkle a 14-inch pizza pan with cornmeal. Or, if you are using a pizza stone, sprinkle cornmeal on a wooden peel (paddle) or a rimless baking sheet. Set aside.

In a medium skillet, warm 1 tablespoon of the olive oil over medium heat. Add the onion and cook until limp, about 5 minutes. Add the thyme and salt and pepper to taste. Set aside.

Prepare the dough (see page 130).

Brush the rim of the dough with olive oil. Distribute the cheese and then the onion over the dough, leaving about a 2-inch rim. Bake for 8 to 10 minutes, or until the cheese is brown and bubbly. Serve immediately.

Serves 6 to 8 as an appetizer; 4 as a main course

Note: The pizza will cook more quickly with a pizza stone. Allow an extra 5 minutes' baking time if you're not using a stone.

## PERFECT PAIRS

**THE ASSERTIVENESS OF** the cheese is contrasted by the sweetness of the onions, which makes for several wine possibilities. For white wine, try a Chenin Blanc, a slightly oaked Viognier, or a dry Riesling. For red, choose a lighter variety such as Dolcetto or Carignane.

# Patricia Green Cellars

**THE FIRST THING YOU HEAR WHEN YOU GET WITHIN A COUNTRY MILE OF PATRICIA** Green is her laugh. Although she stands less than five feet tall, the air around her vibrates with energy because of her strong and engaging presence. And Green's wine is unquestionably a reflection of its maker.

The bold-spirited winemaker has long been drawn to the outdoors, having salmon-fished off the Oregon coast and later done reforestation work in southern Oregon's Umpqua Valley. Her relocation to the Umpqua Valley and one season's grape harvest led her to her current occupation. In 1988, two years after working her first harvest, Green became winemaker at Hillcrest Vineyard winery—a remarkable assignment given that she had no formal training. Eventually she made her way to Oregon's Willamette Valley, where she worked as a consulting winemaker for

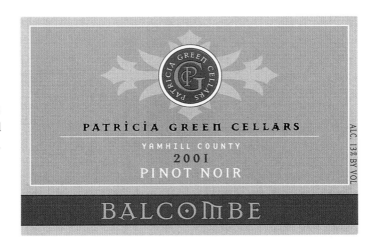

various wineries. Finally, she landed at a then-new winery called Torii Mor Vineyards. It was there where she developed her reputation—and the winery's—for making outstanding Pinot Noir. It was also at Torii Mor where she hooked up with her collaborator and winery co-owner, Jim Anderson.

Together, this team managed to create quite a sensation at Torii Mor Vineyards, producing award-winning Pinot Noirs that were highly sought after for their deep, rich flavors and gorgeous color extraction. Eventually, though, Green and Anderson decided that they wanted a winery of their own, and, at that time,

Autumn Wind Winery, in the heart of Yamhill County, was up for sale. They snatched it up and turned it into Patricia Green Cellars.

Although Green and Anderson are not life partners—Anderson is married and retains a good sense of humor when asked about working with such a strong woman and being married to another: "It's like having two wives; we just argue about different things"—they are, indeed, united in their intense dedication to their new enterprise.

While Pinot Noir may be their primary focus, Green has managed to bottle a Sauvignon Blanc unlike any other. It is nearly sweet, although it has no residual sugar, and it has fine acidity to keep it from losing its sharp focus. Green does not barrel age her Sauvignon Blanc, and the result is a wine that is citrusy, with hints of green apple and honey. Since Sauvignon Blanc is not a traditional grape in the Willamette Valley, it's more than surprising that she's working with the grape and finessing it so well. It is a perfect wine for cheese.

Green's most impressive talent, though, lies with her Pinot Noirs. A random barrel tasting reveals distinct differences between them because she, like so many of her colleagues, barrel-ferments her different vineyard lots separately and bottles most of them that way too. As a result, the majority of her output is single-vineyard.

Green and Anderson source grapes from seven different vineyards, and from those grapes they make ten vineyard-designated wines and one blend of three vineyards. Two of their stand-out single-vineyard wines are those from the Shea Vineyard near Carlton and the Balcombe Vineyard. Both of these vineyards produce blockbuster wines but of very different character. While the Shea is ripe and round, the Balcombe is a bit darker and edgier. "If you don't express the vineyard site, you're doing something wrong," Green says. Part of her method for showing site involves using native yeasts. These are naturally occurring yeasts produced in the vineyard, inextricably linking them with the grapes themselves. Using natural yeast is a means of furthering the terroir, or site-specific qualities, so that the final wine will embody as many characteristics as possible from the vineyard from which it has come. "You've got yeast, grapes, a site—it's bringing the essence of the vineyard into the wine," Green says.

Perhaps most intriguing about the Patricia Green wines is the power behind them. Green's Pinot Noir is silken yet strong, jarring yet smooth, suave yet bold. And that color. While Green claims ignorance about her wine's hue, other than the fact that she cold-soaks her grapes in the Burgundian style, it's hard to imagine that sheer luck is the excuse year after year. The explanation hardly matters, though, when the end result is so breathtaking.

Green and Anderson are just putting the finishing touches on their winery in the heart of the Willamette Valley. They have built it in anticipation of growing to a seven- to eight-thousand-case annual production from their current five-thousand-case output. The winery is perched above beautiful North Valley Road in the Ribbon Ridge area, in the heart of Oregon's wine country. Across from the winery, horses, cows, and roosters amble about, but grapevines provide the dominant vista in this verdant valley. Many prominent wineries, including Beaux Freres and Willakenzie, are a stone's throw away.

Although Patricia Green Cellars is still a start-up in the wine world, the factors driving it—Anderson's extreme dedication to the business side and Green's immense talent as well as equal dedication—make it a winery to watch. Through their own label, Green and Anderson are making a big splash in the field of Oregon wines and helping give Pinot Noir new definition.

## WHAT THEY MAKE

**Red wines**
Pinot Noir (*Balcombe, Balcombe Block 1B, Bonshaw, Eason, Estate, Four Winds, Shea*)

**White wines**
Chardonnay
Sauvignon Blanc

## HOW TO REACH THEM

Newburg, Oregon
503-554-0821 (*phone*)
503-538-3681 (*fax*)
www.patriciagreencellars.com

# GRUYÈRE, WILD MUSHROOM, AND ARUGULA PIZZA

ONCE OR TWICE A YEAR, A VARIETY OF WILD MUSHROOMS APPEARS IN THE MAR-
KETS AT THE SAME TIME. In June, morel season is ending, but usually not before chanterelles and porcini or cèpes have made their way to store shelves. What a perfect time to make this pizza. This recipe also works perfectly fine with common button mushrooms and/or portobello mushrooms. When you roast these mushrooms, though, you will likely have a good amount of liquid, so be sure to drain the mushrooms before adding them to the pizza. Or you can use dried mushrooms. Select a variety of morels, porcini, and perhaps shiitake mushrooms. Reconstitute them in boiling water, drain, and proceed according to the directions below. Your pizza will be just as hearty and ultra-satisfying as one made with fresh mushrooms.

Cornmeal

½ pound mixed wild mushrooms, such as morels, chanterelles, and porcini, washed well and dried, stems removed (you can save the stems for a mushroom or vegetable stock)

2 tablespoons olive oil, plus extra for brushing

Salt and freshly ground pepper

2 cups packed arugula leaves

1½ teaspoons fresh lemon juice

Dough for one 14-inch pizza (see page 130)

4 ounces Gruyère cheese, coarsely grated

Preheat the oven to 500°F. If you are using a pizza stone, place it in the oven. Sprinkle a 14-inch pizza pan with cornmeal. Or if you are using a pizza stone, sprinkle cornmeal on a wooden peel (paddle) or a rimless baking sheet. Set aside.

Slice all of the mushrooms ¼ inch thick. If some of the mushrooms are quite large, cut them in half crosswise after slicing. In a medium-size ovenproof pan, combine 1 tablespoon of the oil and the mushrooms. Add salt and pepper to taste. Shake the pan vigorously to coat the mushrooms and place in the oven. Roast for 10 minutes, or until the mushrooms have softened and are beginning to develop a caramel color around the edges. Remove from the oven. Taste and add more salt if necessary, but remember that the cheese and the arugula will also have salt.

In a small bowl mix together the arugula, lemon juice, and remaining 1 tablespoon of olive oil. Add salt and pepper to taste. Set aside.

Prepare the dough (see page 130).

Brush the rim of the dough with olive oil. Distribute the cheese and then the mushrooms over the dough, leaving about a 2-inch rim. Slide the pizza onto the stone, if using. Bake for 8 to 10 minutes, or until the edges of the crust are a deep golden brown and the cheese is bubbling. Remove from the oven and let sit for 5 minutes. To serve, slice into wedges and top each serving with a handful of the arugula salad.

Serves 6 to 8 as an appetizer, 4 as a main course

Note: The pizza will cook more quickly with a pizza stone. Allow an extra 5 minutes' baking time if you're not using a stone.

## PERFECT PAIRS

THE RICHNESS OF THIS pizza adds up to Chardonnay for a white wine, and for a red wine, the mushrooms and spicy arugula call for an earthy Oregon Pinot Noir.

# Pedrozo Dairy & Cheese Co.

THE METEORIC RISE OF GREAT AMERICAN CHEESEMAKING NEVER CEASES TO BE astounding. It has become an unstoppable force, in large part because of people like Jill and Tim Pedrozo who are propelling the movement forward. Their farmstead Northern Gold, a raw Jersey milk cheese, is a study not only in great cheese, but also in the great palates that are now guiding this movement. The beautiful golden color of this cheese is reminscent of butter, and the flavor runs a parallel course.

Tim Pedrozo is a third-generation dairyman, having grown up in Merced, in California's Central Valley. Like many California dairy farmers, Tim and Jill Pedrozo were in search of an enterprise that went beyond the unprofitable fluid milk business. Cheese held the answer; all they needed was to find a dairy of their own, since Tim and his father had already sold off their cows. A search led them to Bob and Karen Parker, owners of the Parker Dairy in Orland, California, about a hundred miles north of Sacramento. The Parkers had a Holstein dairy and a cheesemaking facility, but they were looking to retire. The Pedrozos bought the dairy, acquired their own herd of Jersey cows, and on December 31, 1998, started moving those cows at 4 A.M., finishing just as the new year was rung in.

Karen Parker had been making a Gouda-style cheese, and she taught the Pedrozos cheesemaking, but because so much of the process is art rather than skill, it was not a seamless switch. The Pedrozos' first batches of cheese were fine, Jill says, but they needed refining. That refinement came quickly, though, and a short time later Jill was able to leave her job as an elementary school teacher and become a full-time cheesemaker. Tim manages the herd and does much of the cleaning in the cheesemaking room.

The Pedrozos' day begins at 5 A.M., when milking gets under way. At that hour, Jill's only job is to sit in the cheese room and catch the first few drops of milk as they are transported from the milking barn to the cheesemaking room. Because the pipe that carries the milk is cleaned after every use, it is imperative that the first drops of milk to pass through the pipe are thrown out so that the chlorine in the cleaning solution won't make its way into the cheese. After Jill throws it out, she gets to retreat inside for another couple of hours.

The making of Northern Gold cheese gets under way in earnest when the approximately 150 gallons of milk are filtered into the vat and the two French starter cultures are added. The milk sits for one hour, after which time the vegetable rennet is added. Thirty minutes later, Jill cuts the curds into lima-bean size and drains off one-third of the whey. (The whey is fed to the calves.) Hot water is then added to the curds, which are stirred for ten minutes and drained. At this point, a little salt is added, the curds are stirred again, and they are then packed into the net-lined molds for further drainage. Finally, the curds are put under a hydraulic press to remove more whey, but they are turned every one to two hours. If they're not turned, they will stick to the pressing rack.

By now, anywhere from three to six hours (depending on the cheese) have passed, and the cheese is ready to go into the aging room overnight. The next day, the cheese is placed in a salt brine, where it is left for as long as four days, depending on the size of the cheese. Finally, the cheese is aged for from sixty days to over six months, depending on the size of the cheese. The Northern Gold that eventually emerges from the aging room is a semi-hard cheese that is relatively mild but with sweet overtones. Its buttery complexion and flavor, combined with its fruitiness and long finish, make it a near-perfect food. Think melted butter over a baked apple.

Northern Gold's rare cousin, Black Butte Reserve, is another story altogether. Aged a minimum of six months, Black Butte Reserve is a twenty-pound embodiment of springtime. The cheese is made only once a year, in the spring, when the cows have just given birth and are eating the lush spring grasses. The high quality of the pasture at this time of year is reflected in the cows' milk, and the Pedrozos have figured out a way to capture all of the springtime nuances in their cheese. Word has traveled quickly about the Black Butte Reserve, and now nearly all of it is spoken for before it emerges from the aging room.

That just means it's showing up on more store shelves around the nation than ever before.

Another Pedrozo gem is the Northern Gold Winemakers Cheese, made in two-pound wheels. Tim Pedrozo makes his own version of red wine using Portuguese grapes from the Central Valley and immerses the cheese in it for a week or two. The cheese emerges a deep burgundy color and, unlike some wine-soaked cheeses, maintains a perfect balance between a not-overpowering wine flavor and the rich flavors of the cheese. Cheese and wine in one bite—now that's perfection.

Like many cheesemakers, Jill and Tim Pedrozo are decidedly modest about their contribution to the American cheese repertoire. Their cheese, though, is worthy of applause not only because of its magnificent flavor, but also because each new batch is better than the last. That does not happen with good luck; it happens because of high standards. The Pedrozos are continually honing their skills, and the result is cheese that is now consistently excellent and always exciting.

WHAT THEY MAKE

Northern Gold
Black Butte Reserve
Tipsy Cow

HOW TO REACH THEM

Orland, California
530-865-9548 (*phone and fax*)
www.pedrozodairycheese.com

# SWISS PIZZA

THIS IS A GREAT PIZZA TO MAKE IN THE WINTERTIME, WHEN MUCH OF THE AVAILABLE PRODUCE IS CONFINED TO A FEW ROOT VEGETABLES AND SOME BITTER GREENS. This recipe uses the latter to great effect, especially if you can find the red variety of Swiss chard. It will brighten any wintertime table. The addition of the pungent Swiss cheese brings this "Swiss" pizza full circle, but if you'd prefer to use Emmentaler or Gruyère, you won't sacrifice any flavor. It is equally good with either (or both!) of these cheeses. The addition of Parmesan cheese lends a nutty flavor to the pizza, not to mention that it extends its international theme.

This pizza is also simple to put together. Once the dough is made, it takes only about 30 minutes to get it from the kitchen counter to the kitchen table. To expedite preparation, you can grate the cheese and make the topping up to 2 hours in advance, leaving them covered and at room temperature.

Cornmeal

1 large leek, white and light green part only

1 tablespoon olive oil, plus extra for brushing

1 large bunch Swiss chard, preferably red, large stems removed, cut crosswise into 3-inch-long strips

¼ teaspoon red pepper flakes

Kosher or coarse sea salt

Dough for one 14-inch pizza (see page 130)

4 ounces Swiss cheese or Northern Gold, coarsely grated (or use Emmentaler or Gruyère)

3 tablespoons finely grated Parmesan or aged Asiago cheese

Preheat the oven to 500°F. If you are using a pizza stone, place it in the oven.

Sprinkle a 14-inch pizza pan with cornmeal. Or, if you are using a pizza stone, sprinkle cornmeal on a wooden peel (paddle) or a rimless baking sheet. Set aside.

Cut the leek in half lengthwise, leaving the root intact. Wash it thoroughly and slice it crosswise into ¼-inch-thick slices.

In a large sauté pan, warm the oil over medium-high heat. Add the leek and cook for 2 minutes. Add the chard, pepper flakes, and salt to taste. Cook, stirring occasionally, until the chard is wilted and cooked through but not completely limp. (Overcooking will cause the chard to discolor and lose some of its vibrant flavor.) Set aside.

Prepare the dough (see page 130).

Brush the rim of the dough with olive oil. Distribute the Swiss cheese then the Swiss chard mixture over the dough, leaving about a 2-inch rim. Sprinkle on the Parmesan cheese. Slide the pizza onto the stone, if using. Bake for 8 to 10 minutes, or until the edges of the crust are a deep golden brown and the cheese is bubbling. Serve immediately.

Serves 6 to 8 as an appetizer, 4 as a main course

Note: The pizza will cook more quickly with a pizza stone. Allow an extra 5 minutes' baking time if you're not using a stone.

## PERFECT PAIRS

BITTER GREENS ARE difficult to pair with wine. Nevertheless, a lean, herbaceous Sauvignon Blanc will go just fine with this pizza, as will a dry Chenin Blanc. For red wine, choose Sangiovese or an earthy Merlot.

# Bingham Hill Cheese Company

IN THE FOOTHILLS OF THE ROCKY MOUNTAINS, ABOUT AN HOUR NORTH OF Denver, is a local landmark known as Bingham Hill. It is the natural marker that signifies the region's geological diversity, from the plains on one side to the picturesque Pleasant Valley on the other, the latter of which was home to the area's first French settlers. The knoll's historical significance as well as its prominence led Tom and Kristi Johnson, of nearby Fort Collins, Colorado, to name their cheese company after it.

Bingham Hill Cheese Company was begun by the Johnsons when both were looking to make a change in their jobs and lifestyle. Kristi, a microbiologist, was working as a patent attorney in the biotech field, and Tom, who had a master's degree in watershed science, was the director of a river restoration project. "We were less and less enchanted working in intangible fields," says Tom Johnson.

One day Kristi took a rare day off from work to care for one of the couple's children who was sick. She turned on the television to see the iconic Martha Stewart making cheese. Kristi had grown up in Wisconsin, where her father was a consultant for a cheese manufacturer; consequently she was familiar with cheesemaking. Seeing cheesemaking on television struck a chord. This would turn out to be a seminal moment and the beginning of the Bingham Hill Cheese Company.

Sensing that the American consumer was being "shortchanged" on the cheese front, the Johnsons felt compelled to do something about it while enhancing

their own lives at the same time. First they took a few short courses in cheesemaking and settled on making a Stilton-style cheese because "it wasn't being made in this country," says Tom Johnson. Other types of blue cheese were being produced, but not specifically a hard, almost cheddar-like blue. Their first batch of Rustic Blue was ready in March 2000. By August of the same year, it had won a blue ribbon in the blue cheese category at the prestigious American Cheese Society competition.

The Johnsons met their objective to make a great-tasting cheese a short time out of the gate, and they did so, in part, because they had a very specific goal, they had some scientific background, and they knew the flavor profile they were after.

Rustic Blue is a very firm, somewhat crumbly blue cheese that is tannish gold in color and pockmarked with blue spots alternating with vertical blue-gray streaks throughout the cheese. The raw-milk cheese, which is aged five to six months, has some cheddar overtones with an almost chocolaty finish. There are also little crystals that occasionally form inside the cheese, lending a faint, agreeable crunch to the otherwise firm texture.

Made from the Holstein milk from a nearby dairy, Rustic Blue manages to develop extraordinary richness, largely as a result of the hands-on care the Johnsons give to it. Each wheel is turned and inspected daily, and because the Johnsons have learned how delicate their product is, they are now tasting every wheel before it goes to market. That type of dedication

Poudre Puff, named after the Poudre River, is shaped by hand and misted with brie mold to create the bloomy rind.

bagel, stirred into hot polenta, or piped into the groove of a celery stalk. They are also making a Roquefort-style blue cheese, called Sheepish Blue, using sheep's milk from a Colorado sheep farmer. The cheese is crumbly and a bit salty, and, like their cows' milk blue, rustic. Tom is also making two fantastic yet difficult-to-make washed-rind cheeses called Harvest Moon and Angel Feat. The latter is made with sheep's milk and earned a much deserved blue ribbon in the 2002 American Cheese Society competition.

The most striking characteristic of both Kristi and Tom Johnson is their intense interest in their craft. Bingham Hill Cheese Company is a business, and one that the Johnsons approach as deliberately as any CEO does his or her own company, but it is also something more than that. The Johnsons realize they are part of the greater American cheese community, and because of their eagerness to learn, they have ingratiated themselves within that community. Their cheese is excellent yet they convey a guileless interest in learning how to improve not only their own product but also the image and quality of American cheese as a whole. Their attitude is refreshing and inspiring—just like their cheese.

helps define the moniker "micro-cheesery," which Tom Johnson uses to describe his operation. Like a microbrewery, Bingham Hill Cheese Company offers a unique product made with great care in small quantities, designed to echo the local culture, tastes, and flavors.

The Johnsons have now embarked on a couple of new projects, including making excellent cheese spreads, plain and flavored, which are enhanced by the addition of cream. These spreads are fantastic on a

WHAT THEY MAKE

Angel Feat (*sheep's milk*)
Cheese spreads (*Plain, Basil Garlic, Dill, Garlic Parsley and Chive, Roasted Green Chile, Tuscan Herb, Wasabi*)
Ghost Town

Harvest Moon
Poudre Puff
Rustic Blue
Sheepish Blue
Tumbleweed

HOW TO REACH THEM

Fort Collins, Colorado
970-472-0702 (*phone*)
970-472-0622 (*fax*)
www.binghamhill.com

# MEDITERRANEAN PIZZA

**A LITTLE BIT OF THE MEDITERRANEAN COMES HOME WITH THIS PIZZA BECAUSE OF THE FETA CHEESE AND GARBANZO BEANS.** It is definitely rich, so a little goes a long way. The roasted red peppers called for here are now easily found in jars in most supermarkets. If you want to make your own, simply char a fresh red bell pepper over a gas flame or under the broiler, and then place it in a paper bag for about 15 minutes. Next, cut it in half, remove the seeds, and peel off the skin. Proceed as directed.

Preheat the oven to 500°F. If you are using a pizza stone, place it in the oven.

Sprinkle a 14-inch pizza pan with cornmeal. Or, if you are using a pizza stone, sprinkle cornmeal on a wooden peel (paddle) or a rimless baking sheet. Set aside.

In a small bowl, mix together the beans, vinegar, olive oil, and salt. Set aside.

Prepare the dough (see page 130).

Brush the rim of the dough with olive oil. Distribute the Fontina cheese over the dough, leaving about a 2-inch rim. Lay the pepper strips in a spoke pattern over the cheese. Scatter the garbanzo beans over the peppers and cheese. Bake for 7 minutes. Remove the pizza from the oven and scatter with the feta and mint. Bake for 3 to 5 minutes longer, or until the edges of the crust are golden brown and the cheese is bubbling. Let the pizza sit for 5 minutes before serving.

Serves 6 to 8 as an appetizer, 4 as a main course

Note: The pizza will cook more quickly with a pizza stone. Allow an extra 5 minutes' baking time if you're not using a stone.

Cornmeal
½ cup canned garbanzo beans, drained
1 teaspoon sherry vinegar (or red wine vinegar)
1 teaspoon olive oil, plus extra for brushing
Dash of salt
Dough for one 14-inch pizza (see page 130)
3 ounces Fontina cheese (or a washed-rind cheese such as Bingham Hill's Harvest Moon, which should add a nice strong flavor), coarsely grated
1 red pepper, roasted, skinned, and cut lengthwise into ¼-inch strips (or roasted peppers from a jar)
4 ounces feta cheese, crumbled
2 tablespoons chopped fresh mint

## PERFECT PAIRS

**THERE ARE MANY FLAVOR** components in this pizza, but most of them lean toward red wine. If you want something refreshing, opt for a rosé to bring out the acidic flavors in the pizza, or choose a Sangiovese to go with the more assertive roasted peppers and salty feta.

# John Folse's Bittersweet Plantation Dairy

AS AMERICAN CHEESEMAKERS CONTINUE TO RAISE THE OVERALL STANDARD OF American cheese, they are not only creating unprecedented cheeses, they also introduce us to the idea of "place" by way of their products. We are now learning that a farmstead cheddar from California is different from the same cheese made in Vermont. In Gonzales, Louisiana, about twenty miles east of Baton Rouge, cheesemaker Michael Levy is contributing to this regional distinction through the cheeses he makes at Chef John Folse's Bittersweet Plantation Dairy. Products like Creole Cream Cheese, Evangeline, and Parmesan Lorenzo—to name a few of the cheesemaker's offerings—are meant to conjure up images of the diverse ethnicities and lore that have come together to establish this colorful part of the South. All the same, they offer modern flavors for today's cheese buyer.

Chef John Folse, founder and chef of the area's popular Lafitte's Landing restaurant and owner of Bittersweet Plantation Dairy, has built a business based on the Cajun and Creole heritage of the area. He founded his restaurant in 1978 in a building that used to be his home, in Donaldsonville, Louisiana, about halfway between New Orleans and Baton Rouge. He also owns the historic White Oak Plantation in Baton Rouge, the centerpiece of which is a colonial-style mansion that serves as a special events center as well as home base for Folse's catering and food product manufacturing business. Now he has set his sights on making cheese, and he has hired Levy to make it happen.

A guy as enthusiastic and knowledgeable as Levy is a rare combination in the cheesemaking world. His interest in cheese and dairying began while he was living on a kibbutz in Israel. He moved from his native Chicago to Israel in 1990, and when he returned home in 1993, he had a new vision for his future. Rather than pursuing a postgraduate degree in psychology, he decided to focus on food and dairy and earned an M.S. in dairy food technology at Louisiana State University. That formal education has contributed to the relatively quick startup of the Bittersweet Plantation Dairy cheese operation.

The goats' and cows' milk cheeses made at the Bittersweet Plantation Dairy take inspiration from the seven cultures to be found in the area—African-American, Native American, English, French, German, Italian, and Spanish. The milks come from carefully chosen nearby sources—just one goats' milk producer and and one cows' milk producer, the latter being the locally heralded Klinepeter Farms dairy.

One of Levy's goats' milk cheeses, Evangeline, is named for the Henry Wadsworth Longfellow poem of the same name, which chronicles the exile of the Acadians from Nova Scotia. (The Acadians settled in Louisiana and were called Cajuns by the local Creoles, who were the native offspring of the French settlers.) The cheese is a lovely three-ounce soft-ripening goats' milk cheese with a thin layer of edible vegetable ash bisecting it horizontally. It is relatively mild yet flavorful, and the texture is soft and creamy. The molds used to make Evangeline, and all of Levy's cheeses, are from France. Levy says he has several hundred molds in forty different shapes—a small cheesemaker's dream.

Gabriel, a cheese named for Evangeline's hero

and lost lover, is aged about twice as long as the Evangeline; it is larger, a one-pound wheel; and, like Evangeline, it has a layer of ash in the middle. It too is mild, but at the same time it has lovely complexity and depth, making it a surprisingly good companion for a wide variety of wines, white and red alike.

Moving away from the Acadian to the area's Creole roots, Levy makes a cheese called Creole Cream Cheese. He says this cheese was first produced about 250 years ago in Louisiana and is therefore a major part of the region's food history. Already Slow Food USA, an organization dedicated to preserving and promoting artisan foods, has inducted the Creole Cream Cheese into its so-called Ark of Taste. Creole Cream Cheese is kind of a cross between farmer's cheese and sour cream. Unlike the more familiar cream cheese, it is quite liquidy; but like cream cheese, it has cream in it. It is mild in flavor and is traditionally sweetened with sugar or honey and topped with a little fruit. It can also be used in savory applications, including as an adornment for the humble baked potato.

Another exciting cheese emerging from Levy's "kitchen" is Bayou Blue, a rare goats' milk blue cheese. The pasteurized cheese is aged for about three months and has a soft brown rind. It is very creamy. Many other cheeses, such as Parmesan Lorenzo, a Guernsey milk Parmesan; Del Escondido, a Spanish-style cheese made with both goats' milk and Guernsey milk; Fleur de Lis, a buttery triple-crème; D'Arensbourg, named after the leader of the 18th-century German settlers in the New Orleans area; and a Tilsit-like Guernsey cheese, are eventually going to be the mainstays of the Bittersweet Plantation Dairy operation.

For the first year of operation, 2002–03, Levy is projecting he will make about 75,000 pounds of cheese, quite a lot for a start-up. Still, he hopes to maintain the artisan side of what he does while also looking toward higher production. If he is successful at maintaining quality at that level—and there's every reason to think he will be—then he will not only be accomplishing something that most cheesemakers, American and foreign alike, find tremendously challenging; he will also be filling a need for consistently made, great-tasting cheese from coast to coast.

WHAT THEY MAKE

**Cows' milk cheese**
Creole Cream Cheese
D'Arensbourg
Del Escondido (cows' and goats' milk)
Enrico Tonti Blue
Fleur de Lis
Parmesan Lorenzo
St. Francis White Cheddar

**Goats' milk cheese**
Chèvre de Bayou
Fresh chèvre

**Flavored chèvres**
Crescent City Herb Chèvre
Fire-Roasted Sweet Pepper Chèvre
Nice n' Spicy Chèvre

**Other goats' milk cheeses**
Bayou Blue
Evangeline
Gabriel
Jolie Blonde'

HOW TO REACH THEM

Gonzales, Lousiana
225-644-6000 (phone)
225-644-1295 (fax)
www.jfolse.com

# SPICY SPANISH PIZZA

**"EXOTIC" AND "SPICY" BEST CHARACTERIZE THIS UNUSUAL PIZZA.** I first had a version of this pizza at a lively restaurant in Oakland, California, called A Côté, which is worth seeking out for the flatbreads alone. I don't know how they made their traditional Spanish sauce known as Romesco, but the version I came up with has quickly become a household favorite. Make it a day or two in advance so that this pizza will be even more convenient. Be sure to buy Spanish—not Mexican—chorizo. If you can't find it, then substitute linguica or andouille.

## FOR THE SAUCE

2 tablespoons whole almonds, toasted

1 tablespoon coarsely chopped roasted red pepper (use the type that comes in a jar or make your own; see page 143)

2 small cloves garlic

1 medium Roma tomato (about ¼ pound), quartered

¼ teaspoon kosher salt

⅛ teaspoon cayenne pepper

Freshly ground pepper

1 tablespoon red wine vinegar

1 tablespoon extra-virgin olive oil

Cornmeal

Dough for one 14-inch pizza (see page 130)

2 ounces finely grated Parmesan cheese (or use extra-aged Asiago or Provolone)

¼ pound chorizo sausage, sliced ⅛ inch thick

Preheat the oven to 500°F. If you are using a pizza stone, place it in the oven.

Sprinkle a 14-inch pizza pan with cornmeal. Or, if you are using a pizza stone, sprinkle cornmeal on a wooden peel (paddle) or a rimless baking sheet. Set aside.

To make the sauce: In the bowl of a food processor, combine the almonds, red pepper, garlic, tomato, salt, cayenne, and a dash of black pepper. Process until the mixture is smooth. Add the vinegar and olive oil and process until well incorporated. Add more salt, if necessary. Set aside. (This mixture can be made up to 2 days in advance and refrigerated. Bring to room temperature and stir well before using. Makes ¾ cup.)

Prepare the dough (see page 130).

Brush the rim of the dough with the remaining olive oil. Slather on the Romesco to within 1 inch of the edge. Distribute the cheese, then the chorizo on top. Bake for 8 to 10 minutes, or until the crust is a rich golden-brown with a few dark spots and the cheese is bubbly. Serve immediately.

Serves 6 to 8 as an appetizer, 4 as a main course

Note: The pizza will cook more quickly with a pizza stone. Allow an extra 5 minutes' baking time if you're not using a stone.

## PERFECT PAIRS

**THIS SPICY DISH CALLS** for a spicy wine. Choose a Gewürztraminer, or for a taste of the exotic, a dry sherry. If you're interested in a red wine, a fruity Zinfandel will soothe the heat nicely as long as it isn't too high in alcohol.

# Waterbrook Winery

JANET AND ERIC RINDAL ARE AWFULLY YOUNG TO BE THE OWNERS OF ONE OF THE older Washington wineries. Having started Waterbrook Winery in 1984 in Walla Walla, they were unquestionably ahead of their state's wine trends. But once you learn a little about each of them, it is no longer surprising that they were out in front of the pack.

Janet Rindal grew up on a farm in the area, and Eric grew up with an interest in wine. When they got married, the wine industry was just getting under way in this part of eastern Washington. Janet says there was a building on her family's farm that was going unused, and she and Eric thought it would be a good place to put a winery. In no time, the Rindals' first Sauvignon Blanc received a gold medal at the prestigious Seattle Enological Awards. They were off and running.

As pioneers, they faced challenges. The main one was the relative lack of available fruit in the area. Rindal says most of the farmers in the Walla Walla area grew wheat and alfalfa. The Rindals decided to plant some of their own grapes, but their plants took time to mature. They also had to contend with the public's lack of familiarity with Washington wines, which meant that they had to develop a market. Through it all, they managed to stay ahead of the curve and carve out a reputation for making consistently excellent wine.

The award-winning Sauvignon Blanc is noteworthy partly because of its low price—around nine dollars—and also because of its far more "expensive" flavor. It is crisp with hints of melon and pear, and is thankfully devoid of oakiness. "Our goal is to have people enjoy wine and after finishing say, 'That was a good buy,' " says Janet Rindal, aware of the fact that many people don't have a lot of money to spend on wine.

There is little question that the Waterbrook wines offer value, especially because they are so skillfully made by winemaker Brian Carlson. The Viognier expresses typical apricot and pineapple flavors, which are bolstered by good acidity and a nice finish. The Mélange, a red table wine, provides loads of bang given its reasonable price tag. It is consistently good, demonstrating good structure, fruit, and a nice finish, even though the particular blend changes from year to year.

As "project-oriented" people, the Rindals have taken on a few rather unusual projects in addition to the winery. In 2000 and 2001, Janet Rindal earned the title of the United States BMX, or Bicycle Motocross, champion in her age group. This is not a sport for sissies. Rindal can be seen hurling her specially outfitted bike over jumps and turning on a dime on her hometown track, which was built by her husband. Eric flies planes.

It may be their thrill-seeking nature that helps the Rindals to keep their business and the product they make in perspective. Although obviously driven, Janet Rindal maintains refreshing humility. "It's a big ole' world out there—wine is not the end all. There are lots of important things going on," she says. Be that as it may, she and Eric, along with winemaker Carlson, have raised the bar—and visibility—of Washington wine, and they have done so with amazing energy and, especially, grace.

WHAT THEY MAKE

**White wines**
Chardonnay
Sauvignon Blanc
Viognier

**Red wines**
Cabernet Sauvignon
Mélange
Meritage
Merlot

HOW TO REACH THEM

Walla Walla, Washington
509-522-1262 (phone)
509-529-4770 (fax)
www.waterbrook.com

# BACON, TOMATO, AND MOZZARELLA PIZZA

**BACON AND TOMATO ARE A CLASSIC COMBINATION, ESPECIALLY WHEN LETTUCE IS THROWN IN.** Although this recipe does not call for lettuce, if you wish, you can use 1 cup of arugula leaves to create your own "BLT." Just add the arugula as soon as the pizza comes out of the oven. With or without the greens, this pizza is a winner because of both simplicity and full flavor.

Cornmeal

8 slices bacon, cut into 1-inch pieces

Dough for one 14-inch pizza (see page 130)

1 tablespoon olive oil

1 teaspoon coarse sea salt

8 ounces fresh mozzarella cheese, coarsely grated (if it is too watery to grate, use a sharp knife to chop it into small pieces)

1 large tomato (about ¾ pound), seeds and most of the juice removed, coarsely chopped

Preheat the oven to 500°F. If you are using a pizza stone, place it in the oven.

Sprinkle a 14-inch pizza pan with cornmeal. If you are using a pizza stone, sprinkle cornmeal on a wooden peel (paddle) or a rimless baking sheet. Set aside.

In a medium skillet, cook the bacon over medium heat just until the edges begin to brown but the bacon is still soft and pliable, about 6 to 7 minutes. Drain on paper towels.

Prepare the dough (see page 130).

Brush the rim of the dough with the olive oil and sprinkle with the salt. Distribute the cheese over the dough and sprinkle with the bacon pieces. Bake for 5 minutes. Scatter the tomatoes over the surface of the pizza and continue baking until the cheese is golden-brown and bubbly and the bacon is crisp, about 5 to 10 more minutes. Serve immediately.

Serves 6 to 8 as an appetizer, 4 as a main course

Note: The pizza will cook more quickly with a pizza stone. Allow an extra 5 minutes' baking time if you're not using a stone.

## PERFECT PAIRS

**THE BACON AND TOMATO** on this pizza serve a great purpose. In addition to adding flavor, they bring a mild cheese like mozzarella into the realm of the assertive, allowing it to be paired with more weighty wines such as Sangiovese, Zinfandel, and Grenache.

# Meadow Creek Dairy

HELEN FEETE IS A WONDER. THE PETITE
REDHEAD HAS A MODEST AND SEEMINGLY
laid-back demeanor that absolutely belies her steadfast
commitment to the land, her animals, and, ultimately,
her cheese. She and her husband, Rick, along with
their two grown children, have created an admirable
model farm—and cheese.

The Feetes have been practicing sustainable agriculture and rotational grazing for twenty years,
although neither Helen nor Rick came from a dairy
background. They studied their art by traveling to New
Zealand and observing rotational grazing techniques
there. Once they started their farm in
Virginia, they sold fluid milk exclusively. In 1998 they made the decision to undertake cheesemaking
using the milk from their Jersey cows.
Although they had been making
cheese on and off, it was too difficult
to do so consistently with the demands
of the dairy. But as with many American
cheesemakers, the Feetes' decision to
devote themselves to cheesemaking
happened to coincide with America's
increasing appetite for artisan cheese.
Lucky them, and lucky us.

The Meadow Creek Dairy
cheese has had an exceptional
ascent. When Helen Feete first began
making cheese, she was able to sell it fairly well in her
immediate area of Galax, in southwest Virginia, but
her cheeses were still works in progress at that point.
After all, she had had virtually no cheesemaking experience. Just a couple of years later, though, the
Meadow Creek Dairy cheeses have become the ones
people are seeking out.

While Rick Feete manages the pasture—a task
that takes tremendous skill since the Jerseys eat the
grass faster than the Feetes can grow it—Helen toils

**Mountaineer**
*Aged over 90 days*
**Net Wt.:**
Ingredients:
Cultured Raw Milk
Salt, Rennet

Meadow Creek Dairy, Galax, Virginia 24333
**KEEP REFRIGERATED**

away in her new cheesemaking room, experimenting
with new cheeses and making more familiar cheeses
at the same time. Among the "familiar" cheeses is her
Mountaineer. Styled loosely after a Beaufort—one of
the finest European alpine cheeses, owing to its nutty,
buttery, and rich character—Mountaineer is a raw-
milk cheese aged for anywhere from three months to
as long as eighteen months. Feete admits, though, that
she usually winds up selling the cheese a little sooner
than she'd like because of demand.

Likewise, her Appalachian Jack goes out the door
quickly, but a sample of an aged version proves how
incredible such a common cheese
can be in the right hands. It has layer
upon layer of flavor, with a firm,
slightly crumbly texture and a lovely
brownish gold color. It gives conventional Jack cheese new meaning.

One of the most exciting cheeses
Feete produces is Grayson, named after
the county in which she and Rick live.
Inspired by a trip the Feetes took to
Ireland in 2000, Grayson is a raw milk
washed-rind cheese that is aged a
minimum of three months. To make
it, Feete cuts the curds fairly small
and then washes them, retaining
about three-quarters of the whey.

She then drains off a little more of
the whey and scoops the moist curds into hoops or
molds for shaping and draining. After it has been left
to drain for as long as thirty hours, the cheese is
flipped quickly to keep the rind smooth—a trick
Helen learned in Ireland. She then puts the cheese in
the cooler for half a day before putting it in brine for
two days. Finally, it is moved to the aging room. The
eight-pound wheels are smeared with yeast and bacteria to facilitate ripening and the development of a pronounced flavor in the cheese. Since not many

American cheesemakers are creating this type of difficult-to-make cheese, given the inherent difficulties in making it, Feete's undertaking is to be commended. She is helping fill a real gap in the American-made cheese market.

Helen Feete is also working on a blue cheese, although the vagaries of making blue cheese have proven trying. Nonetheless, she's persevering, with extremely good results. Hers is a natural rind blue cheese, medium-firm in texture with a thin skinlike rind. Although she calls it "pretty assertive," the cheese, christened New River Blue, is a crowd-pleaser. One can only imagine how much of a crowd she'll have when she's got a little more blue cheese experience under her belt.

Although cheesemaking is the reason the Feetes are part of a book on American cheese, their devotion to the land and to their animals is equally noteworthy. Without that, the milk to make the cheese would be inferior, to be sure. Among the factors that make their farm exceptional is their closed herd; that means that all of the breeding is done from within, enabling them to maintain far more control over the health and genetics of the herd. In addition, they grow only grass, and they do not use pesticides or herbicides. The cows' feed is supplemented with legumes, perennial grasses, and some grain. Finally, the Feetes have designated a finite milking period for their cows, allowing the cows (and the Feetes!) a midwinter rest of at least two months.

Helen Feete says she would like to try making an aged raw-milk Gouda to capture the caramelized flavor inherent in that type of cheese. For now, she makes a variety of fantastic raw-milk Monterey Jack-style cheeses, feta cheese, and other self-styled creations. Although she had no real idea of how to make cheese just a few years ago, Feete now feels more confident. "I can actually see a direction. I'm not just floundering anymore," she says. The proof is in the lovely cheeses she produces.

### WHAT THEY MAKE

Appalachian Jack (*Plain, Hot Pepper, Rosemary, Shiitake Leek*)
Grayson
Meadow Creek Feta (*Plain, Peppered, Tomato and Herb*)

Mountaineer
New River Blue

### HOW TO REACH THEM

Galax, Virginia
276-236-2776 (phone)
276-236-2776 (fax)
www.meadowcreekdairy.com

# MONTEREY JACK AND ROASTED ASPARAGUS PIZZA

**PIZZAS DON'T HAVE TO BE COMPLICATED TO BE GOOD.** This pizza proves that. You can roast the asparagus while you're preparing the dough and grating the cheese, and next thing you know, the pizza is finished. This recipe also offers maximum flexibility. If you don't have any Monterey Jack, then use mozzarella. Or, if you feel like a more unusual twist, head toward the aged goats' milk or sheep's milk cheese section of the cheese department.

Cornmeal

2 tablespoons olive oil

2½ teaspoons finely chopped fresh rosemary (or 1¼ teaspoons dried rosemary)

¼ teaspoon kosher salt

¼ pound asparagus (about 8 spears) ends trimmed, cut into thirds

Dough for one 14-inch pizza (see page 130)

4 ounces Jack cheese, coarsely grated

Preheat the oven to 500°F. If you are using a pizza stone, place it in the oven.

Sprinkle a 14-inch pizza pan with cornmeal. Or, if you are using a pizza stone, sprinkle cornmeal on a wooden (paddle) peel or a rimless baking sheet. Set aside.

In a small baking pan, mix together 1 tablespoon of the olive oil, the rosemary, and salt. Add the asparagus to the pan and shake it around to coat it with the mixture. Roast for 12 minutes, or until brown on the edges.

Prepare the dough (see page 130).

Brush the rim of the dough with the remaining olive oil. Distribute the cheese over the dough, then the asparagus pieces, leaving a 1-inch border. Bake for 8 to 10 minutes, or until the crust is a rich golden-brown with a few dark spots and the cheese is bubbly. Serve immediately.

Serves 6 to 8 as an appetizer, 4 as a main course

Note: The pizza will cook more quickly with a pizza stone. Allow an extra 5 minutes' baking time if you're not using a stone.

## PERFECT PAIRS

This is a relatively mild pizza, although it by no means lacks flavor. Instead the flavors are buttery and almost caramel-like because of the roasted asparagus. For white wine, this points to a California Chardonnay or Pinot Blanc, and for red wine, a medium-bodied Barbera. You could also opt for a dry, vintage sparkling wine.

# CHEESE PLATES

Kumquat-Peppercorn Compote with Sheep's
Milk Cheese, recipe on page 167

# THE CHEESE BAR

Few party offerings get people more revved up than do cheese and wine. Both are innately festive, and the very appearance of cheese and wine is fundamentally alluring. It seems part of the human condition to have a primordial response to a spread of beautiful cheeses. Oh, how wonderful it will taste! The poetic shape of a wine bottle and the knowledge of what lies beneath the cork only helps further this reaction. Side by side, cheese and wine constitute the "fifth food group" for many adults.

The appeal of cheese and wine together lies also in the simplicity of the combination. A few cheeses, a few wines, a few accompaniments, and a long afternoon or evening are the fundamental ingredients. By the same token, as we grow more sophisticated in our cheese tastes, it may no longer be enough simply to set out a few cheeses along with some clusters of grapes, a few nuts, and a bottle of wine. Instead, as culinary adventurers, we are constantly seeking new ways to serve and enjoy our food. This brings us to the next entertaining option: the cheese bar.

Think back to the 1970s, when salad bars were all the rage. Here we are taking that concept into the 21st century and creating our own cheese bar. In addition to serving as many as ten or twelve cheeses, you can include an assortment of nuts—spiced, sugared, or just toasted—two or three compotes, a chutney or two, some fresh and dried fruits, and one or two types of bread. It's a cheese buffet, of sorts, but it is far more exotic than a simple platter of cheeses. It serves as a learning experience, since all who partake can mix and match the ingredients and come up with their favorite combinations. It is also a convenient way to offer a variety of wines without worrying whether or not they will make good companions to the cheese. With the many flavors on the "buffet," you almost can't go wrong with the wine. Surely some combinations will find perfect harmony.

One of the best things about staging your own cheese buffet is that everything can be prepared well in advance. In the case of the chutneys, they can be prepared as much as a week ahead, and the compotes one or two days in advance. The cheeses can be purchased a day or two ahead, depending on the particular types, and the nuts can be made as much as a month in advance and frozen. The only items you may need to purchase the day of your party are fresh bread and fresh fruit, should you decide to use it, although even then, apples and pears will certainly last a few days. Of course, the dried fruit will last for months.

Following are a few ideas for your next cheese bar, although you can stage your offerings any way you want. You might want to include your own cheese creations, such as adding herbs to fresh chèvre, or creating your own "torta" by simply layering some goat cheese with pesto and sun-dried tomatoes. Or, if you want to draw on the original salad bar idea, include a few salad makings such as arugula, dried cherries, roasted and chopped fresh beets, and a light mustard-based vinaigrette. Not only do these ingredients make for a nice salad, each of them enhances most types of cheese. The sky's the limit. Just be sure to provide several options so that people will have ample opportunity to mix and match.

Although the way you put out your cheese bar components isn't essential, it's a good idea to arrange the cheeses from mild to strong and soft to hard. Following are suggestions for three cheese bars featuring recipes in this chapter.

## CHEESE BAR #1

- Four styles of cheddar cheese, four styles of blue cheese

- Apple-Pear Butter, Port-Roasted Grapes, Plum-Mango Chutney, honey

- Roasted almonds, Candied Walnuts

- Thin-sliced apples, grapes, fresh figs

- Dried dates, dried plums (*prunes*)

Sweet Grass Dairy's Lumiere is a goat's milk cheese that pairs nicely with Chenin Blanc.

* Sparkling wine, Chardonnay (*older vintage*), Riesling, Dolcetto, port (*tawny*), sherry (*medium-dry*)

* Toasted walnut bread slices, fresh baguette slices

### CHEESE BAR #2

* A variety of soft-ripened cheeses (*Brie, Camembert, goats' milk Camembert, sheep's milk Camembert*); one semi-hard goats' milk cheese, one semi-hard sheep's milk cheese, two cows' milk cheeses (*dry Jack and Gruyère*)

* Kumquat-Peppercorn Compote, Dried Fruit Compote, Quince Paste, purchased or homemade apricot chutney

* Spicy Pecans, toasted hazelnuts

* Fresh pear slices, ripe kiwi

* Dried figs, dried cherries

* Sparkling wine, Chardonnay, Pinot Blanc, Pinot Noir, Sangiovese, sherry (*dry*)

### CHEESE BAR #3

* Four washed-rind cheeses, four hard cheeses, two semi-soft cheeses

* Cherry Compote, purchased or homemade fig compote, Fennel-Honey Marmalade

* Spiced nuts, toasted walnuts

* Fresh nectarine slices, fresh plum slices, fresh melon slices

* Dried dates, dried figs

* Chenin Blanc, Gewürztraminer, Grenache, Zinfandel, sparkling wine

* Rosemary bread (*for hard cheeses*), sweet baguette, walnut toasts

# CLASSIC CHEESE PAIRS

These cheese pairs are not called "classics" for nothing. They are timeless in their appeal, transcending food trends and proving that what has satisfied the appetite of generations past is likely to do so for generations to come. The following are loose guidelines for these classics and are meant to serve six people.

## DATES AND PARMESAN

- 2 or 3 dates per person (or prunes—"dried plums," as they're now called)
- Six 1-ounce chunks of highest-quality Parmesan cheese

### PERFECT PAIRS

For this cheese classic, choose a medium-dry sherry, ruby port, or light white dessert wine, such as Muscat.

## FIGS AND BLUE CHEESE (FRESH OR DRIED)

- 4 or 5 dried figs, or 2 or 3 fresh figs, halved
- 6 ounces of creamy or aged blue cheese, coarsely cut

### PERFECT PAIRS

A glass of port is often found alongside this classic combination. If you're using dried figs, another good choice is an off-dry sparkling wine, which cuts through the saltiness of the cheese and brings out the earthy and toasty qualities of the figs.

## APPLES AND CHEDDAR

- 2 tart-sweet apples, such as Braeburn, Gala, or Jonagold, cored and sliced thin
- 6 ounces aged, earthy cheddar cheese, cut into 6 pieces

### PERFECT PAIRS

Apples and cheddar together make for a challenge when it comes to wine. That said, a late-harvest Sauvignon Blanc will work very nicely, as will Cayuga White, a hybrid grape.

## GOAT CHEESE AND HONEY

- Three 4-ounce crottins, cut in half
- 2 tablespoons honey (use any type you prefer; lavender honey works particularly well)
- 1 medium-firm ripe pear, such as Bosc, cut into 24 slices

Drizzle honey over each piece of cheese and serve along with 6 slices of pear per serving.

### PERFECT PAIRS

A late-harvest Chenin Blanc would be great with this combination, as would a late-harvest Semillon.

## RICOTTA AND HONEY

- 2 pounds best-quality ricotta cheese, preferably sheep's milk or Jersey milk
- 6 tablespoons best-quality honey

Distribute the ricotta among 6 bowls. Drizzle honey over the ricotta as you would fudge sauce over ice cream. Serve immediately.

### PERFECT PAIRS

Ricotta is sweeter than goat cheese, although it still retains a hint of tanginess. A cream sherry will match the creaminess of the cheese, and it will add a slight earthy component to go with the honey. A late-harvest Muscat is a good choice too.

# GOING NUTS

ROASTED NUTS ARE THE PERFECT ACCOMPANIMENT TO CHEESE. They match the nutty flavors in some cheeses, and for others they provide a wonderful flavor contrast. No matter what, their crunchy texture is a natural companion to the various textures of cheese. The recipes that follow are just guidelines, so feel free to use whatever spices and herbs you like. Also, you may want to experiment with different types of nuts. All of the nuts can be frozen for up to three months.

## CANDIED WALNUTS

THESE VERSATILE NUTS GO BEAUTIFULLY WITH FRESH OR AGED GOAT CHEESE, BLUE CHEESE, OR GRUYÈRE.

Preheat the oven to 350°F.

In a medium-sized bowl, mix together the sugar, cayenne, and salt.

Bring a small saucepan of water to a boil. Add the walnuts and blanch them for 3 minutes. Drain well and then immediately roll the walnuts in the sugar mixture until thoroughly coated. The sugar will melt slightly. Line a baking sheet or pan with parchment or a silicone mat such as Silpat. Transfer the walnuts to the sheet and bake, stirring occasionally, until they are a deep golden-brown, about 12 to 15 minutes. Watch carefully because the sugar can burn easily. Let cool completely before serving.

Makes 1 cup

¼ cup powdered sugar

⅛ teaspoon cayenne pepper

⅛ teaspoon salt

4 ounces walnuts halves (about one heaping cup; don't use pieces)

## SPICY PECANS

SERVE THESE NUTS WITH DRY JACK CHEESE OR AGED SHEEP'S MILK CHEESE.

Preheat the oven to 325°F.

In a small bowl, whisk together all of the ingredients except the pecans. When blended, add the pecans to the bowl and coat well. (It won't look like much coating, but don't worry. It is enough.) Spread the pecans out on a small baking pan and bake until they start to release a nutty aroma and are beginning to turn a light brown color, about 8 minutes. Remove from the oven and let cool completely before serving.

Makes ¾ cup

2 teaspoons canola oil

¼ teaspoon kosher salt

¼ teaspoon ground cumin

⅛ teaspoon ground coriander

3 peppermill twists of fresh pepper

¾ cup pecan halves

## CARAWAY ALMONDS

**THESE NUTS ARE PARTICULARLY GOOD WITH CHEDDAR, GOUDA, AND HAVARTI CHEESE.**

1 cup whole almonds
1 egg white
½ teaspoon coarse salt
½ teaspoon caraway seeds, crushed

Preheat the oven to 300°F.

To blanch the almonds, in a small pan, add the nuts and enough water to cover by 1 inch. Bring to a boil. Boil for 1 minute and then drain. As soon as the almonds are cool enough to handle, slip them out of their skins by holding them at one end and squeezing. They will come right out.

In a small bowl, whisk the egg white until it begins to get foamy. Add the salt and caraway and whisk until they are incorporated. Add the almonds and stir to coat. Spread the almonds out on a baking sheet and roast, stirring frequently, for 15 to 20 minutes, or until the almonds are golden-brown. Some of them will stick together, but that is fine. Remove from the oven and let cool completely before serving.

Makes 1 cup

## SPANISH ALMONDS

**THERE'S NOTHING BETTER THAN A FEW SALTED AND ROASTED ALMONDS WITH AN AGED CHEESE AND A GLASS OF SHERRY.** Or serve these nuts with some olives and fresh goat cheese.

1 cup whole almonds, blanched
  (see instructions above)
1 tablespoon grapeseed, light olive, or canola oil
1 teaspoon coarse salt

Preheat the oven to 300°F.

In a small bowl, combine all the ingredients. Spread the nuts out on a baking sheet and roast for 15 to 20 minutes, or until they are a deep golden-brown. Remove from the oven and let cool completely before serving.

Makes 1 cup

# Cadence Winery

**IT IS SURELY PARADOXICAL TO DESCRIBE A WINE AS EXPLODING WITH ELEGANCE.** Yet, Cadence wines—with their sultry blue label, their meticulously chosen fruit, their finesse, and their irreproachable character—exemplify that very contradiction. The Bordeaux-style wines practically defy any description at all; easier to explain is the story behind the wine and its enchanting name.

Cadence winery was started by Gaye McNutt and Ben Smith in 2000, although preparation for their enterprise began years earlier. During the decade that preceded Cadence, Smith was a winemaker-in-training. He just didn't realize it. He had tried his hand at winemaking a few years before, when a friend asked him to participate in a harvest. The experience hooked him, and he began making his own wine at home. Officially, Smith was an employee at Boeing in Seattle, where he worked on flight control systems. One of the perks of being a Boeing employee was membership in the exalted Boeing Winemaker's Club. Smith says this club had access to some of the best vineyards in the state, so he could make wine with high-quality grapes.

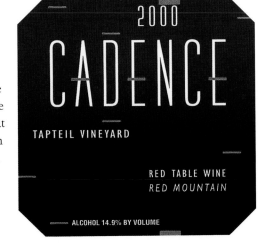

Two important things happened for Smith during this time: He earned a "Best of Show" award for his wine and was told that it was of commercial quality. Second, he recognized that all the best Boeing-made wines came from the same vineyards. McNutt and Smith were inspired to write a business plan. McNutt says they saw it could work if they could get the fruit they wanted. They approached the growers and learned that the fruit was indeed obtainable.

In 2000 Smith quit Boeing, although McNutt kept her job as an attorney at Microsoft. It was a justifiably scary move, but McNutt says they realized that once the ball started rolling, they couldn't look back. Their goal was to make top-notch Bordeaux blends, using fruit from the Columbia Valley. This appellation, along with the Walla Walla Valley, is primarily responsible for Washington's stellar reputation for red wine.

The word "blend" can connote many things. Cadence does not blend grapes from different vineyards, with the exception from its Reserve; instead it blends grapes that come from within the same vineyard. Cadence produces three wines that are single-vineyard designates, and the Reserve is a blend of the grapes from those three vineyards, all of which are on Red Mountain. McNutt and Smith have also purchased their own vineyard on Red Mountain. The first wine from that vineyard will probably not be released until 2005.

Smith and McNutt's approach to starting their own wine label was deliberate and methodical. They organized tasting groups, talked to people at wine shops, hosted numerous dinner parties, and bought Washington and French wines. Smith says that for him, desirable wine comes down to one thing: balance. "I don't go for hugely extracted wines. I don't think they're food friendly—they're monolithic," he says. This winemaking philosophy bucks the trend in a country where such "monolithic" wines represent the quintessential wine experience for many people.

Although Cadence wines are made in the heart of Seattle, the grapes come from the Columbia Valley in eastern Washington. Specifically, they come from the Tapteil Vineyard, Ciel du Cheval Vineyards, and Klipsun Vineyards. Although all of the vineyards are in the same area, each has its own unique characteristics, which is why Smith sources from all of them.

The wine from the Taptiel Vineyard, which is on a slope on upper Red Mountain, shows black fruits, a lovely balance, just as Smith intends, and a nice long finish. It also has quite a bit of tannin. In contrast, the wine from the Ciel du Cheval Vineyards, on the lower part of Red Mountain, has softer tannins and slightly more prominent fruit. As a result, the wine is a little more approachable earlier. The grapes from the Klipsun Vineyards, which are known for being big, bold, and powerful, have been reined in nicely by Smith. But regardless of the vineyard from which each wine has been made, the common characteristic of all Cadence wines is their remarkable power within a restrained framework. The phrase "iron fist in a velvet glove," used by Warren Winiarski, founder of Stag's Leap Wine Cellars in Napa Valley, embodies the essence of Cadence wines.

What is particularly striking about the Cadence wines is not just the wines themselves but the people behind them. Both McNutt and Smith are extremely approachable and strikingly serene, even though the pace of their life as burgeoning winemakers is frenetic. In the midst of the harvest of 2001, when all winemakers accept frenzy as their daily routine, they sat calmly, explaining the story of their wines. (Never mind that McNutt was more than nine months pregnant and would be going to the hospital two days later to have her baby.) The two are not strangers to challenges or pressure. McNutt is a devoted triathlete, and Smith is an avid cyclist. These athletic interests, along with the couple's passion for music, can be seen in the name they chose for their wine. In music the word "cadence" speaks to the beat of a rhythmic movement, and in cycling it refers to a precise rhythm in pedaling. The word evokes a graceful image in both contexts, and, now, it graces what is easily one of Washington state's most elegant families of wines.

WHAT THEY MAKE

Red table wine
Ciel du Cheval
Klipsun
Reserve
Tapteil

HOW TO REACH THEM

Seattle, Washington
206-381-9507 (phone)
206-860-9906 (fax)
www.cadencewinery.com

# EMMENTALER WITH FENNEL-HONEY MARMALADE AND PUMPERNICKEL BREAD

**THIS MARMALADE IS DOWNRIGHT ADDICTIVE AND GOES WELL WITH MANY FOODS, IN ADDITION TO CHEESE.** Try it over roast pork or on a piece of rye toast. No matter what, you won't mind having this on hand, especially when you're looking to jazz up a cheese. Note that it is easiest to slice the cheese when it is cold; bring it to room temperature before serving.

To make the marmalade: In a medium nonreactive saucepan, combine the fennel, wine, honey, ¼ cup of the water, orange juice, lemon juice, and currants. Bring to a boil for 1 minute. Reduce the heat to low and cook, uncovered, stirring occasionally, for 1 hour. Be patient!

Meanwhile, in a small pot, bring 1 cup of the water to a boil. Add the orange zest and cook for 30 seconds. Drain the zest in a small strainer and bring the remaining cup of water to a boil in the same pot. Once again, add the orange zest and cook for 30 seconds. Drain again and let cool. (This method all but eliminates bitterness in the zest while retaining its orange flavor.)

After the fennel has cooked for 1 hour, add the zest to the fennel mixture and cook for 10 to 20 more minutes, or until the fennel has cooked through but is still holding its shape, and most of the liquid has evaporated. The mixture will become almost glazed. Remove from the heat and let cool to room temperature. The marmalade will keep, refrigerated, for about 3 weeks.

When ready to serve, toast the bread slices on one side under the broiler. Turn, butter, and toast until the bread turns a shade darker. Let cool briefly. (Note: Because of its high moisture content, pumpernickel takes a total of 15 to 20 mintues to toast.)

To serve, place 3 pieces of the cheese on individual serving plates, and place three pieces of toast next to the cheese. Top each piece of toast with a spoonful of the fennel mixture. Serve immediately.

Serves 4

## FOR THE MARMALADE

1 large fennel bulb (about ¾ pound), as on page 104, quartered lengthwise, cored, and sliced crosswise ¼ inch thick, to make about 3 cups

½ cup white dessert wine, such as Robert Mondavi Moscato d' Oro

¼ cup plus 2 tablespoons honey

2¼ cups water

2 tablespoons orange juice

1 tablespoon plus 1 teaspoon fresh lemon juice

¼ cup currants

1 heaping tablespoon julienned orange zest

12 pieces pumpernickel bread squares (use the heartiest, densest bread you can find)

1 tablespoon unsalted butter, at room temperature

4 ounces Emmentaler cheese (or use Gruyère), cut into 12 paper-thin slices

## PERFECT PAIRS

**THE ORANGE, CURRANT,** and sweetened fennel come together to create a caramel-like flavor. The Emmentaler cheese also has some caramel overtones, and because of that a sweet dessert wine is a great choice. An orange Muscat, such as California's Quady Essensia, is an obvious choice, but a late-harvest Vignoles from New York or an ice wine will also be quite nice.

# Uplands Cheese Company

WHEN MIKE AND CAROL GINGRICH WON "BEST OF SHOW" FOR THEIR CHEESE AT the American Cheese Society's 2001 annual conference, the shouts of joy that erupted in the room could probably be heard for miles. That enthusiasm came not just from the Gingrichs, but particularly from the people who had tasted their Pleasant Ridge Reserve. The complex flavors in the cheese unquestionably wowed the judges, but the story behind this cheese is much more remarkable.

In 1994 the Gingrichs, who had been living in southern California, were interested in returning to farming, something they had done many years before. In partnership with their friends Dan and Jeanne Patenaude, they bought a three-hundred-acre farm in southwest Wisconsin with the intention of setting up a rotational grazing system for about two hundred dairy cows. As it was, the Patenaudes had already been practicing this innovative type of grazing for about ten years on a much smaller scale.

"Rotational grazing" means moving cows to a different part of the pasture each day, so that the grass in the pasture has a chance to grow back. The reason is twofold: First, if the cows are not allowed to overgraze, the land remains significantly healthier. Second, when the grass reaches a height of between eight and twelve inches, it is at its optimum nutritional level, at which it produces milk with the best flavor. By establishing this system and subsequently testing their milk, the Gingrichs and Patenaudes knew they had a superior milk supply. Their only limitation was that pasture was available to the cows only for two seasons—spring and summer.

Nonetheless, the Gingrichs and the Patenaudes were convinced that because their milk was special, it was worthy of special attention. Deciding to put it to good use is how their cheesemaking efforts got under way.

They began by studying the cheeses of the world that were made specifically from grass-fed, pastured cows. They came up with an even dozen. They then placed orders with New York cheese shops, since those cheeses were not readily available in their area. Many cheese parties ensued, and the final vote was for a French Alps cheese called Beaufort. To be called Beaufort, the cheese has to be made only from the milk of a particular type of cow that is pastured above eight thousand feet. While the Gingrichs couldn't replicate this environment, they did draw upon the archives of the Wisconsin Milk Marketing Board for a Beaufort recipe, convinced that they could create a similar cheese. Together with the Center for Dairy Research at the University of Wisconsin (UW), they made eight batches of Beaufort-style cheese using slightly different procedures. From that cheesemaking session, they came away with thirty-two wheels. They took the cheese home, put it in brand-new coolers, and tended to it, just as their recipes instructed. Every so often, they would return to the Center for tastings. Finally they determined that one of the eight recipes was superior to the rest. That became their recipe for Pleasant Ridge Reserve.

By this time, they needed a place to make their cheese on an on going basis, and Bob Wills, owner of nearby Cedar Grove Cheese, graciously offered his factory for them to use on weekends. Indeed, so supportive was Wills of the Gingrichs' project that he even accompanied them to UW as their cheese experiment progressed. Shortly after determining what cheese they were going to make, the Gingrichs rented refrigerator space in a commercial kitchen to use as an aging room. In 2000 they made their first cheese: 603 ten-

pound wheels of it. Amazingly, this was the source of their "Best of Show" cheese—their very first season as cheesemakers!

Although the Gingrichs understandably keep a few details to themselves, their cheesemaking method is not nearly as unique as their milk source is. Their cheese is made in a traditional mountain style, in which the curds are cooked slowly, the whey is drained, and the remaining curds are then scooped into molds and pressed, turned, and pressed again. The wheels of cheese are then brought to the coolers, where they are dry salted and washed and turned for two to three weeks. They are then left to age for anywhere from four to ten months—or longer—although demand for this cheese so far has precluded an aging period longer than ten months.

The flavor of their cheese nearly defies description. Because of the particular bacteria applied to the cheese, the cheese takes on astoundingly deep, somewhat musty flavors, but at the same time it has a pleasant floral quality. The color of the paste is a yellowish gold, owing, in part, to the grass, and also to the breeds of cows, which include Jerseys, Ayreshires, Brown Swiss, New Zealand Fresians, French Normandes, and Holsteins. Several of these breeds

have high concentrations of butterfat in their milk, and this translates to a more golden color in the cheese. The cheese is semi-hard with a distinct buttery flavor and texture, despite its long aging period, and the rind ranges from light pink to tan.

Since he is a computer expert, Mike Gingrich's dream of living on a farm probably seemed foreign to many of his and Carol's southern California friends. But to see how the Gingrichs have embraced their rural lifestyle, and especially how they have demonstrated a strong commitment to the land, it now seems as if it was an instinctive calling all along. Naturally, this is a business for them, but that does not diminish the end result, which is exemplary milk, healthy land practices, a life they and their partners enjoy, and in the end, unparalleled cheese that we can all enjoy as well.

WHAT THEY MAKE

Pleasant Ridge Reserve

HOW TO REACH THEM

Dodgeville, Wisconsin
866-588-3443 (toll-free)
608-935-7030 (fax)
www.uplandscheese.com

# GRUYÈRE WITH ARTIE'S CHERRY COMPOTE

**MY HUSBAND IS THE ONE WITH THE SWEET TOOTH—AND DESSERT-MAKING SKILLS—IN THE HOUSE.** One night, during the height of cherry season, he created this versatile compote. It is excellent served over Crème Fraîche Sorbet (see page 257) or Lemon Ricotta Cake (page 255), and equally good served with a mountain-style semi-hard cheese such as Roth Käse's Gruyère, Uplands Cheese Company's Pleasant Ridge Reserve, Three Sisters' Serena, or an Emmentaler.

Although there are more kitchen gadgets on the market than anyone could possibly use, a cherry pitter is one of those kitchen helpers that I highly recommend. It also comes in handy for pitting certain types of olives.

Preheat the broiler.

To make the compote: In a medium saucepan, combine the water and sugar over high heat. Bring to a boil and cook for 1 minute. Add the cherries and cook for 1 more minute. Reduce the heat to medium and cook for 7 to 10 more minutes, or until the cherries begin to soften slightly. Since they will continue to cook, it is better to take them off the heat sooner rather than later, because they will get mushy. Remove from heat, add the lemon juice, and let cool to room temperature. The cherries will continue to soften and create some of their own liquid as they cool. Set aside. (Makes 1 cup.)

Place the bread slices on a baking sheet and broil for 1 to 1½ minutes, or until the bread is lightly browned. Turn the slices and brush with butter. Broil about 30 seconds, or until the butter is bubbling and the bread is lightly brown. Let cool completely.

Distribute the bread slices among 4 serving plates. Top the bread with cheese slices. Spoon some compote over the cheese and sprinkle with nuts.

Serves 4

## FOR THE COMPOTE

½ cup water

½ cup sugar

1 pound Bing cherries, stemmed and pitted

¼ cup fresh lemon juice (from about 1 lemon)

4 slices brioche or egg bread, crust removed, and cut into 4 equal pieces

1 tablespoon plus 1 teaspoon unsalted butter, melted

4 ounces Emmentaler or Gruyère cheese, cut into 12 thin slices

¼ cup whole blanched (skinless) almonds, lightly toasted (see page 158 for blanching method)

## PERFECT PAIRS

**CHERRIES, ALMONDS, AND** Gruyère all call for Kirsch, a cherry *eau de vie*, which is the traditional accompaniment to these components. But we're talking about wine here—not brandy—so a good choice with this cheese plate would be any fruity, medium-bodied Pinot Noir, Zinfandel, or at the other end of the spectrum, an off-dry Riesling.

# Andrew Rich

**YOU KNOW WHEN THE WORDS "RENEGADE" AND "WINEMAKER" ARE USED TO DESCRIBE** the same person that you're in for something special. Winemaker Andrew Rich fits that description perfectly, and his wines—and even one of his labels—are demonstrable proof of the magic that can occur when a trailblazer takes on the challenge of winemaking.

A self-avowed Francophile from an early age, Rich decided to quit his postcollege job as a travel editor and writer in New York City and head to Beaune, in the heart of Burgundy, France, to study viticulture and enology. When he returned to the United States, he landed a job at California's Bonny Doon Winery, whose owner, Randall Grahm is well known for his outspoken, unconventional views on just about everything, although he is intensely serious about the Rhône-style wines he makes. Rich, a renegade himself, found a kindred spirit in Grahm.

At Bonny Doon Rich started out as a cellar rat—the highly unglamorous point of entry for many would-be winemakers, who spend hours in the cellar pulling hoses, cleaning barrels, and doing any number of undesirable but necessary tasks in a winery. A short time later, Rich was promoted and put in charge of white wine production at Bonny Doon. At the time, that meant making Chardonnay (no longer produced there), Marsanne, and Rousanne. During this time, Grahm introduced his Vin de Glaciere, an ice wine of sorts made from the Muscat Canelli grape; it is a sweet though not cloying dessert wine (and it's a marvelous cheese wine). This exposure to making a dessert wine would come in handy when Rich would one day lend his own name to an Oregon wine.

Eventually, some friends and a passion for Oregon persuaded Rich to make the move north, although he had no job or any prospects. It turned out, however, that he didn't need any. Soon after arriving in Oregon, Rich was lured to Western Australia, where he served as assistant winemaker for one season. When he returned to Oregon, after a short stint with Ponzi Vineyards, he started his own label.

This is when the word "renegade" really came into play. Unlike most Willamette Valley producers, Rich is not particularly passionate about Pinot Noir. His real passion lies with Rhône grapes, although he makes a fine Pinot Noir. "I like Pinot Noir, but I find a really good Syrah from the northern Rhône to be more satisfying." Coming from a Willamette Valley wine producer, this comment could be construed as heresy.

The names of some of Rich's wines may qualify as eccentric, but a few sips tell you that their maker's quiet, almost self-effacing demeanor belies the power and quality in the bottle. Rich named one of his wines Tabula Rasa, or "blank slate," as a reference to his approach to winemaking. "An everyday blend stylistically is similar every year, but I had this idea that you could play with a blend starting with a tabula rasa," he says. Extending this free-wheeling theme, Rich includes on the Tabula Rasa label a stamp from Oenotria, the original Greek name for a place in southern Italy where it is believed the Greeks found grapes. "I think of myself as working in Oenotria—a land of wine and honey where I'm not tied down to making [necessarily] Oregon or strictly Washington wines." So he makes both.

"I like the freedom to play with cool-climate and warm-climate grapes. It's more interesting," he says. "Freedom" seems to be the key word, which is why Rich will tell you that he doesn't like the idea that so many people are tied into varietal labeling. "It's

*Les Vigneaux*

**2001 GEWURZTRAMINER ANDREW RICH VINTNER**

unfortunate since so many blended wines are good ones."

With Tabula Rasa, what's on the bottle is as alluring as what's in it. On the label is a hand-written correspondence between two individuals, A and Z. The nature of the relationship between A and Z and their genders are unknown. The story is meant to be mysterious, and its author (Rich) will reveal no details. The whole idea is delightfully intriguing, not to mention clever, since each new vintage includes a new chapter in the ongoing travails of A and Z. So there is an enticement to buy the next year's vintage.

As to what's in the bottle, the Vin de Tabula Rasa White Wine varies. In 1999 it was an unusual blend of Chenin Blanc and Sauvignon Blanc. In 2000 it consisted entirely of Chenin Blanc. Two-thirds of the grapes came from Washington and one-third came from Oregon. Rich did this because he wanted to get riper grapes, which Washington could provide, but he also wanted the Oregon grapes to keep the wine racier and more minerally. The white wine is an extremely refreshing, crisp wine, with melon and citrus flavors countered by nice structure and a pleasant, round mouthfeel. It's an ideal summer wine and quite good with fresh cheeses.

His other label, Les Vigneaux, which means "little vineyards" and was originally meant to refer to the small growers, designates these wines as varietals rather than blends. Under this label, Rich makes Sauvignon Blanc, Pinot Noir, Syrah, Cabernet Sauvignon (with Washington grapes), a Cabernet-Merlot blend he calls Mésalliance, or "marriage of unequals" (Rich's opinion of the two varietals), and a late-harvest Gewürztraminer, which is an absolutely lovely wine full of spice, fruit, and acidity.

Andrew Rich now makes about four thousand cases, up from five hundred cases in 1995. But despite this very small production, the self-described "vinarchist" does not miss a chance to weigh in on the topic of high-end wine scarcity. "I don't like the idolatry that creeps in. I don't like the cult of wine." Still, he is very serious when he talks about the true value of the fruit of the vine. "With the Tabula Rasa label, I am trying to convey that wine is something that can make your world into Oenotria for a few minutes at the table. Wine does improve your life. It won't change your life, but momentarily it will make life more enjoyable. I hope it does anyway."

WHAT THEY MAKE

**Les Vigneaux**
Cabernet Sauvignon
Cabernet Sauvignon/
Merlot "Mésalliance"
Gewürztraminer
Pinot Noir

Sauvignon Blanc
Syrah

**Vin de Tabula Rasa**
Red Wine
White Wine (Chenin Blanc)

HOW TO REACH THEM

Newberg, Oregon
503-284-6622 (phone and fax)
www.andrewrichwines.com

# KUMQUAT-PEPPERCORN COMPOTE
# WITH SHEEP'S MILK CHEESE

**THIS EASY-TO-MAKE COMPOTE WORKS NICELY WITH MANY DIFFERENT CHEESES, BUT AN AGED SHEEP'S MILK CHEESE IS PARTICULARLY GOOD.** Although the compote is sweet, you can easily turn this into a savory course by adding a bit of prosciutto along with the cheese. In that case, think about serving this cheese plate before the meal, as an hors d'oeuvre.

Preheat the oven to 450°F.

To make the compote: In a medium heavy-bottom pot, bring the water and sugar to a boil. Continue cooking until the mixture is reduced by half, about 5 minutes. Turn the heat to medium-low and add the remaining ingredients except the cheese and bread. Cook, stirring occasionally, until the kumquats are soft, 5 to 6 minutes. Let cool to room temperature. (Makes about ½ cup.)

Cut the bread slices into three pieces each. Place on a baking sheet and toast in the oven until light brown. Turn the slices and toast. Let cool completely.

To serve, place a little compote on each slice of bread. Serve the cheese alongside.

Serves 6

### FOR THE COMPOTE

1 cup water

¼ cup sugar

¼ pound kumquats, cut crosswise into ⅛-inch-thick slices and seeded

2 teaspoons whole peppercorns

1 star anise

6 ounces aged sheep's milk cheese (or use any aged goats' or cows' milk cheese)

6 large slices hearty Italian-style bread

## PERFECT PAIRS

**THE PEPPERCORN IS** mellowed slightly by the cheese, although it still adds a bite, and the orange flavor calls for a like characteristic in the wine. The best accompaniment is an orange or black Muscat dessert wine, a late-harvest Sémillon, or a late-harvest Gewürztraminer.

# Andante Dairy

**THE LYRICAL NATURE OF CHEESEMAKING HAS NEVER BEEN PLAYED OUT QUITE SO** literally as it is at Andante Dairy in Santa Rosa, California. There cheesemaker Soyoung Scanlan is making cheeses like Nocturne, Adagio, Cadenza, Largo, and others whose names—and styles—are borrowed from musical phrasing and the tones and tempos that they imply. Andante is often the tempo used in more languid, songlike classical music pieces, and for Scanlan this meaning captures both an ideal and a necessity: to be able to maintain a slower pace in life and to make cheese at the more traditionally languorous speed. As a name for her cheesemaking operation, Andante captured these ideals and her love of music.

Scanlan has indisputably taken one of the more unusual paths to cheesemaking. She grew up in Korea, which is not a country where cheese is commonplace. But her father traveled the world and would regale her and her brother with stories, including ones about the "fungus-covered cheeses" he would see in other countries. Scanlan says that the idea of such food wasn't entirely foreign to her because Koreans are quite familiar with fermented foods like soy and miso. Still, cheese was not part of the national culinary lexicon.

While in Korea, Scanlan studied biochemistry and molecular biology. She then decided to come to the United States to get her Ph.D.—a plan she abandoned almost as soon as she arrived, owing to an unexpected turn of events. As fate would have it, two weeks after arriving in the United States, while attending a concert at Boston Symphony Hall, Scanlan sat next to a man with whom she began talking, despite her limited English. Her vocabulary must have been sufficient, though, because this man, James Scanlan, ultimately became her husband.

The newly married couple soon moved from Boston to California, and Soyoung, who had had an interest in saving small farms in Korea, realized she could pursue that aim here. She drew on her educational background and decided to pursue dairy science studies at California Polytechnic State University. There she studied milk chemistry for two years, after which not only did she know the physical and chemical properties of milk, but she also had become a die-hard cheese fanatic. She and James had taken several trips to France, where she fell in love with the "fungus-covered" French icons. With her science and academic background, as well as a continuing interest in farming, she decided to try making cheese herself.

Her foray began at the well-regarded goat cheese operation in the Napa Valley called Goat's Leap. Owner Barbara Backus allowed Scanlan to use her cheesemaking room when she wasn't using it. To do so, Scanlan would first have to travel from her San Francisco home to Petaluma, about an hour's drive, and pick up her Jersey milk from Spring Hill Dairy. She then drove another forty-five minutes to Napa to make cheese. At the time, she was making cows' milk cheeses exclusively, although she later began to experiment with goats' milk cheeses too.

In 2001 Scanlan found her own space to make cheese, in Santa Rosa, California. The cheeses she has produced are as unique as her journey to becoming a cheesemaker has been. Her cheeses are informed by her technical background and, equally important, her innate sensibility. Like her, they are soft-spoken yet willful, and each little puff on the snow-white rinds seems to represent a mark of punctuation symbolizing the slow passage of time in their development. They are the ultimate representations of "andante."

One of the loveliest soft-ripened cheeses is one Scanlan calls Nocturne. It is named after her favorite musical pieces by Chopin; the cheese is soft, creamy, and elegant—much like the music. It is square-shaped and, because it is made with the milk of Jersey cows (she still sources from Spring Hill Dairy), it is richer than many comparable cheeses. In appearance, it is similar to some French goats' milk cheeses, but in taste it bears the mark of cows' milk.

Another cheese, called Mélange, is a mix of cows' and goats' milk. The goats' milk makes the cheese whiter in color and adds a bit of tartness to the otherwise rich and creamy cheese. It, too, is a soft-ripening cheese and a real crowd-pleaser. Surprisingly, there aren't a lot of mixed milk cheeses in this country, but Scanlan says she was inspired by her exposure to these cheeses commonly made in Europe. She now makes several such cheeses.

One of the best cheeses made anywhere is the Andante Dairy Picolo. It is a small, cylindrical-shaped triple-crème cheese. Scanlan adds crème fraîche, sourced from Kendall Farms on California's central coast, to her cows' milk and ages the cheese for about one month. The result is a cheese with a thin white rind and an oozing, buttery interior. It is magnificent and seems to last a little longer than most cheeses in this category. It will harden, but it tends to keep for about a month.

Scanlan is continually experimenting, so one never knows what cheese might appear next under the Andante label. She makes Figaro, a mixed-milk cheese wrapped in fig leaves that have been soaked in Sauvignon Blanc, an extraordinary cheese in the St. Marcellin style called Pianoforte; and Adagio, which is a heart-shaped cows' milk cheese. She is passionate about Camembert and is striving to make the quintessential one. There is little doubt that she will achieve that goal. She is tireless in her pursuit, and if her motivation continues to outpace her stamina, the cheese-buying public stands to benefit greatly from the outcome.

## WHAT THEY MAKE

**Cows' milk cheeses**
Adagio
Cadenza
Largo
Legato (Camembert)
Nocturne
Pianoforte
Picolo

**Goats' milk cheese**
Acapella

**Mixed-milk cheeses**
Figaro
Mélange
Metronome
Minuet
Musette
Rondo

## HOW TO REACH THEM

Santa Rosa, California
707-526-0517 (phone and fax)
www.andantedairy.com

# DRIED FRUIT COMPOTE WITH BRIE

**THIS IS PERHAPS AN UNUSUAL CHEESE PLATE IN THAT IT IS NOT FINGER FOOD.** It is meant to be eaten with a knife and fork, since there is no bread with which to scoop it up. If, however, you prefer a few bread slices with your cheese plate, then by all means include them. You may want to choose a hearty bread, perhaps one with walnuts, as an accompaniment. Either way, you're sure to love the way the sweet but tart dried fruit acts as a wonderful flavor and textural contrast to the creamy cheese.

To make the compote: In a medium-sized saucepan, combine all the compote ingredients except the cherries. Bring to a simmer over medium-high heat until the sugar is dissolved. Reduce the heat to medium and simmer for 5 minutes. Add the cherries and continue simmering, stirring occasionally, until the fruit is tender and the juices are reduced to a medium-thick syrup, 15 to 20 minutes. Let cool to room temperature. (Compote can be made 2 days in advance and refrigerated. Bring to room temperature before serving. Makes about 4 cups.)

To serve, place a wedge of cheese on its side on each of 8 individual serving plates. Spoon some compote over the cheese.

Serves 8

Note: It is easiest to cut the cheese when it's cold; bring it to room temperature before serving.

## FOR THE COMPOTE

1¾ cups water

1 cup sugar

¾ cup sweet white wine, such as Robert Mondavi's Moscato d'Oro

⅓ cup fresh lemon juice (from about 1 large lemon)

6 strips lemon peel, each one inch long and ¼ inch wide (a vegetable peeler works best for this)

One 8-ounce package dried Black Mission figs

One 6-ounce package dried apricots

1 cup dried tart cherries (about 4½ ounces)

8 ounces Brie cheese, Camembert, or other soft-ripened cheese, cut into 8 wedges

## PERFECT PAIRS

**THE DRIED FRUITS** together with the soft-ripened cheese call for a wine with raisiny, darker tones. You can go one of two ways: choose an Oregon or Central Coast (California) Pinot Noir, or look to a dessert wine. In the latter category, a natural choice would be to use the same wine with which you made the compote, or one that is similar. Or you might choose a lighter-style port.

# Cabot Creamery

be all too easy to take its product for granted. Cabot has been making good cheese for more than eighty years, and the expectation now is for nothing less than exceptional cheese. But, in fact, making great cheese for such a long time does not just happen—there must be a deliberate plan, with the cheese passing over innumerable refined taste buds along the way, so that it will remain a high-quality item. Cabot Creamery cheddar has passed the test of time and taste buds, and, to a large extent, established the outstanding reputation for Vermont cheddar.

Cabot got its start in 1919, when the owner of a creamery in Cabot, Vermont, decided to get out of the business. Local farmers, upset that they would have no place to sell their milk, banded

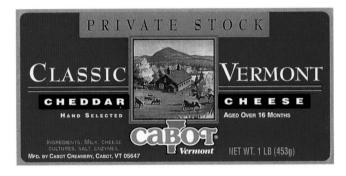

together and bought the creamery. It cost each of them five dollars plus a cord of wood to fire up the furnace, and fire it up they did—all ninety-four farmers. They also ignited a new dairy co-op, which set the stage for the business model that is still in operation today.

Since Cabot Creamery's beginnings, the dairy co-op has grown to include 1,400 farm families throughout New England. Rather than selling on the open market, co-op members sell the milk to the co-op, which, in turn, markets their milk for them. The idea is that the farmers will get a better return from the co-op than if they were to sell their milk on the open market. They also get a so-called "patronage refund" at the end of the year if the co-op finishes with excess revenue. Since much of the milk goes into Cabot Creamery cheese, the farmers enjoy the added bonus that their milk is marketed as a value-added product: cheese. The association of their milk with good cheese helps both them as well as Cabot.

Cheesemaking at Cabot Creamery is done on a grand scale. In just the Cabot plant alone (the other plant is in Middlebury, Vermont), about fourteen million pounds of cheese are made every year. And while the operation has many mechanized elements, it is surprisingly reliant on so-called cheese cooks and cheesemakers—human beings—to bring the cheese to its high quality and ensure its great taste. Many of these hands-on cheese experts at Cabot have been there for decades, including the plant manager, Marcel Gravel, who's been with Cabot for over a quarter of a century.

The cheesemaking facility at Cabot is divided into three main areas. The milk is pumped from the milk trucks to the lower plant. There the milk undergoes initial handling, whether that be removal of fat for making low-fat cheeses, pasteurization, heat treatment, or the like. From there the milk is sent up to the cheddar room, where the cheese cook oversees the bulk of the cheesemaking process. In this phase, the starter cultures and rennet are added to facilitate the formation of the cheese curds. All the while, the cheese cook is monitoring the acid level of the cheese. Although the acidity is always important in cheesemaking, it is particularly so in the making of cheddar cheese. When the mixture has reached the proper acidity, the curds are pumped, along with the remaining whey, to the finishing table. There the whey is drained and the curds are stirred until they once again reach the proper acidity level. Salt is then added, which stops the acidity from rising any further.

Next the cheese curds are put into forty-pound blocks or thirty-eight-pound rounds, all by hand. The blocks and wheels are pressed overnight, after which they are aged for varying amounts of time, depending on the kind of cheddar that is being made. Along the way, the Cabot cheese graders will taste the cheese and determine whether it will be designated as the Cabot Private Stock, which is aged for about two years, the Vintage Choice, which is made somewhat differently but is aged for the same amount of time, or any of the many other cheddar cheeses made by Cabot.

As for Cabot's other specialty cheddars, they truly embody the flavor—and spirit—of cheddar cheese. The Private Stock is one that can be likened to a vintage wine. Just as winemakers will designate certain vintages as particularly special, so, too, will the Cabot graders with certain cheese. The Private Stock's texture is solid rather than crumbly, and its flavor is clean, creamy, and not excessively sharp. It has lovely depth and complexity and is one of those cheeses you will be thinking about long after you have consumed it.

The Vintage Choice is equally good. Rather than being smooth-textured, this cheese is a little more crumbly and its flavor is sharper. It has the unmistakable bite of American cheddar—the very quality that Americans have grown to love—but that sharpness does not enter the realm of bitterness as sometimes happens with other cheeses. It is a truly lovely cheese.

Cabot Creamery also makes a line of low-fat cheddars. In the case of most cheesemakers, such cheese is not usually worth mentioning—not so with Cabot. Their reduced-fat and low-fat cheddars are remarkably flavorful, and what is particularly surprising is that they melt well. Usually, low-fat cheeses do not melt well because they lack fat.

The list of awards garnered by Cabot over the years is too long to mention, but it reflects a company that has shown tremendous commitment to making great cheese and, no less, keeping an eye on improving its products. Some products will never change. Take the Hunter's Cheddar. This harks back to the days when hunters, before heading out, would stop at the plant and ask for the "stinkiest" cheese to hang in their deer camp. The "cheddar-gone-wild," according to a company spokesman, sustained the hunters throughout their hunt. Although hunters may not be stopping by the plant to pick up this sharp and bitter cheese, plenty of people still do. Other Cabot products are possibly more civilized, if just as flavorful and memorable. Perhaps most important, with its long history and superior reputation for quality, Cabot has created and fostered our love for Vermont cheddar.

WHAT THEY MAKE

Cheddar (Mild, Sharp, Extra Sharp, Hunters, Private Stock, Vintage Choice, Light, Organic)
Flavored Cheddar (Feta Cheddar, Five Peppercorn, Garlic & Herb, Habanero, Mediterranean, Roasted Garlic, Salsa, Smoked, Smoky Bacon)
Butter
Cottage Cheese
Sour Cream
Whipped Cream

HOW TO REACH THEM

Montpelier, Vermont
888-792-2268 (toll-free)
802-371-1200 (fax)
www.cabotcreamery.com

# APPLE-PEAR BUTTER ON CHEESE TOASTS

**FEW FOODS ARE MORE COMFORTING THAN CHEESE TOASTS.** The buttery smell that wafts through the kitchen while they're cooking and the visual and flavor transformation of the cheese from solid to melted is heavenly. Apple-Pear Butter is another type of comfort food, and with the cheese toasts, creates a truly memorable cheese plate. The butter can be made up to two weeks in advance and refrigerated.

## FOR THE BUTTER

4 medium apples (about 1½ pounds), such as Gala or Braeburn, peeled, cored, and cut into 1-inch chunks

2 medium pears (about ¾ pound), such as Bosc, peeled, cored, and cut into 1-inch chunks

1 cup apple cider

¼ cup plus 1 tablespoon brown sugar

1 teaspoon fresh lemon juice

¼ teaspoon cinnamon

9 slices white bread, crusts removed

8 ounces cheddar cheese, thinly sliced

To make the butter: In a large, heavy-bottomed pot, combine the apples, pears, cider, sugar, lemon juice, and cinnamon and turn the heat to high. Bring to a boil, then immediately reduce the heat to low. Cook, stirring occasionally, until there is no liquid left, about 2½ to 3 hours. Stir fairly vigorously to smooth out the mixture and then let it cool to room temperature. (The butter will keep, tightly covered, for 2 weeks in the refrigerator. Makes about 1½ cups.)

Preheat the broiler.

Place the bread slices on a baking sheet and toast on one side until light brown, about 2 minutes. Turn the bread and top each slice with some cheese slices. Broil until the cheese is golden-brown and bubbly, about 2 minutes. Cut each slice into quarters.

To serve, spoon some apple-pear butter into the center of each of 6 plates. Surround with 6 pieces of cheese toast and serve. (You will have extra butter.)

Serves 6

## PERFECT PAIRS

**THE CHEESE TAKES ON A** rich, caramel-like flavor once it is toasted. In combination with the sweet butter, a wine with honey and butterscotch flavors is in order. Look for a Washington state or New York ice wine, or any late-harvest wine, such as a late-harvest Sémillon.

# South Mountain Products (Berkshire Blue)

IT'S A FAR CRY FROM NEWSPAPER PUB-
LISHING TO CHEESEMAKING, BUT THAT
is exactly the road Michael Miller has taken. When he sold his Pittsfield, Massachusetts–based newspaper, *The Berkshire Eagle*, in 1995, he knew he wanted to embark on cheesemaking. "A long time ago, I reached the end of a meal with most of my faculties," he relates with a chuckle, "and we had a cheese course of Stilton, roast-ed walnuts, raisins, and port." That cheese course led to a gastronomic epiphany for Miller. He loved the combination of flavors, and he especially liked the cheese. After that, Miller says, there was no turning back.

At first, he thought he want-ed to re-create a Stilton in his scenic part of western Massachusetts. He read the history of Stilton "twice," he says, and he visited the Stilton factories in England. But even after eating some very good Stilton, he wasn't con-vinced that that was the cheese for him. So he put an advertisement in the Specialty Cheesemaker newslet-ter, "Retired newspaper publisher wants to make a raw milk Jersey blue cheese." He ended up answering the summons of Dr. Alan Duffield, who was making just that sort of cheese in Somerset, England.

Miller went to Duffield's Willett Farm Dairy and visited his 16th-century farmhouse. As Miller tells it, not only did he and Duffield hit it off, so did their wives—an important part of the equation, Miller says. Duffield had been making a series of blue cheeses for about twelve years, all with Jersey milk, although he occasionally made goats', buffalos', sheep's, and

organic cows' milk cheeses as well. His Exmoor Blue, however, was the cheese that caught Miller's attention.

The raw-milk cheese, aged forty-five days in England, had that certain something—it could have been the creaminess, the little crystals interspersed throughout, the buttery yet tangy flavor, or all of the above—but this was the cheese Miller wanted to make. He hired Duffield as a consultant, and Duffield made a series of trips to America to teach Miller how to make his Exmoor Blue. In May 1999, Berkshire Blue made its first trip to market.

The reception to this blue cheese has been nothing short of ecstatic. It won first place at the 2002 American Cheese Society competition. This enthusiastic welcome is owing in part to the uniqueness of Berkshire Blue but mostly the praise comes in recognition of the magnificent flavor of the cheese, thanks to Miller's rather extraordi-nary dedication.

On cheesemaking days (there are three of them each week), Miller travels to High Lawn Farm in Lee, Massachusetts, a unique three-thousand-acre Jersey farm that not only has its own milk bottling plant but also is one of the last remaining American farms that still sports its own fleet of delivery trucks. At one time, the historic family-owned farm was known for its high-quality Jersey stock and served as the starting point for a great deal of Jersey breeding for the world market.

Miller picks up his milk at the farm at one o'clock in the morning (his choice because then he can enjoy time at home later in the day), pumps it into his truck, and then returns to the cheesemaking facility in Great Barrington, just up the road. There, he begins the cheesemaking process by adding two starter cultures to the milk. He lets the cultures go to work for three hours, during which time he takes a nap. At about six in the morning, he adds a vegetable rennet, waits for the milk to coagulate, adds the Italian and French mold powders he uses (three in all), and then scoops the curds into five-by-eight-inch molds. The curds stay there for a day or two to drain, and then the cheese is unmolded and put in a saltwater brine overnight. Again, the cheese is left to drain for a couple of days. (This time, the fluid that is draining is mostly salt water. The first draining is mostly an expulsion of whey.) Next the cheese is placed in a maturing room, where it is regularly turned over for the first couple of days, and then is left for about two weeks. It is transferred to the cold room for the next month and a half, after which it is finally ready for market. The end result is a somewhat delicate and intensely creamy rather than crumbly blue cheese. All in all, it certainly does justice to Miller's memories of his first cheese course.

It is rather startling to realize that this publisher-cum-cheesemaker makes over two thousand pounds of Berkshire Blue a month, mostly by himself. Even when things go well, it is a monumental effort. But when things don't go well, his effort is all the more remarkable. The nature of the challenge he faces was underscored in a phone conversation I had with him. In the middle of the conversation, Miller blurts out a non sequitur: "You know, this four-thousand-dollar vat I just bought is leaking," he says casually. "It came from a New York State prison." The vat, of course, holds the milk to make his cheese. Undaunted and no stranger to physical work, Miller calmly stated that he hoped the leak could be spot welded. This "inconvenience" was all in a day's work for Miller, and it unquestionably makes his Berkshire Blue all the more impressive.

WHAT THEY MAKE

Berkshire Blue

HOW TO REACH THEM

Great Barrington, Massachusetts
(no mail order)
413-528-9529 (phone)
413-445-5935 (fax)

# PORT-ROASTED GRAPES ON BLUE CHEESE TOASTS

**WHEN I WAS FIRST MAKING THESE TOASTS, MY HUSBAND ASKED, "WHY ARE YOU USING MASCARPONE?"** My answer was simple: It tastes good. But, actually, taste isn't the only important thing when it comes to good food; texture matters too. As creamy as the blue cheese might be, the addition of mascarpone really smooths out the mixture to give it a lovely mouthfeel. Not to be overlooked, though, the flavor of mascarpone, while mild, serves an important purpose here because it cuts the sharpness and saltiness of the blue cheese. This not only makes for a nice after-dinner cheese plate and segue into dessert, but it also turns it into an ideal companion for the roasted grapes. Although you can use any type of hearty bread you wish, walnut bread really gives this cheese plate a nice rustic element.

1 cup seedless red grapes

2 tablespoons port

1 teaspoon sugar

3 ounces creamy blue cheese, such as Point Reyes Original Blue or Bel Gioioso Gorgonzola

3 tablespoons mascarpone cheese (or cream cheese)

Twelve ⅛-inch-thick slices walnut bread, toasted

Preheat the oven to 400°F.

In a small pan, mix together the grapes, port, and sugar. Roast, shaking the pan occasionally, until the grapes begin to soften and the skins start to shrivel but the grapes are still partially holding their shape, 25 to 30 minutes. Remove them from the oven and let cool.

In a small bowl, beat together the blue cheese and mascarpone.

To assemble, spread about 2 teaspoons of the cheese mixture evenly over each toasted bread slice. Place 3 slices touching in the center of a plate and top with a spoonful of roasted grapes, being sure to include a little bit of syrup from the pan in each serving.

Serves 4

## PERFECT PAIRS

**SINCE THERE IS PORT IN** this dish, and since that is a classic match for blue cheese, the obvious wine choice here is port. If you're not a port fan, select a late-harvest Zinfandel, which you can also use to roast the grapes.

# Goat Lady Dairy

WHEN GINNIE TATE MOVED FROM THE BIG CITY OF CHICAGO TO THE TINY TOWN OF Climax, North Carolina, her only goal was to get a place large enough for one goat. Although she and her brother, Steve, grew up on a farm, Ginnie had chosen nursing as a profession—not farming. She found the place of her dreams in North Carolina: an old tobacco farm where no one had lived for ten years, and where there was no plumbing or electricity. She joined the local Y so she could take regular showers. Although her home was not discussed among the places of the "rich and famous," it was hers.

Ginnie con-
tinued to practice
nursing in nearby
Greensboro, and she
finally did acquire her
one goat—and more.
She also improved her
land, using local

GOAT LADY DAIRY
3515 Jess Hackett Road
Climax, NC 27233
336-824-2163
www.goatladydairy.com

craftspeople to help her restore the buildings on her homestead, which included a one-room schoolhouse. In the meantime, Ginnie's brother, Steve Tate, and his wife, Lee, were living in England, where Steve says he began to see food in a whole new way. "If you change people's philosophy of food, you really can change their life," he says. Seeing the daily shopping ritual at the individual markets abroad was the source of his revelation.

When he and his family returned to the States, Tate immediately got involved in a Community Supported Agriculture (CSA) program, which is a program that helps create a close link between the farmer and the consumer. City-dwellers agree to buy produce each week from the same farm, and a box of that week's bounty is delivered to a volunteer's home for pickup. Working with a CSA furthered Tate's food- and land-based interests, and with that came the inspiration for what would be his and his family's eventual life change.

Tate says that whenever he, Lee, and their sons would visit his sister in North Carolina, he would begin to play the "wouldn't it be fun if . . ." game. The Tates were intrigued with country life and fantasized about adopting it for themselves. Finally, the Tates developed a business plan around the idea of making goat cheese, since Ginnie had already begun to make some cheese in her home (which, by that time, had electricity). Ginnie was also president of the North Carolina Herb Grower's Association, and in that role, she often held basil festivals on the farm. Realizing the success of these festivals, and judging from the small amount of cheese Ginnie was selling, the Tates decided they could create a viable business.

The name Goat Lady Dairy came about because Ginnie, who had been raising goats and was a single woman, was perceived as a bit of an oddity in her part of the country. Since her neighbors weren't exactly sure how to characterize her, they began calling her the "goat lady." The name stuck.

Cheesemaking under this name began in 1995. Ginnie became the cheesemaker, Lee Tate took on goat-tending duties, and Steve learned the art of ripening the cheeses ("It took three years to learn to make a good Camembert," he says); helped with the farming, gardening, and goats; and at that time, continued working part-time as a pastoral therapist, which had been his profession before farming. Today all the Tates maintain their original duties.

The Goat Lady Dairy plain chèvre, called "Fromage," is a lovely, mild, fluffy cheese; it is a perennial favorite. In addition to the plain, they make several herbed varieties. But their standout cheeses— the Camembert, their smoked four-ounce "medallion," and especially their Gray's Chapel cheese—are worth a trip to North Carolina.

The Smokey Mountain Round is quite unlike most smoked cheeses. It is as much a textural as a flavor experience, owing to its surprising creaminess. Many smoked cheeses have a tendency to be firm and even rubbery. This one is actually a fresh cheese done in a hot-smoked style. Tate says he uses different woods to smoke it—whatever is available—and the end result is an unmistakably smoky cheese, but not overwhelmingly so.

Gray's Chapel, named after an old crossroads in the Goat Lady Dairy area of Randolph County, is a rare raw-milk washed-rind cheese. Tate uses an old Trappist monk recipe to make it, and the process is extremely labor-intensive because the cheese must be stirred by hand . . . literally. That does not mean that Tate uses a device to stir the curds. Rather, he uses his own (sterilized) hands and arms to do the stirring, because, he says, he must *feel* how the curd changes to determine when it is ready. "I can tell if it is right by the way it sticks to my arm. It will fall off when it is right," he says. When the curds are ready, he drains off the whey and refills the vat with hot water. He then stirs the curd mixture for ten minutes before scooping it into six-inch molds. He must turn the cheese three to four times within the first three to four hours, and he then presses it lightly for two to three hours. The cheese will dry overnight before it is placed in brine for five hours. It then goes onto fir boards in the ripening room, where he hand-washes and rubs the cheese twice a week with an "aromatic" solution of brine and so-called *Brevibacterium linens*. Aromatic is a polite way of characterizing the downright smelly solution he rubs on this cheese. He turns the cheese every day in order to catch the "good" bacteria and stave off the bad.

The final cheese, aged exactly sixty days, is hugely flavorful, earthy, sweet, and wonderfully creamy. Gray's Chapel straddles the line between semi-soft and semi-hard and has an ivory-colored paste. The rind is pinkish-orange, owing to the wash solution. It is truly a sophisticated cheese, and its only limitation is the small quantities in which Steve makes it.

Although they have shown in their products that they could satisfy even the most discerning cheese aficionado or retailer, the Tates have held their legume-, grass-, and alfalfa-fed herd at fifty goats and have chosen to make only enough cheese to satisfy demand in and around their area of North Carolina.

Their brochure says, "Nurturing the land, our family and our guests through creative work and quality products." They are a family farm that "walks their talk," and their exemplary cheese is convincing proof.

---

WHAT THEY MAKE

Chèvre Camembert
Chèvre Taleggio
Climax Crottin
Feta

Fromage (plain and flavored)
Gray's Chapel
Smokey Mountain Round

HOW TO REACH THEM

Climax, North Carolina
336-824-2163 (phone)
www.goatladydairy.com

# BALSAMIC-DRIZZLED STRAWBERRIES WITH WASHED-RIND CHEESE

LIKE THE SEASON ITSELF, THIS SPRINGTIME CHEESE PLATE IS BURSTING WITH COLOR AND FLAVOR. The strong-flavored, aromatic cheese is a perfect foil for the sweet strawberries and caramel-like balsamic vinegar. Like most cheese plates, the components of this one can be made up to two hours in advance. To do this, make sure the toasted bread slices are cool and then place them in an airtight container; keep the strawberries at room temperature, and, if you have a squeeze bottle, put the reduced vinegar in that once it has cooled. Otherwise be sure the vinegar is in some type of airtight container to keep it from hardening.

½ cup strawberries, sliced lengthwise ¼ inch thick

½ teaspoon sugar (depending on the sweetness of the strawberries)

1 loaf French bread (baguette or round)

2 tablespoons unsalted butter, melted

¼ cup balsamic vinegar

4 ounces aged washed-rind goat cheese, cut into 12 thin slices (use Goat Lady Dairy's, Gray's Chapel, Capriole's Mont St. Francis, Bingham Hill's Angel Feat, Cowgirl Creamery's Red Hawk, or any semi-soft, full-flavored cheese)

Preheat the oven to 400°F.

In a small bowl, mix together the strawberries and sugar. Set aside.

Cut the bread into twelve ¼-inch-thick slices (if using a round loaf rather than a baguette, cut the slices in half crosswise to make pieces that measure about 3 inches wide by 2 inches high). Place the bread slices on a baking sheet and bake just until they are light brown around the edges, about 7 minutes. Turn and brush with melted butter. Bake 2 more minutes, or until light brown. Let cool.

In a small sauté pan, heat the vinegar over low heat. Let simmer until reduced to 2 tablespoons, about 10 to 15 minutes. Cooking it over low heat will help prevent the vinegar from taking on a burnt flavor.

To serve, place 3 toast slices along the edges of each of 4 plates. Using a slotted spoon, spoon the strawberries onto the toast slices. Drizzle the vinegar over the strawberries. Place the cheese slices in the center of the plate in a spokelike arrangement so the slices extend out toward each slice of bread. Serve immediately.

Serves 4

## PERFECT PAIRS

THE EARTHINESS OF THE cheese is countered by the sweetness of both the strawberries and the vinegar. These flavors make several wine options possible, including a fruity Pinot Noir, a medium-bodied Zinfandel, or a white dessert wine, such as a late-harvest Sémillon.

# Chinook

KAY SIMON AND CLAY MACKEY HAVE A REPUTATION THAT EXTENDS FAR BEYOND their home in central Washington. While they are known for their wine, never mind the woefully small quantity in which it's made, they are equally known for their incomparable warmth and hospitality. They have opened their home to legions of people—often strangers—and on weekends, when their tasting room is open, it is Simon and Mackey, not hired help, who are pouring the wine and answering questions. They have no desire to change the way things are.

The couple's sales approach is one indication of their unconventional yet admirable style. They have no salespeople. Although they have been making wine under the Chinook label since 1984, they have held steadfast to the notion that no one can sell their wine as well as they can. They are proud of the relationships they have developed with restaurants and retailers, and they are reluctant to give those up—even when that means making an un-planned trip to Seattle, some four hours away, to fill an emergency order. That happens a lot, but they don't mind.

Both Simon and Mackey have relatively long histories in the wine industry. Mackey grew up in Napa, and Simon studied enology at the University of California at Davis. They met at Chateau Ste. Michelle Winery in Washington, where Simon was a wine-maker and Mackey was a vineyard manager. Their duties at Chinook fall along these lines today, although they also do sales as well as distribution these days.

Simon and Mackey's first Chinook vintage was in 1984—the same year they were married. At that time, their winemaking facility, housed in the original farm buildings on their property, was bare-bones. In 2001 they finished building their new winery, which, although compact, is efficient and state-of-the-art. It shares space with fruit orchards, vineyards, nut trees, an herb and vegetable garden, a quaint tasting room, and a fully equipped kitchen where Simon bakes bread, often made with herbs and nuts from the property, for visitors to the tasting room. The tasting room is also where the couple do most of their entertaining, preferring to keep their nearby Prosser, Washington, home more casual.

Although they make only about three thousand cases per year, Simon manages to put out quite a few different wines. Among those is her Chardonnay. It spends ten months in the barrel, but only 30 percent of the wood is lightly toast-ed new oak. This translates to a wine that has subtle vanilla notes and pear and pineapple flavors. This light oak style, among other qualities, is the basis of the couple's winemaking—and sales—approach. "We sell on the basis of our wines being approachable, regional, drinkable, and that they express the character of the region because we don't over-oak," says Mackey. It is fact rather than hyperbole.

In addition to selling the wine themselves, Simon and Mackey have made the surprising decision to withhold their wines from wine journalists who assign scores to wines. They are more interested in another type of critic. "What has changed our wine the most is the reaction from people in our tasting room," says Simon. She and Mackey get instant customer feedback because they are the ones pouring the wine. They also have the opportunity to hear people's general comments about wine, including their fear of it. "Every weekend," says Mackey, "people apologize about their lack of knowledge." He blames the wine press for this. "[The rating system] has led to a whole group of people who are uncomfortable with their likes and dislikes. It's a shame," he says. Mackey qualifies his statement, saying that if people wish to rely on a third party to sift through the huge number of wines that exist, that's fine. But he discourages people from allowing the final ratings to determine what is good and what isn't. Choosing the right wine is simply too subjective for that, Mackey says.

The Chinook wines are not the least bit daunting. The Cabernet Franc is a particular standout, with layers of raspberries, plums, vanilla, and wisps of smokiness. Simon also makes an unusual Cabernet Franc Rosé, which is a great food wine, especially in the middle of summer, when a cool and crisp wine is in order.

As refreshing as the Chinook wines is the attitude of the winemakers. Kay, Clay, and their two golden retrievers live a simple life making an agricultural product. They are fundamentally content with their lifestyle and grateful for it too. "We're doing what we love, we're making a living, we're interacting with great people. What's more exciting than that?" asks Mackey. Hard to imagine.

## WHAT THEY MAKE

**White wines**
Chardonnay
Sauvignon Blanc
Sémillon

**Rosé**
Cabernet Franc

**Red wines**
Cabernet Franc
Cabernet Sauvignon
Merlot

## HOW TO REACH THEM

Prosser, Washington
509-786-2725 (phone)
509-786-2777 (fax)

# GOUDA, SAUTEÉD APPLES, AND CUMIN-OIL CROSTINI

**IN HOLLAND ONE OF THE OLDEST AND MOST POPULAR CHEESES IS CALLED LEYDEN.** It is a Gouda-style cheese that is flavored with cumin seed. This cheese plate is a variation on that theme. Instead of using a Leyden-like cheese, this plate separates out the cumin from the cheese through the use of easy-to-make cumin oil. Sweet apples, Gouda's other popular companion, take this dish from savory to sweet. You can save any leftover bread for another use, or make extra bread slices for this dish.

½ teaspoon ground cumin

1 tablespoon plus 1 teaspoon olive oil

1 large (about ½ pound) tart-sweet apple, such as a Braeburn, Gala, or Jonagold, cored and cut into ½-inch slices to yield 16 slices

2 tablespoons sugar

1 tablespoon unsalted butter

1 walnut or other hearty-style baguette, cut into twelve ¼-inch slices

6 ounces best-quality medium-aged Gouda cheese, such as Winchester Gouda, cut into 12 thin slices

Preheat the oven to 400°F.

In a small bowl, vigorously whisk the cumin and olive oil together. Let rest for at least 15 minutes and up to 6 hours to allow flavors to meld.

In a medium bowl, toss together the apple and sugar. In a large sauté pan, heat the butter over medium-high heat until bubbly. Add the apples and cook, turning often, until they are heated through but still hold their shape, 4 to 5 minutes. Let cool to room temperature.

Place the baguette slices on a large baking sheet and bake until golden-brown, about 6 minutes. Turn the slices and brush them with the cumin oil. Bake until light brown, 3 to 5 minutes. Let cool. The toasted bread slices can be made up to 2 hours in advance, cooled, and kept in an airtight container.

To serve, place 3 slices of bread side by side on one side of each of 4 individual serving plates, with the slices slightly overlapping. Put the slices of cheese in the center of the plate, and spoon the apples onto the side of the plate opposite the bread.

Serves 4

Note: The apples and cheese can be plated up to 1 hour before serving. Cover loosely with plastic wrap. Do not add the bread slices until ready to serve, or they will get soggy.

## PERFECT PAIRS

**THE SPICE OF THE CUMIN** and the creamy yet slightly pungent cheese coupled with the tart-sweet apples makes this plate a good match for a spicy, floral Gewürztraminer, a late-harvest Sauvignon Blanc, or late-harvest Sémillon.

# L'Ecole Nº 41

**WINEMAKER MARTIN CLUBB WALKS INTO A ROOM AND HE INSTANTLY LIGHTS IT UP.** His wine has a smiliar effect. L'Ecole Nº 41 is one of Washington's better-known wine labels, and Clubb has been instrumental in making it so.

The winery, located in the Walla Walla Valley, was begun in 1983 by Jean and Baker Ferguson. Ahead of their time, the Fergusons had purchased an old schoolhouse in the late 1970s with the intention of turning it into a winery, although neither of them had experience in the business. They released their first wines, consisting of Chenin Blanc, Sémillon, and Merlot, and with them they launched what would become a family business.

The Fergusons made about one thousand cases each year for the first six years. But deciding that the business presented more of a challenge than they wanted as retirees, they invited their daughter Megan and her husband, Martin (Marty), Clubb to come up and make the wine. The Clubbs had high-powered jobs in San Francisco, and the allure of country life was compelling. They packed their things, grabbed the kids, and headed north.

Having no experience as a winemaker, Marty took courses in winemaking at the University of California at Davis. He also credits nearby winemakers Rick Small from Woodward Canyon and Rusty Figgins from Glen Fiona Winery for helping him get his start. In 1989 he released his first vintage of Merlot.

L'Ecole Nº 41 is named for its setting at Number 41 Lowden School Road in the town of Lowden. At one time Lowden was called Frenchtown because of the large number of French Canadians who settled there. *L'Ecole* translates as "school." Wine is made in the basement of the school, which was built in 1915, and the recently renovated tasting room is located in a former classroom. The creaky wood remains, and the room is awash in sunlight that streams in through the large picture windows.

The story of the colorful L'Ecole label, which features a schoolhouse, captures part of the magic of the larger L'Ecole story. In 1984 the family asked all of the elementary school children in the extended family to draw an image that could be used on a wine label. Eight-year-old Ryan Campbell won the friendly competition, and his schoolhouse drawing remains the focus of the L'Ecole Nº 41 label (today Campbell is an architect). The label has since been slightly embellished by the work of Megan and Marty Clubb's two children and by the addition of a guardian angel drawing in memory of Jean Ferguson, Megan's mother.

L'Ecole Nº 41 is best known for its Sémillon and Merlot. Although few American wineries make Sémillon, L'Ecole makes three. All are distinctive and eminently drinkable as well as outstanding cheese wines. The Barrel Fermented Sémillon is the only one of the three that is a blend. Although it varies from year to year, it contains about 15 percent Sauvignon Blanc. The wine is crisp and fall-like with hints of figs and honey and a whisper of vanilla. Although Sémillon is often thought of as a blending grape or the star of

France's heralded Sauternes, Clubb has given it such meaning that one wonders why more American winemakers don't make Sémillon.

Clubb's Merlots (he makes three) also demonstrate how one grape can be elevated to exceptional levels, owing to the winemaker's skill. It begins in the vineyard, where Clubb spends much of his time. He is intent on having one grape cluster per shoot and adequate spacing between vines to let the sunlight in. "If you do your work in the vineyards, there's no need to sort," he maintains. L'Ecole is a partner in the highly regarded Seven Hills Vineyard in the Walla Walla Valley, and many of the winery's grapes are grown there.

Like all of the L'Ecole Merlots, the Columbia Valley Merlot contains small amounts of Cabernet Sauvignon and Cabernet Franc. The bright berry overtones along with hints of oak are its dominant features. The Walla Walla Valley Merlot, which is aged in 50 percent new oak, is complex, deeper, and richer; and the single-vineyard Seven Hills Vineyard Merlot, which is aged in 55 percent new oak for eighteen months, has the most tannins and also the greatest complexity. The dark fruit is incredibly alluring, and it is clear that the wine will hold its own nicely for years to come.

Another wine, Pepper Bridge Apogee, is a favorite among the wine press for good reason. It, too, is a Merlot blend, although it has a greater concentration of Cabernet Sauvignon, and the grapes come from the highly acclaimed Pepper Bridge vineyard. The wine is aged in both French and American oak and its flavor is reminiscent of spice, plums, cherries, and chocolate. It is another wine one can enjoy now or later.

No doubt, when the Clubbs moved to Washington they couldn't imagine that the little schoolhouse-turned-winery would be the source of a 25,000 annual case output. And although Megan Clubb has maintained a job outside the wine industry as an executive in a Walla Walla bank, Marty Clubb reports to work at the schoolhouse in shorts and wearing a smile. If only school had been that much fun.

---

WHAT THEY MAKE

**White wines**
Chardonnay
Semillon (*Barrel Fermented / Columbia Valley, Fries Vineyard, Seven Hills*)

**Red wines**
Cabernet Sauvignon (*Columbia Valley and Walla Walla*)
Merlot (*Columbia Valley, Seven Hills, Walla Walla*)
Pepper Bridge Apogee

HOW TO REACH THEM

Lowden, Washington
509-525-0940 (phone)
509-525-2775 (fax)
www.lecole.com

# MOM'S PLUM-MANGO CHUTNEY WITH AGED ASIAGO

**MY MOTHER LOVES SWEET AND SALTY COMBINATIONS, SO, NOT SURPRISINGLY, SHE CAME UP WITH THIS SWEET RECIPE AS THE PERFECT CONTRAST TO SALTY CHEESE.**

## FOR THE CHUTNEY

1½ pounds medium-sized plums (about 6), such as Santa Rosa

1 large mango (about 1 pound), peeled, pit removed, cut into ½-inch pieces

1 cup packed light brown sugar

1 scant cup cider vinegar

1 cup coarsely chopped onion (about ½ large onion)

⅓ cup golden raisins

2 tablespoons chopped fresh ginger

1 large clove garlic, minced

½ teaspoon red pepper flakes

2 tablespoons balsamic vinegar

Dash of salt

½ French bread baguette, cut into 18 slices

6 ounces aged Asiago cheese, cut into 6 wedges (or use Parmesan, cheddar, dry Jack, or other aged, full-flavored, slightly salty cheese)

---

## PERFECT PAIRS

**THE SALTY, NUTTY CHEESE,** together with the tropical flavors in the chutney, is probably best paired with a fruity wine such as an off-dry Riesling or Gewürztraminer. If you would prefer a dry wine, then again, choose a Gewürztraminer or the hybrid, Cayuga White.

As it turns out, the mango, ginger, and plum make a wonderful combination with almost any full-flavored cheese. One other direction you can go is to spread a little mascarpone or cream cheese on a cracker and top it with a dollop of the chutney. Although it takes about three hours to make the chutney, it will last, refrigerated, for two months.

To make the chutney: Cut the plums in half lengthwise. Gently twist the halves in opposite directions to dislodge the pit. Slice the plums about ½-inch thick and then cut each slice in half.

Cut the mango into ¾-inch pieces, avoiding the fibrous material around the pit.

In a large nonreactive pot, combine the plums with the remaining chutney ingredients and bring to a boil. Reduce the heat to low and simmer very slowly, stirring occasionally, until the mixture is quite thick and most of the juice has evaporated, 2 to 3 hours. Taste the chutney. You may need to add a little more sugar or vinegar to strike the proper balance. Remove from the heat and let cool to room temperature. (The chutney will keep in the refrigerator for up to two months. Makes about 2 cups.)

Preheat the broiler.

Place the bread slices on a baking sheet and toast on both sides in the broiler.

To serve, place a wedge of cheese on each of 6 plates and top with about 2 tablespoons chutney (you will have extra chutney). Pass toasted bread slices separately.

Serves 6

# Three Sisters Farmstead Cheese

ALTHOUGH IT IS NAMED FOR THREE SIS-
TERS, THREE SISTERS FARMSTEAD CHEESE
is really a company consisting of just one of the three
sisters and her dad—so far. At age nineteen, Marisa
Hilarides began learning about farmstead cheese side
by side with her father, Rob, at a weeklong cheese
course given by California Polytechnic State University
at San Luis Obispo. Although the family had a dairy,
they had never made cheese before. For a variety of
reasons, not the least of which was because Rob
Hilarides wanted to develop a business that his daughters would be interested in, the family decided
cheesemaking would be a good enterprise
to pursue.

Marisa recalls the decision-
making process in the earliest
days of the fledgling cheese
business. "As a family, we sat
down and tasted every cheese
in the book," she says. Rob
and his wife, Jeannie, and
the three girls, Marisa,
Lindsay Jean, and Hannah—
homed in on the cheese characteristics and textures they
liked the most. They then called in
an expert from a company that provides starter culture bacteria, who
helped them make their first batch of cheese
based on the criteria they'd given him. From there,
Serena—a loose amalgam of the three sisters' names as
created by their grandmother—was born.

The time was August 1999, and the Hilarideses
had no cheesemaking room of their own. So Marisa
would drive thirty minutes to the town of Visalia to
use the cheesemaking equipment at another acclaimed
cheesemaking operation, Bravo Farms. And because
Bravo Farms' owner, Bill Boersma, made cheese during
the day, Marisa was confined to nighttime cheesemak-

ing. Complicating matters was the fact that her cheese
was quite different from the cheddar and other
cheeses Boersma was making. Serena requires a higher cooking temperature, and Boersma's vats were slow
to climb to that temperature. For Marisa, that meant
she had to wait longer between the stages of cheese
production, so she ended up working long hours into
the night. Fortunately, all that is changing.

After a long, hard battle, the Hilarideses have
gotten permission to build a new dairy that will house
a state-of-the-art cheese room and milking parlor, a
room from which to view the cheesemaking and
milking, and two or three cheese-aging and
-storage rooms. The Hilarideses are planning to have a very large herd of nine
thousand cows, which will supply
milk for far more than their
cheese! For Marisa, it will mean
working closer to home and
being able to increase the
amount of cheese she makes,
because she will have a place
to store it.

Like many American arti-
san cheeses that are unique to
the cheesemaker, Serena too, has
no exact equal. It is a hard cheese that
can fall comfortably in both the grating
and eating categories. It is neither a sharp nor a
salty cheese, but it is extremely flavorful. It captures
the slight bite that Parmesan imparts, and it also has
the sweetness and nuttiness that is typical, perhaps, of
a Gruyère. Its texture falls between the two as well—a
little crumbly, but also somewhat smooth.

To make Serena, the milk is slowly heated along
with the rennet. Once the curds are ready, they are cut
and the whey is drained. Hilarides then scoops the
curds into twenty-pound hoops, which are lined with
cheesecloth so that the curds won't stick to them. The

wheels of cheese are pressed for twenty-four hours, after which time they are brined for another twenty-four hours. The wheels are then aged on metal racks for two months before they are transferred to vertical wooden slots, where they are aged for approximately five more months. Hilarides says that most people prefer the cheese when it is a little older, and she is experimenting with aging the cheese for as long as two years. She says it mellows as it ages—the sharpness becomes rounder, yet the cheese retains its nutty and assertive flavors.

Although it remains to be seen whether Marisa's sisters will decide to don cheesemaker hats, for now Marisa is doing an admirable job of starting and running the business virtually by herself. At any given moment, she might be making the four-hour drive to San Francisco to conduct an in-store tasting, or she might be zipping home to make cheese. Or she and her mother might be designing a label or packaging the cheese together. It's a growing business, and Marisa's father hopes that one day she and her sisters will eventually buy it back from him. His own interest is in the larger dairy operation.

Serena has been met with nothing but accolades and awards. As the Hilarideses gear up for higher production and better facilities, it appears that the cheese with the three sisters' names will become a household word sooner than we think.

WHAT THEY MAKE

Serena

HOW TO REACH THEM

Lindsay, California
559-562-2132 (phone)
559-562-9596 (fax)
www.threesisterscheese.com

# MELON, MACADAMIA NUTS, HONEY, AND PARMESAN CHEESE

ONE AFTERNOON WHEN I WAS CUTTING SOME MELON FOR LUNCH, I SUDDENLY HAD THE IDEA TO COMBINE A SALTY CHEESE WITH IT. The cheese I chose has a particular nutty flavor that reminded me of macadamia nuts so I sprinkled a few macadamia nuts on the cheese to enhance that flavor. I then drizzled a little honey over the nuts, which was no great stretch, since the melon I was eating was honeydew. That's how this refreshing cheese plate came about, and now it is one of my favorites. Since there's virtually no preparation time involved, you can make this recipe at the last moment, or get everything ready ahead of time and assemble it in no time. Also, when choosing a cheese, it is important to select one that is aged, has an element of nuttiness to it, and is salty enough to contrast with the honey and melon. Fortunately, there are many choices of cheese in this category, including cheeses from all three milk types—cows', sheep's, and goats'. Simply choose the one you like the most.

1 pound ripe honeydew melon or cantaloupe (about ½ a small melon)

One 2-ounce piece of aged nutty cheese, such as Serena, Parmesan, extra-aged Gouda, Asiago, or aged sheep's milk cheese, shaved into 16 thin slices

1 tablespoon honey

2 tablespoons roasted, lightly salted macadamia nuts (preferably dry-roasted), finely chopped

Cut the melon into twelve ¼-inch-thick slices. Cut the flesh away from the rind in one piece.

Arrange 3 slices of melon on each of 4 individual dessert or salad plates. Arrange 4 slices of cheese, overlapping, on the melon slices. Drizzle the cheese with the honey and top with macadamia nuts. Serve immediately.

Serves 4

## PERFECT PAIRS

THE MELON AND HONEY call for similar flavors in the wine. Opt for a sweet white dessert wine such as an ice wine, made from Muscat or Vignoles or a late-harvest Chenin Blanc or Sémillon.

# Hunt Country Vineyards

**LIKE MANY OF THE WINERIES IN NEW YORK'S FINGER LAKES AREA, HUNT COUNTRY VINEYARDS** is steeped in regional history. Art Hunt, co-owner of the winery with his wife Joyce, is the sixth generation to live on the hilly land perched above the west side of Keuka Lake. The Hunts before him planted orchards, hay, and grapes. They also raised sheep and ran a dairy farm. Although Art did not grow up on this fertile land, he was the only one of his siblings who was interested in continuing to cultivate it. The dream became a reality when he and Joyce moved to the family land in 1973.

At that time the vineyards covered just eighteen acres, and the grapes were the native Concord and Niagaras. The Hunts expanded the grape growing after being told that their land on Italy Hill Road was the best in the county for grape growing because of its glacially formed shale soils. Like many of their cultivating grapes neighbors, the Hunts sold their grapes to the Taylor Wine Company. But when that huge company stopped sourcing their grapes locally, Art Hunt converted his home winemaking hobby into a business. Shortly after doing so, he came upon a revelation—that it was the quality of the fruit that was important to the quality of the wine, not so much his expertise as a winemaker. He was convinced his grapes were notable.

In 1986 the Hunts hired Tim Benedict to be their winemaker. Benedict had trained under the winemaker at nearby Goosewatch Cellars, and the music-major-cum-winemaker turned out to be the perfect fit for the Hunts. Since then Benedict has grown the winery, making ten thousand cases of fifteen different wines. Many of those wines are consistent award-winners.

Among them is a dessert wine that is made from the hybrid grape Vidal. Called Vidal Ice Wine, this wine with 17 percent residual sugar makes as much of an impression as the cobalt blue bottle in which it comes. Despite its high sugar content, it is not syrupy—just pleasantly sweet. Joyce Hunt, who does the public relations and marketing for the winery, explains that the Vidal grape has nice acid and because it is a tough-skinned grape, it is able to hang on the vine longer, where it can develop more sugar. In this case, the grapes are harvested and pressed in December. As Hunt says, the grape has "staying power." That's true in the bottle as well, Hunt says, pointing to ten-year-old Vidal Ice Wines she's tried that have developed honey flavors, as opposed to the younger ones, which taste a little like burnt sugar.

The feature that stands out above others in the Hunt Country wines is their delicacy. No "in your face" wines here, although they are by no means mousy. Benedict uses a deft touch to carefully craft the wines, exploiting the full potential of the grapes rather than masking them with winemaking tricks. So while there's a pleasant amount of oak in the Hunt Country Chardonnay, it is not the first feature to jump out. Instead, the stainless-steel-fermented and oak-aged wine unfolds, exposing buttery and light vanillin qualities, while the fruit maintains full expression.

The same is true with another hybrid wine the Hunts make called Cayuga White. The grape, which was developed at nearby Cornell University in the 1970s, is somewhat similar to Riesling, with its hints of peaches and apples. The Hunt Country version is sweet but not cloying, maintaining 1 to 2 percent

residual sugar. Joyce Hunt says she likes to drink this wine with any food that might have a fruit glaze, such as duck.

In the summer of 2001, the Hunt Country Vineyards sherry, consisting of Chardonnay and Riesling, won "Best Dessert Wine" at the Atlanta International Wine Summit. Taking into account that this sherry is not made in the Spanish *solera* tradition—where the wine is continually cared for and aged in special barrels—taking top honors was quite a feat. Rounding out the dessert wine category, Benedict makes a port and a wonderfully refreshing late-harvest Vignoles.

When Benedict isn't working magic on his grapes, he's making music on his set of drums. Reluctant to render his Eastman Music School education completely useless, he lends his talent to the community all-star big band. Art Hunt is general manager, and is not only running the business. On any given day, he can be found repairing a tractor, painting some siding, or most recently, expanding the tasting room.

One of the older wineries in the region, brimming with history, Hunt Country Vineyards has its footing very much in the future. The subtle hand behind the wines has created extremely memorable ones; they are balanced and interesting, and they are marvelous examples of the quality wines that New York is clearly capable of producing.

WHAT THEY MAKE

**White wines**
Cayuga White
Chardonnay
Classic White
Cream Sherry
Foxy Lady (*second label; Blush, Red, White*)
Late-Harvest Vignoles
Riesling

Seyval Blanc
Vidal Ice Wine
Vignoles

**Red wines**
Cabernet Franc
Classic Red
Hunter's Red

HOW TO REACH THEM

Branchport, New York
800-946-3289 (*phone*)
315-595-2835 (*fax*)
www.huntcountryvineyards.com

# QUINCE PASTE WITH DRY JACK CHEESE

QUINCE PASTE, KNOWN AS *MEMBRILLO* IN SPANISH, IS THE TRADITIONAL ACCOMPANIMENT TO SHEEP'S MILK CHEESE IN SPAIN. Here, though, it is paired with another aged cheese, the perennial favorite dry Jack. You can, of course, pair it with any aged cheese you like. Quince paste will last, refrigerated, for up to six months, making it a perfect cheese accompaniment anytime.

The paste is simple to make, calling for only four ingredients. It does, however, take some planning ahead, as it needs to set overnight. Once made, though, it will last for up to three months, so the effort really pays off. Besides, it's a great way to stretch out the short quince season, which extends from November to early January. Quince can be found in produce markets, farmers' markets, and some grocery stores.

> 1¼ pounds quince (about 3 medium), cut into eighths, tops and seeds removed
>
> ½ cup water
>
> 1¾ cups sugar
>
> 1 tablespoon fresh lemon juice
>
> 6 ounces dry Jack cheese (or any flavorful aged cheese), sliced

In a large, heavy-bottom pot, place the quince and the water. Bring to a simmer, cover, and reduce the heat to low. Cook, stirring occasionally, for 35 to 45 minutes, or until the quince are quite soft. Let cool to room temperature.

Put the quince in a food mill or sieve (do not use a food processor), and mill or press the quince back into the same pot. Add the sugar and lemon juice, and cook over medium heat, stirring constantly, until the mixture thickens considerably and pulls away from the sides, 30 to 35 minutes.

Scoop the mixture onto a flat plate, platter, or baking sheet and smooth to a uniform ½-inch thickness. Let cool to room temperature. Cover the quince paste with plastic wrap and refrigerate overnight. (If you are making the quince paste in advance, after it has set overnight, wrap it well in waxed paper and then in plastic wrap and keep refrigerated. It will last up to six months.)

When ready to serve, cut the quince paste into 3-inch squares or 3-inch x 1-inch rectangles, allowing 1 to 2 slices per person. (You may have some quince paste left over.) Serve the cheese alongside the quince paste.

Serves 6

## PERFECT PAIRS

QUINCE PASTE IS QUITE sweet, but with the dry Jack, it takes on a savory note. This sweet and savory combination is mirrored nicely by sherry. The nuttiness in the cheese and the wine and the sweet notes of the wine make this combination about perfect. Choose a medium-dry sherry. If you'd rather have a dessert wine, then select a late-harvest Muscat, Sémillon, or Vignoles.

PICNICS

# P R O F I L E S | R E C I P E S

Camembert with Honey-Rhubarb Compote
on French Rolls, recipe on page 215

# Behrens & Hitchcock

LES BEHRENS HAS A DISTINCT ADVANTAGE AS A CUTTING-EDGE WINEMAKER. "I HAVE this inability to know my limits," he confesses. It is this "handicap" that has catapulted his wines into ninety-point and above scoring territory as judged by the esteemed wine critic Robert Parker. It is also this tendency that has made the Behrens & Hitchcock wine label one that is constantly sought out by those in the know.

Behrens and his wife, Lisa Drinkward, met Bob (aka Joe Bob) Hitchcock and his wife, Lily, when they all lived in Humboldt County, the northernmost county in California. Behrens was a carpenter by trade, but when his wife, an accomplished cook, wanted to open a restaurant, he promptly put down his tools and became host and manager of the establishment, Folie Douce. (The name is French for "sweet madness," and apparently it aptly characterized Behrens and Drinkward's highly successful restaurant from the day it opened.) Drinkward was the chef.

As host and manager, Behrens needed to know something about wine. "My experience with wine went pretty much from zero to sixty," he says. In fact, Drinkward remembers her first date with Les when he knew enough only to order a glass of the "house white." Winery partner and general manager Bob Hitchcock jokes, "You know, maybe if he'd ordered the house red…" But things soon changed, as Behrens immersed himself in learning everything he could about wine.

Behrens and Drinkward's highly acclaimed restaurant (which remains in business today, although they sold it to one of their waitresses) soon became known for its seasonal, French-influenced food as well as its expanding, well-chosen wine list. Behrens estab-

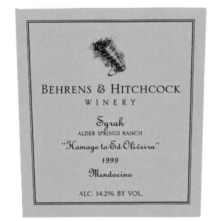

lished personal relationships with many wineries in Napa and Sonoma counties, and rather than having the wine sent to the restaurant in Humboldt, he would drive the five hours to pick it up. Although he did not know it at the time, these contacts would serve him well down the road.

In the meantime, Behrens was so bitten by the wine bug that he decided he wanted to try making his own. Enter Hitchcock, who had done some accounting work for Behrens and Drinkward. Behrens went to Hitchcock, told him his "harebrained" idea, and asked Hitchcock if he would finance the start-up costs.

After running the numbers, Hitchcock thought the scheme made sense, and in 1993 he and Behrens became formal partners.

With their tabletop crusher and purchased grapes, the partnership produced 175 cases of Cabernet, Merlot, Zinfandel, and Petite Sirah the first year. The next year, they increased production to 750 cases, but in between, Behrens says, he asked just about everyone he knew exactly how to make wine.

Behrens says his primary winemaking education came from a longtime winemaker in the Humboldt area named Ed Oliveira of Oliveira Winery. Although Oliveira died in 1999, Behrens remembers the education he got from the man fondly and with reverence, and he has named one of his wines after his friend and teacher. It is a Syrah and is called The Homage to Ed Oliveira. The wine is made from Mendocino County grapes (Mendocino County is south of Humboldt County, and about 100 miles north of San Francisco), aged in new French oak, and captures the notorious blackberry and coffee flavors typical of great Syrahs.

The bright orange Behrens & Hitchcock label is eye-catching and elegant, a standout in a sea of hundreds of Napa Valley wines. The wine inside might be a Cabernet Sauvignon, or the highly acclaimed blend of Syrah, Cabernet Sauvignon, Merlot, and Cabernet Franc they call Ode to Picasso, or possibly a Merlot—Behrens & Hitchcock's flagship wine. Few winemakers manage to coax out the intrigue of the Merlot grape the way Behrens does. While it has the silky elegance of many West Coast Merlots, it has a complexity that few of them capture. It is at once fruity and dry, and its almost-black color carries the notion of color extraction to new heights.

The winery produces more than one Merlot, and the difference in styles makes the wines seem like they are made from different grapes. The Oakville Merlot, from the heart of the Napa Valley, is their benchmark wine—rich, ripe, and luscious—while the Merlot grapes from their Las Amigas vineyard, at the much cooler southern end of the Napa Valley, produce a more austere, less fruit-forward wine, although one that is equally interesting.

Behrens & Hitchcock has managed to be successful since its first vintage, but the turning point for the winery came when their wine made its way to wine critic Robert Parker. A New York distributor who happened upon the Behrens & Hitchcock wine urged the two partners to send him their Cuveé Lola, a blend consisting mostly of Cabernet Franc. The distributor was going to be seeing Parker and wanted him to taste their wine. At 8 A.M. the day after Parker tasted the Behrens & Hitchcock wines, Behrens received a call from the distributor. On the other end he heard no "hello," only the words "Robert Parker is going to make you a star." Apparently Parker had uttered two comments: "I am blown away," and "Who are these people?" To say that Behrens and Hitchcock were buoyed by this response is a serious understatement.

Behrens & Hitchcock now produces nearly five thousand cases annually, and the partners have no desire to grow any larger. "All the fun would go out of it," says Drinkward. Each of their mostly vineyard-designated wines is made in small lots, much like at the very beginning of their operation. They do very little to manipulate their wine, believing that the grapes tell the story—not the winemaker. During Drinkward's frequent visits to the vineyards some of the bad fruit is eliminated, although once the fruit reaches the winery, they still hand-sort every cluster to make sure each

grape that goes into their wine is top quality.

The winemakers' homey attitude is further reflected in their sales philosophy. They prefer to place their wines in small local markets rather than in high-end restaurants because "those are the real people—the people I want at my dinner table," says Behrens.

Drinkward, Behrens, and Bob and Lily Hitchcock display a rustic, can-do attitude that has helped them transcend challenging economic hurdles and their decided lack of experience. Hitchcock puts it best when he says, "Fortunately, we're all people who can look at something and see the possibilities." Indeed.

### WHAT THEY MAKE

Cabernet Sauvignon (*Alder Springs, Kenefick Ranch*)
Cuveé Lola
Homage to Ed Oliveira Syrah (*Alder Springs*)
Merlot (*Alder Springs, Las Amigas,*
*Oakville*)
Ode to Picasso (*Blend—Syrah, Cabernet Sauvignon, Merlot, Cabernet Franc*)
Petite Sirah

### HOW TO REACH THEM

St. Helena, California
707-942-4433 (phone)
707-942-5919 (fax)

# TWO-CHEESE PANINI

**THIS ITALIAN-INSPIRED SANDWICH CALLS ON TWO COMPLEMENTARY CHEESES TO MAKE IT SPECIAL.** In this case, the mild, creamy cows' milk Fontina is countered by the richer sheep's milk cheese. The peppery arugula gives the sandwich a nice edge, as does the freshly ground black pepper. Although this recipe calls for focaccia, if you cannot find a quality focaccia, then opt for a traditional French baguette instead.

In a small bowl, toss the arugula with 1 tablespoon of the olive oil. Set aside.

Cut the focaccia or baguette in half horizontally. Use the remaining 2 tablespoons of olive oil to brush on the bottom side of the bread. Layer on the tomatoes, arugula, sheep's milk cheese, then the Fontina cheese. Sprinkle with pepper to taste, and top with the other slice of bread. Wrap in parchment to transport.

Serves 4

## PICNIC TAKE-ALONGS
- Marinated peppers and olives
- Pasta salad
- Extra chunks of sheep's milk cheese
- Cantaloupe
- Amaretti (light almond cookies)

1 cup arugula leaves

3 tablespoons olive oil

4 pieces of focaccia, measuring about 4 x 4 inches, or use a French baguette

2 Roma tomatoes, cut into ¼-inch-thick slices, seeds removed

2 ounces aged sheep's milk cheese (or use aged goats' cheese or cows' milk cheese such as Serena, Parmesan, or Asiago)

4 ounces Fontina cheese

Freshly ground pepper

## PERFECT PAIRS

**THE CREAMY FONTINA** provides the dominant texture in these panini, while the arugula adds a bit of a bite. Choose a crisp, slightly fruity Arneis or Pinot Gris for white wines. Or, for a red wine, think about a Carignane, Sangiovese, or medium-bodied Merlot.

# Hedges Cellars

OF ALL THE COUNTRIES IN THE WORLD, THE SCANDINAVIAN COUNTRY OF SWEDEN would seem like one of the least likely to provide the inspiration for an American businessman to start a winemaking business—in Washington state, no less. But Sweden was apparently looking for good red wine, and Tom Hedges, who was a Washington state food broker, was approached by a client to produce it. Hedges and his wife, Anne-Marie, enthusiastically embraced the idea, and in 1987 they started Hedges Cellars.

The wine they created, a blend now called Hedges Columbia Valley after the location where the grapes are grown, still constitutes the bulk of the 55,000-case output of Hedges Cellars. For many wineries, a lower-priced blend is often an afterthought following the making of the premium varietals, but Hedges Cellars was founded on producing this wine. It is far above average in both concentration and flavor. Although the makeup of the blend varies, the Columbia Valley red wine now contains a small amount of Cabernet Franc and Syrah, as well as the two main grapes, Cabernet Sauvignon and Merlot. Altogether the wine is multilayered, with flavors ranging from bright raspberry to chocolate notes. The moderate oak adds complexity to the wine, making it an enjoyable wine to drink now or to cellar for a few years.

Hedges Cellars is a family affair, with Tom's brother, Pete, running the day-to-day operations at the winery and Tom and Anne-Marie heading up the business at their new tasting room and winery offices in Issaquah, Washington, east of Seattle. Hedges Cellars is

not a typical Washington winery. While most of the northwest state's wineries are relatively small, the Hedges' French chateau-like winery built in 1995 makes a grand statement. The majestic edifice contrasts with its rather shy and intense winemaker, Stephen Lassard. Although he is a quiet man who seems intent on staying out of the spotlight, his wines are pushing him to the forefront in spite of himself.

It was Lassard, for example, who requested that aerial photographs be taken of the Red Mountain Vineyard in order to see where the areas of low and high vigor were within the vineyard. The aerial view helped him to pinpoint exactly which grapes to pick—and when—for his high-end Red Mountain Reserve, and he also used the photographs to figure out which blocks within the vineyard to focus on for making this particular wine in the future.

The mostly Cabernet wine, blended with about 15 percent Merlot, comes from one of Washington state's most highly regarded vineyards, located within the state's recently designated American Viticultural Area (AVA)—Red Mountain. The grapes for this wine are thicker-skinned and more intense. This intensity naturally translates to the spicy, deep berry-colored wine. The Red Mountain Reserve is aged in both new and old French oak. But just because the fruit is from Red Mountain does not necessarily mean that all of the wine will end up in this vineyard-designated bottle. After one year, Lassard tastes through the barrels and selects the final Red Mountain Reserve from among the barrels. This wine consistently garners high scores from the wine press.

The Hedges' only white wine is the hugely popular Fumé-Chardonnay. Winemaker Lassard spares this uncommon blend from an overdose of oak, thereby allowing the pear and apple flavors from the Chardonnay and the citrus flavors from the Sauvignon Blanc to come through. "There's enough oak coming out of California. We're trying to represent Washington state by making this style of wine," says Lassard. The Fumé-Chardonnay accounts for about 20 percent of the winery's total production.

Even though Hedges Cellars makes a lot of wine, the winery produces only four different wines. Pete Hedges says limiting the number of wines they produce helps the winery retain its focus and maintain the high quality of the wines. The Hedges' other wine, Three Vineyards blend, is a blend of Cabernet Sauvignon, Merlot, and Cabernet Franc. The grapes come from the Hedges' own vineyards in the Red Mountain district and from the Red Mountain Vineyard itself. The idea, Hedges says, is to make a wine that shows a strong sense of place. With its layers of cherries and blackberries, herbs, and dessert-like chocolate and vanilla flavors, this wine accomplishes that.

It's a long way from Sweden to Benton City, Washington, but when a wine is good, it doesn't take much to attract international attention. Hedges Cellars has really done Washington state a service by producing excellent wine in a relatively large quantity. The Hedges and Lassard have shown that good business practices, forward-thinking, and, most of all, focused and talented winemaking, can be done on almost any scale, and the end result is truly excellent wine.

## WHAT THEY MAKE

**White wine**
Fumé-Chardonnay

**Red wines**
Columbia Valley
Red Mountain Reserve
Three Vineyards

## HOW TO REACH THEM

Issaquah, Washington (*tasting room and offices*)
425-391-6056 (*phone*)
800-859-WINE (9463) (*toll-free*)
425-391-3827 (*fax*)

Benton City, Washington (*winery*)
509-588-3155 (*phone*)
509-588-5323 (*fax*)
www.hedgescellars.com

# CAPRESE SALAD ON A STICK

**I CALL THIS A PICNIC ON A STICK BECAUSE STICKS, OR SKEWERS, ARE WHERE ALL OF THE MAIN INGREDIENTS RIDE, MAKING THE DISH ESPECIALLY EASY TO TRANSPORT.** Just put the sticks in airtight containers and you're ready to go. Although the recipe calls for bocconcini, which are small balls of mozzarella about 1 inch in diameter, you can also use a regular hunk of mozzarella and cut it into chunks. The basil oil can be made up to 1 week in advance, and leftover oil can be used to flavor a risotto or marinate vegetables.

1 cup packed basil leaves, stems discarded

1 cup olive oil (not extra-virgin)

½ baguette, sourdough or plain, cut into 1-inch squares (bring the other half of the baguette along on the picnic)

½ pint cherry tomatoes

1 pound whole-milk mozzarella cheese, preferably bocconcini (the small balls of mozzarella; or cut a large mozzarella into ¾-inch chunks)

Salt and freshly ground pepper

20 wooden (soaked in water for 1 hour prior to use) or metal skewers

Preheat the broiler.

In a blender, place the basil leaves along with the oil. Blend well. Pour the basil oil into a jar and set aside. (The oil will keep, refrigerated, for 1 week.)

In a large bowl, toss the bread squares with 2 tablespoons of the basil oil. Thread the bread squares onto 8 skewers so that the chunks of bread are barely touching, about 6 squares per skewer. Broil, turning occasionally, until all sides are light brown. Let cool completely. Store the bread skewers in an airtight container.

Assemble the tomatoes and mozzarella on the remaining skewers. Alternate 5 tomatoes and 4 pieces of cheese on each skewer. Place these skewers in 1 or 2 large airtight containers. (Do not store in the same container with the bread skewers.) They should fit in one layer. Pour the basil oil over the cheese and tomato skewers, turning to coat. Sprinkle with salt and pepper to taste. (Remember that mozzarella has little or sometimes no salt, so make sure to use salt fairly liberally.) Let the skewers sit for at least 1 hour and up to 6 hours before serving.

Each person will have 2 skewers of bread and 3 skewers of tomatoes and cheese.

Serves 4

## PERFECT PAIRS

**MOZZARELLA IS A VERY** mild cheese, but the tomatoes manage to bring out the best in the cheese. Because of the tomatoes and the basil, a light-bodied Sangiovese, Dolcetto, or a refreshing rosé is your best bet.

## PICNIC TAKE-ALONGS
- Roasted chicken
- Remaining baguette plus extra, if desired
- Carrot, jícama, and fennel sticks
- Parmesan chunks
- Brownies

# Westrey Wine Company

**WITH HER DEGREE IN PHILOSOPHY, AMY WESSELMAN, WINEMAKER AND CO-OWNER** of Westrey Wine Company in McMinnville, Oregon, waxes philosophical about her approach to winemaking. "It's all about two things, yum and yuck." The wines made by the winemaker along with her partner, David Autrey, unquestionably fall into Wesselman's category of "yum."

Wesselman and Autrey, both graduates of Reed College in Oregon, began working in the wine industry while they were students, although Autrey's exposure to wine began much earlier because his parents were good friends with some of Oregon's founding wine families. "I grew up around the Adelsheims and Ponzis as a child. I played in the vineyards," he recalls. During their senior year, Wesselman and Autrey helped John Paul at Cameron Winery doing odd jobs around the winery. Not long after, they headed off to Burgundy to learn the art of making Pinot Noir.

Wesselman says this trip to France was a "soul-searching experience." It was the first time she really understood loyalty to the greater good because of the intense hard work and team effort involved in transforming grapes into wine. But even more, she liked the idea of being oriented toward smell and taste in a world geared largely toward sight and sound. Autrey echoes this sentiment, adding, "Burgundy confirmed something we loved, and the ability to make great Pinot was something we wanted to pursue."

At age twenty-five and twenty-eight, respectively, Wesselman and Autrey were possibly Oregon's youngest winemakers in 1993, the year they produced their first vintage under the Westrey label. (The name is a combination of their two last names—WESselman and autTREY.) They chose to create their own winery in addition to working for other winemakers (Autrey still works very closely with Bethel Heights winemaker Terry Casteel) because they, like most winemakers, wanted complete control over their product. A look inside the building that houses their facility, in downtown McMinnville, reveals a small but well-planned space filled with barrels, and an adjacent, equally small, room where the wine is made. It is a no-frills spectacle. Clearly the Westrey glamour is reserved for what goes inside the bottle.

For the two winemakers, the quality of the bottle's contents begins with their carefully chosen vineyards. So important are the vineyard sites to them that the two are naming their newly purchased vineyard (the only one they own) Oracle. Autrey, also a philosophy major, believes that the word "oracle" is consistent with the idea and his belief in the notion of terroir. According to Autrey, wines communicate the symbiosis that exists between the vine and the land. If you're getting mixed signals from a wine, he says, you have to go back and look at the land the vines are growing on and see how the vines are interpreting the growing conditions. He and Wesselman buy grapes from several other highly regarded vineyards throughout Yamhill County, including Abbey Ridge (just above their new Oracle vineyard), Bethel Heights, Freedom Hill, Temperance Hill, and Shea Vineyards.

Once the grapes are harvested, winemaking becomes a joint and equal effort for Wesselman and Autrey. Although Wesselman has a demanding "day job" as executive director of one of the world's best wine events, the International Pinot Noir Celebration, and Autrey handles "90 percent" of the marketing, he says that all the decisions about the wine are made jointly. This unified philosophy of winemaking results not only in fine wine, but in some rather daring decisions as well. For example, they make Chardonnay from two different clones—one that is made for the type of climate found in the Willamette Valley and another that is really meant for warmer climates. Why struggle with the latter? They have figured out how to tame that particular clone's excessively tart qualities and turn it into a gorgeous wine that expresses the grape. Autrey believes that a good Chardonnay is very much about good texture and richness. He and Wesselman also believe in a long, cool fermentation for their Chardonnay. Although they risk minimizing the wine's aromatic qualities, by striking a balance they can bring forth the wine's textural qualities. Westrey's method also helps keep the yeast cells (or lees) in suspension longer, which develops the wine's richness. Their Chardonnays are 100 percent barrel-fermented in 25 percent new oak.

The Westrey Pinot Noir is unquestionably their raison d'être. Autrey puts his affection for it succinctly: "I love it," he says. He and Wesselman are likely also drawn to the inherent challenge in making Pinot Noir. It is an extremely difficult grape to finesse, yet they have figured out how to get maximum color extraction and a firm structure to the wine. Given that their second favorite wine to drink is Burgundy (after their own, of course), it is no surprise that their wine is similar in style—multilayered, earthy, with tobacco, tar, as well as dominant black fruit characteristics.

Although both Autrey and Wesselman are extremely deliberate in their winemaking style, they are also drawn to the art because of the unknowns. "When you think about it," Autrey says, "great winemakers have between thirty and forty shots to get it right in a lifetime—that's pretty unique." Wesselman feels similarly. "Winemaking as farming keeps you really sane with respect to how you feel control in the world," she says. She and Autrey have learned to work with nature by listening to it, responding intuitively to its output, and eventually turning it into liquid magic.

WHAT THEY MAKE

Pinot Gris
Chardonnay (*Reserve, Lane, Temperance Hill*)
Pinot Noir (*Abbey Ridge, Oracle, Shea, Temperance Hill, Willamette Valley*)

HOW TO REACH THEM

McMinnville, Oregon
503-434-6357 (*phone*)
503-474-9487 (*fax*)

# CUCUMBER SOUP WITH MINT PESTO AND FETA CHEESE

**THIS SOUP, WHILE EXCELLENT TO TAKE ON A PICNIC ON A WARM SUMMER DAY, IS EQUALLY GOOD EATEN RIGHT AT HOME.** No matter where you are, you'll enjoy the cool flavors punched up by the tart, refreshing mint pesto. Both the soup and the pesto can be made in advance. Make the soup the day before and prepare the pesto up to a week ahead. Drizzle the pesto with a thin film of olive oil before refrigerating it.

### FOR THE SOUP

3 medium cucumbers (about 2 pounds), peeled, seeded, and cut into chunks

1⅔ cups sour cream

⅓ cup plain yogurt

1 medium jalapeño chile, seeded and coarsely chopped

1½ tablespoons lime juice (about ½ lime)

Kosher salt

### FOR THE PESTO

3 cups mint leaves (about half a large bunch)

2 tablespoons slivered almonds, lightly toasted

½ small (about 6 ounces) red onion, coarsely chopped

2 tablespoons white wine vinegar

1½ tablespoons lime juice (about ½ lime)

3 tablespoons olive oil

Kosher salt

3 ounces feta cheese, crumbled

To make the soup: In the bowl of a food processor or blender, combine all the ingredients except the salt. (If using a blender, cut the cucumber into ¼-inch dice before blending.) Process until smooth and creamy, about 30 seconds. Taste and add a small amount of salt. Process again just until the salt is mixed in. Taste again and add more salt or lime, if needed. Put in a thermos and refrigerate.

To make the pesto: Combine all the pesto ingredients in a food processor or blender and process until smooth. Add just enough salt to bring out the flavors in the pesto. (Don't forget that both the soup and the cheese have salt.) Mix and taste. Process again. You will still have flecks of mint, but the pesto should be fairly runny. (Makes about ⅔ cup; save any extra for another use. It will keep, covered and refrigerated, for 1 week or frozen for up to 1 month.)

To serve, pour the soup into bowls or cups. Place a large dollop of pesto in the center of the soup and sprinkle on a generous portion of cheese.

Serves 4

## PERFECT PAIRS

**THE SOUP, ALONG WITH** the rest of the menu, calls out for a refreshing Pinot Gris or Sauvignon Blanc.

### PICNIC TAKE-ALONGS

- Baguette or other bread, sliced
- Rice or couscous salad (a nice salad might include raisins or currants, nuts, cilantro, some orange peel, and maybe a little extra feta cheese)
- Grilled prawns
- Fruit on a stick (fresh fruit slices on skewers)
- Angel food cake

# Green Mountain Blue Cheese

JUST TWO MILES FROM THE CANADIAN BORDER IN NORTHEAST VERMONT STANDS the eight-hundred-acre Boucher farm. A third-generation Vermont farming family (and twelfth-generation of a North American farming family), the Bouchers have long been in the business of producing milk and meat, among other farm products.

Dan Boucher and his wife, Dawn, live on a seventy-five-acre parcel of the Boucher family farm, which belongs to Dan's parents. (The senior Bouchers as well as Dan's brother and sister-in-law live there too.) A few years ago the family convened to devise a long-term business plan for the farm. The brothers and their spouses came up with independent plans. Dan and Dawn were convinced they needed to lessen their dependence on the fluid milk business, as they saw milk prices continuing to decrease. Their solution was twofold: sell veal and make cheese. Dawn Boucher was already making cheese and butter for home consumption, and she was an avid cook, making—rather than purchasing—almost everything they ate. The idea was to become entirely self-sufficient.

Dawn put together a business plan for a cheesemaking operation. To get started, she cashed in her life insurance policy and borrowed money from family members. She then began designing her cheesemaking room, visiting every cheese operation that would open its doors to her. On her own she came up with a generic design for a plant and began building it (on little bits of paper), although she did not yet know what type of cheese she would be making. It was a solid design, and in the end the only change that was made was the addition of a window in the cheese aging area. She outfitted the cheesemaking room with hand-hewn and used equipment, save for one plastic shovel. Because of this low-cost approach, the Bouchers have been able to pay down their debt in a much shorter time than many such start-up cheese operations can.

To determine the type of cheese to make, Dawn says she and Dan did extensive market research. They visited their local cheese shop and literally bought every cheese there. They continued to buy new cheeses as they came in, and eventually they were able to create a list of cheeses that met their taste and price criteria. Fifty-two experimental recipes later, Dawn Boucher settled on the three blue cheeses she now makes: Vermont Blue, Gor-dawn-zola, and Wild Blue. She sold her first cheese in March of 1998.

Vermont Blue is a dark-blue-veined stirred-curd cheese. To make it, Dawn starts at 5:30 in the morning, when the cows are milked. The milk is sent via a pipe directly from the milking parlor into the cheese room. A starter is added to the milk, and the milk is left for forty minutes. Boucher then adds a vegetable rennet and allows the curds to set up for well over an hour. She then stirs the curds at intervals, to help extract the whey. Once most of the whey is drained off, the remaining curds are put in molds that were fabricated by the Bouchers. The curds are then left to drain further. The cheese is then unmolded and placed in pans, where it is hand-salted and drained for two to three days. After this time, the cheese is taken out of the pans and placed on mats until it is dry to the touch. Boucher then pierces the cheese to allow for oxygen to circulate, which promotes the veining. Then she places the cheese in the curing room, where it is turned constantly for two weeks. Finally, it is wrapped in foil and put in the cold aging room for about three months.

The cheese that emerges is an extensively veined cylindical cheese on which a thin blue mold rind has formed. It is fairly dry and has a musty, earthy flavor and loads of complexity. It is modeled loosely after the French cheese called Fourme d'Ambert, which is a classic. It is neither strong nor mild with a distinguishable yet not overpowering blue "flavor." Vermont Blue was a favorite of the judges at the American Cheese Society just one year after its debut.

The flavor of Boucher's Gor-dawn-zola, named after its maker, is a bit stronger. Although it is a blue cheese, Boucher says the goal in this cheese is to capture the meaty, beefy qualities of Italy's well-known Taleggio cheese. Gor-dawn-zola is similarly creamy, and it has tinges of the peach-colored rind found on Taleggio, but it is distinctly a blue cheese. Boucher

ages it for four months or more, and during that time the cheese attracts different types of molds (all good ones) that serve to develop its appealing flavors.

The milk for the Green Mountain Blue Cheese comes from 165 Holsteins and Holstein crossbreeds. The Bouchers are working on increasing the protein and butterfat levels of their milk, and they believe that crossing their cows with Jerseys and Normandes will help them achieve that goal. The cheese production is rather small—about four hundred pounds a month—but it's enough to keep the operation viable and to stock select stores around the country.

Dawn Boucher says the business has grown just large enough that she is in need of an assistant. That help may be Dan Boucher, who is contemplating relinquishing his milking duties and donning a cheesemaker hat. At this point, the Bouchers' meat business, which has grown to include pork and beef, along with the cheese, is fulfilling their business plan. And Dawn's cheesemaking skills are fulfilling the needs of this country's ongoing love affair with blue cheese.

WHAT THEY MAKE

Gor-dawn-zola
Vermont Blue
Wild Blue

HOW TO REACH THEM

Highgate Center, Vermont
802-868-4193 (phone)
802-868-7395 (fax)
www.vtcheese.com/vtcheese/vtblue/htm

# CHICKEN "WALDORF" PITAS

**HERE IS A MODERN TWIST ON A SALAD CLASSIC.** The addition of blue cheese is a natural when it is paired with refreshing grapes and apples, and the chicken adds a pleasant toothsome element. This easy-to-assemble salad is lighter than the traditional Waldorf because it has far less mayonnaise, which makes it welcome fare during hot picnic weather.

1 whole chicken breast (about 1 pound), broiled or grilled and cut into ½-inch dice

2 large green apples (about ¾ pound), such as Pippin or Granny Smith, cut into ½-inch dice

1 cup red or green grapes, halved

⅔ cup diced celery

½ cup pecan halves, lightly toasted

½ cup blue cheese (crumbly or creamy style—both are fine)

2 tablespoons mayonnaise

4 large leaves butter lettuce

4 pita pocket breads

In a medium bowl, mix together all of the ingredients except the lettuce and bread.

Carefully cut a 3-inch slit in each pita. Gently guide your fingers into the bread to create a pocket. Be careful not to tear the bread. Insert 1 piece of lettuce and follow with a scoop of the salad mixture. Repeat with the remaining bread, lettuce, and salad. Wrap each sandwich separately in parchment or butcher paper. Keep as cool as possible before serving.

Serves 4

## PICNIC TAKE-ALONGS
- Pita chips, or a plain or sourdough baguette, sliced
- Extra blue cheese
- Red potato salad
- Mixed olives
- Lemon squares

## PERFECT PAIRS

**THE BLUE CHEESE IN** these sandwiches provides the most pronounced flavor, so choose a wine accordingly. Knowing that most red wines do not go well with blue cheese, stick with a white wine, sparkling wine, or rosé. Specifically, Pinot Gris is a good choice, as is a Viognier. Or you might want to select a sweeter wine with a little bit of effervescence, such as Muscat.

# MouCo Cheese Company

CHEESEMAKER AND FORMER BREWMASTER ROBERT POLAND SAYS THE NAME OF HIS company, MouCo, came about by asking some cows how to spell their favorite word. "M-o-o," he says, was pronounced "mo," which wasn't right. So he sounded out the name and came up with M-o-u. Okay, so he didn't exactly have a conversation with a cow, but Poland was looking for a name that would be catchy, playful, and capture a bit of European styling, owing to his wife, Birgit's, heritage.

Birgit Halbreiter grew up in Germany in a cheesemaking family. Her father, Franz, has been making cheeses like Camembert, Limburger, and ricotta for nearly fifty years. He also makes the hugely popular Camembert-Gorgonzola hybrid cheese called Cambozola at the Champignon Cheese Factory in Germany. Birgit also made cheese, although when she met her future husband, a professional brewer working for New Belgium Brewing Company in Fort Collins, Colorado, she was working in the brewing business. The couple met at a brewing conference.

Poland and Halbreiter remained in the brewing business, but they gradually set their sights on another fermentation business—cheese. The couple had access to exactly one gallon of raw Jersey milk once a week through a Community Supported Agriculture (CSA) program, and with that milk they began to make cheese. They maintained their jobs in the brewing business, but they worked on their cheese and were able to transform the butterfat-rich Jersey milk into a cheese that Poland says was like a quadruple-crème Brie. Those who were lucky enough to taste it knew that Poland and Halbreiter were on to something. For the next few years, they continued making cheese at home, soliciting input from Birgit's father and honing

their skills along the way. Finally, they turned their home cheesemaking hobby into a business and sold their first official MouCo cheese in June 2001.

Today, the milk for MouCo Camembert comes from a few nearby farms (it is now Holstein milk instead of Jersey). Because of Poland's knowledge of fermentation and Halbreiter's cheesemaking heritage, they are turning out a Camembert that has the flavor and texture of a double- or triple-crème soft-ripening cheese, even though the MouCo cheese has no added cream.

One of the distinguishing characteristics of the MouCo Camembert is how the flavor develops as the cheese ages. Although it is made in a fashion similar to other soft-ripening cheeses, Poland set out to create a cheese whose salt and acidity remain in balance throughout its six-week shelf life. Achieving such a balance is not easy. Usually, a Camembert or Brie is rather bland when it is young, and by the time it is at the end of its life, it has become ammoniated and salty. (The "in-between" time of a week or two is the best time to eat these types of cheeses.) While Poland cannot prevent the cheese from becoming ammoniated because of the bacteria in soft-ripened cheeses, he has figured out a way—through the use of certain cultures—to keep the cheese flavors in balance.

The texture of the MouCo Camembert is another noteworthy characteristic. Again, because of the types of bacterial cultures Poland uses, the cheese develops a soft and creamy texture almost from the beginning. Usually soft-ripened cheeses start out quite firm. Achieving this soft consistency is very difficult and quite possibly explains why there aren't more artisan Camemberts and Bries made in the United States. (The relatively short shelf life and difficulty in shipping these cheeses when they are ripe are other factors that limit the production of these cheeses in this country.)

Poland makes twenty-one batches of cheese at a time, all by hand. The milk is put in small buckets where it is cultured and renneted. Once the curds have formed and developed the firm texture Poland is looking for, they are scooped into the molds, where the excess whey drains for about twenty-two hours. The cheese is then unmolded and immersed in a brine. Poland then puts the cheese on racks and wheels it into the curing room where it stays for about two weeks. After that, the five-ounce Camemberts are ready for market.

As a former musician and professional snowboarder, Poland is no stranger to adventure. Moving from beer making to cheesemaking is an example of that adventurous spirit. As for the future, Poland hopes to draw on his father-in-law's experience and eventually make a soft-ripened blue cheese similar to Cambozola. If he is successful, Poland can be sure that the name MouCo Cheese Company will become a household name.

## WHAT THEY MAKE

Camembert

## HOW TO REACH THEM

Fort Collins, Colorado
970-498-1017 (phone)
www.mouco.com

# CAMEMBERT WITH HONEY-RHUBARB COMPOTE ON FRENCH ROLLS

**RHUBARB IS A HARBINGER OF SPRING, APPEARING IN THE STORES AROUND MARCH AND STAYING THROUGH JUNE.** In this compote, the bright red stalks become a lovely shade of pink, which is also reminiscent of the season. This tart-sweet compote can be made up to a week in advance and refrigerated, making it an easy do-ahead item for a picnic. All you need to do is pick up some bread and cheese (and wine, of course), and you're ready to go.

To make the compote: In a large sauté pan, combine the rhubarb, water, and honey over medium heat. Cover and cook, stirring occasionally, for 10 to 15 minutes, or until the rhubarb is very soft and falling apart. Remove from the heat, add the vinegar, and let cool to room temperature. Allow the flavors to meld for at least 1 hour and up to 6 hours. Or refrigerate overnight. Bring to room temperature before using. (Makes about 1 cup. You will have extra compote.)

To assemble the sandwiches, spread about 2 tablespoons of the compote onto the bottom half of each roll. Add 3 slices of cheese and top with the other half of the roll. Wrap in parchment paper.

Serves 4

## PICNIC TAKE-ALONGS

- A grain and herb salad, such as tabbouleh or a barley salad
- Crudités
- Aged sheep's milk cheese and crackers
- Whole strawberries
- Slices of lemon-poppyseed cake

### FOR THE COMPOTE

1 pound rhubarb, cut in ¼-inch-thick pieces

2 tablespoons water

6 tablespoons honey

1 teaspoon balsamic vinegar

6 ounces Camembert cheese, cut into 24 equal-sized slices (or use Brie)

Four French rolls (approximately 6-inches long), cut in half lengthwise

## PERFECT PAIRS

**RHUBARB IS ONE OF THOSE** vegetables that is not known for its wine-friendliness, but the honey helps rectify that problem. The sweet-sour combination, although challenging, can usually find its match with a high-acid wine that has some sweetness. Try a Washington state or New York Riesling, or even a chilled Muscat. Although the latter is normally a dessert wine, it goes beautifully with savory dishes, too. Besides, what's better for a picnic than a cool, crisp, slightly sweet glass of wine?

# DeLille Cellars

IF THE STATE OF WASHINGTON SET OUT TO GENETICALLY CONSTRUCT THE QUINTESSENTIAL wine spokesperson, it would be Chris Upchurch, the winemaker at DeLille Cellars in Woodinville, Washington. Upchurch is positively evangelical about the wines and the grape-growing conditions of his adopted state, and he is not reluctant to share his enthusiasm. "Nobody believes in Washington state fruit more than I do," he says emphatically.

Originally from the East Coast, Upchurch grew up in a wine-drinking family. While working at a restaurant while in college, he learned that he had a genuine passion for wine. He got involved in wine retailing, a vineyard and grape brokerage business, worked as a sommelier, and dabbled in winemaking. This latter pursuit, he says, was his calling.

DeLille Cellars is located about twenty-five miles northeast of Seattle. No grapes are grown in the cold, wet area—they come from eastern Washington—but the small town of Woodinville is home to several wineries nonetheless. Although perched above a busy stretch of road, the driveway to DeLille Cellars transports a visitor to a different world. Modeled after small Burgundian estates, the DeLille property features a little pond surrounded by a few goats, sheep, chicken, and even a peacock. It is wooded, and the building itself is lodgelike with its wood interior, cross beams, and fireplace. Below the common area is where Upchurch performs his alchemy.

The signature DeLille wine is called Chaleur Estate, and like almost all of the DeLille wines, it is a

blend. Upchurch says that the goal with this one was to create a wine that did not yet exist in Washington—a high-end blend. Chaleur Estate is made up of Cabernet Sauvignon, Merlot, and Cabernet Franc, and as such it is a typical meritage, or Bordeaux blend. Also as in Bordeaux, Upchurch has created a so-called declassification system, where only the finest lots go into the Chaleur Estate.

Chaleur Estate, says Upchurch, begins in the vineyard—not in the winery. From the very beginning, he is looking at the vineyards with an eye toward the final blend—he is not focusing on any single variety. Once the grapes are picked, they are pressed and separated out into twenty different lots. Then the blending trials begin. Upchurch says he will look at all the lots and know that somewhere in the winery is the very best blend. The road to making Chaleur Estate has begun, but it is not an easy road. Upchurch explains making the finest blend is not simply a matter of taking the best of those twenty lots and combining them. It is like working a puzzle, where the pieces must fit together precisely. No single grape should overpower the others; each should complement the others, and, together, the grapes should create an explosive "whole."

Underscoring the inherent difficulties of the task, Upchurch talks about one time when he could not figure out why his blend wasn't working the way he had hoped. He brought in a winemaker from a nearby winery who immediately told him that he had too much of an exceptional lot in the blend. By reducing the amount of the standout lot, he was able to bring the entire wine into balance. All along, he had thought that the good lot was the one that should be emphasized—not minimized.

The consumer is the unquestionable beneficiary of DeLille's declassification system. To make Chaleur Estate a near-perfect blend, some of the good lot excess has to be reserved for another use. That excess then goes into making wines in DeLille Cellars' second label, D2, another very respectable family of wines. Just like in Bordeaux, the lots that do not make it into the first label wines are bottled under a second label. And also as in Bordeaux, the declassified wines are usually exceptional in their own right.

The qualities of Chaleur Estate are nearly indescribable. Just as Upchurch intends, no single feature jumps out and declares its prominence. Instead his wine consists of a polite selection of lots in which each delicately holds up the other, ensuring that no particular one gets undue attention. Together they form an elegant deep-burgundy-colored wine with appealing black cherry notes bolstered by gorgeous but not overbearing oak and light vanilla flavors.

Upchurch also makes a white wine in the Bordeaux style. Called Chaleur Estate Blanc, it is a Sauvignon Blanc–Sémillon blend that is barrel-fermented sur lie and unfiltered. The bottle alone is regal, owing to its French-influenced cursive label, and the contents are equally noble. Crisp yet round hints of oak but not overpowered by wood—the blend is luscious, not to mention somewhat unusual in this country because of the use of the Sémillon.

The DeLille Cellars production is small, and in its decade or so of production, the winery has developed a fiercely loyal following and garnered exceptionally positive critical acclaim. Although Upchurch focuses on Bordeaux varieties, he has also kept a keen eye on the Syrah grape since making his first vintage in 1997 with this grape. He firmly believes that the future of Syrah in Washington state is practically unlimited.

Upchurch's winemaking skill cannot be overemphasized. His approach is highly intellectual, but it is equally visceral. No wine has captured the personality of its maker more than Chaleur Estate. It is the essence of Upchurch in its complexity, and at the same time it manages to be eminently approachable.

## WHAT THEY MAKE

**White wine**
Chaleur Estate Blanc

**Red wines**
Chaleur Estate
D2
Doyenne (Syrah)
Harrison Hill (single-vineyard blend)

## HOW TO REACH THEM

Woodinville, Washington
425-489-0544 (phone)
425-402-9295 (fax)
www.delillecellars.com

# GRILLED SHRIMP AND CRANBERRY BEAN–GOAT CHEESE SALAD

WHILE FALL IS THE TIME WE TRADITIONALLY SEE FRESH CRANBERRRY BEANS, THEIR SEASON ACTUALLY BEGINS EARLIER, IN THE MIDDLE OF SUMMER—JUST IN TIME FOR A PICNIC. But the beauty of these red speckled pods is not only their appearance; they're also easy to shell and cook. To make this salad out of season, use canned and drained white beans, or dried cranberry beans. For dried beans, soak ¾ cup beans in water overnight, drain, and cook in 2 quarts of salted water until tender, about 1½ hours. Follow recipe directions from there.

### FOR THE VINAIGRETTE

1 tablespoon plus ¼ cup extra-virgin olive oil

1 shallot, finely chopped

1 tablespoon sherry vinegar

2½ teaspoons finely chopped fresh rosemary

Salt and freshly ground pepper

### FOR THE SALAD

4 cups water

1 pound fresh cranberry beans, shelled (about 1 cup)

Salt and freshly ground pepper

1 pound medium-sized shrimp (20–24 count)

4 wooden or metal skewers or rosemary branches

Olive oil

2 ounces Black Forest Ham, cut into ½-inch pieces

½ fennel bulb (about ¼ pound), sliced paper-thin

½ cup French green olives, pitted and sliced ¼-inch thick

2 ounces fresh goat cheese, crumbled or pinched into small pieces

If using wooden skewers or rosemary branches, soak them in water for at least 30 minutes.

To make the viniagrette: In a medium sauté pan, warm the 1 tablespoon of oil over low heat. Add the shallot and cook until translucent but not brown, about 7 minutes. Turn off the heat and stir in the vinegar, the ¼ cup oil, rosemary, and salt and pepper to taste. Let cool to room temperature. (You can make this up to 1 day in advance and refrigerate it. Bring to room temperature before using.)

To make the salad: In a small saucepan, combine the water and cranberry beans. Bring to a boil, reduce the heat to low, and cover. Cook for 25 minutes, or until the beans are tender but still holding their shape. Do not overcook, or they will get mushy. Remove the beans from the heat and drain. Add salt and pepper to taste and let cool to room temperature.

Meanwhile, light a grill or barbecue. Thread 5 shrimp onto each skewer. (Rosemary branches work especially well for this!) Brush the shrimp with olive oil and sprinkle with salt and pepper. Grill, turning to cook evenly, until the shrimp have turned pink, about 5 minutes. Let cool to room temperature.

In a large bowl, combine the beans, ham, fennel, olives, and vinaigrette and toss. Gently mix in the cheese. The bean mixture can be prepared ahead and then chilled for up to 6 hours. Bring to room temperature before serving. To serve, distribute the cranberry bean salad on each of 4 plates and top each with 1 skewer of shrimp.

Serves 4

## PICNIC TAKE-ALONGS

- ◆ Italian-style bread (Pugliese or Ciabatta work well; otherwise use any style country bread)
- ◆ Slices of cantaloupe and honeydew melon
- ◆ Cheese assortment including crottin (cylindrical aged goat cheese), Brie, and Parmesan
- ◆ Biscotti

# Merry Edwards Wines

AT THE END OF A NONDESCRIPT CUL-DE-SAC MARKED BY PICK-UP TRUCKS AND casual one-story homes sits a fire-truck-red 1968 Camaro. It is stationed in front of a home toward the end of the U, where it stands as a colorful beacon and a visual cue proclaiming its owners as creative and whimsical. Appropriately, it belongs to winemaker Merry Edwards, who is not short on fancy, imagination, or talent.

Her home, in Forestville, California, in Sonoma County, is situated in the heart of the Russian River Valley—an area known for its outstanding Chardonnay and Pinot Noir. It is the former grape on which Edwards made her name as a winemaker, and it is the latter on which she is establishing a reputation that is single-handedly transforming the entire image of Russian River Pinot Noir. The Russian River Valley has had no greater booster—nor tacit spokesperson—than Edwards.

Edwards has been making wine for nearly thirty years, and it is a career that, only in retrospect, seemed preordained. She had been exposed to wine as a child because her mother often cooked with it, and she had an interest in fermentation, although her focus was bread and beer. She even dabbled in home winemaking. Still it wasn't until a weekend getaway to the University of California at Davis from her graduate studies in nutrition at UC Berkeley that Edwards learned from her friend Andy Quady (a fantastic dessert wine-, port-, and vermouth-maker under the Quady label) that one could actually study winemaking. Almost immediately she dropped her nutrition studies and moved to Davis, and her illustrious career took off.

Although enrolling in school was not difficult,

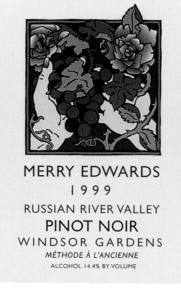

MERRY EDWARDS
1999
RUSSIAN RIVER VALLEY
PINOT NOIR
WINDSOR GARDENS
MÉTHODE À L'ANCIENNE
ALCOHOL 14.4% BY VOLUME

getting a job as a winemaker was. Edwards recalls the constant rejection because of her gender—no one trusted a female winemaker. Finally, in 1974, Mount Eden winery in California hired her. She worked at the Santa Cruz Mountain winery for a couple of years, but, again, it was a visit to a friend, this time in Sonoma County, that would change her course. She was so enamored of the Sonoma area's fruit that she left Mount Eden and took up residence in Sonoma County. Then, in 1977, Edwards helped launch what would become one of this nation's most highly regarded and best-known wineries, Matanzas Creek.

There she became firmly entrenched in the annals of exemplary winemakers.

At Matanzas Creek, Edwards earned numerous awards for her outstanding Chardonnay. But even then, she says, her real love was Pinot Noir. In a fortuitous turn, Merry, whose formal name is Meredith, was sent by Matanzas Creek to the University of Beaune in the Burgundy region of France to learn about the various clones used to grow that region's beloved Pinot Noir and Chardonnay. It was there that she had the revelation that it wasn't enough to plant just any Chardonnay or Pinot Noir. What mattered was the particular clone that was used. In order to grow properly and to yield the optimum flavors, the clone had to be suitable for the soil and climate of the region. This was a novel idea in the United States, and when Edwards shared her newfound knowledge here, she encountered skepticism. Nonetheless, her wisdom prevailed, and she is now credited with no less than helping change the course of the entire California wine industry.

After she was thwarted in her attempt to start her

own winery as well as to become the winemaker at a large winery, she signed on as a consultant winemaker to several wineries. Finally, in 1997, along with investor Bill Bourke, she cofounded Meredith Vineyard Estate Inc., under which she now produces Merry Edwards wines. These wines are exclusively Russian River–area Pinot Noir, Edwards' first love.

Edwards is wholly committed to the Russian River Valley as the place to grow Pinot Noir. "The Russian River," she says, "produces wines that are deep, layered, chocolate, bing cherry, dark fruit—plum—and earthy and rich on the palate." Her Pinot Noirs, of which she makes several, display these characteristics, although each one is distinct.

Her Klopp Ranch Pinot Noir is reminiscent of cherries and plums, and it is also emblematic of Edwards' intense commitment to her growers and to the vineyard. Ted Klopp and Edwards began their collaboration in 1989. At the time, Edwards suggested two clones for Klopp to plant in his vineyard, which is situated in the heart of the Russian River Valley. She and Klopp have been working together ever since, and in a relatively unconventional arrangement, Edwards purchases Klopp's grapes by the acre—not by the ton. That way she can do the essential crop-thinning on the finicky Pinot Noir grapes.

Once the grapes are harvested, Edwards employs the Burgundian method of cold-soaking the grapes. She also does whole-cluster fermentation, and she insists on laborious hand punch-downs of the cap. About three-quarters of the wine is aged in new French oak for ten months.

Edwards' operation is a family affair. Her outgoing husband, Ken Coopersmith, handles the labor-intensive shipping as well as numerous other crucial tasks, and her sister, Marcia Edwards, is the "ace" bookkeeper. Marcia also contributes Pinot Noir–friendly recipes to the Edwards family gatherings and to the website.

Edwards says her interest in making Pinot Noir dovetailed with the public's interest in it. She also notes that wine drinkers are now seeking out Pinot Noir because it is a wine that is just as rich as Merlot, yet more consistently fruit-oriented and lower in tannins. "I think that what's happening is that we're redefining Pinot Noir—not in terms of a French Burgundy," Edwards says. This means primarily that her Pinot Noir is richer and more fruit-forward.

Edwards is unquestionably at the forefront of this redefinition, and in striving to make each of her several Pinot Noirs distinct, she is giving consumers a choice and a varied taste of the outstanding fruit of the Russian River Valley. She is also conveying her zeal in liquid form. "I'm totally passionate about Pinot Noir, and that's the end of the story," she says.

WHAT THEY MAKE

Pinot Noir (Klopp Ranch, Meredith
    Vineyard, Olivet Lane, Russian River
    Valley, Windsor Vineyard)

HOW TO REACH THEM

Forestville, California
888-388-9050 (toll-free)
707-887-0322 (fax)
www.merryedwards.com

# ROASTED CHILE AND CREAM CHEESE SANDWICHES

EVERY SUMMER THE PICTURESQUE TOWN OF ASPEN, COLORADO, IS HOST TO ONE OF THE WORLD'S MOST RENOWNED MUSIC FESTIVALS. One of the highlights of the festival is the Sunday afternoon concert. It is held in a state-of-the-art tent in which the louvered walls are opened to let the mountain breezes in and to allow the sound to carry over the surrounding lawn area. While most festival-goers gather inside, hundreds of people take to the lawn—and take a picnic along with them. One summer my talented friend Susan Walker, a jewelry maker and accomplished cook, brought these simple but flavorful sandwiches she'd created from that morning's farmers' market offerings. I told her they belonged in a book, so here they are.

2 fresh Anaheim or New Mexico chiles

8 ounces best-quality cream cheese, at room temperature

4 small plum (Roma) tomatoes (about ¾ pound), cut lengthwise into 4 slices each

Eight ½-inch-thick slices hearty Italian or French bread (each piece should measure about 6 inches by 3 inches)

If you have a gas stove, turn the flame to medium-high. Using tongs, hold a chile over the flame and char it until it is blackened almost completely on all sides. Repeat with the second chile and place both in a plastic bag. Let them sit for 15 minutes. If you do not have a gas stove, place the chiles under the broiler, turning frequently to char all sides. Place in a plastic bag and proceed as directed.

Using a paring knife, scrape the skin off each chile. Remove the stem and cut the chile in half lengthwise. Discard the seeds and inner membranes. Cut each half into 4 pieces.

To assemble the sandwiches, spread about 2 ounces of cream cheese on 4 slices of bread. Follow with 4 chile slices, and then add 4 slices of tomato. Lightly salt the tomato and top with the remaining slices of bread. Cut the sandwiches in half and wrap them in parchment or waxed paper. They will keep, wrapped, for 3 to 4 hours unrefrigerated, unless the outside temperature is quite hot. In that case, do not let the sandwiches sit out for more than 2 hours.

Makes 4 sandwiches

## PERFECT PAIRS

THE SLIGHT HEAT FROM the chiles in these sandwiches is soothed by the cream cheese—although the pronounced flavor still comes through. As a result, choose a fruity wine such as Riesling, Gewürztraminer, and Chenin Blanc or, for a red wine, a fruit-forward Russian River Pinot Noir will go along just fine.

## PICNIC TAKE-ALONGS
◆ Black olives
◆ Marinated cucumbers and onions (or bring sliced English cucumber)
◆ Semi-hard cheeses such as Gruyère and cheddar
◆ Water crackers
◆ Devil's food cake

# Linden Vineyards

EXPOSURE TO WINE WHILE HE WAS GROW-ING UP AND A STINT IN THE PEACE CORPS teaching fruit-, cocoa-, and coffee-growing in the former Zaire were the seeds of inspiration for wine-maker and winery owner Jim Law. The founder of Linden Vineyards in Linden, Virginia, Law says he returned to the United States from his two-year Peace Corps service with a decided interest in applying his agricultural skills to grape growing and wine making.

He started out working as a cellar rat at a winery in his native Ohio. Although this job was integral to his wine education, Law knew that to further his knowledge he would have to go to one of the Coasts. But as a self-avowed trail-blazer, Law bucked conventional wisdom by ruling out the obvi-ous choice of the West Coast as the place to pursue his passion for winemaking. Instead, he answered an ad for a job as a winemaker in Virginia. He got the posi-tion, and only in retrospect does he see how remarkable that was. "If I'd known then what I know now, I wouldn't have had the audacity to do that," he says.

That was in 1981. Two years later, he decided to strike off on his own by buying land on which to plant his own vineyards. He was particularly impressed with the flavors of the grapes that were coming from the mountains of Virginia. They were high in acidity, and that was a quality he was looking for because he drank mostly European wines. (Many European wines tend to be higher in acidity because they are made with grapes grown in cooler regions.) He found the site he was seeking in an orchard on top of the Blue Ridge Mountains, at an altitude that ranges from 1,200 to 1,400 feet. The land featured different soils and climatic conditions, and, knowing that, he planted different varieties, including Cabernet Sauvignon, Cabernet Franc, Seyval, Vidal (both hybrids), and Chardonnay. The hybrid plantings made sense because, with their hearty nature, they were more likely to withstand the cold winters. (Law says that improved viticulture practices have now made vinifera planting more viable.) In 1987 he released the first Linden Vineyards wines.

Almost every winemaker modestly defers to the quality of the vineyards as the basis for the quality of his or her wines, but Law's intense devotion to man-aging vineyards, both his own and those that, in an unusual arrangement, are owned by his staff, has unquestionably paid off in the flavor, structure, and intensity of his wines. The growing conditions in his part of Virginia—hot and often rainy during the spring and summer and very cold in the winter—are challenging at best, and one would not expect wines with fruit inten-sity to come from there. But Law's attention to details such as leaf-thinning (to allow for greater sun exposure on the grapes), shoot management, fruit dropping (to increase the intensity of the fruit left hanging), and myriad other techniques have enabled him to maximize the flavors in his wines.

Take his Bordeaux blends. Law's nearly chauvin-istic devotion to European wines has informed his winemaking style, and in the case of his elegant Bordeaux-style wines (he makes five), they capture flavors like raspberry, black pepper, blackberry, cherry, and black currant, among others. They're buoyed rather than dominated by oak. Indeed, Law is adamant about the overuse of oak. "If you can taste the oak, then there's something wrong with it," he says.

Law's own Hardscrabble Vineyard Red Wine is a big, brash wine, while his Glen Manor is a little more refined and tame, although no less interesting and complex. It has very soft tannins, beautiful color, and a gentle, smoky flavor. Glen Manor is owned by one of Law's staff members, Jim White, who also manages the vineyard situated at 1,100 feet. The Reserve Red Wine, which comes from the Hardscrabble Vineyard, is smooth and elegant, yet assertive. It's a truly gorgeous wine, both in color and in flavor. All of the blends are harvested, fermented, and aged in the barrel separately. The blending decisions come later. In the end, each wine will consist of Cabernet Sauvignon and Cabernet Franc, and some will also have Petite Verdot and/or Merlot.

Although Law does not own all of his own vineyards, he still makes most of the decisions about grape growing. It is he, not the vineyard owner, who decides when to pick the grapes, and he also weighs in on trellis systems, leaf thinning, how the grapes are picked (they're all hand-harvested), and the like. He likes the French term for a winery owner and winemaker, such as himself—*vigneron*—which translates as "wine grower." Law says the word encapsulates what he does—works in a vineyard *and* makes the wine.

Linden Vineyards is about an hour's drive from Washington, D.C. Law says that his style of winemaking dovetails nicely with the Washington set, who are very Euro-focused. When it comes to the food products he promotes at the winery, it's Virginia all the way. In particular, Law has started a cheese and wine pairing program in which visitors to the winery can choose from a selection of Virginia-made cheeses, including Meadow Creek Dairy cheeses, accompanied by suggested Linden Vineyard wines. Law says he's particularly fond of pairing older vintage (five- or six-

year-old) Chardonnay with aged cheese because the wine has what he calls a "cheesy-leesy" character. He is referring to the lees, or dead yeast cells, to which the wine was exposed when it was made. The lees create a creamy character in the wine. As the wine ages, that creamy character remains, while the bright fruit quality is replaced by a slightly caramel and nutlike flavor. Because they share these qualities, aged cheeses and older wines make a winning combination.

Although Law has enjoyed success with his wines, he takes nothing for granted when it comes to winemaking. It is as if every vintage is a blank slate, and he approaches each one as if he is learning all over again. His red wines, in particular, are more impressive than perhaps any east of the Mississippi, and that can only be attributed to the way Law "listens" to the cycles of the vineyards and the weather that influences them. It is not as if Virginia is an easy place for winegrowing—just ask Thomas Jefferson, whose many ill-fated attempts to make wine were a source of great disappointment to the wine-loving president.

Law makes only five thousand cases a year, and although Virginia's shipping laws are among the most strict, it is possible to come by Linden Vineyards' wines. But it may be best to pay a visit to the winery, high in the Blue Ridge Mountains, and take in its outdoor deck, the fine Virginia cheeses, and, you may get the chance to meet Law himself. And should that happen, Law will not hesitate to give you an impromptu introduction to his wines and the qualities that make Virginia wines worth drinking.

WHAT THEY MAKE

HOW TO REACH THEM

**White wines**
Chardonnay (*Avenius, Glen Manor, and Hardscrabble*)
Riesling-Vidal
Rosé
Sauvignon Blanc
Seyval
Late-harvest Vidal

**Red wines (Bordeaux Blends)**
Glen Manor
Hardscrabble
Red
Reserve
Rush River

Linden, Virginia
540-364-1997 (*phone*)
540-364-3894 (*fax*)
www.lindenvineyards.com

# WATERMELON-FETA SALAD

**FEW FOODS CONJURE UP THE WORD "SUMMER" MORE THAN WATERMELON DOES.** When mixed with grapes, mint, and salty feta cheese, the bright red fruit becomes more than just a summertime treat. The watermelon is also earthy, a little salty, and herbaceous because of the fresh mint. It is sure to be a crowd-pleaser.

Although this is meant for picnics, it's equally good right at home. Put some chicken, pork, or hamburgers on the grill and serve this salad alongside. You'll love the combination of the refreshing salad and the savory flavors from the grill.

If you'd like to make this in advance, you can mix together all of the ingredients except the nuts and dressing. Add those just before you're ready to serve.

2 tablespoons olive oil

1 tablespoon plus 1 teaspoon champagne vinegar (or use white wine vinegar)

2 tablespoons julienned fresh mint plus extra mint sprigs

One 3-pound wedge watermelon (about ¼ of a large melon), preferably seedless

1 cup red and green grapes, halved

¾ cup feta cheese, crumbled

¼ cup pine nuts, lightly toasted

In a small bowl, whisk together the oil, vinegar, and mint. Set aside.

With a sharp knife cut the wedge of melon in half lengthwise. Cut the fruit away from the rind. Then cut the fruit into cubes ¾-inch.

In a large bowl, toss the watermelon together with the grapes and cheese. When ready to serve, toss with the dressing and nuts. Garnish with a mint sprig and serve immediately.

Serves 4

## PICNIC TAKE-ALONGS

If you are going to have access to a grill, then bring along some chicken, a pork tenderloin, or hamburgers to cook and serve with this salad. Otherwise purchase (or make) the following items:
- Pita bread
- Barbecued chicken
- Mixed greens with avocado
- Aged sheep's milk or goats' milk cheese
- Coconut Black-Bottom Cupcakes (see page 252) or store-bought chocolate cupcakes

## PERFECT PAIRS

**THE SALTY FETA AND** sweet watermelon, along with the sweet and savory chicken, makes this a pretty wine-friendly menu, although a white wine or rosé is probably best. Choose a Chenin Blanc, Sauvignon Blanc, Seyval Blanc, Riesling, Vignoles, or rosé.

# Fiscalini Farmstead Cheese

**IT'S A LONG JOURNEY FROM PARAGUAY TO THE UNITED STATES AND BACK TO PARAGUAY—** only to return once again to the United States. But that is the route esteemed cheesemaker Mariano Gonzalez has taken, almost entirely in the name of cheese.

Gonzalez grew up on a dairy farm in Paraguay and learned to make fresh cheese as a boy, out of economic necessity. Since his family lived out in the country, where the roads were full of potholes, the milk trucks sometimes could not make it to the farm. Rather than throw away the milk, Gonzalez's father would ask him to turn it into cheese. The next day, Gonzalez would take the fresh cheese to the market where it would be sold. This routine set the stage for his career.

While in Paraguay, Mariano met an American woman from Vermont whom he followed to the United States. This woman, Margaret Conquest, was from Shelburne, Vermont, and had a job at the well-known Shelburne Farms. She helped Mariano secure a dishwashing job there, and because Shelburne Farms also had a thriving cheddar cheese operation, Mariano was called upon to help wrap cheese during the Christmas holidays. Ever curious, and encouraged by his father and uncle back home in Paraguay to learn all about cheesemaking, Gonzalez talked to the head cheesemaker about the craft. Gonzalez's hope was to bring his knowledge back to Paraguay. Before he could do that, though, his uncle died and the family farm was sold. Gonzalez learned cheesemaking anyway, and in 1989 he became the cheesemaker at Shelburne Farms.

Gonzalez worked at Shelburne until 1997, when he, along with Margaret, who was by that time his wife, decided to return to Paraguay. Although their life there was good, the political situation in Paraguay was unstable. Concerned about the future for themselves and their children, Gonzalez and Conquest made the difficult decision to return to the United States.

Once back in the United States, Gonzalez learned of a dairy farmer in Modesto, California, who was already making cheese but was looking to hire an experienced cheesemaker. The farm was called Fiscalini, and almost immediately after he met with owner John Fiscalini, Gonzalez was hired. The man who had been making the cheese at Fiscalini, Tom Putler, was a former chef and food science major at the University of California at Davis, but his cheesemaking experience was limited. He needed someone more experienced to show him the ropes. Gonzalez was a perfect fit, so he and Putler have been working in tandem at Fiscalini Farms ever since.

For owner John Fiscalini, a successful third-generation farmer in California's Central Valley, making a high-quality aged farmstead cheese was a sensible goal. His family, which hails from Switzerland near the Italian border, had been cheesemakers for several generations. He was also interested in developing a business for his children.

The Fiscalini Farmstead Cheeses include bandage-wrapped cheddar, plain and flavored wax-rind cheddars, and a specialty cheese called San Joaquin Gold. Like many good cheeses, San Joaquin Gold came about as a result of a mistake. Cheesemaker Putler had been asked to make a Fontina d'Aosta, a highly prized cheese from the Piedmont region in Italy. Unfortunately for him, he did not have the proper molds to make the cheese, nor did he have the proper recipe. What he ended up with was a very different cheese, but Fiscalini decided to solicit feedback anyway. The response was so positive that Putler and Gonzalez figured out a way to replicate the cheese. The aged raw-milk cheese became an instant hit.

The real shining light for Fiscalini Farmstead Cheese is its bandage-wrapped cheddar. Gonzalez made this English-style cheese for Shelburne Farms and won many awards for it. Now he is making it with California milk and with an innovative and eminently practical aging room, thanks to the support of Fiscalini, who worked with Gonzalez to design it.

The cheddar room is outfitted with wooden shelves and a moisture control system. The pièce de résistance, though, is the mechanical shelves. After the cheeses have been pressed, they are placed in this room for two months. While there, the cheeses must be turned regularly, but doing so is a Herculean task, given that each wheel weighs an average of sixty pounds. With Gonzalez's system, all he has to do is flip one lever—and boom—all the shelves turn 180 degrees, dropping the cheeses onto the opposing shelves. There is about four inches of room between the cheese and the shelves to which they fall, so when they make contact with the shelves, they do so with a bang. This violent drop is intentional, explains Gonzalez, as the weight of the cheeses hitting the shelves causes the mold spores to fan out. The more such spores spread, the better the cheese will develop. The process is truly ingenious.

The cheese is called bandage-wrapped because cheesecloth is placed in the molds before the cheese curds are poured in. The cheesecloth stays on the cheese for the duration of the aging process. At the beginning of that process, Gonzalez spreads lard on the cloth to inhibit cracking and to keep unwanted molds away from the cheese.

At this point, Gonzalez is planning to age his bandage-wrapped cheddar for between fourteen and thirty months. Like an English cheddar, this cheddar has deep earthy flavors—no super-high acid notes—and hints of butter and hay. It has a firm yet somewhat granular texture and it leaves a lingering sweetness. These qualities earned it a blue ribbon in the 2002 American Cheese Society competition.

The Gonzalez-Fiscalini-Putler team may very well be one of the best and perhaps most important cheese teams in the country. They are proving that commitment to a great product and, equally important, innovation can bring cheese to new heights without compromising one ounce of Old World charm and, most of all, flavor.

WHAT THEY MAKE

Cheddar (Bandage-wrapped, Wax Rind)
Seasoned Cheddar (Caraway, Dill,
   Garlic, Red Pepper, Saffron, Sage, Tarragon)

San Joaquin Gold

HOW TO REACH THEM

Modesto, California
209-545-6844 (phone and fax)
www.fiscalinicheese.com

# PORK AND CHEDDAR SANDWICHES
# WITH PLUM SALSA

IT MAY SEEM LIKE A LOT OF WORK TO COOK A TENDERLOIN BEFORE HEADING OUT ON A PICNIC. Really, though, it just takes some advance planning. Have the rub ingredients mixed and ready to go, and make the salsa the night before. Then, on the day of your picnic, all you have to do is cook the pork and assemble the sandwiches. The flavors of the orange-scented pork, bright plum salsa, and earthy cheddar will make it all worthwhile.

## FOR THE SALSA

¾ pound firm but ripe plums, pitted and coarsely chopped

1 small shallot, finely chopped (about 2 tablespoons)

¼ cup chopped cilantro

1 tablespoon fresh lime juice

1 tablespoon fresh orange juice

2 teaspoons finely chopped fresh jalapeño chile (about ½ large chile)

Salt

## FOR THE PORK

1 pork tenderloin (about ¾ pound)

2 tablespoons olive oil

1 tablespoon fresh orange juice

2 garlic cloves, minced

1 teaspoon salt

Freshly ground pepper

6 round crusty French rolls, cut in half lengthwise

4 ounces cheddar cheese, shaved thin (a vegetable peeler works well for this)

Light a grill or barbecue, or preheat the oven to 450°F.

To make the salsa: In a small bowl, combine the salsa ingredients. Set aside.

To prepare the pork: Rub the pork with the olive oil. Mix together the remaining ingredients and rub over the pork. Let it sit for 15 to 30 minutes.

Place the pork on the grill or, if pan-roasting, place the pork in a large ovenproof skillet set over high heat. Sear quickly on all sides, about 5 minutes total. Transfer the pork to the oven. Grill or roast the pork until medium-rare, or until a thermometer inserted in the center registers 140°F, 15 to 20 minutes. Remove from the oven or grill, tent loosely with foil, and let cool to room temperature.

To assemble the sandwiches: Slice the pork into very thin slices, between ⅛ and ¼ inch thick. (You may have a little left over. If so, save it for later use or make more sandwiches.) Place about 4 slices of pork on the bottom half of each roll. Follow with cheese and about 1 tablespoon salsa. Top with the remaining roll halves. Wrap in parchment paper and place in a cooler or refrigerator until ready to go. If possible, remove from the cooler about 1 hour before serving.

Serves 6

## PICNIC TAKE-ALONGS
- Tortilla chips plus extra plum salsa
- Mexican rice salad
- Grapes and orange slices
- Blue cheese and cheddar
- Berry pie

## PERFECT PAIRS

SPICY, FRUITY SALSA, the lightly-spiced pork, and the earthy cheddar calls for a fruity wine. Head toward Gewürztraminer, or, if a red wine suits you better, then think about a Dolcetto or a light-bodied, fruity Sangiovese or Zinfandel.

# DESSERTS

Pear and Goat Cheese Tart, recipe on page 260

# Marin French Cheese Company

AS CALIFORNIA'S LONGEST CONTINUOUSLY OPERATING CHEESE FACTORY, MARIN FRENCH Cheese Company has a storied past and may be looking forward to an even brighter future. The company began in 1865, when a man named Jefferson A. Thompson, who owned a seven-hundred-acre ranch in the verdant hills of Marin County, north of San Francisco, decided to acquire cows and make cheese. The San Francisco market was growing, and Thompson believed he could create a business that would serve that market. At the time he was making hard Italian-style cheese.

In 1900 the Thompson family took the lead from a cheesemaking neighbor and began making soft-ripened cheeses—in particular, Camembert. Now, over one hundred years later, Marin French Cheese Company continues to make the same style of cheese.

For five generations, Marin French Cheese Company remained in the Thompson family. But around 1990 the heirs apparent, who were involved in other professions, reluctantly decided to sell it. In line to buy the operation were Jim and Chris Boyce. The Boyces were cattle ranchers in the White Mountains on the California-Nevada border, businesspeople, and people with a fierce devotion to good farming practices. Although they had spent many years in the white-collar world, their true passion was the land. Nearly fifteen years before becoming the owners of Marin French Cheese Company, the Boyces had been told the company might come up for sale. From that time forward, they kept a keen eye on it, and in 1997 it finally became theirs.

Prior to buying the company, Jim and Chris were intent on figuring out the reason for its longevity. The secret, they learned, was as traditional as the company: goodwill. The commitment the company had to its customers, thousands of whom pass through its retail store annually, and especially its employees, was reflected in the quality of the cheese.

The traditions at Marin French Cheese Company are best seen through the cheese. Although long-time cheesemaker Howard Bunce makes beautiful Camembert and Brie, amazingly, his most popular cheese is simply called Breakfast Cheese. The small, soft, square cheese is mild and a tinge buttery. Jim Boyce explains that this cheese was first made in 1865, when the company began. It was sold on the docks of San Francisco and in nearby bars where stevedores would go for sustenance. The traditional protein at English bars (or pubs) was pickled eggs, but since there were no such eggs in San Francisco, cheese had to suffice. The cheese was shipped from Marin down the Petaluma river on a boat called the *California Gold*. Today, more than a hundred years later, Breakfast Cheese remains the company's biggest-selling cheese. The company has come out with a nearly identical breakfast cheese called "Le Petite Dejeuner," designed to attract consumers who may not find something called "breakfast cheese" as enticing. The traditional "Breakfast Cheese" will continue to be sold as well.

The other surprisingly popular cheese for Marin French Cheese Company is called Schloss. This very aromatic cheese is smeared with whey as it ages (similar to brick cheese), and it ranges in flavor from mildly strong to very strong. Interestingly, as it gets past a certain point in its aging, perhaps a few months old, the cheese becomes harder and takes on a dessert-like butterscotch flavor. Schloss is unique in the world of cheese, and because of that it is often overlooked at the grocery store. For Marin French Cheese Company visitors, though, it has become an insider's favorite. The company is in the process of developing another similar cheese called California Liederkrantz. This news will come as a pleasant surprise to all of this country's Liederkrantz fans, who have long lamented the demise of the aromatic cheese in our country.

The label under which Marin French Cheese Company has always produced its cheese is called Rouge et Noir, and it is echoed in the red and black label on the cheese. But in an effort to bring new attention to their product, the Boyces have resurrected another line called Yellow Buck. This name was originally used in the early 1900s, and in 2000 the cheese was brought back as part of a commemorative line. The Camembert carries both the Yellow Buck and Rouge et Noir labels.

Among the most exciting cheeses now being made at Marin French Cheese Company is La Petit Crème, a soft-ripened triple-crème that earned a blue ribbon at the 2001 American Cheese Society conference. As the description implies, this cheese is creamy, buttery, and rich. A little goes a long way, although despite its richness, it is hard to stop eating. This soft-ripened cheese comes in a three-ounce cylindrical shape, and as a relative newcomer to the line of cheeses at Marin French, it provides a window into the forward-thinking philosophy of the Boyces as well as the cheesemakers.

The cheesemaking plant and retail store are perched on top of a hill on the green-carpeted land that stretches across Marin and Sonoma counties, and the milk for the cheese comes from four nearby dairies. The plant is open 365 days a year. Jim Boyce says they used to be closed on holidays, but invariably people would knock on his door and ask if they could pick up a little cheese for their holiday meal. He decided to formally open the doors, and he says he gets a real kick out of working holidays.

Sadly, just as the Boyces were hitting their stride as cheese company owners, Chris Boyce was stricken with cancer and passed away in the summer of 2002. Jim, with the help of his son Max, will continue running the business and in so doing, will not only carry on the legacy of the founding Thompson family but also now that of his wife.

## WHAT THEY MAKE

Breakfast Cheese
Brie (*Plain and Flavored*)
California Liederkrantz
Camembert
Le Petit Bleu
La Petite Crème

Le Petit Dejeuner
Le Petit Vin
Quark (*Plain and Flavored*)
Schloss
Triple Crème Brie

## HOW TO REACH THEM

Petaluma, California
707-762-6001 (*phone*)
800-292-6001 (*toll-free*)
707-762-0430 (*fax*)
www.marinfrenchcheese.com

# BRIE AND NECTARINE TURNOVERS

**ALTHOUGH THIS RECIPE CALLS FOR NECTARINES, THIS SIMPLE DESSERT CAN BE MADE WITH A VARIETY OF FRUITS, CREATING A TREAT THAT CAN BE ENJOYED YEAR-ROUND.** If you use apples, a dash of cinnamon along with the sugar makes a nice addition.

The exact amount of sugar you'll use in this recipe will depend on the sweetness of the fruit. If your fruit is quite sweet, add just a little bit of sugar to bring out the juices.

A few notes on the cheese: First, be sure to smell your Brie before buying it. If it is the least bit ammoniated, it will ruin this dessert. The aroma should be fresh. Second, although a ripe, creamy Brie is nice to eat on its own, it's actually better to use a slightly underripe cheese for this dish. Finally, whenever you're cutting the rind off of a soft-ripened cheese, be sure the cheese is very cold, otherwise the cheese will be too difficult to cut.

2 medium firm but ripe nectarines (about ½ pound), peeled and cut into ½-inch dice

2 tablespoons plus 1 teaspoon sugar

One 17.3-ounce package frozen puff pastry, thawed

6 ounces Brie cheese, rind removed, cut into thin slices (or use ripe California Teleme; do not use a salty cheese)

1 egg, lightly beaten

¼ cup decorative large-granule sugar (or 2 tablespoons regular sugar)

Preheat the oven to 400°F.

In a small bowl, mix together the nectarines and 1 tablespoon of the sugar. Let sit for about 15 minutes, gently stirring once or twice.

Using a sharp knife, cut each sheet of puff pastry into four squares. Roll out each square into a 5- x 5-inch square. Put each square on a large baking sheet. Sprinkle the squares with the remaining 1 tablespoon plus 1 teaspoon sugar. Place a few slices of cheese in the center of each square. Pile about 2 tablespoons of the nectarines over the cheese on each pastry square. Repeat with remaining pastry, cheese, and fruit.

Next, brush the edges of each square with a small amount of egg. Fold one corner of each square toward the opposite corner to form a triangle and press the edges with the tines of a fork to seal the turnovers and to create a decorative edge. Brush the turnovers with the remaining egg and sprinkle with decorative sugar.

Place the turnovers on a baking sheet and bake for 20 minutes, or until the pastry is a rich golden color. Serve warm or at room temperature.

Serves 8

## PERFECT PAIRS

**THE SWEET NECTARINE** and flaky texture point to a light, sweet wine, perhaps with a little effervescence. A Muscat would be a nice choice as would a late-harvest Riesling.

# Sweetwoods Dairy

ABOUT MIDWAY BETWEEN ALBUQUERQUE AND SANTA FE, NEW MEXICO, LIES THE minuscule town of Peña Blanca. Even during the week, the block-long group of stores there may or may not be open. The town doesn't seem to worry about keeping pace with the rest of the world. Perhaps its setting in the shadow of red craggy rocks under a crystalline sky is enough. Within this flat, high-desert valley lies Sweetwoods Dairy, home of about sixty goats and one horse. The story of how this dairy came to be is as intriguing as the operation's unique location.

Patrice Harrison-Inglis and her husband, Larry Harrison, were living in San Jose, California, in 1981 when their eighteen-month-old son, Ben, was diagnosed with a very serious form of leukemia. The family spent their days at Stanford Children's Hospital as he underwent treatment. During the time that Ben was in treatment, the Harrison-Inglises had their second child, Les. But by that time, their attitude about the life they were leading had changed dramatically. Their experience with nearly losing a son (Ben made it through the treatment and today is a healthy adult) convinced them that they should abandon their life as a two-career, upwardly mobile couple and instead alternate their work duties. Patrice worked as a secretary for a Silicon Valley company, and Harrison alternately worked as an orchard manager.

During the time their son was being treated, the family left San Jose and took up residence in a cabin in the Santa Cruz Mountains, above San Jose. Patrice says they had no running water, no electricity, and no phone. Although she had grown up with these creature comforts, she did not miss them. While Ben was in the hospital, Patrice and Larry met a couple who farmed in California's Central Valley. That couple offered them two goats, which Patrice gladly accepted.

Although she did not have electric power, she did have land. With the milk from those goats, she began making cheese, which she would occasionally bring to work to share with her office mates. They ate the cheese enthusiastically and told Patrice that she ought to consider making her cheese commercially. She sloughed off the suggestion, but finally, she says, it stuck. She worked out a quasi business plan, which required accumulating fourteen more goats. (By this point she had a brood of six.) But the Harrison-Inglises needed more space. Larry Harrison, who was from New Mexico, decided to scout out a parcel in his home state.

Within a few short weeks, their retirement money had been used as a down payment on a small parcel of land, and they were headed east. The adventure had just begun. To move, they got a forty-foot trailer and loaded the first twenty feet or so with their household items and furniture. The back half was loaded with goats. In this fashion, they traveled to New Mexico, stopping along the way to milk their goats daily and to let the goats stretch their legs. Patrice recalls the kindness of the families they met throughout their journey. Some offered them warm showers, and others helped them to milk the goats. It must have been a bizarre road show indeed.

Once they arrived in New Mexico, the family set up camp. They had no home—just a five-acre parcel surrounded by a barbed-wire fence. Harrison had laid the foundation for their one-room adobe home as well as one for the dairy, but that was all they had. So they and their two sons, aged ten and six at the time, roughed it until their home was built.

At this point, Patrice says their "one and only" plan was to create the dairy. Once that was accomplished, they assumed that Harrison would find a regular job. It never happened. The work was so all-consuming that all four members of the family became involved in the operation.

Patrice was and is the cheesemaker. She began by making her Red Ribbon fresh goat cheeses, which remain her mainstay today. These fresh cheeses are made over the course of three days, beginning in large pots rather than in vats. She makes these cheeses three times a week and sells them at various farmers' markets and two supermarkets in the area. The biggest of the farmers' markets is held in Santa Fe, and to see the hordes of people congregating at her booth is quite a sight. These food-savvy people know a good thing when they see it.

The Red Ribbon cheeses are so-named because each hand-wrapped disk of goat cheese, which Patrice packages by herself, is finished off with a decorative red ribbon. This flourish distinguishes her cheese and also provides a visual representation of the handwork that goes into making that cheese.

A cheese that Patrice is particularly proud of is her Snow Rose, a Camembert-style goat cheese that is ripened for about two weeks before it is sold. It is a soft-ripening cheese, and as it ages it develops a creamy translucence just under the rind that signifies that it is perfect for eating. Patrice says, though, that it is also at this stage that she sometimes takes the cheese down a different path. Rather than keeping it in the cellophane in which she packages it, she will wrap it in a breathable paper. This covering dries out the cheese, and while the outside becomes hard, the inside, she says, becomes crumbly, like an aged crottin. This is her favorite cheese, and it's a favorite among her customers too.

Harrison-Inglis has now begun making sheep's milk cheese, after some sheep owners in Colorado began to make their milk available to her. Given that she knew nothing about sheep's milk, it is all the more remarkable that she is making such a go of these new cheeses. The Black Sheep cheese is an aged, hard cheese that shaves like a Parmesan and is covered with edible vegetable ash. "It looks like a rock," she says. It doesn't taste like a rock, though. It's buttery, with layer upon layer of flavor. She also makes a sheep's milk ricotta from the whey that comes from making the Black Sheep.

Although Harrison-Inglis's son Les helps her tremendously, she is the lone milker for her sixty-some-odd goats. That's a day-and-night job, seven days a week, from March through November. In between milkings, she has to make cheese and run the operation. There is so much work that she has decided to look for part-time help.

Despite these inherent difficulties, Harrison-Inglis speaks of the challenges of her business in the same upbeat way she speaks of the rewards. That positive outlook has sustained her and her business. It has also made the Sweetwoods Dairy cheeses emblematic of one family's commitment to a lifestyle that was born out of a special appreciation for life.

WHAT THEY MAKE

**Goats' Milk Cheeses**
Red Ribbon Fresh Goat Cheese
  (Plain, Herbed)
Snow Rose

**Sheep's Milk Cheeses**
The Black Sheep
Ricotta
Sheep Butter Cheese

HOW TO REACH THEM

Peña Blanca, New Mexico
505-465-2608 (phone)
505-465-0904 (fax)
Limited mail order

# BLUE CHEESE–CAMEMBERT FONDUE WITH PHYLLO-PEAR "CIGARS"

CHEESE FONDUE COMES IN MANY FORMS AND CAN VARY ACCORDING TO THE DIF-FERENT CHEESES USED AS WELL AS THE INGREDIENTS CHOSEN TO DIP INTO THE FONDUE. While bread is the traditional "dipper," you can use a variety of fruits or vegetables, depending on the type of fondue. In this fondue, the phyllo cigars, so called because of their shape, make for a tasty and unique dipper. You can roll the cigars one day ahead and cover and refrigerate them before baking. Just plan a little extra baking time because they will be cold when you put them in the oven.

Preheat the oven to 350°F.

To make the cigars: In a large pan, stir together the pears, water, and sugar. Turn the heat to medium, cover the pan, and cook, stirring occasionally, until the pears are quite soft, 10 to 15 minutes. Set aside.

Stack the phyllo sheets and cut them in half cross-wise. Cover with a damp kitchen towel. Set 1 phyllo sheet with the short end toward you and brush it with butter. Spread about 2 tablespoons of the pear mixture in a thin line in the center of the sheet, parallel to the ends. Fold the sheet in half, enclosing the pear mixture. Fold in both sides about ¾ inch. Starting at the end closest to you, gently roll up the phyllo. Brush the end with butter to seal. Place seam side down on a baking sheet and continue with the remaining phyllo and pear mixture.

Bake the cigars for 20 to 25 minutes, or until deep golden-brown. Let cool at least 15 minutes or to room temperature.

Warm a fondue pot by filling it with hot water. Pour out the water and wipe the pot dry.

To make the fondue: In a medium bowl, toss together the cheeses and flour. In a medium-sized heavy-bottomed pot, heat the wine over medium heat. When the wine is simmering, add a small amount of the cheese mixture and stir until smooth. Continue with the remaining cheese, adding small amounts at a time. Transfer the fondue to a fondue pot and serve, with phyllo cigars and fruit slices.

Makes 16 cigars; serves 4 to 6

## FOR THE CIGARS

4 large Bosc pears (about 2 pounds), peeled, cored, and cut into ⅛-inch dice

1 tablespoon plus 1 teaspoon water

1 tablespoon plus 1 teaspoon sugar

8 phyllo sheets

1 stick unsalted butter, melted

## FOR THE FONDUE

9 ounces Camembert cheese, rind removed, cut into chunks (this is easiest to do when the cheese is cold)

4 ounces creamy-style blue cheese, cut into chunks

1 tablespoon plus 1 teaspoon flour

1 cup white dessert wine, such as Robert Mondavi Moscato d'Oro

Pear slices, Asian pear slices, and apple slices, for serving

## PERFECT PAIRS

THE OBVIOUS CHOICE OF wine for this dish is the wine you used to make the fondue. A Muscat or a late-harvest Riesling are good choices. Just be sure that the wine has enough sweetness to stand up to the pears and to contrast with the strong flavors of the blue cheese.

# Bookwalter Winery

THE FIRST THING YOU NOTICE ABOUT JOHN BOOKWALTER IS THAT HE IS STRIKINGLY down to earth. For someone who has been charged with the job of running his family's winemaking business, with all the inherently heady prospects that accompany that responsibility, Bookwalter retains refreshing charm and accessibility.

John Bookwalter is the son of Bookwalter Winery's founders, Jerry and Jean Bookwalter. Jerry started the winery in 1983 after managing some of Washington state's largest and most prestigious vineyards and identifying the need for more high quality wine producers in the state. He opened his winery doors to immediate critical acclaim and set Bookwalter Winery on its path toward ongoing national recognition.

The first vintage from Bookwalter Winery included Riesling and Chenin Blanc. Later Merlot and Cabernet Sauvignon, among other wines, were made. All this time, Jerry Bookwalter continued working as a vineyard manager on other properties on a consultant basis, which also gave him access to some of the fruit from those properties. In a way, he had the inside track on the locations of Washington's best grapes.

In 1997 Jerry's son, John, who had worked in sales and marketing for such large companies as Pepsi, Gallo, and Coors, returned to the winery to lend his expertise there. Not long after rejoining the family business, John says he identified the need to fundamentally improve what Bookwalter Winery did. He enrolled in winemaking classes and took seminars to bone up on the how-to of winemaking. At the same time, he recognized that his own wine experience might not be enough, so he brought in top-notch wine consultant Zelma Long to help get him and the winery on track. Long rose to prominence at the helm of Simi Winery in Healdsburg, California.

Since joining the business, John has changed the course of the winery, steering it primarily toward red wines. "I prefer to drink them, and therefore I prefer to make them," says Bookwalter. He is an ardent promoter of Washington Cabernets, believing they can be the best in the world. Nonetheless, his winery continues to put out several white wines, especially sweet ones, partly because those are the wines that originally brought the winery its recognition. They are excellent wines.

The Bookwalter Winery is located in Richland, Washington, in the heart of the Columbia Valley. It is an arid part of the state, yet 98 percent of the state's wine grapes are grown there. The long growing season, hot days, and cool nights all conspire to create ideal conditions for grape growing. The Bookwalters own ten acres in the vicinity of their winery, and they continue to buy fruit from other vineyards as well. John Bookwalter says he and Jerry are as hard on their growers as anyone can be and are fastidious about what takes place in the vineyard. To further ensure quality, they pay their growers by the acre—not by the total weight of fruit. The purpose behind this system is to encourage the grower to "drop fruit," that is, to get rid of some of the fruit in order to channel all of the plant's energy into the clusters that remain. The flavor of the grapes that are harvested is naturally intensified; ultimately those grapes make a better wine.

The fruits of this diligence are present in the Bookwalters' glorious wines. The Cabernet Sauvignon, which is perhaps their flagship wine, is evidence of John Bookwalter's commitment to red wine. It is rich, full-bodied, with blackberry highlights and overall elegance. Bookwalter racks his wines frequently—that is, he moves the wine from barrel to barrel so that it does not sit on the bitter sediments for too long. Frequent racking keeps the wine smoother and less tannic. He is also adamant about getting the best barrels possible, preferring ones that are tight-grained and have a medium toast.

Despite the younger Bookwalter's gradual emphasis on red wines, the winery's sweet wines play an important role in the overall American wine vocabulary. All three—the JOCAT (a blend of Muscat and Johannisberg Riesling), Chenin Blanc, and Johannisberg Riesling—are appealing to anyone who enjoys a wine with obvious sweetness but equally important acidity. They are excellent food wines and go particularly well with cheese.

Bookwalter Winery also puts out a Merlot as well as a marvelous red table wine that consists of Merlot, Cabernet Franc, Cabernet Sauvignon, and Sangiovese. The help of consultant Long is certain to raise the wines to the level John Bookwalter has set. But Bookwalter himself is making his own valuable contributions with his sales and marketing expertise, savvy, and above all, palate. He knows how good wine should taste, and he's ushering the Bookwalter winery toward that goal.

## WHAT THEY MAKE

**White wines**
Chardonnay (*Columbia Valley, Vintner's Select*)
Chenin Blanc

**Red wines**
Cabernet Sauvignon
Merlot
Red Table Wine

**Sweet wines**
Chenin Blanc (*Ciel du Cheval Vineyard*)
JOCAT
Johannisberg Riesling

## HOW TO REACH THEM

Richland, Washington
509-627-5000 (*phone*)
877-667-8300 (*toll-free*)
509-627-5010 (*fax*)
www.bookwalterwines.com

# WINE-SOAKED MELON WITH HERBS AND SHEEP'S MILK RICOTTA

**THIS LIGHT DESSERT LOOKS AS LOVELY AS IT TASTES BECAUSE IT'S SERVED IN THE MELON ITSELF.** You will need a melon baller to scoop out the melon while still preserving the shell as a bowl. If you do not have one, then simply cut the melon flesh into 1-inch cubes. Serve in a shallow bowl instead of the melon.

This recipe calls for sheep's milk ricotta. If you cannot find it, you can substitute regular cows' milk ricotta. Just be sure to select as creamy and rich a ricotta as you can find because you do not want a grainy or chalky consistency. For a different texture and richer flavor, you can substitute mascarpone cheese. But if you do, do not add the milk as called for. Add only the sugar.

½ cup late-harvest Muscat, such as Robert Mondavi Moscato d'Oro, or other white dessert wine

2 tablespoons sugar

1 tablespoon plus 1 teaspoon fresh lemon juice

2 small cantaloupes (about 2 to 3 pounds each), cut in half, seeds and strings removed

2 tablespoons basil, cut into thin strips or chiffonade

1½ tablespoons mint cut into thin strips or chiffonade, plus whole sprigs for garnish

½ cup sheep's milk ricotta cheese (or use cows' milk ricotta, fromage blanc, or mascarpone. See headnote.)

2 teaspoons milk

In a small nonreactive pot, place the wine, 1 tablespoon plus 1 tablespoon of the sugar, and lemon juice. Bring to a boil, stirring constantly, and cook for 1 minute. Turn off the heat and let cool to room temperature.

Using a melon baller, carefully scoop out the melon flesh from the shell, leaving about ½ inch of melon along the rind. Reserve the melon shells. Place the melon balls in a medium bowl and gently mix in the herbs. Pour the cooled wine mixture over the melon and let sit for 1 hour at room temperature, stirring occasionally. Or refrigerate for up to 3 hours.

In the meantime, in a small bowl, mix together the cheese, remaining sugar, and milk.

To serve, spoon the melon, along with some of the wine mixture, into each of the 4 reserved melon shells. Place a dollop of the cheese mixture on top of the melon and put a mint sprig in the middle of each mound of cheese. Serve immediately.

Serves 4

## PERFECT PAIRS

**IT MAKES THE MOST SENSE** to accompany this dish with the wine that you used to make it. If you used a Muscat, then drink that alongside, too. Likewise, if you've used a late-harvest Sauvignon Blanc, then by all means, drink that. You just don't want a wine that is drier than the one you used to make the dessert or the wine will taste bitter.

# S. Rhodes Winery

**ON THE EASTERN SIDE OF McCLURE PASS, A STRETCH OF ROAD THAT CREEPS OVER** the mountain from Aspen, Colorado's, bedroom community of Carbondale to the high desert town of Paonia, lies a small vineyard. There, at 5,800 feet, is the home where ex-Californian Steven Rhodes lives—and prays every year that a cold frost won't come too early. In that event, the solution is to buy grapes from growers in the "lower" elevations—about three or four thousand feet.

Colorado has about forty wineries, but it is nothing short of a marvel that people would venture to grow grapes there. The freezing winters, spring frosts, and the early falls that inevitably accompany the high altitude would be enough to discourage most sane individuals, but not determined winemakers like Rhodes.

Steven Rhodes moved to Colorado from Sonoma County in California in the early 1990s to look after his aging parents. They owned about forty acres in Hotchkiss, Colorado, and Rhodes was interested in farming it. He says he always had an interest in wine, stemming from the days when he played guitar at a French restaurant on California's northern coast. Since the restaurant could only afford to pay him in French wine, he learned to drink—and appreciate—wine. Living near wine country as he did, he began to make "garage wine"—a term he uses loosely to describe the Zinfandel wine he made to drink rather than to sell. At the time, in the early 1980s, grapes were cheap and easy to come by.

Rhodes' mentor was a man named Americo Rafanelli, whose eponymous Sonoma County winery had a reputation for making stellar Zinfandel. (It still does.) Rafanelli, Rhodes said, was a winemaker who used intuition as his guide. That informal method

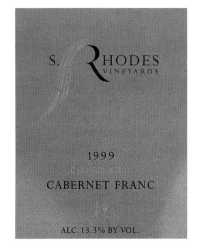

rubbed off on Rhodes, shaping both his winemaking style and his approach to the business. "If I make a mistake, it's not the end of the world," he says. Given his small annual production level, about one thousand cases, Rhodes says that even a bad year is not devastating for him.

Out in the vineyards, Rhodes is especially at home. "I really like to grow grapes," he says. "Winemaking is a hobby." On his east-facing slopes are his cooler-climate grapes, Pinot Noir and Gewürztraminer, and on his south-facing slopes are Merlot and Cabernet Sauvignon. It's hard to imagine having two cool-climate grapes on the same piece of land where two warmer-climate grapes are grown, even when the crops are facing in different directions. Nonetheless, when the weather cooperates, Rhodes gets good yields from both slopes. His first harvest was in 1996.

Because his operation is so small and is self-financed, Rhodes cannot afford new barrels in which to age his wines. Instead, he adds toasted oak cubes to a few of his French oak barrels to impart some of the new oak flavor and the tannins associated with new oak. Many winemakers—especially those who are well financed—scoff at this method, but the results Rhodes gets are astoundingly good. He has figured out how to integrate just the right amount of oak into the wine.

Rhodes, along with one helper, built his small winery himself. The fermentation tanks are open cement (not the usual steel or wooden ones), and the barrel room is a small, cool subterranean area. His tiny crusher-destemmer looks like it would take days to do its job, but he says it can crush a ton of grapes in just a few hours.

Because of Rhodes' background with Zinfandel, he really knows what he's doing, in spite of his attempt to downplay his expertise as a winemaker to a visitor. The care he takes in his hands-on winemaking methods, including everything from harvesting the grapes, to punching down the cap by himself, to racking, and many other functions in between, is ultimately reflected in the layers of flavor that emerge in his wines.

His Cabernet Franc is a study in integration. The tannins are present but integrated, and the fruit is perfectly in balance with those tannins. It isn't a huge wine; instead it's slightly toned down, a little silky, and reminiscent of dark fruits. Rhodes' Merlot is an amazing wine. A barrel sample (no oak cubes here) from the 2000 vintage revealed a rich, beautifully structured, dark berry wine. Rhodes had considered blending the Merlot with a little of his Cabernet, which had a little more edge to it, but he decided that the Merlot, destined for a Reserve bottling, deserved to be showcased independently.

If a particular crop isn't stellar, Rhodes sees that as a learning experience. "If it's tart," he says, "I remember what happened." Or, if it's a year when the acids are low, then that's fine too, he says. The point is that he believes the wine is made in the vineyard and it's simply up to him to take what nature gives him and do the best he can.

His small aerie above the Colorado high desert is at once beautiful and lonely. The main industry in the area is coal mining, and the people haven't changed much, even as technology and modern-day conveniences have moved in around them. The vista encompasses a farm here, a gas station there, and a ridge of snow-topped peaks, each of which seems to have etched out a piece of sky. Rhodes vascillates between expanding his operation or moving to a place like California where it would be easier to make wine, yet far more expensive. For now, the renegade winemaker is doing just fine making a name for himself in a state known more for its geological marvels than for its viticultural ones.

## WHAT THEY MAKE

Cabernet Franc
Cabernet Sauvignon
Gewürztraminer

Merlot
Pinot Noir
Late-Harvest Chardonnay

## HOW TO REACH THEM

Hotchkiss, Colorado
970-527-5185 (*phone and fax*)

# GRILLED PEACHES WITH BASIL CRÈME FRAÎCHE

**THIS VERSION OF PEACHES AND CREAM GIVES AN OLD IDEA A WHOLE NEW MEANING.** The tart crème fraîche is as refreshing as the summer day is long, and the sweetness of the peaches provides the perfect contrast. Because of the addition of basil, this dish bridges the gap between main course and dessert. If you'd like to make it more dessert-like, you can serve some light cookies alongside.

A couple of important notes: First, the peaches must be the freestone variety. (The pit is not attached by fruit fibers.) Otherwise it can be very difficult to extract the pit while keeping the peaches intact. Second, choose peaches that are ripe but still firm. You don't want them to be soggy after they're cooked, but you do want them to be sweet. The peaches can be prepared 2 hours in advance and kept at room temperature.

4 medium peaches (about 1½ pounds), cut in half lengthwise
2 tablespoons unsalted butter, melted
¼ cup balsamic vinegar
1 teaspoon sugar
½ cup crème fraîche
1 teaspoon fresh lemon juice
2 tablespoons julienned basil leaves, plus basil sprigs

Set a grill to medium-high or preheat the broiler.

Brush the cut sides of the peaches with the melted butter. Place the peach halves cut side down on the grill, or, if using the broiler, cut side up. Grill or broil until grill marks form, or, if using the broiler, until the butter is bubbling and the peaches begin to turn golden-brown. Remove from the heat and set aside to cool.

In a small heavy-bottom pot gently warm the vinegar and sugar over medium-low heat. Bring to a boil slowly and cook until the vinegar is reduced by about half and takes on the consistency of molasses, about 10 minutes. Watch carefully, as it can burn easily. Let cool.

Meanwhile, in a small bowl mix together the crème fraîche, lemon juice, and basil. Set aside.

To serve, place two peach halves on each plate grilled side up. Fill the centers and coat the tops of the peaches with the crème fraîche mixture. If you have a squeeze bottle, place the vinegar mixture in that and squeeze thin lines of the mixture over the peaches and onto each plate. Otherwise, use the tip of a spoon to drizzle the vinegar. Garnish each plate with a sprig of basil and serve immediately.

Serves 4

## PERFECT PAIRS

**SINCE FRESH PEACHES** are the focus of this dessert, make that the focus of your dessert wine too. A late-harvest Riesling would be a natural choice, as would a rare late-harvest Viognier. A late-harvest Vidal Blanc would also be quite nice with this dessert.

# Chimney Rock Winery

ALMOST ALL WINEMAKERS ARE CONCERNED ABOUT HOW THEIR GRAPES ARE GROWN, but few have taken the time to write a primer on the subject. But not only has Chimney Rock winemaker Doug Fletcher done that, he has also revolutionized the way grapevines are grown. In the process he has created spectacular wines.

His vinegrowing primer, called "Creating Balanced Vines," is straightforward, easy to grasp, and totally pragmatic. Not surprisingly, Fletcher is the same way.

A microbiology major from the University of Oregon, Fletcher never really had designs on becoming a winemaker, although as a child he made hard apple cider and was intrigued with the fruit wines made by his neighbors. In the 1970s he met Peter Martin Ray, the son of Martin Ray, who was one of California's leading pioneers in the wine industry. Fletcher volunteered to work a harvest at the Martin Ray winery and was instantly hooked. Part of the reason, he says, was the camaraderie among all the workers that was fostered by Martin Ray's wife, Eleanor, who would make "wonderful breakfasts" daily for everyone. At about that time, the revelation hit: "Why would anyone want to do anything other than this?" he recalls asking himself. "Back then it was a lifestyle choice. It still is."

After becoming the winemaker at the Santa Cruz mountain winery, Fletcher was summoned by Dick Steltzner in the Stags Leap District of the Napa Valley to become his winemaker. The position turned out to be more than just a winemaker job, though, because Fletcher effectively started the Steltzner winery, too. He left two years later, but not before the tough wine critic Robert Parker compared Fletcher's Steltzner Cabernet with that of one of Bordeaux's finest appellations, St. Julien. In 1987 Fletcher applied for the winemaker position at another Stags Leap District winery that was then in the planning stages. It was to be called Chimney Rock.

Sheldon "Hack" Wilson was the owner, a self-made businessman who had made his fortune starting Pepsi franchises in Africa and running a beer company, among other enterprises. Wilson had always been interested in wine and decided to purchase the eighteen-hole Chimney Rock golf course with the idea of converting part of it into an estate vineyard. The first wines made at Chimney Rock were Chardonnay, Sauvignon Blanc, Merlot, Cabernet Franc, and Cabernet Sauvignon, although it was never Fletcher's desire to make Chardonnay. He preferred to stick with strictly Bordeaux varietals. (Chardonnay is a Burgundian grape.)

In 1991 Fletcher got his wish, although for somewhat dubious reasons. The phylloxera-ridden Chardonnay vines at Chimney Rock had to be removed, and rather than replanting the same grape, Fletcher was able to convince Wilson to let him plant Bordeaux varieties instead. Chimney Rock still produces marvelous Sauvignon Blanc (one of two white grapes grown in Bordeaux; Sémillon is the other), although the wine is called Fumé Blanc as an homage to one of Wilson's favorite wines, the Loire Valley's Pouilly Fumé. Like the French wine, it has no oak exposure. It is unquestionably one of Napa Valley's best Sauvignon Blancs, with its tart but not grassy characteristics and the melon, peach, and citrus flavors that emerge. It is a wonderful match for food, especially light, fresh cheeses.

The silkenness of Fletcher's wines makes them seem as if they were effortless to make, as if they simply slipped right into the bottle. In part, that is true, because Fletcher has a firm grasp on the concept that the wine is made in the vineyard—not the winery.

Chimney Rock®

*Cabernet Sauvignon*

*Stags Leap District*
*Napa Valley*
*1999*

PRODUCED & BOTTLED BY CHIMNEY ROCK WINERY
NAPA, CALIFORNIA • ALCOHOL 14% BY VOLUME

Part and parcel of Fletcher's methods is the ability to manage the tannins in the field rather than "retroactively" in the winery. Fletcher allows the grapes to mature physiologically, often beyond the point when the sugar content of the grapes indicates they are ripe for picking. This means leaving the grapes on the vine longer.

The wine itself, like most wines, is very much a reflection of its maker. In the case of Fletcher, he prefers fruit flavors and therefore tries to emphasize them in his wine. He is able to create the flavors he is after because he has managed his vines—and the tannins—so well in the vineyard. A barrel sample of Merlot underscores this. The wine, which had been in barrel for a few short months, was as smooth as a decades-old wine. But the bright fruit flavors and nice acid structure portended a wine of the utmost interest and complexity, now and certainly for years to come.

His Reserve Cabernet Sauvignon is a study in fruit and spices, such as vanillin, that come from the oak aging. When asked whether he thinks fruit-forward wines, as most American wines are, are somehow less interesting or less complex than many of the less fruity European wines, Fletcher points out that since our natural inclination as humans is toward fruit, why not emphasize that in a product that's made from a fruit? Fortunately that emphasis is not at the expense of essential acidity.

Chimney Rock Winery is now a partnership between the Wilson family (Hack Wilson died in 2000) and the Terlato family, who own Paterno Imports—a company that handles marketing for several other wineries, including Alderbrook and Rutherford Hill. This ownership shift has not changed much at the winery, except the new owners are overseeingthe conversion of the remaining nine holes of

## BALANCING THE VINES

**The magic of Fletcher's wines is in his so-called "Balanced Vine Theory,"** which is based on the notion that how a vine looks is fundamentally most important. If it looks right, then it indicates that the vine is planted to the appropriate rootstock and in the appropriate soil for that rootstock. So what constitutes an "ideal" vine?

According to Fletcher, the proper vine will consist of the following: A shoot or cane height of three to four feet, fifteen to eighteen leaves on each cane, and spacing of four-and-a-half canes per foot.

By "balancing the vines" each grape cluster (intentionally, there is usually only one cluster per shoot) gets the plant's maximum amount of energy. If the vines are busy sending energy to the production of too many leaves on the shoots, then that's energy—and sugar—that isn't going into the grapes, while an underproducing vine will not sufficiently ripen the fruit.

It's quite a marvel to walk though the Chimney Rock vineyards and observe Fletcher's theory in practice: The height of the shoots is indeed more or less the same not because they have been snipped—but because Fletcher has effectively limited their growth. Likewise, if you count the number of leaves on each shoot, you see that there are fifteen to eighteen—just the way he wants it. The vines simply won't grow beyond this point because of Fletcher's earlier decisions governing rootstock and pruning, among other things.

Fletcher has also figured out a way for his grapes to get consistent sun exposure. For every two rows of parallel vines, the vines on the north side are trellised higher than those on the south side. Fletcher has devised it so that at this latitude in east-west vineyards, the sun will hit the grapes at the same angle all day long since the south row of vines is not shading the north row. This method, named the Fletcher Lyre (although he did not name it himself), creates even ripening and development of the grapes.

the Chimney Rock golf course to Cabernet Sauvignon acreage. In fact, the majority of grapes that go into Chimney Rock wines come from the Chimney Rock estate.

While unusual in the United States this allows a hands-on winemaker like Fletcher to control most of the variables inherent in grape growing as well as winemaking. The results are wines that are seamless, with balanced fruit flavors, a lot of structure, and exceptional elegance. Best of all, since the winery produces 22,500 cases a year, although still a relatively small output, one does not need to be on a waiting list nor among the rich and famous to buy a bottle of this truly memorable wine.

### WHAT THEY MAKE

Cabernet Franc Rosé
Cabernet Sauvignon (*Blend, Reserve*)

Elevage (*Merlot*)
Fumé Blanc

### HOW TO REACH THEM

Napa, California
707-257-2641 (*phone*)
800-257-2641 (*toll-free*)
707-257-2036 (*fax*)
www.chimneyrock.com

# CHOCOLATE-MASCARPONE TART

**THIS IS ONE OF THE EASIEST YET MOST SATISFYING DESSERTS YOU'LL EVER MAKE.**
All you need to do is toast some nuts, make a crust out of them, and fill the crust with the simple cheese mixture. The end result is kind of a cross between ice cream and frozen custard, even though this recipe has no eggs. Like ice cream, it hits the spot on a hot summer day. Best of all, this tart can be made well in advance and will last about two weeks in the freezer.

### FOR THE CRUST

2 cups whole almonds with skins,
    toasted and cooled
Scant ½ cup packed dark brown sugar
4 tablespoons (½ stick) unsalted butter, melted

### FOR THE FILLING

8 ounces mascarpone cheese, softened
⅓ cup plus 1 tablespoon sugar
1 teaspoon vanilla
3 tablespoons cocoa powder, sifted
½ cup heavy cream
About ¼ ounce semisweet or milk chocolate

Preheat the oven to 350°F.

To make the crust: In the bowl of a food processor, process the almonds and sugar together. Pour in the melted butter and pulse until incorporated. Press the mixture into a 9-inch fluted tart pan with a removable bottom. Bake for about 15 minutes, or until the crust has turned a slightly darker shade of brown. Remove from the oven and let cool completely.

To make the filling: In the bowl of a stand mixer, or in a large bowl using a hand mixer, beat together the cheese, sugar, and vanilla until smooth. Turn the mixer to low and add the cocoa powder. Mix until creamy, about 1 minute. In a separate bowl, whip the cream until stiff peaks form. Gently fold the whipped cream into the cheese mixture and stir just until the ingredients are blended. Pour into the prepared crust and, using a vegetable peeler, shave the chocolate over the top of the tart. Freeze for at least 2 hours.

To serve, let the tart sit at room temperature for 10 minutes and then cut. After serving, return the remaining tart to the freezer. Wrapped well, the tart will keep for up to 2 weeks in the freezer.

Serves 10 to 12

## PERFECT PAIRS

**THE CREAMY TEXTURE** of the cheese, the chocolate flavor, the nutty crust, and the overall sweetness in this tart add up to tawny port and cream sherry as your best choices for dessert wines. Some people like the combination of Cabernet Sauvignon and chocolate too, although the wine has to have enough fruit to stand up to the sugar in the dessert.

# Rollingstone Chèvre

KAREN AND CHUCK EVANS HAVE BEEN QUIETLY MAKING CHEESE FOR OVER fifteen years, but that does not mean that they haven't made a loud splash in the process. People talk about Rollingstone Chèvre with near reverence, and a conversation with Chuck Evans shines some light on why.

Although he is a goat owner and goat lover, he speaks with utter disdain about the smell of his goat bucks. He doesn't want that odor on his clothes, and, most of all, he says, he doesn't want it on his plate. He is referring to the goaty flavor that can sometimes be the negative hallmark of some people's goat cheese, due to the influence of the male goats. So he and his wife, Karen, set out to acquire goats that were least inclined to impart this flavor, as well as to learn to handle their goats and milk in a way that would minimize this "buckiness." For that reason, the Evanses own only Saanen goats, which are a quieter, calmer breed, and they handle the milk minimally, so as not to stir up those unwanted flavors.

The Rollingstone Chèvre operation is located in the small town of Parma, which lies in an agricultural valley in the southwest corner of Idaho near the Oregon border. The area gets about eight to twelve inches of rain a year, making it a good place for goats, which can feed on pasture most of the year. It is also the site of the farm where Chuck Evans grew up, although he left it for many years to pursue his passion for art. At the age of 34, he was the youngest-ever art department chairman at Winona State University in Winona, Minnesota.

Over the years, the Evanses began to buy goats' milk, because that was the only milk their daughter could drink. One day when there was no goats' milk at the store, the Evanses made a trip to the milk supplier's farm. That was a turning point for them. The supplier sat down on the cold, dirty ground, milked a goat, and handed them the plastic holder containing the milk. It was a far cry from a sanitary dairy. Unnerved by the conditions, they politely thanked the woman and promptly fed the milk to their dog. That experience convinced the Evanses that they should buy a goat themselves. They did so, and over time, they purchased several more.

In 1980 they moved to Parma, leaving the university life behind, although both continued their crafts as potters. Karen Evans began making cheese at home and, some seven years later, did so commercially for the first time. A friendship with a Boulder, Colorado, food critic led to introductions to chefs, and this contact helped give birth to the commercial endeavor. Today Karen creates between fifteen and twenty cheeses at any given time. And true to Chuck Evans' word—and preference—none of the cheese is goaty. Instead, each one is pleasantly mild with a wonderful fresh milk flavor and creamy, or rather, dreamy texture.

Among the particularly notable Rollingstone Chèvre cheeses, all of which are pasteurized, is the Wheel with Anise and Lavender. As the name suggests, it is a floral cheese, but, unlike many such flavored cheeses, it is enhanced by the herbs and spices but not overwhelmed by them. The cheese has such nice body and flavor that it holds its own yet acts as a perfect host for the lovely flavorings.

Another great cheese is the Pyramide with

Pepper Medley. The aged Pyramide has four different kinds of peppercorns—black, green, white, and pink—that create a speckled effect in the bright white cheese. The Torta with Fresh Basil and Pistachios is a real standout. It is particularly good with summer tomatoes, as the Evanses' winemaking friends, Kay Simon and Clay Mackey from Chinook Winery, demonstrated one summer evening with their homegrown tomato crop. What a memorable combination.

The Evanses now own about 200 goats, of which about 150 are milked. They have just recently hired one part-time person to help with the goats, but Karen, who is self-taught, continues her solo enterprise as cheesemaker. She is frequently experimenting with new cheeses, among which is one that is aged on grape skins, called Late Harvest Chèvre. The Evanses saw a similar cheese being made in Italy, and they couldn't get over the lush fruitiness imparted by the grapes in combination with the flavorful cheese. For now, they are using Merlot, although that may change, depending on the flavor of the cheese as well as the availability of the grape skins. Here is one instance when deciding on the perfect wine to pair with the cheese would not be a challenge—it would be a delight.

It's a long way from university life to farm life, but returning to the farm is a route often taken by folks who have grown up there. The Evanses have carved out a nice, though hardworking life, creating wonderful cheese in this rural part of the west. Anyone who has tried it knows how good this cheese is, and those who haven't should certainly make the effort.

## WHAT THEY MAKE

### Fresh cheeses
Brandywine Banon Style Chèvre
Chèvre (plain and flavored)
Chèvre Crottin
Chèvre Log
Chèvre in Grapeleaf
Chèvre with Roasted Garlic in Grapeleaf
Fromage Blanc de Parma
    (plain and flavored)
Late Harvest Chèvre
Tortas (Fresh Basil and Pistachios,
    Sundried Tomatoes and Basil Pesto,
    Fines Herbes)

### Aged chèvres
Bleu Agé
Chèvre Agé
Idaho Goatster
Orange Zest Pecan
Pyramide with Pepper Medley
Wheel with Anise and Lavender

### Oil chèvres
Chèvre Provençal
Feta with Calamata Olives and Rosemary

## HOW TO REACH THEM

Parma, Idaho
208-722-6460 (phone and fax)
www.rollingstonechevre.com

# COCONUT BLACK-BOTTOM CUPCAKES

ONCE AGAIN, MY MOTHER-IN-LAW SAVES THE DAY WITH ANOTHER "BEST OF" RECIPE. In this case, her black-bottom cupcakes are tried and true, highlighting the best of both chocolate and cream cheese. One night when I was making them, I was trying to think of ways to vary the classic recipe, and my husband weighed in with just one word: "coconut." It turned out to be an excellent idea, turning these cupcakes into the ultimate candy bar. If you want to continue with the tropical theme, you can also add half of a ripe, mashed banana to the cream cheese mixture. The banana-chocolate combination can't be beat.

## FOR THE BATTER

1½ cups flour

1 cup sugar

¼ cup cocoa

1 teaspoon baking soda

½ teaspoon salt

1 cup water

⅓ cup vegetable oil

1 tablespoon white vinegar

1 teaspoon vanilla

## FOR THE FILLING

8 ounces cream cheese or fresh goat cheese

⅓ cup sugar

1 egg

Pinch of salt

1 cup chocolate chips

½ cup sweetened coconut

Preheat the oven to 350°F.

To make the batter: In a medium-sized bowl, mix together all the batter ingredients. Set aside.

To make the filling: In another bowl, beat together the cream cheese, sugar, egg, and salt. When the mixture is thoroughly combined, stir in the chocolate chips and coconut.

To assemble: Place paper liners in each of 12 cupcake tins. Or, if you don't have paper liners, then lightly grease the tins. Pour the batter into the tins, filling them about three-fourths full. Place a heaping tablespoon of the filling in the center of each cupcake. (You may end up with extra filling. If so, simply put it into an extra cupcake tin and bake it along with the chocolate cupcakes. You'll end up with a cheesecake-like dessert.)

Bake for 15 to 20 minutes, or until a toothpick inserted in the center of the cupcake comes out with just a few crumbs clinging to it. Don't overcook! Let cool completely in the pan. The cupcakes can be stored in an airtight container for up to 1 week, or frozen for up to 2 months.

Makes 12 cupcakes

## PERFECT PAIRS

THESE CUPCAKES HAVE A fairly intense chocolate flavor. Some people love a glass of Cabernet Sauvignon with their chocolate, and that's just fine. For those who don't, a not-too-sweet port would work well or, if you can find it, a late-harvest Zinfandel. Although sweet, this wine will often have some earthiness to it, which goes nicely with the cocoa flavor of the cupcakes.

# Navarro Vineyards

**IN THE HEART OF THE ANDERSON VALLEY, AMONG ENDLESS STRETCHES OF VINEYARDS,** and about twenty miles east of the oceanside town of Mendocino, a loose cluster of wineries is set among the rolling hills. Within this area lies Navarro Vineyards, the area's oldest continuously operating family-owned winery, named for the nearby river. Through its exceptional winemaking and direct customer sales emphasis, Navarro Vineyards has brought deserved recognition to the Anderson Valley's unique winegrowing attributes and ultimately, to its renowned products.

Founded by Ted Bennett and Deborah Cahn in 1974, Navarro Vineyards is the result of a passion. Bennett, who owned a successful chain of stereo stores in southern California, was smitten with Alsatian wines—particularly Gewürztraminer. Through two years of careful analysis, he and Cahn learned that the conditions in the Anderson Valley were nearly identical to those in Alsace. In particular, the valley was cooler than most of the other California winegrowing regions, and its conditions were optimum for growing Gewürztraminer. Bennett sold the stereo stores, and he and Cahn exchanged the fast life for the country, later becoming life partners.

They started by planting eighteen acres of Gewürztraminer and seven acres of Pinot Noir and Chardonnay. With the help of now well-known winemakers Robert Stemmler and Jed Steele, Bennett and Cahn made their first wines in 1976. Unfortunately, there were few people to sell these wines to. They reasoned that it might be easier to bring the people to the wine rather than the other way around, so they created a tasting room. Although it wasn't part of any preconceived business plan, this approach ended up setting the stage for the way they would do business from then on: direct sales. They were inspired to add other wines to their repertoire, specifically Riesling and Pinot Gris, because at their tasting room they could solicit instant feedback on their experimental wines, as well as listen to the wish lists of customers.

While both Bennett and Cahn shared the duties of the winery, much of the marketing fell into Cahn's hands. She knocked on the doors of every restaurant and slowly built a mailing list from a pile of names held safely in a shoebox. Low-tech record-keeping notwithstanding, the list grew (as did her computer expertise), especially as people who visited the Navarro tasting room were put on Navarro's mailing list. Today 90 percent of Navarro Vineyards' sales are direct—through the tasting room and mailing list—and the remainder are through restaurants.

Navarro makes several noteworthy products from the Gewürztraminer grape. In addition to their standard-bearing dry wine, they also make a *vendange tardives* (late-harvest) Gewürztraminer and a non-alcoholic Gewürztraminer grape juice. This latter product has been on the beverage list at Berkeley's Chez Panisse restaurant since its inception, and has gained popularity partly as a result. There aren't too many varietal grape juices, and this one is spicy yet sweet—decidedly not cloying like grape juice can be. It's a real adult beverage, although children like it, too.

One of the standout Navarro wines is the dessert Riesling. Bennett and Cahn make two—Vineyard Select and Cluster Select. The Vineyard Select is 100 percent botrytis—that is, the grapes used for the wine have developed the so-called noble rot that works to concentrate the sugars in the grape. This wine has 15 percent residual sugar and, although very sweet, has a nice undercurrent of acidity. The extraordinary wine, though, is the Cluster Select Riesling. For this one, they hand-select every cluster that will go into the final wine. Like the Vineyard Select, the Cluster Select consists of 100 percent botrytis, but the difference is that the grapes within the clusters are all at the same level of ripeness, and in this wine the result is a very high sugar level, 28 percent residual sugar. The depth and complexity of this wine practically defy description. Although the sugar level is high, there is enough acidity to keep the wine from being cloying. The wine tastes of orange and honey and earth, and, best of all, it ages astoundingly well. The older ones are amber colored and have caramel, burnt sugar, and orange flavors.

The Anderson Valley is well-known Pinot Noir territory, and Navarro makes its contribution to this reputation. Bennett and Cahn make Pinot Noir the old-fashioned way, which they call "Méthode à l'Ancienne." The grapes are handled gently from start to finish. In particular, pumps are not used to press down the cap; instead the cap is pressed down by hand three times a day. Also, they use small, open-topped fermenters, which help with color and flavor extraction. Navarro's extraordinary winemaker, Jim Klein, usually filters and fines the wine, but it's a year-by-year decision—he has no set way of making his wines, and, instead, makes decisions based on the qualities he finds in a particular vintage.

The 910-acre ranch Bennett and Cahn own had been a sheep farm before they purchased it, and Cahn has continued that tradition, although on a smaller scale. The wine business is the couple's cash cow, as is evident by the popularity of the Navarro tasting room. Rarely is it empty, and even more rarely does anyone leave without making a purchase. Cahn says that she and Bennett love the business, and, by the looks of it, the oldest family-owned winery in the Anderson Valley is likely to remain vibrant. Their daughter is now studying winemaking, and one can safely assume she is doing so with an eye toward taking on the family business.

## WHAT THEY MAKE

**White wines**
Chardonnay
Edelzwicker (*blend of Gewürztraminer, Riesling, and Muscat*)
Gewürztraminer (*dry, sweet; non-alcoholic grape juice*)
Muscat Blanc
Pinot Gris
White Riesling (*dry and sweet*)

**Red wines**
Cabernet Sauvignon
Pinot Noir (*dry and nonalcoholic grape juice*)
Valdiguié (*known as Brocol in France*)
Zinfandel

## HOW TO REACH THEM

Philo, California
800-537-9463 (*toll-free*)
707-895-3686 (*phone*)
707-895-3647 (*fax*)
www.navarrowine.com

# LEMON RICOTTA CAKE WITH BLUEBERRY COMPOTE

**LEMON AND RICOTTA CHEESE ARE A NATURAL PAIR—LIGHT AND INVIGORATING.** In this case, the ricotta makes the cake more dense and moist, but it is still very refreshing. The fresh blueberry compote, with the addition of dessert wine, adds depth and sophistication. The crème fraîche sorbet on page 257 is the perfect accompaniment to this dessert, but if you don't have time to make that, this cake is equally good with regular crème fraîche or slightly sweetened whipped cream. This is a cake for company, since all of the components can be made ahead, and when assembled it looks as if you've worked all day.

Preheat the oven to 350°F. Butter an 8-inch round cake pan and dust with sugar. Set aside.

To make the cake: In the large bowl of a stand mixer, or in a large bowl, using a hand mixer, combine the dry ingredients and the lemon zest. Add the butter and mix on low until creamy. Turn the mixer to medium speed and add the sour cream, mixing until smooth and almost pastelike. Next, add the egg yolks, again mixing until smooth. Add the cheese and vanilla and beat at high speed until fluffy. Turn out into the prepared pan and smooth the top.

Bake the cake for 35 to 45 minutes, or until a toothpick inserted comes out with a few crumbs still clinging to it. You do not want the toothpick to come out completely clean, as this will indicate the cake is overdone. Cool for 15 minutes in the pan on a cooling rack and then remove the cake from the pan to cool completely.

To make the compote: In a medium-sized, heavy-bottomed pot, combine the water, sugar, lemon juice,

## FOR THE CAKE

1½ cups cake flour, sifted

¾ cup superfine sugar (or use regular sugar) plus a little extra for dusting

¾ teaspoon baking powder

¼ teaspoon baking soda

Pinch of salt

1½ teaspoons grated lemon zest (about half a medium lemon)

8 tablespoons (1 stick) unsalted butter, at room temperature, cut in small pieces

½ cup sour cream, quark, or plain yogurt

3 large egg yolks

½ cup whole-milk-ricotta cheese (not low-fat. If the ricotta is quite watery, drain it by lining a colander with cheesecloth or with a double layer of paper towels. Place cheese in the colander and let it sit for about 15 minutes.)

1 teaspoon vanilla

## FOR THE COMPOTE

½ cup water

¼ cup sugar

2 teaspoons fresh lemon juice

¼ teaspoon vanilla

2 cups fresh blueberries

Crème Fraîche Sorbet (page 257), crème fraîche, or whipped cream (optional)

and vanilla. Bring to a boil over medium-high heat. Cook for 1 minute. Turn the heat to medium-low and add 1 cup of the blueberries. Cook until some of the skins start to come off, 3 to 5 minutes. Remove the pot from the heat and add the remaining 1 cup blueberries. (The second half of the berries will be plumped rather than cooked, resulting in a slight crispness on the outside of the berry and a soft, creamy interior.) Stir to coat the second half of the berries in the group and let cool.

To serve, cut thin slices of cake (a little goes a long way), drizzle with a spoonful of compote, and top with a small scoop of sorbet, a dollop of crème fraîche, or whipped cream.

Serves 10 to 12

Note: The compote can be made 1 day in advance and refrigerated. Bring to room temperature before using.

## PERFECT PAIRS

**THE BLUEBERRY COMPOTE** that tops the cake is light and sweet, so the best wine for this dessert is one that mirrors those qualities. Muscat and a sweet sparkling wine are two good choices; so, too, is a late-harvest Sauvignon Blanc, which will find a particular affinity with the cake as well as the compote.

# CRÈME FRAÎCHE SORBET

**ALTHOUGH MOST SORBETS ARE VEHICLES FOR RIPE, SEASONAL FRUIT, THIS ONE TRANSCENDS THE SEASONS.** With crème fraîche as the main ingredient, it is a year-round option that makes a creamy, rich, and welcome finale to any meal. Best of all, it is the ultimate garnish on any cake, such as the Lemon Ricotta Cake with Blueberry Compote (see page 255), a great foundation for fresh or dried fruit compotes (see page 171), or for cut-up fresh fruit. The sorbet is best when it is just made, but it can be frozen for one week with little ill effect.

⅔ cup sugar

1½ cups water

2 cups (16 ounces) homemade crème fraîche (see below) or two 8-ounce store-bought containers

1 teaspoon vanilla extract

2 teaspoons fresh lemon juice

In a medium-sized heavy pot, bring the sugar and water to a boil, stirring constantly, until the sugar dissolves, about 2 minutes. Let cook for 1 more minute. Transfer the syrup to a large heat-proof bowl and chill until completely cold, about 1 hour. When cold, whisk in the remaining ingredients. Transfer to an ice cream maker and process according to the manufacturer's instructions. You can serve the sorbet right away, or it will keep in the freezer for a week if transferred to an airtight container. Let soften slightly before serving.

Makes about 1½ pints to serve 6 to 8

## PERFECT PAIRS

**THE TARTNESS OF THIS** sorbet makes choosing a wine a bit tricky. You don't want to strip away the sweetness of a wine—or let a too-sweet wine overwhelm the sorbet. A good wine would be a semi-dry Riesling or semi-dry Gewürztraminer. These wines are not super sweet, but they are not bone dry either. You could also choose a full-fledged dessert wine as long as it isn't overly sweet.

# CRÈME FRAÎCHE

**MAKING YOUR OWN CRÈME FRAÎCHE IS SIMPLE.** The only thing you need to remember is to plan ahead, since it might take as much as 36 hours for the mixture to set up completely.

In a small stainless-steel bowl, mix together the ingredients. Cover the bowl with cheesecloth or with a light dish towel and place it in a cool, dry place such as a pantry or kitchen counter for at least 12 hours, gently stirring the mixture occasionally. You want the mixture to become quite thick; there should be very little liquid remaining. It could take as long as 36 hours for the mixture to set up, depending on the temperature in your home. When the mixture is thick, stir it once more. Place it in an airtight container and refrigerate. It will last 2 to 4 weeks. If any liquid comes to the surface, simply stir it back in.

2 cups heavy cream

⅓ cup sour cream (do not use nonfat, but low-fat is okay)

# Port Madison Farm

OCCASIONALLY, A NEW CHEESE WILL APPEAR THAT, IN THE MIDST OF ALL THE other magnificent cheeses, still manages to attract the spotlight. Port Madison Farm's goat cheese is one of those rare gems. The intense focus owners Beverly and Steve Phillips place on the quality of their milk translates to the quality of cheese. "We did double-blind taste tests to determine the best milk," says Beverly, when describing how they selected their goats.

The Port Madison Farm is named for the northern part of Bainbridge Island, where the Phillipses live. It is the oldest settled part of the island, and at one time it was the center of most of the activity in that part of Washington because of its bustling port. In fact, people in Port Madison used to describe Seattle as "that village across the sound." Now the farm is the only dairy in Kitsap County.

The Phillipses began farming on Bainbridge Island, in the late 1980s. They built a Grade-A goat dairy and started providing the Seattle market with fluid goats' milk—a niche that had not been filled. The natural offshoot of producing milk was making cheese, and Steve Phillips says they fell in love with cheesemaking. Because the focus of their business was fluid milk, Phillips says they bred their goats to produce a milk without goaty overtones. Their excellent-tasting milk later produced wonderful cheese.

It began with one goat: Eloise. Phillips says this Nubian produced over four thousand pounds of milk in her time, and that her milk had the seventh-highest percentage of protein of any goat in the country. It also had a high concentration of butterfat. Phillips says that although the milk output was low, the trade-off was that it had an exceptionally sweet taste. Eloise, in effect, set the standard for the Port Madison Farm cheese, and the Phillipses have taken measures to perpetuate her gene pool in subsequent generations.

The best way to discern the quality of any milk, other than to drink it, is to eat a fresh cheese made from it. The Phillipses' fresh chèvre is a prime example. It looks like fresh powder—a look that is enhanced by its snowball shape—and, unlike many fresh chèvres, its texture is neither crumbly nor wet. The painstaking way it is made explains its fine texture.

"No bags!" is Beverly Phillips' motto. Fresh goat cheese is usually made by piling the curds into burlap bags or cheesecloth and leaving them to drain. The end result can be cheese with a texture that alternates between lumpy and smooth. The Port Madison chèvre is made by ladling the curds into small individual molds. The curds are then left to drain for several hours before they are turned. They are then salted and left to drain in the refrigerator for two more days before they are wrapped for market. Packaging the cheese any sooner, Bev Phillips says, results in a cheese that is too wet.

Although fresh chèvre is their main seller, the Phillipses also make two other cheeses, including a rare goats' milk mozzarella. Made in approximately two-inch balls, the mozzarella is a big hit at the Seattle farmers' market. The Port Madison Farm Spring Cheese is another outstanding cheese. Made in a havarti style, it is a washed-curd cheese interspersed with lots of tiny holes, and its color is somewhere between ivory and cream. The flavor is like butter. Although it is normally aged for between two and four months, the pasteurized milk cheese shows hints of tremendous flavor even when it's younger than that. Spring Cheese is made in seven-pound wheels.

The Phillipses are intent on "milking" the best flavors from their goats' milk, and a low-stress environment for their goats is vital to their effort. That is why they keep their goats twelve to a pen, with each pen containing goats from the same generation. That arrangement keeps the goats from fighting, Steve says, and it also keeps them in the same lactation cycle. He explains that stress stimulates the production of adrenaline, which lends an unpleasant flavor to the milk. When harmony is maintained in the pen, the goats are less stressed, so they give better milk, he says.

As they go along, the Phillipses will be adding a blue cheese to their repertoire, and they've begun making a soft-ripened cheese they're rightfully proud of called Baby Brie. And who knows what else? With such fantastic milk and proven cheesemaking talent, the sky's the limit. In the meantime, Seattleites are now looking back across the sound at Bainbridge Island and its lone dairy and taking notice of the big splash it is making with some of the nation's best goat cheese.

WHAT THEY MAKE

Baby Brie  
Chèvre (*Plain and Flavored*)

Mozzarella  
Spring Cheese

HOW TO REACH THEM

Bainbridge Island, Washington  
206-842-4125 (*phone and fax*)  
www.portmadisonfarm.com

# PEAR AND GOAT CHEESE TART

**ALTHOUGH THIS MAY BE A DESSERT, IT IS NOT TERRIBLY SWEET.** Because of that, you want to choose pears that are very ripe, as they will provide the necessary sweetness. Peggy Smith, co-owner of Cowgirl Creamery in California and a long-time chef at Chez Panisse restaurant gave this recipe a subtle but powerful boost by suggesting the addition of pine nuts.

## FOR THE DOUGH

1 cup flour

1 tablespoon sugar

¼ teaspoon salt

8 tablespoons (1 stick) unsalted butter, cut in small pieces

3 to 4 tablespoons cold water

## FOR THE FILLING

6 ounces fresh goat cheese, at room temperature

2 tablespoons sugar

1 egg

½ teaspoon vanilla

¼ cup pine nuts

2 medium-sized pears (about 1 pound), preferably Comice or very ripe Bosc, peeled, cored, and sliced ⅛ inch thick

2 tablespoons unsalted butter, melted

1½ teaspoons large-granule decorative sugar, or use regular sugar

To make the dough: In the bowl of a food processor, combine the flour, sugar, and salt. Pulse twice. Add the butter and process just until the mixture looks a little like cornmeal, 8 to 10 seconds. Don't overprocess or your crust will turn out tough. Add the water, 1 tablespoon at a time, pulsing between additions. The dough should begin to hold together, but you do not want it to form a ball. This will mean there's too much water. Turn the dough out onto a large piece of plastic wrap. Pat it into a flattened disk, wrap with the plastic, and chill for at least 1 hour or overnight.

Preheat the oven to 375°F. Place the rack in the bottom third of the oven. Have a fluted 9-inch tart pan with a removable bottom ready.

Remove the dough from the refrigerator and let it sit for 10 minutes. Roll out a 13-inch circle of dough and carefully place it in the tart pan. Gently push the dough into the crevices of the pan, leaving some overhang. Roll the rolling pin over the edges of the tart pan to remove the extra dough. (It is fun to roll out the scraps and dot them with jam. Bake them alongside the tart but only for a few minutes. They will burn easily.) Line the bottom and sides of the dough with foil and fill the tart pan with pie weights or dried beans. Bake for 30 minutes. Remove the foil and weights and let the crust cool.

To make the filling: In a medium bowl beat together the cheese, sugar, egg, and vanilla. Stir in the pine nuts. Spread a thin layer evenly over the prepared tart shell. Lay the pear slices over the filling, close to the edges, slightly overlapping, in a circular pattern, continuing in toward the middle of the tart. Brush the pears with the melted butter and sprinkle with the sugar. Place the tart pan on a baking sheet and bake for 35 to 45 minutes, or until the edges of the tart are golden-brown and the pears have softened and turned brown around the edges. Remove from the oven and let cool completely before serving.

Serves 8 to 10

## PERFECT PAIRS

**THIS RUSTIC NOT-TOO-SWEET** tart is best paired with a medium-sweet sherry or a late-harvest Sémillon.

# Lazy Lady Farm

IT IS IMPOSSIBLE TO KNOW WHETHER OPPORTUNITY OR DESTINY PLAYS A BIGGER role in a person's future. Or whether either does. In the case of Laini Fondiller, the owner of Lazy Lady Farm, a strong case could be made for the contribution of both. A week after Fondiller graduated from Ball State University, she moved from Indiana to Massachusetts to join some high school friends for the summer. While there, she took a job helping a family with their ill son, but in her heart she yearned for a job on a nearby hog farm. After many bicycle rides past the farm, she eventually mustered the nerve to stop and ask for a job. She was hired "as a joke," she later learned. But that joke lasted four years, during which time Fondiller became a sow expert and knowledgeable about crop farming.

Farming proved to be a calling, a passion that rose to the surface as sure as the corn she was helping to grow. Although she was working for nothing, that first summer on the farm convinced her that she should forsake any prospective ivory tower future; she had found contentment on top of a Caterpillar. Her express desire to devote her life to the land met with consternation from her family, but the strong-willed Indiana native was not to be swayed.

She made her way to Vermont, where she worked on dairy farms for a few years. But a desire to work with something else besides cows led her to seek out small goat and sheep farms in France. Although she couldn't speak French at the time, she managed to secure work on dairy farms, and eventually on the island of Corsica. There she milked 250 goats "for some grumpy guys who yelled at me," she says good-naturedly. She also made cheese, learned French, and became irreversibly hooked on the life of a farmer. She went from the island to the highlands, tending 400 sheep (and two dogs) at 6,000 feet in the Alps. "That was the best job I ever had," she recalls. She returned to Vermont and worked on a few farms before finally calling one of them her own.

About seven miles from the Canadian border in Westfield, Vermont, Lazy Lady Farm is an anomaly in several ways. The standout feature is the low-tech means by which Fondiller makes her high-quality organic cheese. Laini and her partner, Barry Shaw, who Fondiller says does not like farming, live in a solar-powered environment, because their farm is located too far from the electricity lines. The remote, scenic, and silent area has kept them there.

In this bare-bones world, Laini rises at 5:30 to milk her twenty goats and makes her way to the cheese room about half an hour later. By day's end, she will have made three of her eleven cheeses, all in five-gallon batches. Because of space constraints, she cannot make larger batches.

At any given time, Fondiller may be working on La Roche, a cylindrical three-ounce marvel of pasteurized sweet, firm goat cheese with a soft, velvety white rind. Or she could be working on her aged raw-milk Capridose. This cheddar-like cheese, which is aged for two months, has an earth-toned rustic rind. The crevasses, ridges, and sandy features of the rind protect the semi-firm ivory-toned interior, whose flavor speaks more of fruit orchards than its rustic rind would suggest. Fondiller says that Capridose has been evolving for about ten years. It does not have a hint of goatiness, and its complexity seduces the taster to try it again and again.

Just as a popular chef has a signature dish or two, so too does a cheesemaker. For Fondiller, it is her La Petite Tomme. This Camembert-Brie hybrid, as she describes it, is unquestionably unique in the world of cheese. It has a favorable split personality: It trembles between soft and creamy—like a pinball, it bounces over the taste buds to register salty, sweet, and tart flavors—and it culminates in a textural and flavor sensation that will carry any true cheese aficionado to the level of connoisseur. To preserve the delicate integrity of this cheese, Fondiller wraps it in special paper. Because of the craftsmanship that goes into this cheese, as well as the special wrapping, it comes at a higher price. That does not deter its legion of regular buyers.

In addition to goats, Fondiller keeps two cows, a flock of sheep, some chickens, and half a dozen pigs, which drink the whey and eat any leftover cheese that is not salable. What is salable is sold primarily at the Montpelier, Vermont, farmers' market as well as in select places around the country and by mail order. But the small quantities go fast, and as a one-person operation, Lazy Lady Farm is unlikely to ever produce cheese for the masses.

Given the demands of running a solar-powered farm in the northern reaches of the country, the name Lazy Lady Farm is a humble paradox. Fondiller explains she liked the name because it's "kind of like my goal—to be a truly lazy lady." One wonders when she'll find the time to live up to her name.

## WHAT THEY MAKE

| | |
|---|---|
| Boursin | La Roche |
| Capridose | Mon Jardin |
| Capriola | Pyramid |
| Chèvre | Sage Brush |
| Feta | Valencay |
| La Petite Tomme | |

## HOW TO REACH THEM

Westfield, Vermont
802-744-6365 (phone)
802-744-2223 (fax)

# PORT-POACHED FIGS WITH PRESERVED LEMON AND GOAT CHEESE

**AS YOU CAN SEE, THIS RECIPE CALLS FOR PRESERVED LEMONS.** These are lemons that are preserved in salt and lemon juice and are, as a result, naturally very salty. Once rinsed, though, they impart an earthy, lemony flavor that mirrors the tart goat cheese. They are available at gourmet food stores or you can make your own. If you don't wish to use them, simply blanch finely sliced lemon peel in two changes of boiling water for thirty seconds, drain well, and pat dry. Chop and use according to the directions below.

1⅓ cups port

⅔ cup plus ¾ teaspoon water

½ cup plus ¾ teaspoon sugar

1 teaspoon vanilla

One 5-inch-long sprig fresh rosemary, plus 4 small sprigs for garnish

8 figs, stemmed and cut in half lengthwise

¼ cup fresh goat cheese

2 teaspoons finely chopped preserved lemon rind, rinsed well (optional), or use blanched, sliced lemon peel

¾ teaspoon milk

In a flat-bottomed, nonreactive pot, bring the port, water, ½ cup of the sugar, vanilla, and long rosemary sprig to a boil, stirring until the sugar is dissolved. Cook for 1 minute. Reduce the heat to medium-low. Add the figs, cut sides down, and cook for 5 minutes. Carefully remove the figs from the pot and arrange them on a plate, cut sides down, in a single layer to cool. Turn the heat back to high and boil the port mixture until it thickens and becomes syruplike, about 5 minutes. Remove from the heat and let cool to room temperature. (It will continue to thicken a little as it cools.)

In the meantime, in a small bowl mix together the cheese, lemon rind, milk, and ¾ teaspoon sugar.

To serve, place 4 fig halves, cut sides up, in a spoke-like pattern, on each of 4 plates. Spoon about 1½ teaspoons of the cheese mixture on top of each fig. Remove the rosemary sprig from the syrup and discard. Drizzle the syrup over the cheese. Arrange a small fresh rosemary sprig in the center of the figs on each plate. Serve immediately.

Serves 4

## PERFECT PAIRS

**LOOK NO FURTHER THAN** port as the wine to pair with this dessert. Anything else will pale in comparison.

# APPENDIX

# CHEESE TERMS

**Acidic:** A slightly sour and sometimes biting flavor in cheese.

**Acidification:** When the milk is becoming acidic due to the introduction of starter culture bacteria.

**Acidity:** The level of acid in raw milk. It also refers to the level of acid in the milk after starter culture bacteria have been added. The cheesemaker must know the acidity level before proceeding to the next phase.

**Affineur:** The "cheese finisher," or person whose specialty and responsibility is to age cheese.

**Aged:** Describes a cheese that has been left to mature, and in the process to lose moisture and develop flavor. The term can refer to a cheese that is as young as three weeks, as in the case of a crottin, but usually it refers to cheeses that are allowed to mature for a minimum of two months.

**Aging:** The process cheese undergoes as it evolves from its wet to its solid state. The longer cheese ages, the less moisture it will have and usually the more flavor it will develop.

**Ammoniated:** The condition of overripeness, usually of soft-ripened cheese, where the aroma and taste are similar to ammonia. An undesirable quality.

**Annatto:** A seed from which color is extracted to create the orange hue found in some cheddar and Colby cheeses.

**Aroma:** The smell that emanates from a cheese. It can be mild to overpowering, though it does not always translate directly to the flavor.

**Asadero:** A mild, fresh Mexican-style cheese, either processed or natural, that is often molded into a log and sliced.

**Asiago:** A pressed-curd salted cheese that is sold as a fresh cheese as well as an aged, or grana-style, cheese. It has a sweet, mild flavor when young and a piquant flavor when aged.

**Baby Swiss:** A smaller, milder version of Swiss cheese. The holes, or eyes, in the cheese are smaller than those found in the large wheels of Swiss cheese, and the wheels are usually only five pounds or less. Baby Swiss is also higher in moisture than Swiss.

**Bacteria:** The microorganisms that circulate just about everywhere, including cheese aging rooms, which contribute to the cheese's final flavor. Bacteria also occur naturally in the cheese, fostering the aging and flavor of the cheese.

**Bacterial cultures:** Starters that bring the milk to the proper acid level. They also contribute to the flavor and texture found in cheese.

**Bacterial-ripened cheese:** See Surface-ripened cheese.

**Bakers' cheese:** Also known as pot cheese, bakers' cheese is a nonfat, dry, soft-curd cheese used in baking. It is also the favored ingredient for cheese blintzes.

**Balanced:** Concentration of milk and acid in a cheese. If it is balanced, the milk flavors and acid level in the cheese are correctly proportional.

**Barnyardy (sometimes called barny)**: Describes a flavor and aroma in some cheese that is reminiscent of the smells that emanate from a barn or barnyard. Usually it is similar to a strong, musty, and even sometimes dirtlike flavor or aroma, and despite that description, can be a favorable quality in many cases. Some aged goat cheeses and some sheep's milk cheeses might be described as barnyardy.

**Beer Kaese (also Beer Käse):** Also known as beer cheese, beer kaese is a surface-ripened cheese that is usually quite strong in both flavor and aroma. Some believe it was invented to accompany beer, giving it its name. It is made primarily in Wisconsin.

**Bitter:** An unfavorable component in cheese that is often detected after the cheese has been swallowed. It leaves a lingering off-taste in the mouth. This bitter flavor can be likened to the taste of caffeine.

**Blind:** A Swiss cheese with very few holes, or eye formation. The traditional Swiss cheese flavor might also be missing from a blind cheese.

**Bloomy rind:** The white, flowery, and desirable downlike surface of a soft-ripened cheese such as Camembert or Brie, the result of a bacterial spray or powder, usually Penicillium candidum.

**Blue-surface cheese:** A cheese that has blue mold characteristics on the outside, usually due to the addition of both internal and external molds, but is not pierced to allow blue veins to form.

**Blue-veined cheese:** A cheese in which a mold (usually *Penicillium roqueforti*) is added to the curds. Once the cheese is pressed and formed, it is skewered to create veins, allowing air to penetrate the cheese and foster mold growth. The mold that is formed in those veins and throughout the cheese is blue or blue-green, resulting in the name for the cheese. Blue cheese can be made from cows', goats', or sheep's milk.

**Body:** The texture of the cheese.

**Brick cheese:** A surface-ripened cheese that is mild when young, but when aged becomes very pungent. It is made in the form of a brick, although it is said it got its name because of the brick-like shape of the weights that were originally used to press the cheese.

**Brie:** A round, creamy, soft-ripened cheese with a bloomy rind. American-made Brie is usually four- to six-ounces.

**Brine:** A solution, usually salt and water, in which certain cheeses are soaked for anywhere from a few hours to several months. It is a means of salting the cheese as well as creating a protective exterior for longer aging. Gouda, Emmentaler, Gruyère, and dry Jack are cheeses that are brined before they are aged. Feta cheese is often stored and sold in brine and can be kept that way for over a year, while mozzarella is often briefly soaked in brine before it is packaged.

**Brushed rind:** A process where the rind of a natural-rind cheese is brushed to keep mold from forming and to keep the interior of the cheese moist.

**Butterfat:** The fat portion of milk. This varies according to animal, with sheep's milk having the highest proportion of butterfat.

**Butter Kaese (or Butterkäse):** A mild, semi-soft cheese that in some cases is spreadable and firmer in other cases. It is up to the individual cheesemaker how it is made. It is made in a loaf shape for easy slicing and usually found in the Midwest.

**Butterscotch:** The caramel-like flavor that develops in some aged cheeses. It is most often found in a well-aged Gouda.

**Buttery:** Can apply to both texture and flavor. In the case of texture, it is the quality of butter: creamy yet with body. A ripe California Teleme or a ripe Camembert might be described as buttery in texture. When used to describe the flavor, buttery pertains to the cream-like, rich flavor in the cheese. Again, a ripe Camembert could be described as butter as could many aged cheeses such as Gruyère.

**Camembert:** A creamy, bloomy-rind, soft-ripened cheese that originated in Normandy, France. The desirable outer mold is usually created by the spraying of the *Penicillium candidum* or *P. camemberti* mold. Sometimes, though, it is not sprayed and instead mold forms naturally as the result of particular molds that have been added to the curds. American Camemberts are usually made in four- to six-ounce wheels. Traditionally this is a cheese made with cows' milk, but many American cheesemakers are making Camemberts from goats' and sheep's milk as well.

**Casein:** The protein in milk that coagulates to form curds. This coagulation is brought about by the introduction of cultures to the milk. These cultures raise the acid level, causing the casein proteins to clump together or coagulate. Rennet is then introduced, which causes the protein bonding or coagulation to intensify, leading to curd formation.

**Caves:** Aging rooms that are usually built underground. These subterranean spaces allow for greater control over temperature, light, and humidity.

**Cellar:** Similar to a cave, a cellar is a room used for aging or ripening cheese. It is usually underground, but it may be part of a home, barn, or cheese plant, similar to a basement.

**Chalky:** Refers to the texture of a cheese, often a goat cheese, where the consistency is dry, crumbly, and leaves an undesirable coating on the tongue.

**Cheddar:** A natural cream-colored or dyed orange cheese that is usually classified by its age and is the result of a process of cheesemaking called cheddaring. The classifications are mild (usually two to four months old), medium (four to eight months old), sharp (nine to twelve months old), and extra-sharp (over one year up to as much as four years old).

**Cheddaring:** The process by which cheddar cheese is made. The curds are formed into long sheets and stacked to promote the draining of the whey. They are usually restacked several times to allow for maximum whey drainage. They are then milled, or cut into tiny pieces, and pressed into molds.

**Cheese board or cheese course:** A grouping of cheeses that is served before, after, or instead of a meal.

**Cheesecloth:** Thin cotton cloth used to drain cheese curds and/or line cheese molds.

**Chèvre:** The French word for "goat," chèvre refers to a fresh cheese made with pasteurized goats' milk. It comes in many shapes, including logs and rounds, or it can be sold in small tubs or in bulk at some cheese shops. It is a soft, spreadable cheese that is equally good on its own or as an ingredient in salads or cooked dishes, both sweet and savory.

**Chontaleño:** A semi-hard Central American–style cows' milk cheese, similar in texture and taste to the salty, crumbly cheese known as cotija.

**Citrusy:** A flavor characteristic that is similar to the tart, sometimes sour, and sometimes herbal qualities found in citrus fruits. It might be specific, such as orange-like or lemony. It often pertains to high-acid cheeses, such as a young goat cheese.

**Clean:** A flavor characteristic in a cheese that shows a bright, pronounced flavor with no aftertaste.

**Cloth-wrapped or bandaged:** Describes a cheese, usually cheddar, that is "bandaged" or wrapped in cloth and then aged.

**Coagulation:** The state in cheesemaking when the casein, or milk protein, clumps together to form curds.

**Coffee-flavored:** A flavor characteristic, often of a well-aged Gouda, that is similar to the taste of coffee.

**Colby:** A cheese thought to have been invented near the town of Colby, Wisconsin. It is similar to cheddar but differs in the cheesemaking process. The curds are washed with cool rather than hot water and they are not stacked and drained. Colby is a higher-moisture cheese that is generally mild. Some Colby is aged, in particular the Colby-like cheese called Crowley.

**Cooked curds:** A process in cheesemaking where the curds are heated, sometimes to very high temperatures, to help expel the whey. Examples of cooked-curd cheeses include Emmentaler and Gruyère.

**Cotija:** A hard, aged, white, crumbly Mexican cheese. Similar to feta, it is often sprinkled on dishes such as black beans or enchiladas or can even be used as a salt substitute in salads and potatoes. It is a very dry cheese that does not melt when heated. Cotija is also sometimes called queso añejo.

**Cottage cheese:** A fresh washed-curd cheese to which cream, milk, or nonfat milk is added to create a creamy consistency. The curds vary in size from small to large. It may be eaten plain or with fruit.

**Crescenza:** A fresh, runny cows' milk cheese that looks melted even when it hasn't been heated because of its creamy consistency. It is used in a variety of savory dishes because it melts so well, but it also pairs nicely with dried or fresh fruit. The flavor is similar to a mild Jack cheese.

**Crumbly:** Describes a cheese that literally crumbles when cut. Older blue cheeses may be crumbly, as are some fetas, cotija, queso blanco, and enchilado.

**Cracked:** When a cheese has visible fissures running through it. Sometimes this is the natural result of aging, but sometimes it signifies that the cheese has dried out and is likely past its eating prime.

**Creamy:** A favorable textural consistency and/or flavor of certain cheeses. It indicates a smooth and often runny consistency, and usually refers to the ripe forms of Brie, Camembert, California Teleme, and crescenza, among others. It can also refer to certain fresh cheeses, such as some cottage cheese, mascarpone, and crème fraîche. Creamy is also used to describe a flavor denoting rich or buttery characteristics.

**Crème fraîche:** Cultured milk or cream, or a combination of both. The result is a thick fresh cheese similar in consistency to sour cream. The flavor is buttery and a little tangy, which makes it good on fruit tarts or pies instead of whipped cream. It is also used in cooked dishes, both sweet and savory.

**Crottin:** A cylindrical cheese with a brownish, yellowish rind, made from goats' milk. Crottins are generally mild and are sold anywhere from ten days to three weeks old. If kept well, they can become hard grating cheeses in about eight weeks.

**Crowley:** A unique cheese invented in the mid-1800s. It is made by America's oldest continuously operating cheese factory, the Crowley Cheese Company in Vermont. It is a natural-colored cheese similar in texture and flavor to Colby.

**Curds:** The solid or coagulated portions of the milk. Curds are the result of the casein or milk proteins clumping together after they are exposed to starter bacteria. The starters raise the acid level of the milk, causing the casein molecules to bond together. The curds undergo further solidifying once rennet is introduced, and eventually the curds become cheese.

**Curing:** Synonymous with aging or ripening. The period when a cheese is left in a cave, or curing or aging room, to mature and lose some of its moisture.

**Cutting the curd:** After the rennet has been introduced and the curds have begun to form, the curds are then cut with various-shaped metal wires to help expel the whey.

**Delicate:** Describes the light, gentle aroma and/or flavor that comes from some young cheeses. The aroma from a young Jack, Teleme, or Fontina might be considered delicate.

**Dry Jack:** Monterey Jack cheese that has been aged at least one year to become a hard grating cheese.

**Dry matter:** The portion of the cheese that is comprised of solids. Most cheese has at least twenty-five percent of its weight in dry matter or solids. The non-dry matter is the liquid portion of a cheese. For example, a young Jack cheese will consist of about fifty percent dry matter, while the other fifty percent is moisture. This is also the portion of the cheese that is measured for total fat content.

**Earthy:** A generally positive term to describe a depth of flavor that has characteristics of the earth, or soil, of the area where the cheese is made and/or the feed of the animal. It often speaks to a slight mustiness in the cheese.

**Edam:** A mild cows' milk cheese in the family of Dutch cheeses that is usually shaped into an elongated sphere and waxed. It can be eaten as a table cheese while its slight saltiness lends flavor to cooked dishes as well.

**Emmentaler:** Often called Swiss cheese in the United States. Emmentaler is named after a river valley in Switzerland, where the cheese originated. It is usually made in large wheels weighing as much as 200 pounds and is distinguished by its large eye formation and hazelnut flavor.

**Enchilado:** A soft, crumbly Mexican cheese distinguished by its red coating, which is made from either chile powder or paprika. Enchilado añejo is a harder, longer-aged version of enchilado.

**Explosive:** A term used to describe a quality in cheese that simply lights up the flavor sensors. It does not necessarily equate to "strong," and instead refers to a cheese that, when tasted, literally bursts with flavor.

**Eyes:** These are the holes formed in cheese as a result of the introduction of certain bacteria. In the case of Swiss cheese, eyes are encouraged, usually by the introduction of the *Propionicacter shermanii* bacterium. This bacterium produces carbon dioxide, which creates bubbles that eventually burst, leaving the grape-size eyes behind. Other cheeses, such as Havarti, have smaller eyes because the bacteria used in those are not as aggressive.

**Farmer cheese:** A fresh cheese that is similar to cottage cheese, though it is less creamy, the curds are often smaller, and its taste is more sour.

**Farmlike:** The flavor characteristic that might also be described as grassy or hay-flavored. It is often a fresh, milky, or earthy flavor as compared to barnyardy, which can be stronger and more gamy.

**Farmstead:** A cheese that is made exclusively from milk that comes from the cheesemaker's own animals.

**Feed-flavored:** When the characteristics of the feed eaten by the animals are discernible in the taste of the cheese.

**Fermentation:** The process by which milk transforms into cheese and other milk products such as sour cream and yogurt. Technically, fermentation is the process leading to the breakdown of carbohydrates. In the case of milk, Lactococci or Lactobacilli bacteria are introduced to the milk, which causes the breakdown of lactose into lactic acid. This conversion sets up the proper acid levels and textural consistency for the milk to be made into cheese.

**Feta:** A fresh cheese that originated in Greece, where it was traditionally made with goats' or sheep's milk. In the United States it is made with either sheep's, goats', or cows' milk, or sometimes a mixture of two milks. Feta is usually kept in a saltwater brine and can be preserved for well over a year. It is a rindless cheese that, despite the brine, is dry and crumbly.

**Firm:** Refers to the body of the cheese when it is strong and smooth rather than weak or soft.

**Flat:** Indicates that the flavor of the cheese is neutral, with no particular standout characteristics; lacking flavor.

**Floral:** The fragrant quality in cheese that can pertain to both aroma and flavor. A floral flavor is a sweet though not sugary taste, such as in a fresh sheep's milk ricotta. It can also refer to a cheese that might have a floral component added to it.

**Fontina:** Originated in Italy, Fontina is a semi-hard, mild to strong-flavored cows' milk cheese. It is distinguished by its tiny eyes and is a brushed-rind cheese. In the United States, however, Fontina is not always a brushed-rind cheese, and at least one producer is making Fontina from goats' milk.

**Fresh cheese:** Cheese that has not been aged or ripened. Cottage cheese, pot cheese, and mozzarella are a few examples of fresh cheese.

**Fresh milk:** A flavor and/or aroma characteristic that is reminiscent of the pre-fermented milk. A just-made mozzarella, especially one made with the milk from a water buffalo, has this milk or lactic flavor.

**Fromage blanc:** A fresh (unripened) cultured cheese that can be made from cows', goats', or sheep's milk. Its consistency falls somewhere between ricotta and sour cream, and its taste lies somewhere between those two products as well. Tangier than ricotta but not as sour as sour cream, it can be used as a spread and is also very good for cooking since it melts nicely and adds creaminess and body. It can be used in pastas, risotti, pizzas, baked desserts, and with fruit .

**Fruity:** A flavor and/or aroma characteristic that is reminiscent of fresh fruit. The flavor or aroma can be that of a specific fruit, such as an apple-like flavor in a Gruyère, or more general, as in fruity, or with notes of sweetness. The aroma of a cheese might also have the natural sweetness that is associated with fruit.

**Gamy:** Can be a favorable or unfavorable characteristic, depending on the individual and the cheese. Gamy refers to the flavor and/or aroma in a cheese that has strong animal-like characteristics. If a goat cheese tastes gamy, it usually means that it has a strong, earthy flavor that the taster might be associating with the smell or taste of a goat. A young cheese generally should not have a gamy flavor or aroma.

**Garlicky:** Pertains to a garlic flavor occasionally detected in cheese. It usually comes from the feed or grasses that the animal has eaten. It is generally not a favorable characteristic.

**Gorgonzola:** An Italian blue-veined cheese that has been adopted by a few American cheesemakers. Gorgonzola is a cows' milk cheese made from pasteurized milk. It has two distinct styles, based on the length of aging. A young Gorgonzola may be called Gorgonzola dolce. It is creamy (sometimes so creamy it is best eaten with a spoon), with greenish-blue veins and a relatively mild but spicy "blue" flavor. Longer-aged Gorgonzola is firmer, spicier, and stronger-flavored.

**Gouda:** Of Dutch origin, Goudas were originally wax-wrapped mild cows' milk cheeses. While those are still made in great quantities, many American cheesemakers are now making Goudas in the Dutch *boerenkaas*, or farmstead, fashion. These are handcrafted raw milk, cooked-curd, brined Goudas that are aged for as long as two years. Longer-aged Goudas are golden in color and have a nutty, caramel, and sometimes coffee flavor. They can also be earthy, somewhat strong, and salty. Gouda is a good melting cheese, and because of that is good in many cooked dishes. Some Goudas are now made with goats' milk.

**Grana style:** A cheese that is made by cooking, pressing, and salting the curds. The pressed curds are then brushed and turned constantly during the aging process to become a dry, granular ("grana") cheese. Asiago is a type of grana cheese.

**Grassy:** Refers to a flavor, and sometimes an aroma, in a cheese that is reminiscent of grass. It usually relates to a certain acidic element that might even be perceived as sour by some. Fresh goat cheeses often have a grassy element, which is usually considered favorable. The grassy flavor and aroma can also pertain to the flavors and/or aromas that are the result of the grasses eaten by the animals.

**Green cheese:** Term used to describe a cheese just after it has been made and before it goes into the ripening room.

**Gruyère:** A so-called mountain or Alpine cheese because of its origins in the Swiss and French Alps. (French Gruyère is called Comté). Gruyère is a cooked-curd brined cheese that is aged from three months to one year. It has legendary melting qualities and is the usual ingredient in cheese fondue. It can range in flavor from mild to medium-strong and has nutty, earthy, and floral qualities. The most authentic Gruyère in the United States is made by Roth Käse in Wisconsin, which has a sister plant in Switzerland.

**Gummy:** Of or pertaining to a gumlike or chewy quality in the texture of cheese, often due to excessive moisture or condensation. An unfavorable characteristic.

**Hard:** Term used to describe cheeses that have been aged for a long period, and/or salted, and/or pressed, causing them to lose their moisture and become hard. Grating cheeses are hard cheeses.

**Havarti:** A generally mild cows' milk cheese made throughout the United States, but especially in Wisconsin. It has very small eyes and is a very good melting cheese. Havarti is often made with flavorings such as caraway seed, dill, or garlic.

**Heat-treated milk:** Falling somewhere between raw milk and pasteurized milk, this milk is quickly heated at a lower temperature. This might mean that the milk is heated at 130°F for two to sixteen seconds. The goal is to kill off any of the potentially unhealthful organisms that might exist in raw milk yet retain certain flavor and other characteristics that also exist in raw milk.

**Herbaceous:** A term that can apply to the flavor and/or the aroma of a cheese, referring to an herbal quality in the cheese. This quality can be the result of herbs added to the cheese, or herbs used in the curing process, but usually it is the result of the way the cheese is made, the area in which it is made, and the type of feed or grasses eaten by the animals whose milk was used for the cheese. It is often found in aged sheep's milk and goats' milk cheeses.

**Holes:** The same as eyes, holes are the distinguishing characteristic of Swiss or Emmentaler cheese. They are the result of carbon dioxide bubbles that form in the body of the cheese. This carbon dioxide occurs in response to specific bacteria that are deliberately introduced into the cheese. Other cheeses, such as Havarti and Fontina, have smaller holes because of the less aggressive bacteria present in these cheeses.

**Homogenization:** A process which breaks down and incorporates the fat globules found naturally in milk. This prevents the cream from separating and rising to the top. It also helps in cheesemaking because less of the fat is lost in the whey, which means the yield will be higher. Some cheesemakers deliberately avoid homogenization, however, because they believe the larger fat globules are beneficial to the consistency and flavor of their cheese.

**Ivory:** The light cream color in many cows' milk and some sheep's milk cheeses, including several undyed cheddars, the inside or paste of Camembert and Brie, Jack cheese, crescenza, and California Teleme.

**Jack cheese:** See Monterey Jack.

**Kasseri:** Usually a Greek sheep's milk cheese, in the United States it is made by some producers with cows' milk. It is a very mild cheese that is best used in cooking.

**Lactic:** The strong presence of milk flavor and/or aroma.

**Lactic acid:** The acid that is produced by the breakdown of lactose, which results from starter bacteria being added to the milk.

**Lactose:** A natural sugar present in milk.

**Lactose intolerance:** The inability of the body to break down lactose. Symptoms of lactose intolerance can include bloating, diarrhea, and nausea.

**Liederkranz:** Introduced in this country in the late 1800s, Liederkranz is a strong surface-ripened cheese that is made in a small oblong shape. It has a moist rind and a hefty aroma. Currently, it is made only by Marin French Cheese Company in California.

**Limburger:** A very pungent semi-soft surface-ripened cheese made and enjoyed primarily in the Midwest, though it originated in Belgium. Often served with raw onion on dark rye or pumpernickel bread. To some the aroma and taste of Limburger is overpowering.

**Longhorn:** A style of cheddar or Colby cheese that is so named because of its tall cylindrical shape.

**Mascarpone:** A naturally sweet, spreadable cream made with only two ingredients: cream and citric or tartaric acid. These ingredients are combined and left to drain, allowing all of the non-cream components, including the sodium, to separate out. The cream that is left is buttery in taste and texture. It is very rich and is used as an ingredient in both sweet and savory dishes. It also melts well and can sometimes be used in place of cream cheese, though it is creamier. Its best known use is in the Italian dessert tiramisù.

**Metallic:** Refers to a metal flavor detected in cheese. It is an unfavorable characteristic.

**Mold:** Spores that are added to the milk or the curds and/or the surface of a cheese to encourage mold growth as the cheese is formed. Surface molds are sometimes sprayed on the outside of the cheese, as in the case of Camembert. These types of molds are edible. Mold is also the undesirable growth that forms on the outside of old and/or poorly wrapped cheeses. This can often be cut away from the aged cheeses, however, and the cheese can then be consumed.

**Molding:** The step in cheesemaking when the curds are poured or hand-ladled into molds, usually plastic, that are outfitted with tiny holes to allow for drainage of the whey. Molding also contributes to the final shape of the cheese. Sometimes the molds are muslin or nylon bags that are tied in a particular shape. These bags allow for drainage and also create the final shape of the cheese.

**Monterey Jack:** Originated in California in the mid-1800s, Jack cheese is a cows' milk cheese that can be sold as a young, high-moisture semi-soft cheese or aged to become a hard grating cheese. The young version melts very well and is often used in Mexican cooking. It has a fruity flavor and aroma, but it also has a bit of a tang. The aged version, called Dry Jack by California's Vella Cheese Company, becomes golden after two or three years and is nutty, still somewhat fruity, and moderately salty. High-moisture Jack cheese is often made with flavors, including hot peppers, pesto, onion, or garlic.

**Mottled:** Describes a spotty and uneven appearance on the outside of the cheese, or an unevenness of color, usually due to the combining of curds from two different vats.

**Mouthfeel:** The way a cheese feels in the mouth. It might be smooth, dense, granular, buttery, or any number of other possible consistencies.

**Mozzarella:** A mild fresh cheese, made from either cows' milk or, in Italy, the milk of water buffalos. Hot water is added to the curds and whey, causing them to separate. The hot curds are stretched or kneaded for a short period and formed into their final shape, usually a ball. Because of this process, mozzarella is called a pasta filata, or stretched-curd cheese. Fresh mozzarella is sold in brine or water, and is often cut in slices and served in a salad with sliced fresh tomato, basil, and olive oil. In its drier form, mozzarella is packaged in plastic and used primarily as a grating cheese for pizzas and other cooked dishes. For this reason, it is often referred to as a pizza cheese. It can be made with either whole milk or part skim milk.

**Muenster:** Traditionally a strong French washed-rind cheese (spelled Munster). American Muenster is a very mild, slightly sweet cows' milk cheese, used mainly for melting in grilled cheese sandwiches or eaten plain alongside some fresh apples. It is an excellent "beginner's cheese" because of its mildness.

**Mushroomy:** Describes the flavor and/or aroma in a cheese that is reminiscent of mushrooms.

**Musty:** Often due to mold growth, a musty flavor or aroma that can be likened to dirt. It is earthy to the point of dankness, and such flavor often lingers well after the cheese has been consumed. It is not a favorable characteristic.

**Mutton-like:** Describes the aroma or flavor in a cheese that is similar to the taste or smell of sheep or lamb; a strong, gamy flavor or aroma.

**Natural rind:** A rind that develops naturally due to bacteria in the cheese, and/or introduced to the surface of the cheese, and/or found in the cheese aging room.

**Nutty:** A favorable flavor and sometimes aromatic characteristic often found in aged cheeses. As the word implies, nutty refers to the toasty and sometimes woody flavors that are found in nuts. Those same flavors can be found in certain cheeses, including Swiss, Gruyère, and Parmesan.

**Oaxaca:** A mild Mexican cows' milk cheese that is nearly identical in taste to mozzarella. It, too, is a stretched-curd cheese, or pasta filata, but instead of a ball, Oaxaca is formed into the shape of a braid.

**Oniony:** A flavor of onion that comes through in the cheese. This is usually due to the feed or grass that has been eaten by the animals. It is generally an unfavorable characteristic.

**Open:** Refers to the body or texture of a cheese that contains holes or openings.

**Panela:** A Mexican fresh cows' milk cheese that is molded in baskets and gently pressed to release some of its moisture. Panela is an excellent frying cheese because it softens but does not melt when cooked. It can even be sliced and grilled. It can be used in both sweet and savory dishes.

**Parmesan:** A grana-style cheese that, in the United States, is made with pasteurized or heat-treated milk. The curds are then cooked and salt is either added to the curds, or the pressed cheese is placed in a saltwater brine. Domestic Parmesan is aged a minimum of ten months. In Italy, traditional Parmigiano-Reggiano is made from raw milk and is aged for a minimum of eighteen months.

**Pasta filata:** Literally "stretched curd," pasta filata cheeses are those that are hand-or machine-stretched while still warm and made into a variety of shapes. This stretching creates the stringlike characteristic common to all pasta filata cheeses. Examples of pasta filata cheeses are mozzarella, Oaxaca, Provolone, and the well-known string cheese.

**Paste:** The interior of a cheese. In French, the interior is called the *pâte*.

**Pasteurization:** The process by which milk is heated with the intent of killing any unwanted or unhealthful organisms. The standard formula for pasteurization is 160°F for fifteen seconds. This, however, varies according to the pasteurization equipment and sometimes the intended cheese. Fresh, unripened cheeses are heated at 145°F for thirty minutes.

**Pasty:** Describes an unfavorable sticky consistency in the body of the cheese.

**Pencillium camemberti:** A mold spore sometimes used in the production of Camembert cheese.

**Penicillium candidum:** A mold that is often used in certain soft-ripened cheeses to create flavor as well as the growth of a particular type of rind.

**Peppery:** Refers to a spicy flavor often found in some blue cheeses.

**Perfumy:** Term used for the perfume-like aroma that is emitted from certain cheeses. Aged Goudas and Gruyères often have this characteristic.

**Piquant:** A bright, tangy, and sometimes sharp flavor characteristic. It can be detected in certain young goat cheeses and also in some cheddars.

**Pot cheese:** A low-fat plain cottage cheese that has no added salt. It is also called dry curd cottage cheese. The name comes from the time when cheese was made from skim milk and heated in a pot on the stove.

**Provolone:** A stretched-curd, or pasta filata, cheese made with either raw or pasteurized milk. It can be aged for as long as two years, at which time it becomes hard and salty. The younger versions of Provolone are a common sandwich ingredient, but Provolone also melts well in cooked dishes.

**Pungent:** A strong and possibly acrid flavor or aroma found in some cheese. Many surface-ripened cheeses, such as brick and Limburger, might be described as pungent. To some this is a desirable characteristic, and to others it is not. Some cheeses might have a pungent quality because they are poorly made or are too old. In this case, the result is undesirable.

**Quark (or quarg):** A staple for most Germans, quark is a nonfat or low-fat fresh cheese whose consistency lies somewhere between yogurt and a creamy cottage cheese. It is, in fact, similar to bakers' cheese. Some producers make nonfat versions of quark, while others include butterfat in their recipes. It can be used in place of sour cream or yogurt in baking, and it can also be used as a tart topping on toast. It is also a tangy addition to a fresh fruit salad.

**Queso añejo:** See Cotija.

**Queso blanco:** A mild Mexican semi-hard cheese made from cows' milk. Used primarily in cooking.

**Queso blanco fresco:** A mild, fresh Mexican cheese that is very firm yet moist. It can be used in cooking, but it does not melt. It is similar in consistency to feta cheese and can be similarly crumbled. When used for frying, queso blanco fresco is called queso para freir, or "frying cheese."

**Rancid:** Refers to a soapy, bitter, and off flavor that is usually the result of poorly handled milk.

**Raw milk:** The milk that comes directly from the animal. It is milk that has not been pasteurized.

**Red-hued:** The color of the rind on some surface-ripened cheeses, such as brick and Limburger. Also, the undesirable color of an overripe soft-ripened cheese, such as a Camembert.

**Rennet:** An animal, vegetable, or microbial substance that contains the enzyme rennin, which is crucial to the coagulation of milk. Traditionally rennet came from the stomach of a calf, but it also comes from sheep and goats. Non-animal sources include the vegetable known as cardoon, and microbial rennet is the laboratory-made genetic equivalent of animal rennet.

**Rennin:** The enzyme that coagulates milk.

**Rich:** Used mostly to describe a full-flavored, high-butterfat cheese. It can also describe a cheese whose earthiness or saltiness is the predominating characteristic. A Parmesan cheese might be considered rich because it is high both in butterfat and in salt.

**Ricotta:** A slightly granular and mild fresh cheese most often made with cows' milk. It is made in several ways: entirely from the whey; with whole or part skim milk; and without the whey. It can be quite watery or it can be fairly dry, depending on the producer and packager. Although rare in this country, sheep's milk ricotta is particularly flavorful and worth trying.

**Ricotta salata:** The dry form of ricotta. Ricotta salata is made, usually from whey, and then placed in a basket to drain. It is pressed to release further moisture from the cheese and left to dry for weeks or months. It is then used as a grating cheese. Most ricotta salata comes from Italy and is made from sheep's milk.

**Rind:** The outside of a cheese, either natural or artificial. The rind protects the interior of the cheese and often imparts a flavor of its own to the cheese. Some cheeses have no rind at all because the cheesemaker has chosen to package the cheese before a rind has the chance to form. This packaging can be in the form of wax, plastic, or in the case of Washington State University's Cougar Gold, a can.

**Rind rot:** The visible soft spots, discoloration, or rotting of a cheese rind.

**Ripe:** A cheese that is ready to be eaten. Refers to any cheeses that are aged, regardless of the period of time they are aged. A ten-day-old cheese might be considered ripe.

**Ripening:** Synonymous with aging, ripening is the process of maturing a cheese.

**Robust:** Rich and full-bodied. The cheese might burst with a number of flavors, including but not limited to those that are buttery, gamy, herbal, or floral.

**Romano:** A granular-style cheese made almost exclusively from cows' milk in this country. It is quite salty and is used primarily as a grating cheese.

**Rubbery:** A term that pertains to an undesirable quality in the texture of a cheese. It suggests a certain stiffness and a lack of the textural qualities normally found in the particular cheese. Certain bulk-manufactured part-skim mozzarellas are inherently rubbery, as are many low-fat and nonfat cheeses. This is due to the relative lack of fat globules and the particular protein structure in these types of cheeses.

**Runny:** The state of a ripe cheese when it oozes outside of its rind after being cut or is no longer keeping its original shape. Examples might include some soft-ripened cheeses, California Teleme, and crescenza.

**Rustic:** Earthy and/or herbal qualities present in the flavor and/or aroma of a cheese. Certain natural-rind aged sheep's milk cheeses might be considered rustic.

**Saggy:** A cheese that is drooping. In the case of soft-ripened cheese, this can be favorable since it means that the cheese is ripe. However, it can just as easily mean that the cheese is overripe. A quick whiff will usually tell whether it's ripe or ready to be discarded.

**Salting:** The step in cheesemaking when salt is added to the cheese. It varies according to the type of cheese. For example, salt is added to the curds during cheddar making while it is added in brine form to a Gouda after the cheese has been molded.

**Savory:** Loosely defined as the "fifth sense" after sweet, sour, bitter, and salty. Several cheeses are characterized as savory, including aged cheddar and Parmesan. See Umami.

**Scamorza:** A fresh, oval-shaped pasta filata cheese that is made in both plain and smoked styles. It is very similar to mozzarella, though slightly more tangy, and can be used interchangeably.

**Sharp:** A flavor in cheese that straddles the line between piquant and bitter. Many bulk-manufactured American cheddars are labeled sharp. Usually refers to a step in the cheesemaking process where the enzymes are quickly heated to boost the acid level of the cheese. This translates to a sharper cheese. In specialty cheesemaking, the sharpness also comes about because of the acid content, but the full sharp flavor manifests itself slowly as a result of the aging process.

**Silky:** A term used to describe the texture of a cheese if that cheese is particularly smooth or runny.

**Smoked:** The flavor that is produced after a cheese has been subjected to a natural smoking process. Cedar chips, hickory chips, and other types of regional wood are most often used to make smoked cheese.

**Smoky:** Describes a flavor and/or aroma in a cheese that is reminiscent of smoke from a wood-burning fire. More loosely, it might simply mean an earthy component in the cheese.

**Soft cheese:** An unpressed, high-moisture cheese that is aged for a very short time. Crescenza is an example.

**Soft-ripened cheese:** A cheese that ripens from the rind inward due to the mold or bacteria added in the cheesemaking process and/or sprayed on the surface of the cheese. Evidence that a soft-ripened cheese has begun its ripening or softening is that the part of the cheese that lies just under the rind is becoming soft, sometimes to the point of being runny. Camembert and Brie are the best-known examples.

**Solid:** Term used when the texture of the cheese is firm and has no discernible openings. It also shows no weakness or "give" when pressed.

**Sour:** Refers to the condition when a cheese has an overpowering acidic component.

**Sour milk:** Refers to an unfavorable flavor in cheese that is reminiscent of sour milk, which would be sour and possibly musty.

**Spicy:** A characteristic in cheese that might be piquant, pungent, and/or aromatic. Blue cheese is often described as spicy because of its mold characteristics, while a cheese flavored with black pepper or chile peppers is also described as spicy.

**Springlike:** A flavor and/or aromatic characteristic in cheese that is fresh, herbaceous, perfumy, fruity, floral, or any combination of these.

**Squeakers:** Just-made cheddar cheese curds that are scooped up and packaged by the cheesemaker and sold on the day they are made. Squeakers were invented in Wisconsin, where they remain popular today. They are said to squeak when they are eaten, due to their freshness. Technically, if squeakers are sold the day after they are made, they are then called Day-Old.

**Starter:** The bacteria that is added to milk at the beginning of the cheesemaking process to raise the lactic acid level. This in turn creates "sour" milk, which then helps the milk to coagulate. The starter also lends flavor to the final cheese.

**Stravecchio:** Name of Wisconsin's Antigo Cheese Company's aged Parmesan. Meaning "very old," Stravecchio is aged for twenty months.

**Sulfurous or Sulfide flavor:** The flavor and/or aroma in a cheese that is reminiscent of rotten eggs. It is thought to come about when, for some reason, an enzyme found in certain bacteria breaks down two of the sulfur amino acids in cheese.

**Supple:** Refers to a texture that is pliable, smooth, and/or satiny.

**Surface-ripened cheese:** A cheese on which bacteria is encouraged to grow on the surface, such as with brick cheese or washed-rind cheeses, to achieve distinct (usually strong) flavors. Also called bacterial-ripened cheese.

**Sweet:** The flavor or aroma of a cheese that usually signifies a lower-acid cheese and possibly one with a less pronounced sodium component.

**Swiss cheese:** The famous "cheese with the holes." It originated in Switzerland, though in that country it is referred to as Emmentaler, which is a slightly different cheese. In this country, as in Switzerland, it is a cooked- and stirred-curd cheese that is salted after it has been lightly pressed. The large eyes form as a result of carbon dioxide, which is created by the introduction of certain bacteria. Ohio is this country's largest producer of Swiss cheese.

**Tangy:** Used when describing goat cheese, due to its piquant flavor. It often suggests a higher-acid cheese.

**Teleme:** A cheese that is in the brine family of cheeses (of which feta is one), originating in Greece. In this country, it is a soft, sometimes runny cheese (depending on ripeness) that was created in the early 1900s in California, where it is still made today. Similar to Jack cheese, though with more pronounced fruitiness.

**Tilsit:** A semi-soft to semi-hard washed-rind cows' milk cheese that has roots in several European countries. The wheel-shaped cheese is mild when it is young, and when aged becomes strong and favorably earthy. It is a particularly good cooking cheese because of its melting properties and its full flavor.

**Truffly:** A flavor and/or aroma in cheese that is earthy, almost dirtlike, but favorably so. The characteristic pertains to the prized fungus known as a truffle.

**Turophile:** A cheese aficionado.

**Umami:** A term used to describe the "fifth taste," after sweet, sour, salty, and bitter. It was identified by the Japanese and is now being studied in this country. Umami is loosely equated to the term savory. Many foods fall into the umami category that don't fall neatly into the other four taste categories, such as mushrooms, tomatoes, and some shellfish. Aged cheddar and Parmesan, among others, are said to have umami.

**Vegetal:** Describes a plantlike flavor or aroma in a cheese. It can include any type of plant or vegetable.

**Veiny:** Containing an abundance of veins, which are caused by the proliferation of mold in the cheese, brought about by the introduction of oxygen. This is how the veins in blue cheese are formed, where it is a favorable characteristic. It is an unfavorable characteristic in a cheese in which the veins are unintended.

**Velvety:** Pertains to the texture and/or mouthfeel of a cheese. Both the rind and the paste of a ripe soft-ripened cheese might be said to have velvety characteristics.

**Washed-rind cheese:** Cheese in which the rind is literally washed with a solution, usually salt, water, and *Brevibacterium* or *B. linens* to keep the cheese moist as well as to lend flavor. This moisture can translate to a stronger cheese, depending on the cheese. A washed-rind cheese can also be washed with liquids besides saltwater, such as cider, beer, or wine.

**Wax or paraffin:** The wax coating of a cheese. If the wax is applied well and is of good quality, it should adhere tightly to the cheese and show no signs of cracking.

**Weedy:** Refers to a flavor in a cheese that is overly vegetal and/or grassy and/or earthy.

**Whey:** The high-protein liquid portion of milk that forms after the milk protein, or casein, begins to coagulate and becomes curds.

**Yeasty:** A flavor and/or aroma in a cheese that is reminiscent of baking bread, a good Champagne, or brewed beer. A blue cheese might have a yeasty aroma, as might certain soft-ripened cheeses.

# WINE TERMS

**Acetic:** A vinegar-like taste and/or smell that is caused by acetic acid, a by-product of fermentation.

**Acid:** The grape component that gives wine liveliness, freshness, and ageability. The predominant acids are malic, tartaric, and citric acid. Other acids, such as acetic and carbonic, are produced during fermentation.

**Acidic:** Term used to describe a wine with high, and therefore perceptible, acidity. It is often harsh or astringent wine. Some acidity is favorable; too much can result in a harsh or astringent wine.

**Acidity:** An essential component in wine for balance; without it, a wine will usually be fat or flabby.

**Aeration:** The deliberate action of swirling a glass of wine or decanting wine to draw air into the wine. The air helps to release some of the wine's flavor and aroma components.

**Aftertaste:** Different from the finish, the aftertaste refers to the flavors that remain in the mouth after swallowing.

**Aging:** During winemaking, aging refers to the period of time that the unbottled wine is kept in fermentation vats and/or barrels. Generally, the longer the aging period, the more oaky and intense the wine. Aging also refers to the period of time a wine is in the bottle. Wines with big tannins are generally the best candidates for aging, since the aging process will usually help mellow such wines. Aging, however, does not always improve wine; if the wine isn't balanced when it's bottled, it likely won't improve over time, either.

**Alcohol:** Also called ethanol, alcohol is the result of fermentation, or the process by which the yeasts convert the sugar in the grape juice to alcohol and carbon dioxide.

**Alcoholic:** Term used to describe a wine that is high in alcohol. Also called "hot." Too much alcohol in a wine is generally an unfavorable characteristic as it indicates the wine is out of balance.

**American Viticultural Area (AVA):** The official term for a specific wine-growing area, such as Sonoma County. An AVA is designated by the Bureau of Alcohol, Tobacco, and Firearms. It refers only to a geographic area. An AVA does not indicate which type of grape or grapes are grown within that area.

**Anthocyanins:** The pigments of red-skinned grapes.

**Appellation:** In the United States, appellation is synonymous with AVA.

**Aroma:** Usually refers to the smell of the grape variety or varieties in the wine, although it can also refer to the smells that result from the winemaking and aging process. For example, a wine can have an oaky aroma.

**Aromatic:** A term used to describe a wine that is particularly high in herb and/or spice aromas.

**Astringent:** The pungent, "mouth-puckering" flavors of a wine that is very high in acidity or tannins.

**Austere:** A wine that is lacking in fruit, creating a severe quality; usually such wines have excessive tannins and/or acidity that may diminish with age.

**Balance:** A wine is said to have balance when each of the components in the wine—the alcohol, acids, fruit, and tannins (in red wines)—are detectable, yet no single component is dominant. For example, a dessert wine that does not have detectable acidity is likely to be cloying and too sweet. In this case, the wine does not have the proper balance.

**Barrel:** The oak wood vessel used to ferment and/or age wine. It consists of wood staves, which are heated and bent to create the barrel shape. The intensity of the oak ranges from mild to high, depending on how the oak is treated or toasted (light, medium, or heavy). The degree to which the wood is toasted significantly influences the flavors in the wine. Also, new barrels impart the most flavors to the wine.

**Barnyard:** A wine smell that is analogous to a barnyard. It is usually a flaw that occurs during the winemaking process.

**Berries:** Another word for grapes; used most often before the grapes have matured.

**Big:** A catch-all word to describe a wine that is full-bodied, full-flavored, and intense.

**Bitter:** This quality can result from the winemaking process, or sometimes certain grapes are inherently bitter if not handled correctly. A grape, such as Gewürztraminer, is inherently bitter—a quality that is exacerbated if the sugars get too high.

**Blanc de noirs:** Literally "white from black," blanc de noirs refers to a sparkling wine that is slightly pink hued rather than red, even though it is made with red wine grapes (Pinot Noir). Because the wine is not left in contact with the skins, it does not become a red wine and therefore is a "white wine made from black," or blanc de noirs.

**Blanc de blancs:** Literally "white from white," a blanc de blancs is a sparkling wine made entirely from Chardonnay grapes.

**Blending:** The process by which a winemaker combines different lots of wine to create one single, presumably superior, wine.

**Blush wine:** A pink-hued wine made with red-skinned grapes. A blush wine retains its pink color rather than being entirely white, even though skin contact (from which wine gets its color) is kept to a minimum.

**Body:** Technically, body refers to the level of alcohol in the wine, which accounts for the wine's weight, viscosity, and mouthfeel.

**Botrytis:** The so-called noble rot, or beneficial mold, that develops on some grapes. Botrytis shrivels the grapes, intensifying their sugars yet maintaining acidity, which makes for excellent dessert wines. Botrytised wines are used for making some of the world's finest dessert wines; the most famous among them is Sauternes, which is made from botrytised Sémillon grapes. In the United States, such wines are usually referred to as "late-harvest" wines.

**Bottle shock:** The phenomenon whereby a wine that has just been bottled may taste flat and/or have an unpleasant aroma. Bottle shock usually goes away a few weeks after bottling. Also called bottle sickness.

**Bouquet:** Refers to the overall aroma of the wine that comes from the winemaking processes as well as aging, as opposed to one single element, such as the grape(s) used to make the wine.

**Brettanomyces:** In wine parlance, this undesirable yeast is often referred to in its truncated form, "brett." Although no winery can avoid the presence of this yeast, most go to great pains to prevent it from dominating their wine. Brettanomyces is easily detected through its barnyardy or "horsey" aroma. Some people are more sensitive to the presence of brett than others; some actually enjoy this quality while others do not.

**Brix:** Refers to the sugar level of grapes. The word comes from the name of the man who developed the system used to measure the sugar content of grapes.

**Brut:** A measurement of dryness in sparkling wine. Brut is the driest.

**Bud break:** Term used to describe the cycle in grape growing when the buds begin to appear on the grapevines. Bud break is the precursor to flowering, which happens two to three months later.

**Bulk wine:** Refers to a large quantity of wine that is sold in bulk. The buyer rather than the seller bottles the wine.

**Buttery:** The quality in a wine, most often Chardonnay, that is the result of malolactic fermentation. It is specifically owing to the presence of diacetyl, the same compound found in butter.

**Cap:** The accumulation of skins, seeds, and sometimes stems at the top of a tank of fermenting red wine.

**Caramel:** A burnt sugar quality in the flavor and sometimes aroma of the wine.

**Carbon dioxide:** The by-product, along with alcohol, of fermentation. In the making of sparkling wine, carbon dioxide is deliberately harnessed in the bottle to create the wine's distinct bubbles.

**Chapatalization:** The introduction of sugar during the winemaking process to complete fermentation. Sugar is added when the natural sugar content of the grapes is low, usually because they are grown in a cool climate where the grapes cannot sufficiently ripen. Adding sugar to wine is illegal in California, where, because of the hot climate, it is assumed the grapes will reach sufficient sugar levels.

**Character:** Used to describe a wine that has distinctive (positive) qualities.

**Chewy:** A term used to describe a wine that is full-bodied (high in alcohol) with loads of tannins. Such a wine has a distinctive mouthfeel and is therefore described as chewy.

**Citrus(y):** Characteristics in wine that are similar to those found in citrus fruits, such as lemon, grapefruit, and lime. It is partly owing to the variety, and it is sometimes owing to the acidity in the wine.

**Clarity:** The desirable clear quality of a bottled wine, particularly in a white wine. Clarity is most often achieved through filtering. A lack of clarity is not, however, necessarily a flaw.

**Clean:** A straightforward wine with a simple flavor and usually without flaws.

**Closed:** A wine whose qualities are not detectable, either because it is too young, too cold, or simply in need of air to release its aromas and flavors.

**Cloudiness:** Indicates the presence of sediments, usually because they haven't been sufficiently filtered from the wine.

**Cluster:** Group or single bunch of grapes.

**Cloying:** Refers to a wine that is too sweet, usually because of a lack of necessary acidity to bring it into balance.

**Complex(ity):** A favorable term used to describe a wine that is multidimensional in flavor, aroma, and color.

**Corkage:** The fee charged by a restaurant to open a wine that a customer has brought to the restaurant rather than purchased from the restaurant. Some states, such as Colorado, do not allow customers to bring in their own wine, while other states allow or even encourage it.

**Corked:** Refers to a wine that has been ruined owing to the presence of tricloranisole (TCA), a compound that comes from the bleaching process for cork. This compound interacts with natural bacteria in the cork and creates an off smell and taste in the wine. The resulting aroma is often likened to "wet cardboard."

**Creamy:** A term that refers less to taste and more to the texture of some wines. A creamy consistency is owing to the dead yeast cells, or lees.

**Crisp:** A term that usually applies to a wine that is high in acidity.

**Crush:** The time of year when the grapes are being harvested and brought in to have their juice extracted.

**Crusher-destemmer:** A machine used to crush the just-picked grapes and simultaneously remove the stems.

**Crushing:** The action of extracting juice from the grapes.

**Crystals:** The harmless solids sometimes found clinging to the inside of a wine bottle that come from tartaric acid.

**Decant:** To transfer wine from the bottle into another vessel to promote aeration and/or to separate the wine from any sediments in the bottle.

**Depth:** Similar to "complexity," depth refers to a wine that is multilayered. But it differs in that it also refers to a full-flavored wine, while complexity may or may not.

**De-stemming:** The process of removing the stems from grape clusters. This task is usually done in a special machine called a crusher-destemmer.

**Dosage:** The mixture of sugar and wine that is added to sparkling wine just before bottling to give it sweetness. The sweetness of the dosage determines how the wine is characterized—dry, extra dry, or off dry.

**Dry:** A wine that has virtually no residual sugar.

**Earthy:** A usually favorable aroma that is reminiscent of wet earth; slightly musty.

**Elegant:** A somewhat elusive term used to describe a wine that is balanced, often complex, and well made.

**Enology (oenology):** The study of winemaking.

**Estate bottled:** Refers to a wine that is bottled in the same location as the winery. It does not mean, however, that the grapes for the wine have come from the estate.

**Estate grown:** Refers to grapes that are grown on the property owned by the winery.

**Esters:** The slightly sweet aromas produced as a result of the reaction between acids and alcohol during fermentation.

**Ethanol:** (see alcohol)

**Fat:** Term used when a wine is low in acidity and/or is heavy.

**Fermentation:** In winemaking, fermentation is the conversion of sugar to alcohol and carbon dioxide. The process is brought about by the introduction of specific yeasts.

**Filtration:** The process by which the solids are separated from the wine and prevented from making their way into the final wine. Filtration is almost always done with white wines, in which clarity is essential, but some red winemakers choose not to filter their wines because they believe filtration negatively alters the flavor of their wine. Often a non-filtered red wine is imperceptible to the eye.

**Finesse:** Wine with flair, refinement, and elegance in style.

**Fining:** A process that removes harsh tannins in red wines. Many winemakers, however, choose not to fine their wine, believing that it removes flavor and complexity from the wine.

**Finish:** The flavor (and aroma) that lingers after swallowing.

**Flabby:** A wine in which there is a decided lack of acidity.

**Fleshy:** A wine with low tannins, high alcohol, and generally lots of flavor.

**Flinty:** Although technically this term comes from wines grown in certain soil, it is used broadly to describe wines—often Sauvignon Blanc—that are acidic and austere.

**Floral:** A wine whose taste and aroma are reminiscent of flowers.

**Foxy:** A term that refers to a wine made with grapes, such as Catawba, from the native American species Vitis labrusca. "Foxy" is used to describe wines that have a musky and generally unpleasant aroma.

**Free-run juice:** The juice that seeps naturally from grapes as a result of gravity or the weight of the grapes—not from external pressure.

**Fruity:** A term used to describe a wine that tastes of fruit—not one that is sweet; that is, not one that has added or residual sugar.

**Full-bodied:** Wine with a high alcohol level and therefore a big mouthfeel, texture, and usually flavor.

**Gravity flow:** Many wineries use a gravity flow system, in which wine is transferred via gravity, rather than mechanically through pumps. For this to happen, the winery has to be constructed with different levels.

**Grassy:** A characteristic of certain wines, such as Sauvignon Blanc; the quality is reminiscent of grass and herbs.

**Herbaceous:** Term for a wine whose aroma and usually flavor are reminiscent of fresh herbs. Sauvignon Blanc, Cabernet Sauvignon, and Merlot, in particular, are often described this way.

**Honeyed:** Term used to describe some sweet dessert wines owing to their honey-like flavor.

**Hot:** Description for a wine whose alcohol content is its dominant characteristic. It is an unfavorable term since it implies a wine that is out of balance or not well integrated. Fortified wines, however, are deliberately high in alcohol and, as such, are not considered "hot."

**Hybrid:** Term for a grape that is the result of the crossing or breeding between or among two different species. Such crossings can be between the same species, such as two vitis vinifera vines or an American vine (vitis Labrusca) and vitis vinifera, or a French hybrid crossed with an American vine or vitis vinifera. The purpose of such hybrids is usually to create a grape that can withstand certain climatic conditions that either of the two species used to create the hybrid cannot withstand alone.

**Inky:** Descriptive term for a red wine whose color resembles dark ink.

**Integrated:** Sometimes used interchangeably with "balanced," an integrated wine is one in which all of the basic components—tannins, fruit, alcohol, and acid—have total equilibrium.

**Jammy:** Tasting like, jam—intensely fruity. Often Zinfandel and Grenache are described this way, although other varieties, such as Merlot, can be described as jammy, too.

**Lactic acid:** The acid that is produced as a result of malolactic fermentation (ML); during this process, malic acid is converted to lactic acid, which creates a smoother wine.

**Late-harvest:** A term that refers to the very ripe grapes picked after the grapes used for making dry wines have already been harvested. Late-harvest grapes are left on the vine longer to develop their sugars; they are then used to make dessert wines.

**Lean:** A wine that tends to be lacking in fruit. "Lean" may or may not be a favorable term.

**Lees:** The dead yeast cells that fall to the bottom of a fermentation vessel. When wines are left on the lees, they develop a creamy character. Although spelled differently, the term used to describe a wine that is left on the lees is called "sur lies."

**Legs:** The streaks of wine that remain on the inside of the glass after the wine has been drunk. Such streaks are a result of a wine's alcohol content. The higher the amount of alcohol, the more pronounced the legs are.

**Length:** A term used to describe a wine's finish: it can be short, medium, or long, with long being the most desirable.

**Light-bodied:** A term used to describe a wine with relatively low alcohol and therefore light texture.

**Maceration:** Literally, this refers to the time during which the juice is in contact with the skins. Some red wine producers macerate for an extended period in order to extract as much color from the skins as they can. It is a delicate process because macerating for too long can produce bitter flavors.

**Malic acid:** One of the three primary acids in wine. Tartaric and citric are the other two.

**Malolactic fermentation:** Also called ML for short, malolactic fermentation is a secondary fermentation that results in the conversion of malic acid to lactic acid and carbon dioxide. The process makes the wine softer. It is called secondary fermentation because it follows the primary yeast-induced fermentation. Malolactic fermentation, however, is usually naturally occurring—not yeast-induced—and is done with all red wines and many white wines.

**Medium-bodied:** A term used to describe a wine that is neither light nor full. A medium-bodied wine is one that has an average level of alcohol and a resulting medium texture. The mouthfeel will be noticeable but not heavy.

**Mellow:** Usually used to refer to the character of an older wine in which the tannins have softened and the fruit tastes more stewed or caramelized than bright and fresh.

**Méthode Champenoise:** The official method for making Champagne and many other sparkling wines. The method dictates the winemaking process from the pressing of the grapes to secondary fermentation to aging, riddling, disgorgement, and dosage.

**Muscat:** Known variously as muscat blanc, muscat canelli, moscato bianco, moscato d'Asti, and others, the muscat grape is officially called Muscat à Petits Grains Ronds. It is a grape frequently used to make dessert wines, particularly in California.

**Must:** The mixture of stems, seeds, skins, and juice that comes from the crushing of the grapes.

**Non-vintage:** A term most often used in reference to sparkling wine, non-vintage means that the grapes used to make the wine did not come from one single year. Instead, the grapes for the wine came from more than one year.

**Nose:** A term for the aroma and/or bouquet of a wine.

**Oaky:** The flavor and/or aroma that comes from wine fermented and/or aged in oak barrels.

**Oenophile (enophile):** Someone who enjoys wine.

**Off dry:** A term used to describe a wine that has a very small, but detectable, amount of residual sugar.

**Oxidized:** At its most basic, an oxidized wine is one that has been exposed to air. It can happen in the field if the grapes are not processed soon after picking—the juice will effectively turn brown. It can also happen in the bottle. Many times old wines will be oxidized because of natural cork shrinkage. If that happens, air can seep in and oxidize the wine.

**Peppery:** Denotes a black pepper and spicy flavor. It is often used when describing Zinfandel and Syrah.

**Press:** The device into which grapes are placed and then pressed to extract the juice. A press is used either before or after crushing, depending on the type of wine being made and the winemaker's preference.

**Pumping over:** Refers to the means by which the cap (must) that forms on the top of a fermenting red wine is submerged back into the juice to achieve optimum color and flavor extraction. The term "pumping over" generally refers to the method whereby a hose is run from the bottom of a tank and sprayed over the cap. This process also facilitates the release of carbon dioxide, one of the two main bi-products of fermentation.

**Punching down:** A manual means of submerging the cap that forms on red wines as they ferment. As opposed to pumping over, in which the fermentation vessel has been outfitted with a pump that circulates the juice, punching down is done with a long sticklike device that someone uses to literally "punch down" the cap and stir the juice.

**Racking:** The process of transferring clear wine from one vessel, usually a barrel, to another. As sediments settle to the bottom of the barrel, the clear wine is "racked off" to avoid overexposure to the bitter seeds and stems. The racking process also helps aerate the wine, which promotes the red color in red wines.

**Refractometer:** A device used to measure the sugar level of the grapes.

**Residual sugar:** A term that refers to the sugar that remains in the wine after fermentation has stopped.

**Robust:** A term for big, full-flavored, and full-bodied wine.

**Rosé:** A dry, pink, or salmon-colored wine that is made from red grapes. It does not become a red wine because the juice has minimal contact with the skins.

**Short:** A term used to describe a wine's finish, specifically one that lacks body and flavor.

**Soft:** A term used to describe a wine in which the tannins and acid are well balanced; a soft wine is generally mellow. In the case of red wines, a soft wine is also the result of the ripeness of the grapes—if they are picked when they are physiologically immature, the resulting wine will probably lack softness.

**Soften:** A term that can be used interchangeably with mellow, it refers to a wine usually high in tannins that, with aging, becomes better integrated or soft.

**Spicy:** A wine that has spice flavors, for example, cloves or cinnamon, to name just two.

**Steely:** A term that refers to the razor-sharp lean characteristic of an acidic white wine.

**Still wine:** Any wine that is not carbonated.

**Structure:** Refers to how a wine's primary components—alcohol, tannin, acid, and fruit—all come together (or do not, as the case may be). The structure of a wine may also refer specifically to the acidity in the wine.

**Sulfur:** Refers to the sulfur dioxide that is often added to grapes to prevent oxidation and/or added to wine to stop primary and/or secondary fermentation (ML). Because some people are allergic to sulfites—a term that encompasses sulfur dioxide among other sulfurs—all wines that have sulfur dioxide must be labeled as containing sulfites.

**Sur lie:** French term meaning "on the lees," referring to the stage during which a wine is left in contact with the dead yeast cells, to create creaminess in the wine.

**Sweet:** A wine that has residual and/or added sugar.

**Table wine:** Although there are legal definitions for table wines, which refer to the alcohol content, the term table wine generally refers to dry wines as opposed to sweet, dessert, and/or fortified wines.

**Tart:** The sharp, green-like flavors that come from a highly acidic wine.

**Tannin:** The astringent quality of a red wine (usually) that comes from the skins, seeds, and stems of the grapes and, to some degree, from the wood in which the wine is aged. Although tannins create a dry sensation in the mouth, they tend to soften over time—assuming the grapes were mature when they were picked. Tannins are essential to aging.

**Terroir:** In wine, terroir refers to the unique flavors that result from the specific soil, climate, and topography where the grapes were grown. A Cabernet Sauvignon made in Bordeaux will taste different from one made in Napa because of the terroir.

**Tirage:** The mixture of sugar and yeast that is introduced in the bottle of sparkling wines to induce a secondary fermentation.

**Toasty:** The flavor that results from the oak in which the wine is aged. The greater the degree to which the oak has been charred, the greater the level of toasty character in the wine.

**Topping up:** The process whereby the winemaker adds a small amount of wine to the barrel to replace the wine that naturally evaporates. The goal is to minimize the amount of air in the barrel and keep the wine from oxidizing.

**Vanillin:** A term used to describe the vanilla-like quality in a wine that comes from oak barrel in which the wine has been aged.

**Varietal:** The dominant type of grape used to make the wine. For example, Cabernet Sauvignon is a varietal wine.

**Variety:** A term for the type of grape that comes from a particular vine. Cabernet Sauvignon, Chardonnay, Pinot Noir, are all varieties from the vitis vinifera species.

**Vegetal:** A derogatory term for a wine that smells of cooked vegetables, such as asparagus.

**Velvety:** A positive term used to describe a wine that is smooth and rich with minimal tannins.

**Veraison:** The part of the cycle of grape development when the berries are changing from hard to soft, and green to gold or red, depending on the variety.

**Vinifera:** Vine species of the genus vitis from which most of the world's wines are derived. Examples are Cabernet Sauvignon, Chardonnay, Chenin Blanc, and Syrah.

**Vintage:** Refers to the single year in which the grapes were picked to make the wine.

**Vintner:** The person who makes or sells wine.

**Viticulture:** The study and science of grape-growing.

**Yeast:** A single cell organism that, in the case of wine, converts sugar into alcohol and carbon dioxide. As such, it is essential to winemaking.

**Yeasty:** The aroma in sparkling wine that is reminiscent of bread dough. Can also refer to a similar aroma in still wines. Both come from the lees, or dead yeast cells, to which the wine has been exposed.

# CHEESEMAKERS AROUND THE COUNTRY

*(\*denotes cheesemaker profiled in the book)*

## ALABAMA

*Fromagerie Belle Chèvre*
Ardmore, Alabama
256-423-2238 or 800-735-2238

*Sweet Home Farm*
Elberta, Alabama
251-986-5663 (mail order at
Christmas time only)

## ARKANSAS

*Doeling Dairy Goat Farm*
Fayetteville, Arkansas
501-582-4571 or 888-524-4571
501-582-1213 (fax)
www.doelingdairy.com

## CALIFORNIA

*Andante Dairy\**
Santa Rosa, California
707-526-0517 (phone and fax)
www.andantedairy.com

*Ariza Cheese Company*
(Mexican cheeses)
Paramount, California
562-630-4144 or 800-762-4736
562-630-4174 (fax)
www.mexicancheese.com

*Azteca Cheese Company*
(Mexican cheeses)
Gardena, California
310-532-6928
310-532-0009 (fax)

*Belfiore Cheese Company*
Berkeley, California
510-540-5500
510-540-5594 (fax)

*Bellwether Farms*
Petaluma, California
707-763-0993 or 888-527-8606
707-763-2443 (fax)
www.bellwethercheese.com

*Bodega Goat Cheese*
Bodega, California
707-876-3483 (phone and fax)
www.bodegagoatcheese.com

*Bravo Farms*
Visalia, California
559-625-0490 (phone and fax)
www.bravofarm.com

*Cacique Cheese Company*
(Mexican and Caribbean cheeses)
City of Industry, California
626-961-3399 x505 (customer
service)
626-369-8083 (fax)
www.caciqueusa.com

*California Polytechnic University
Creamery*
San Luis Obispo, California
805-756-1243
805-756-6055 (fax)
www.calpolycheese.com

*Cowgirl Creamery / Tomales Bay
Foods*
Point Reyes Station, California
415-663-9335 or 415-663-8153
415-663-5418 (fax)
www.cowgirlcreamery.com

*Cypress Grove Chèvre*
McKinleyville, California
707-839-3168
707-839-2322 (fax)
www.cypressgrovechevre.com

*Fagundes Old World Cheese*
Hanford, California
559-582-2000
559-582-0683 (fax)
www.oldworldcheese.com

*Fiscalini Farms\**
Modesto, California
209-545-5495
209-545-4110 (fax)
www.fiscalinicheese.com

*Formaggi di Ferrante*
Benicia, California
707-746-5454
707-746-5475 (fax)

*Gioia Cheese Co., Inc.*
Pico Rivera, California
562-942-2663
562-942-2962 (fax)
www.gioiacheese.com

*Goat's Leap Cheese*
St. Helena, California
707-963-2337 (phone and fax)
www.goatsleap.com

*Harley Farms Goat Dairy*
*(Sea Stars)\**
Pescadero, California
650-879-0480
650-879-9161 (fax)
www.harleyfarms.com

Joe Matos Cheese Factory
Santa Rosa, California
707-823-4454
707-584-5283

Karoun Dairies Inc.
(Middle Eastern cheeses)
Los Angeles, California
323-666-6296 or 323-666-6222
323-666-1501 (fax)
www.karouncheese.com

Kendall Farms
(crème fraîche)
Atascadero, California
805-466-7252 (phone and fax)

Laura Chenel Chèvre
Sonoma, California
707-996-4477
707-996-1816 (fax)

Loleta Cheese Company
Loleta, California
707-733-5470 or 800-995-0453
707-733-1872 (fax)

Marin French Cheese Company*
Petaluma, California
707-762-6001 or 800-292-6001
707-762-0430 (fax)
www.marinfrenchcheese.com

Marquez Brothers International
(Mexican and Central American cheeses)
San Jose, California
408-960-2700 or 800-858-1119
408-960-3213 (fax)
www.marquezbrothers.com

Mozzarella Fresca
Gardena, California
707-746-6818
707-746-6829 (fax)
www.italcheese.com
www.mozzarellafresca.com

MyTime Ranch
(goat cheese)
Eureka, California
707-442-3209
www.capriciouscheese.com

Oakdale Cheese & Specialties
Oakdale, California
209-848-3139
209-848-1162 (fax)
www.oakdalecheese.com

Pedrozo Dairy and Cheese
Company*
Orland, California
530-865-9548  (phone and fax)
www.pedrozodairycheese.com

Peluso Cheese Company
Los Banos, California
209-826-3744
209-826-6782 (fax)

Point Reyes Farmstead Cheese
Company*
Point Reyes Station, California
800-591-6878
415-663-8881 (fax)
www.pointreyescheese.com

Redwood Hill Farm
Sebastopol, California
707-823-8250
707-823-6976 (fax)
www.redwoodhill.com

Rumiano Cheese Company
Crescent City, California
707-465-1535
707-465-4141 (fax)
www.rumianocheese.com

Sierra Nevada Cheese Co., Inc.
Sacramento, California
916-331-5289 or 916-331-3107
916-331-3164 (fax)
www.sierranevadacheese.com

Skyhill Napa Valley Farms, Inc.
Napa, California
707-255-4800
707-252-9297 (fax)

Sonoma Cheese Factory
Sonoma, California
707-996-1931 or 800-535-2855
707-935-3535 (fax)
www.sonomacheese.com

Spring Hill Jersey Cheese
Petaluma, California
707-762-3446
707-762-3455 (fax)
www.springhillcheese.com

Straus Family Creamery
Marshall, California
415-663-5464
415-663-5465 (fax)
www.strausmilk.com

Three Sisters Farmstead Cheese*
Lindsay, California
559-562-2132
559-562-9596 (fax)
www.threesisterscheese.com

Vella Cheese Company
Sonoma, California
707-938-3232 or 800-848-0505
707-938-4307 (fax)
www.vellacheese.com

Winchester Cheese Company
Winchester, California
909-926-4239
909-926-3349 (fax)
www.winchestercheese.com

Yerba Santa Dairy
(goat cheese)
Lakeport, California
707-263-8131
707-263-8131 (fax)

## COLORADO

*Bingham Hill Cheese Company\**
Fort Collins, Colorado
970-472-0702
970-472-0622 (fax)
www.binghamhill.com

*Haystack Mountain Goat Dairy*
Niwot, Colorado
303-581-9948
303-516-1041 (fax)
www.haystackgoatcheese.com

*MouCo Cheese Company\**
Fort Collins, Colorado
970-498-0107
www.mouco.com

## CONNECTICUT

*Calabro Cheese*
East Haven, Connecticut
203-469-1311 or 800-969-1311
203-469-6929 (fax)
www.calabrocheese.com

*Cato Corner Farm*
Colchester, Connecticut
860-537-3884
860-537-9470 (fax)
www.catocorner.com

*Foxfire Farm*
Mansfield Center, Connecticut
860-455-0739 (phone and fax)

*Highwater Dairy*
(goat cheese)
Glastonbury, Connecticut
860-657-1569

*Rustling Wind Creamery*
(goat cheese)
Falls Village, Connecticut
860-824-7084
860-824-0207 (fax)
www.rustlingwind.com

*Sankow's Beaverbrook Farm*
(sheep's milk cheese)
Lyme, Connecticut
860-434-2843
860-434-2560 (fax)
www.beaverbrookfarm.com

*Town Farm Dairy*
Simsbury, Connecticut
860-658-5362

## FLORIDA

*Turtle Creek Dairy*
(goat cheese)
Loxahatchee, Florida
561-798-4628

## GEORGIA

*Sweet Grass Dairy\**
Thomasville, Georgia
229-227-0752
229-227-1403 (fax)
www.sweetgrassdairy.com

## HAWAII

*Heather Threlfall*
Honokaa, Hawaii
808-775-9787 (phone and fax)

## IDAHO

*Rollingstone Chèvre\**
Parma, Idaho
208-722-6460(phone and fax)
www.rollingstonechevre.com

## INDIANA

*Capriole Inc.*
Greenville, Indiana
812-923-9408 or 812-923-1180
812-923-9408 (fax)
www.capriolegoatcheese.com

## IOWA

*Maytag Dairy Farms*
Newton, Iowa
641-792-1133 or 800-247-2458
641-792-1567 (fax)

## LOUISIANA

*Chef John Folse's Bittersweet
Plantation Dairy\**
Gonzales, Louisiana
225-644-6000
225-644-1295 (fax)
www.jfolse.com/dairy.html

## MAINE

*Appleton Creamery*
Appleton, Maine
(no phone orders)
www.appletoncreamery.com

*Nezinscot Farm*
Turner, Maine
207-225-3231
207-225-3220 (fax)

*State of Maine Cheese Company*
Rockport, Maine
207-236-8895 or 800-762-8895
207-236-9591 (fax)
www.cheese-me.com

*Sunset Acres Farm*
(goat cheese)
Brooksville, Maine
207-326-4741
207-326-4826 (fax)

## MARYLAND

*Gemelli, Inc.*
Silver Spring, Maryland
301-595-7522 or 800-436-3554
301-595-9808 (fax)
www.gemelli.com

## MASSACHUSETTS

*Great Hill Blue*
Marion, Massachusetts
508-748-2208 or 888-748-2208
508-748-2282 (fax)
www.greathillblue.com

*Hillman Farm\**
Colrain, Massachusetts
413-624-3646

*Smith's Country Cheese*
Winchendon, Massachusetts
978-939-5738
978 939-8599 (fax)

*South Mountain Products\**
(Berkshire Blue)
Great Barrington, Massachusetts
413-528-9529 (no mail order; see
Resources)
413-445-5935 (fax)
www.highlawn-farm.com

*Westfield Farm*
Hubbardston, Massachusetts
978-928-5110 or 877-777-3900
978-928-5745 (fax)
www.chevre.com

## MICHIGAN

*Black Star Farms/Leelanau Cheese
Company*
Suttons Bay, Michigan
231-271-4970
231-271-4883 (fax)
www.blackstarfarms.com

*Elk Creek Cheese Company*
(goat cheese)
Applegate, Michigan
810-633-9547 or 800-968-1220
www.elkcreekcheese.com

*Zingerman's Creamery Cheeses*
Ann Arbor, Michigan
734-665-1901 or 888-636-8162
www.zingermans.com

## MINNESOTA

*Amablu*
Faribault, Minnesota
507-334-5260
507-332-9011 (fax)
www.amablu.com

*Dancing Winds Farms*
Kenyon, Minnesota
507-789-6606
www.dancingwinds.com

*Eichten's Hidden Acres*
Center City, Minnesota
651-257-4752 or 800-657-6752
651-257-6286 (fax)
www.fresnomall.com/eichten/

*Shepherd's Way Farm*
Nerstrand, Minnesota
612-448-4457

## MISSOURI

*Stoney Acres Sheep Dairy*
Falcon, Missouri
417-668-5560 (phone and fax)
www.geocities.com/heartland/
bluffs/2479

## NEVADA

*Oasis Farmstead Dairy*
(goat cheese)
Fallon, Nevada
775-867-4683
www.oasisfarmsteaddairy.com

## NEW HAMPSHIRE

*Boggy Meadow Farm/Fanny Mason
Farmstead Cheese*
Walpole, New Hampshire
603-756-3300 or 877-541-3953
603-756-9645 (fax)
www.fannymasoncheese.com

## NEW MEXICO

*Coonridge Organic Goat Cheese*
Pie Town, New Mexico
888-410-8433
www.coonridge.com

*Sweetwoods Dairy\**
Peña Blanca, New Mexico
505-465-2608
505-465-0904 (fax)

## NEW YORK

*Cappiello Dairy Products*
Schenectady, New York
518-398-5325
518-374-4015 (fax)
www.cappiello.com

*Captain Kid Dairy*
(goat cheese)
Mattituck, New York
631-298-5548

*Coach Farm*
Pine Plains, New York
518-398-5325
518-398-5329 (fax)
www.coachfarm.com

*Goat Hill Farm*
Manlius, New York
315-655-3014 (phone and fax)

*Grassland Cheese
Consortium/Sprout Creek Farm*
Duchess County (Hudson Valley),
New York
www.cowsoutside.com

*Hawthorne Valley Farm*
Ghent, New York
518-672-4465
518-672-4887 (fax)
www.hawthornevalleyfarm.com

Lioni Latticini
Brooklyn, New York
800-528-3252
718-259-8378 (fax)

Lively Run Goat Dairy*
Interlaken, New York
607-532-4647
607-532-8759 (fax)
www.livelyrun.com

Northland Sheep Dairy
Marathon, New York
607-849-3328

Old Chatham Sheepherding
Company
Old Chatham, New York
518-794-7733 or 800-SHEEP-60
518-794-7641 (fax)
www.blacksheepcheese.com

## NORTH CAROLINA
Celebrity Dairy
(goat cheese)
Siler, North Carolina
919-742-5176
919-742-1432 (fax)
www.celebritydairy.com

Goat Lady Dairy*
Climax, North Carolina
336-824-2163
www.goatladydairy.com

Shelton Cheeses
Dobson, North Carolina
336-366-3659
336-366-2629 (fax)
www.sheltoncheeses.com

## OHIO
Brewster Dairy
Brewster, Ohio
330-767-3492
330-767-0151 (fax)
www.brewstercheese.com

Caprine Estates
(goat cheese)
Bellbrook, Ohio
937-848-7406
937-848-7437 (fax)
www.caprineestates.com

Miceli Dairy Products
Cleveland, Ohio
216-791-6222
216-231-2504 (fax)
www.miceli-dairy.com

Minerva Cheese Factory
Minerva, Ohio
330-868-4196
330-868-SWIS (7947)
www.minervacheese.com

## OREGON
Bandon Cheese
(cow cheese)
Bandon, Oregon
541-347-2456
541-347-2012 (fax)

Covered Wagon Farm
(goat cheese)
503-628-2447 (phone and fax)
Sherwood, Oregon

Juniper Grove Farm
Redmond, Oregon
541-923-8353 or 888- 376-6243
541-504-2526 (fax)
 Rogue Valley Creamery
(blue cheese)
Central Point, Oregon
541-664-2233
541-664-0952 (fax)

Tillamook County Creamery
Association
Tillamook, Oregon
503-842-4481 or 800-542-7290
(mail order only)
503-815-1309 (fax)
www.tillamookcheese.com

## PENNSYLVANIA
Iron Bridge Farm
(goat cheese)
610-469-4618
610-469-1002 (fax)

LeRaysville Cheese Factory
(cows' milk cheese)
LeRaysville, Pennsylvania
570-744-2554
570-744-2192 (fax)

Menhennett Farm
Cochranville, Pennsylvania
610-593-5726

Pipe Dreams Fromage
(goat cheese)
Greencastle, Pennsylvania
717-597-1877

Woodchoppertown Chèvre
Boyertown, Pennsylvania
610-689-5498

## TEXAS
Cheesemakers, Inc. & Yellow Rose
Goat Dairy
(Hispanic and goat cheeses)
Cleveland, Texas
281-593-1319
281-593-2898 (fax)

Larsen Farms Goat Dairy
Blanco, Texas
830-833-5192

Mozzarella Company
Dallas, Texas
214-741-4072 or 800-798-2954
214-741-4076 (fax)
www.mozzco.com

Pure Luck Grade A Goat Dairy
Dripping Springs, Texas
512-858-7034 or 800-256-8268
512-858-7021 (fax)
www.purelucktexas.com

Texas Jersey Cheese Company
(farmstead cheese)
Schulenburg, Texas
1-800-382-2880
409-743-5019 (fax)

White Egret Farm
Austin, Texas
512-276-7505
512-276-7489 (fax)
www.whiteegretfarm.com

## VERMONT
Blythedale Farm, Inc.
Corinth, Vermont
802-439-6575

Cabot Creamery*
Cabot, Vermont
802-229-9361
802-371-1200 (fax)
www.cabotcheese.com

Crowley Cheese
Healdville, Vermont
802-259-2340 or 800-683-2606
802-259-2347 (fax)
www.crowleycheese-vermont.com

Doe's Leap
(goat cheese)
East Fairfield, Vermont
802-827-3046

Grafton Village Cheese Company
Grafton, Vermont
802-843-2221 or 800-472-3866
802-843-2210 (fax)
www.graftonvillagecheese.com

Green Mountain Blue Cheese*
Highgate Center, Vermont
802-868-4193
802-868-7395 (fax)
www.vtcheese.com/vtcheese/
greenmtn/boucherstory.html

Lazy Lady Farm*
Westfield, Vermont
802-744-6365
www.vtcheese.com/vtcheese/lazy
/lazy.htm

Neighborly Farms of Vermont
Randolph Center, Vermont
802-728-4700 or 888-212-6898
www.neighborlyfarms.com

Orb Weaver Farm
New Haven, Vermont
802-877-3755

The Organic Cow
Tunbridge, Vermont
802-685-3123
802-685-4332 (fax)

Rivendell Meadows Farm
Irasburg, Vermont
802-755-6349

Shelburne Farms
Shelburne, Vermont
802-985-8686
802-985-1233 (fax)
www.shelburnefarms.org

Sugarbush Farm
Woodstock, Vermont
802-457-1757 or 800-281-1757
802-457-3269 (fax)
www.sugarbushfarm.com

Taylor Farm
Londonderry, Vermont
802-824-5690
www.vtcheese/vtcheese/taylor/
taylor.htm

Vermont Butter & Cheese
Websterville, Vermont
802-479-9371 or 800-884-6287
802-479-3674 (fax)
www.vtbutterandcheeseco.com

Vermont Shepherd
Putney, Vermont
802-387-4473
802-387-2041 (fax)
www.vermontshepherd.com

Willow Hill Farm
Milton, Vermont
802-893-2963
802-893-1954 (fax)
www.sheepcheese.com

## VIRGINIA
Blue Ridge Dairy
Lovettsville, Virginia
540-822-4363

Briar-Patch Goat Cheese
Disputanta, Virginia
804-991-2121 or 888-GOAT-MLK
(phone and fax)
www.bent-treefarm.com

Drinking Swamp Farm
(goat cheese)
Haynesville, Virginia
www.cheese-goat.com

Everona Dairy
(sheep's milk cheese)
Rapidan, Virginia
540-854-4159
540-854-6443 (fax)

Gourmet Goat
Red Oak, Virginia
804-735-8250

Iron Rod Chevre
Earlysville, Virginia
804-973-8407

Meadow Creek Dairy*
Galax, Virginia
276-236-2776
276-236-2776 (fax)
www.meadowcreekdairy.com

Monastery Country Cheese
Crozet, Virginia
434-823-1452
434-823-6379 (fax)
www.nmoa.org/Products/
va454.htm

Mountain Hobby Cheeses
(goat cheese)
Willis, Virginia
540-789-4277

Rucker Farm (goat cheese)
Flint Hill, Virginia
540-675-3444

## WASHINGTON

Appel Farms
Ferndale, Washington
360-384-4996 (phone and fax)
360-312-1431(cheese store)
www.appel-farms.com

Port Madison Farm*
Bainbridge Island, Washington
206-842-4125 (phone and fax)

Quillisascut Cheese Company
(goat cheese)
Rice, Washington
509-738-2011 (phone and fax)
www.quillisascutcheese.com

Sally Jackson Cheeses
(goats', sheep's, and cows' milk cheeses)
Oroville, Washington
(no mail order; see Resources)

Samish Bay Cheese
Bow, Washington
360-855-3197
360-766-6707 (fax)
www.samishbaycheese.com

Washington State University
Creamery
Pullman, Washington
509-335-4014 or 800-457-5442
509-335-7525 or 800-572-3289
(fax)
www.wsu.edu/creamery

White Oak Farmstead*
Battle Ground, Washington
360-576-7688
www.white-oak.com

## WISCONSIN

The Antigo Cheese Company
Antigo, Wisconsin
715-623-2301 or 800-356-5655
715-623-4501 (fax)
www.antigocheese.com

Bass Lake Cheese Factory
Somerset, Wisconsin
715-247-5586 or 800-368-2437
715-549-6617 (fax)
www.blcheese.com

BelGioioso Cheese
Denmark, Wisconsin
920-863-2123 (no mail order)
920-863-8791 (fax)
www.belgioioso.com

Butler Farms
Whitehall, Wisconsin
715-983-2285
715-983-2230 (fax)

Carr Valley Cheese
LaValle, Wisconsin
800-462-7258
608-986-2906 (fax)
www.carrvalleycheese.com

Cedar Grove Cheese
Plain, Wisconsin
800-200-6020
608-546-2805 (fax)
www.cedargrovecheese.com

Chalet Cheese Co-op
Monroe, Wisconsin
608-325-4343
608-325-4409 (fax)

Crave Brothers Farmstead Cheese
Waterloo, Wisconsin
920-478-3134
920-478-3809 (fax)

DCI/Salemville Cheese
Mayville, Wisconsin
920-387-5740 x22
920-387-2194 (fax)

Fantome Farm
Ridgeway, Wisconsin
608-924-1266  (phone and fax)

Henning Cheese
Kiel, Wisconsin
920-894-3032
920-894-3022 (fax)

Hook's Cheese Company
Mineral Point, Wisconsin
608-987-3259

Klondike Cheese
Monroe, Wisconsin
608-325-3021
608-325-3027 (fax)

LoveTree Farmstead Cheese
Grantsburg, Wisconsin
715-488-2966
715-488-3957 (fax)
www.lovetreefarmstead.com

Meister Cheese Company
Muscoda, Wisconsin
608-739-3134
608-739-4348 (fax)
www.meistercheese.com

Montchevré (Betin Inc.)
Belmont, Wisconsin
608-762-5878
www.montchevre.com

Organic Valley
LaFarge, Wisconsin
608-625-2602
608-625-2600 (fax)
www.organicvalley.com

Park Cheese
Fond du Lac, Wisconsin
920-923-8484 or 800-752-7275
920-923-8485 (fax)

Roth Käse USA, Ltd.
Monroe, Wisconsin
608-328-2122 or 800-257-3355
608-329-2120 (fax)
www.rothkase.com

Specialty Cheese Company
Lowell, Wisconsin
920-927-3888 or 800-367-1711
920-927-3200 (fax)
www.specialcheese.com

Swiss Valley Farms
Platteville, Wisconsin
888-519-5818
www.swissvalleyfarms.com

Uplands Cheese Company*
Dodgeville, Wisconsin
866-588-3443
608-935-7030 (fax)
www.uplandscheese.com

Widmer Cheese Factory
Theresa, Wisconsin
920-488-2503
920-488-2130 (fax)
www.widmerscheese.com

# WINEMAKERS AROUND THE COUNTRY

(*denotes winemaker profiled in the book)

## CALIFORNIA

A. Rafanelli Winery
Healdsburg, California
707-433-1385

Acacia
Napa, California
707-226-9991
707-226-1685 (fax)
www.acaciawinery.com

Adler Fels
Santa Rosa, California
707-539-3123
707-539-3128 (fax)
www.adlerfels.com

Alban Vineyards
8575 Orcutt Road
Arroyo Grande, California
805-546-0305

Andrew Murray Vineyards
Los Olivos, California
805-686-9604
805-686-9704 (fax)
www.andrewmurrayvineyards.com

Arrowood Vineyards and Winery
Glen Ellen, California
707-938-5170
707-938-1543 (fax)
www.arrowoodvineyards.com

Atlas Peak Vineyards
Napa, California
707-252-7971
707-224-4484 (fax)
http://atlaspeakvineyards.com

Au Bon Climat
Los Olivos CA
805-934-7989 805-686-1016
www.aubonclimat.com

Babcock Vineyards
Lompoc, California
805-736-1455
805-736-3886 (fax)
www.babcockwinery.com

Beaulieu Vineyard
Rutherford, California 94573
707-963-2411
707-967-8228 (fax)
www.beaulieuvineyard.com

Behrens and Hitchcock Winery*
Calistoga, California
707-942-4433
707-942-5919 (fax)

Beringer Vineyards
St. Helena, California
707-963-4812 or 707-963-7115
707-963-8129 (fax)
www.beringer.com

Bernardus
Carmel Valley, California
800-223-2533
831-659-1676 (fax)
www.bernardus.com

Blackjack Ranch
Solvang, California
805-686-9922
805-693-1995 (fax)
www.blackjackranch.com

Blockheadia Wine,
Lorenza-Lake Winery
St. Helena, California
707-963-8593
707-967-9548 (fax)
www.blockheadia.com

Bonterra Vineyards
San Rafael, California
415-444-7442
415-444-7483 (fax)
www.bonterra.com

Bonny Doon Vineyard
Santa Cruz, California
831-425-4518
831-425-3528 (fax)
 www.bonnydoonvineyard.com

Bradford Mountain Winery
Healdsburg, California
707-433-8236
707-433-7398 (fax)
www.bradfordmountain.com

The Brander Vineyard
Los Olivos, California
805-688-2455 or 800-970-9979
805-688-8010 (fax)
www.brander.com

Broman Cellars
Napa, California
707-224-5490 or 800-541-4401
707-224-5497 (fax)
www.bromancellars.com

Byron
Santa Maria, California
888-303-7288
805-937-1246 (fax)
www.byronwines.com

Ca'Vesta
Redwood Valley, California
707-963-1534 or 707-485-0323
707-963-8620 (fax)

Cafaro Cellars
St. Helena, California
707-963-7181
707-963-8458 (fax)
www.cafaro.com

Cakebread Cellars
Rutherford, California
707-963-5222 or 800-588-0298
707-967-4012 (fax)
www.cakebread.com

Carlisle Winery and Vineyards
Santa Rosa, California
707-566-7700
707-566-7200 (fax)

Caymus Vineyards
Rutherford, California
707-963-4204
707-963-5958 (fax)
www.caymus.com

Chalk Hill Estate Vineyards
and Winery
Healdsburg, California
707-838-4306 or 800-838-4306
707-838-1907 or 707-838-9687
(fax)
www.chalkhill.com

Chalone Vineyard
Soledad, California
831-678-1717
831-678-2742 (fax)
www.chalonewinegroup.com

Chappellet Winery
St. Helena, California
707-963-7136 or 800-4-WINERY
707-963-7445 (fax)
www.chappellet.com

Chateau St. Jean Winery
Kenwood, California
707-833-4134 or 800-543-7572
707-833-4200 (fax)
www.chateaustjean.com

Chateau Souverain
Geyserville, California
707-433-5174 or 888-809-4637
www.chateausouvrain.com

Chimney Rock Winery*
Napa, California
800-257-2641
707-257-2036 (fax)
 www.chimneyrock.com

Cline Cellars
Sonoma, California 707-935-4310
or 800-546-2070
707-935-4319 (fax)
www.clinecellars.com

Corison Winery
St. Helena, California
707-963-0826
707-963-4906 (fax)

Cosentino Winery
Yountville, California
707-944-1220
707-944-1254 (fax)
www.cosentinowinery.com

Cuvaison Winery
Calistoga, California
707-942-6266
707-942-5732 (fax)
www.cuvaison.com

Domaine Carneros
Napa, California
707-257-0101
707-257-3020 (fax)
www.domaine-carneros.com

Domaine Chandon
Yountville, California
707-944-8844
707-944-1123 (fax)
www.domainechandon.com

Domaine de la Terre Rouge,
Terre Rouge and Easton Brands
Fiddletown, California
209-245-3117
209-245-5415 (fax)
www.terrerougewines.com
or www.eastonwines.com

Duckhorn Vineyards
St. Helena, California
707-963-7108
707-963-7595 (fax)
www.duckhorn.com

Dry Creek Vineyard
Healdsburg, California
707-433-1000 or 800-864-WINE
707-433-5329 (fax)
www.drycreekvineyard.com

Eberle Winery
Paso Robles, California
805-238-9607
805-237-0344 (fax)
www.eberlewinery.com

El Molino Winery
St. Helena, California
707-963-3632
707-963-1647 (fax)
www.elmolinowinery.com

Elyse Winery
Napa, California
707-944-2900
707-945-0301 (fax)
www.elysewinery.com

Ferrari-Carano Vineyard and Winery
Healdsburg, California
707-433-6700 or 800-831-0381
707-431-1742 (fax)
www.ferrari-carano.com

Fetzer Vineyards
Mendocino, California
707-744-1250 or 800-846-8637
707-744-1437 (fax)
www.fetzer.com

Fife Vineyards
St. Helena, California
707-963-1543
707-963-8620 (fax)
www.fifevineyards.com

Flora Springs
St. Helena, California
707-967-5711
707-967-7815 (fax)
www.florasprings.com

Foxen Vineyards
Santa Maria, California
805-937-4251
805-937-0415 (fax)

Peter Franus Wine Company
Napa, California
707-945-0542
707-945-0931 (fax)
www.franuswine.com

Frog's Leap Winery
Rutherford, California
707-963-4704 or 800-959-4704
707-963-0242 (fax)
www.frogsleap.com

Garretson Wine Company*
Paso Robles, California
805-239-2074
805-239-2057 (fax)
www.mrviognier.com

Geyser Peak
Geyserville, California
707-857-9400 or 800-255-9463
707.857.9402 (fax)
www.geyserpeakwinery.com

Gloria Ferrer
Sonoma, California
707-996-7256
707-996-0378 (fax)
www.gloriaferrer.com

Green and Red Vineyard
St. Helena, California
707-965-2346

Greenwood Ridge Vineyards
Philo, California
707-895-2002
707-895-2001 (fax)
www.greenwoodridge.com

Hanna Winery
Healdsburg, California
707-431-4310 or 800-854-3987
707-431-4314 (fax)
www.hannawinery.com

Hanzell Vineyards
Sonoma, California
707-996-3860 or 800-393-4999
707-996-3862 (fax)
www.hanzell.com

Havens Wine Cellars
Napa, California
707-261-2000
707-261-2043 (fax)
www.havenswine.com

The Hess Collection
Napa, California
707-255-1144
707-253-1682 (fax)
www.hesscollection.com

Hitching Post
Buellton, California
805-688-0676
www.hitchingpost2.com

Honig Vineyard and Winery
Rutherford, California
707-963-5618 or 800-929-2217
707-963-5639 (fax)
www.honigwine.com

Husch Vineyards
Philo, California
707-462-5374 or 800-55-HUSCH
707-895-2068 (fax)
www.huschvineyards.com

Iron Horse Ranch and Vineyards
Sebastopol, California
707-887-1507
707-887-1337 (fax)
www.ironhorsevineyards.com

J. Lohr
San Jose, California
408-288-5057
408-993-2276 (fax)
www.jlohr.com

J Wine Company
Healdsburg, California
707-431-5400 or 888-JWINECO
707-431-5410 (fax)
www.jwine.com

Kendall-Jackson Vineyard and
Winery
Santa Rosa, California
707-544-4000
707-569-0105 (fax)
www.kj.com

Kent Rasmussen Winery
St. Helena, California
707-963-5667
707-963-5664 (fax)

Kenwood Vineyards
Kenwood, California
707-833-5891
707-833-1146 (fax)
ww.kenwoodvineyards.com

Landmark Vineyards
Kenwood, California
707-833-0053
707-833-1164 (fax)
www.landmarkwine.com

Lazy Creek Vineyards
Philo, California
707-895-3623

Lolonis Winery
Redwood Valley, California
925-938-8066
925-938-8069 (fax)
www.lolonis.com

Long Meadow Ranch
St. Helena, California
877-NAPA-OIL
707-963-1956 (fax)
www.longmeadowranch.com

Long Vineyards
St. Helena, California
707-963-2496
707-963-2907 (fax)
www.longvineyards.com

Luna Vineyards
Napa, California
707-255-2474
707-255-6385 (fax)
www.lunavineyards.com

McDowell Valley Vineyards
Hopland, California
707-744-1053
707-744-1826 (fax)
www.mcdowellsyrah.com

MacRostie Winery and Vineyards
Sonoma, California
707-996-4480
707-996-3726 (fax)
www.macrostiewinery.com

Mariah Cellars
San Rafael, California
415-444-7441

Markham Vineyard
St. Helena, California
707-963-5292
707-963-4616 (fax)
www.markhamvineyards.com

Martin and Weyrich Winery
Paso Robles, California
805-238-9234
805-238-6041 (fax)
www.martinweyrich.com

Mason Cellars*
Oakville, California
707-944-9159 or 707-944-1710
707-944-1293 (fax)
www.masoncellars.com

Matanzas Creek Winery
Santa Rosa, California
800-590-6464
707-571-0156 (fax)
www.matanzascreek.com

Merryvale Vineyards
St. Helena, California
800-326-6069
707-963-1949 (fax)
www.merryvale.com

Merry Edwards Wines*
Forestville, California
888-388-9050
707-887-0322 (fax)
www.merryedwards.com

Miner Family Vineyards
Oakville, California
800-366-9463
707-945-1280 (fax)
www.minerwines.com

Monteviña Winery
Plymouth, California
209-245-6942
209-245-6617 (fax)
www.montevina.com

Morgan Winery
Salinas, California
831-751-7777
831-751-7780 (fax)
www.morganwinery.com

Mumm Napa Valley
Rutherford, California
707-942-3434 or 800-Mum-Napa
707-942.3467 (fax)
www.mummcuveenapa.com

Murphy Goode Estate Winery
Geyserville, California
707-431-7644
707-431-8640 (fax)
www.murphygoodewinery.com

Nalle Winery
Healdsburg, California
707-433-1040
707-433-6062 (fax)
www.nallewinery.com

Navarro Vineyards*
Philo, California
707-895-3686 or 800-537-9463
707-895-3647 (fax)
www.navarrowine.com

Newton Vineyard
St. Helena, California
707-963-9000
707-963-5408 (fax)

Parducci Wine Estates
Ukiah, California
707-463-5350 or 888-362-9463
707-462-7260 (fax)
www.parducci.com

Peachy Canyon Winery
Paso Robles, California
805-237-1577 or 800-315-7908
805-237-2248 (fax)
www.peachycanyon.com

Pepi Winery
Oakville, California
707-944-2807
707-944-2824 (fax)
www.pepi.com

Peters Family Winery
Napa, California
707-337-6111
815-346-0614 (fax)
www.petersfamilywinery.com

Peter Michael Winery
Calistoga, California
800-354-4459
707-942-0209 or 707-942-8314 (fax)
www.petermichaelwinery.com

Peterson Winery
Healdsburg, California
707-431-7568
707-431-1112 (fax)
www.petersonwinery.com

Pietra Santa Vineyards and Winery
Hollister, California
831-636-1991
831-636-1929 (fax)
www.pietrasantawinery.com

Pine Ridge Winery
Napa, California
707-253-7500 or 800-575-9777
707-253-1493 (fax)
www.pineridgewine.com

Piper-Sonoma Cellars
Healdsburg, California
707-484-4378
707-539-4863 (fax)

Quady Winery
Madera, California
559-673-8068 or 800-733-8068
559-673-0744 (fax)
www.quadywinery.com

Quivira Estate Vineyards and
Winery
Healdsburg, California
707-431-8333 or 800-292-8339
707-431-1664 (fax)
www.quivirawine.com

Qupé Wine Cellars
Los Olivos, California
805-937-9801
805-937-2539 (fax)

Ravenswood Winery
Sonoma, California
707-938-1960 or 888-669-4679
707-938-9459 (fax)
www.ravenswood-wine.com

Ridge Lytton Station
Healdsburg, California
707-433-7721
707-433-7751 (fax)
www.ridgewine.com

Robert Mondavi Winery
Oakville, California
707-259-WINE or 888-766-6328
707-251-4110 (fax)
www.robertmondavi.com

Robert Sinskey Vineyards
Napa, California
707-944-9090 or 800-869-2030
707-944-9092 (fax)
www.robertsinskey.com

Rochioli Vineyard and Winery
Healdsburg, California
707-433-2305
707-433-2658 (fax)

Roederer Estate
Philo, California
707-895-2288
707-895-2120 (fax)
www.roederer-estate.com

Rosenblum Cellars
Alameda, California
510-865-7007
510-865-9225 (fax)
www.rosenblumcellars.com

Saintsbury
Napa, CA 94559
707-252-0592
707-252-0595 (fax)
www.saintsbury.com

Sanford Winery and Vineyards
Buellton, California
805-688-3300 or 800-426-9463
805-688-7381 (fax)

Schramsberg Vineyards
Calistoga, California
707-942-6668 or 800-877-3623
707-942-5943 (fax)
www.schramsberg.com

Seghesio Family Vineyards
Healdsburg, California
707-433-3579
707-433-0545 (fax)
www.seghesio.com

Sequoia Grove Vineyards
Rutherford, California
707-944-2945 or 800-851-7841
707-963-9411 (fax)
www.sequoiagrove.com

Shafer Vineyards
Napa, California
707-944-2877
707-944-9454 (fax)
www.shafervineyards.com

Showket Vineyards
Oakville, California
877-746-9538
707-944-0131 (fax)
www.showketvineyards.com

Siduri Wines
Santa Rosa, California
707-578-3882
707-578-3884 (fax)
www.siduri.com

Silverado Vineyards
Napa, California
707-257-1770 or 800-997-1770
707-257-1538 (fax)
www.silveradovineyards.com

Sonoma-Cutrer Vineyards
Windsor, California
707-528-1181
707-528-1561 (fax)
www.sonomacutrer.com

St. Supery
Rutherford, California
Rutherford, CA 94573
707-963-4507 or 800-942-0809
707-963-4526 (fax)
www.stsupery.com

Stag's Leap Wine Cellars
Napa, California
707-944-2020 or 866-422-7523
707-257-7501 (fax)
www.cask23.com

Stonegate Winery
Calistoga, California
800-946-6500
707-942-9721 (fax)
www.stonegatewinery.com

Stonestreet
Healdsburg, California
707-433-9463 or 800-355-8008
707-433-9469 (fax)
www.stonestreetwines.com

Stony Hill Vineyard
St. Helena, California
707-963-2636
707-963-1831 (fax)
www.stonyhillvineyard.com

Swanson Vineyards
Rutherford, California
707-967-3500
707-967-3505 (fax)
www.swansonvineyards.com

Robert Talbott Vineyards
Gonzales, CA
831-675-3000
831-675-3120 (fax)
www.talbottvineyards.com

Trefethen Vineyards
Napa, California
707-255-7700
707-255-0793 (fax)
www.trefethen.com

T-Vine Cellars
Calistoga, California
707-942-8685
707-942-8685 (fax)

Vinum Cellars
Oakville, California
415-863-0516 or 888-66-VINUM
415-863-0512 (fax)
www.vinumcellars.com

Voss Vineyards
Napa, California
707-259-0993
707-259-1510 (fax)
www.vossvineyards.com

## COLORADO

*Plum Creek Cellars*
Palisade, Colorado
970-464-7586
970-464-0457 (fax)

*S. Rhodes\**
Hotchkiss, Colorado
970-527-5185 (phone and fax)

*Terror Creek Winery*
Paonia, Colorado
970-527-3484 (phone and fax)

## ILLINOIS

*GenKota Winery*
Mt. Vernon, Illinois
618-246-WINE
618-246-9465 (fax)
www.genkotawine.com

*Owl Creek Vineyard*
Cobden, Illinois
618-893-2557 (phone and fax)
www.owlcreekvineyard.com

## MASSACHUSETTS

*Westport Rivers Vineyard & Winery*
Westport, Massachusetts
508-636-3423
508-636-4133 (fax)
www.westportrivers.com

## MICHIGAN

*Bel Lago*
Cedar, Michigan
231-228-4800
231-228-4888 (fax)
www.bellago.com

*Black Star Farms*
Suttons Bay, Michigan
231-271-4970
231-271-2883 (fax)
www.blackstarfarms.com

*Raftshol Vineyards*
Suttons Bay, Michigan
231-271-5650 (phone and fax)
www.raftsholvineyards.com

*St. Julian Wine Company*
Paw Paw, Michigan
800-732-6002
www.stjulian.com

## MISSOURI

*Mount Pleasant Winery*
Augusta, Missouri
800-467-WINE
636-228-4426 (fax)
www.mountpleasant.com

*Stone Hill Winery*
Branson, Missouri
Hermann, Missouri
888-926-WINE (Branson)
888-909-WINE (Hermann)
417-334-1942 (Branson fax)
www.stonehillwinery.com

## NEW JERSEY

*Tomasello Winery*
Hammonton, New Jersey
800-MMM-WINE
609-561-8617 (fax)
www.tomasellowinery.com

*Unionville Vineyards*
Ringoes, New Jersey
908-788-0400
908-806-4692 (fax)
www.unionvillevineyards.com

## NEW MEXICO

*Gruet Winery\**
Albuquerque, New Mexico
505-821-0055 or 888-857-9463
505-857-0066 (fax)
www.gruetwinery.com

## NEW YORK

*Anthony Road Wine Company, Inc.\**
Penn Yan, New York
315-536-2182 or 800-559-2182
315-536-5851 (fax)
www.anthonyroadwine.com

*Atwater Estate Vineyards*
Hector, New York
607-546-8463
607-546-8464 (fax)
www.atwatervineyards.com

*Bedell Cellars*
Cutchogue, New York
631-734-7537
631-734-5788 (fax)
www.bedellcellars.com

*Chateau LaFayette Reneau*
Hector, New York
607-546-2062 or 800-469-9463
607-546-2069 (fax)
www.clrwine.com

*Corey Creek Vineyards*
Southold, New York
631-765-4168
631-765-1845 (fax)
www.coreycreek.com

*Dr. Konstantin Frank's Vinifera
Wine Cellars and Chateau Frank
Champagne*
Hammondsport, New York
607-868-4884 or 800-320-0735
607-868-4888 (fax)
www.drfrankwines.com

*Fox Run Vineyards*
Penn Yan, New York
315-536-4616 or 800-636-9786
315-536-1383 (fax)
www.foxrunvineyards.com

Hermann J. Wiemer Vineyards
Dundee, New York
607-243-7971 or 800-371-7971
607-243-7983 (fax)
www.wiemer.com

Heron Hill Winery
Hammondsport, New York
607-868-4241 or 800-441-4241
607-868-3435 (fax)
www.heronhill.com

Hunt Country Vineyards*
Branchport, New York
315-595-2812 or 800-946-3289
315-595-2835 (fax)
www.huntcountryvineyards.com

Jamesport Vineyards
Jamesport, New York
631-722-5256
631-722-5256 (fax)
www.jamesport-vineyards.com

Keuka Overlook Wine Cellars
Dundee, New York
607-292-6877
607-292-6820 (fax)
members.aol.com/keukaoverl/
index.html"

Lamoreaux Landing Wine Cellars
Lodi, New York
607-582-6011
607-582-6010 (fax)
www.fingerlakes.net/lamoreaux

McGregor Vineyard and Winery
Dundee, New York
607-292-3999 or 800-272-0192
607-292-6929 (fax)
www.linkny.com/~mcg

Macari Vineyards and Winery
Mattituck, New York
631-298-0100
631-298-8373 (fax)
www.macariwines.com

Martha Clara Vineyards
Mattituck, New York
631-298-0075
631-298-5502 (fax)
www.marthaclaravineyards.com

Millbrook Vineyards and Winery
Millbrook, New York
845-677-8383 or 800-662-9463
845-677-6186 (fax)
www.millbrookwine.com

Palmer Vineyards
Riverhead, New York
631-722-9463
631-722-5364 (fax)
www.palmervineyards.com

Paumanok Vineyards
Aquebogue, New York
631-722-8800
631-722-5110 (fax)
www.paumanok.com

Pellegrini Vineyards
Cutchogue, New York
631-734-4111
631-734-4159 (fax)
 www.pellegrinivineyards.com

Prejean Winery
Penn Yan, New York
315-536-7524
315-536-7635 (fax)
www.prejeanwinery.com

Red Newt Cellars*
Hector, New York
607-546-4100
607-546-4101 (fax)
www.rednewt.com

Standing Stone Vineyards
Hector, New York
607-582-6051 or 800-803-7135
607-582-6312 (fax)
www.standingstonewines.com

Swedish Hill Vineyard
Romulus, New York
315-549-8326 or 888-549-9463
315-549-8477 (fax)
www.swedishhill.com

Wölffer Estate/Sagpond Vineyards
Sagaponack, New York
631-537-5106
631-537-5107 (fax)
www.wolffer.com

## NORTH CAROLINA
Biltmore Estate Wine
Asheville, North Carolina
828-225-1333 or 800-624-1575
828-274-6396 (fax)
www.biltmore.com

RayLen Vineyards and Winery
Mocksville, North Carolina
336-998-3100 (phone and fax)
www.raylenvineyards.com

Shelton Vineyards
Dobson, North Carolina
336-366-4724
336-366-4758 (fax)
www.sheltonvineyards.com

## OHIO
Chalet Debonné Vineyards
Madison, Ohio
440-466-3485
www.debonne.com

Markko Vineyard
Conneaut, Ohio
800-252-3197
440-599-7022 (fax)
www.markko.com

## OREGON
Adelsheim Vineyard
Newberg, Oregon
503-538-3652
503-538-2248 (fax)
www.adelsheimvineyard.com

Amity Vineyards
Amity, Oregon
503-835-2362 or 888-AMITY-66
503-835-6451 (fax)
www.amityvineyards.com

Andrew Rich Wines*
Portland, Oregon
503-284-6622
503-284-6622 (fax)

Archery Summit Winery
Dayton, Oregon
503-864-4300 or 800-732-8822
503-864-4038 (fax)
www.archerysummit.com

Argyle Winery / Dundee Wine
Company
Dundee, Oregon
503-538-8520 or 888-427-4953
503-538-2055 (fax)
www.argylewinery.com

Belle Pente
Carlton, Oregon
503-852-9500
503-852-6977 (fax)
www.bellepente.com

Bethel Heights Vineyard
Salem, Oregon
503-581-2262
503-581-0943 (fax)
www.bethelheights.com

Chateau Benoit
Carlton, Oregon
503-864-2991
503-864-2203 (fax)
 www.chateaubenoit.com

Chehalem
Newberg, Oregon
503-538-4700
503-537-0850 (fax)
www.chehalemwines.com

Cooper Mountain Vineyards
Beaverton, Oregon
503-649-0027
503-649-0702 (fax)
www.coopermountainwine.com

Domaine Drouhin
Dundee, Oregon
503-864-2700
503-864-3377 (fax)
www.drouhin.com

Domaine Meriwether
Eugene, Oregon
541-345-5224
541-431-0476 (fax)

Elk Cove Vineyards
Gaston, Oregon
503-985-7760 or 877-ELKCOVE
503-985-3525 (fax)
www.elkcove.com

Eola Hills Wine Cellars
Rickreall, Oregon
503-623-2405 or
1-800-291-6730
503-623-0350 (fax)
www.eolahillswinery.com

Erath Vineyards Winery
Dundee, Oregon
503-538-3318 or 800-539-9463
503-538-1074 (fax)
www.erath.com

Foris Vineyards Winery
Cave Junction, Oregon
800-843-6747 or 800-84-FORIS
541-592-4424 (fax)
www.foriswine.com

Ken Wright Cellars*
Carlton, Oregon
503-852-7070 or 800-571-6825
503-852-7111 (fax)
www.kenwrightcellars.com

King Estate Vineyards and Winery
Eugene, Oregon
541-942-9874 or 800-884-4441
541-942-9867 (fax)
www.kingestate.com

Patricia Green Cellars*
Newberg, Oregon
503-554-0821
503-538-3681 (fax)
www.patriciagreencellars.com

Ponzi Vineyards
Beaverton, Oregon
503-628-1227
503-628-0354 (fax)
www.ponziwines.com

Rex Hill Vineyards and Winery
Newberg, Oregon
503-538-0666 or 800-739-4455
503-538-1409 (fax)
www.rexhill.com

Sineann Cellars
St. Paul, Oregon
503-538-5894

Sokol Blosser Winery
Dundee, Oregon
503-864-2282 or 800-582-6668
503-864-2710 (fax)
www.sokolblosser.com

Torii Mor Winery
Dundee, Oregon
503-434-1439
503-434-5733 (fax)
www.toriimorwinery.com

Westrey Wines*
McMinnville, Oregon
503-434-6357
503-474-9487 (fax)

Witness Tree Vineyard
Salem, Oregon
888-478-8766
503-362-9765 (fax)
www.witnesstreevineyard.com

## PENNSYLVANIA
Blue Mountain Vineyards
New Tripoli, Pennsylvania
610-298-3068
610-298-8616 (fax)
www.bluemountainwine.com

Pinnacle Ridge Winery
Kuztown, Pennsylvania
610-756-4481
610-756-6385 (fax)
www.pinridge.com

## TEXAS
Alamosa Wine Cellars
Bend, Texas
915-628-3313
www.alamosawinecellars.com

Becker Vineyards*
Stonewall, Texas
830-644-2681
830-644-2689 (fax)
www.beckervineyards.com

Bell Mountain Vineyards
Fredericksburg, Texas
830-685-3297
830-685-3657 (fax)
www.bellmountainwine.com

Cap-Rock Winery
Lubbock, Texas
806-863-2704 or 800-546-9463
806-863-2712 (fax)
www.caprockwinery.com

Fall Creek Vineyards
Tow, Texas
915-379-5361
915-379-4741 (fax)
www.fcv.com

Grape Creek Vineyard, Inc.
Stonewall, Texas
Stonewall, TX 78671
830-644-2710
830-644-2746 (fax)
www.grapecreek.com

Llano Estacado Winery
Lubbock, Texas
806-745-2258
806-748-1674 (fax)
www.llanowine.com

Messina Hof Winery and Resort
Bryan, Texas
979-778-9463
979-778-1729 (fax)
www.messinahof.com

Pheasant Ridge Winery
Lubbock, Texas
806-746-6033
806-746-6750 (fax)
www.pheasantridgewinery.com

## VIRGINIA
Barboursville Vineyards
Barboursville, Virginia
540-832-3824
540-832-7572 (fax)
www.barboursvillewine.com

Jefferson Vineyards
Charlottesville, Virginia
434-977-3042
434-977-5459
www.jeffersonvineyards.com

Linden Vineyards*
Linden, Virginia
540-364-1997
540-364-3894 (fax)
www.lindenvineyards.com
Valhalla Wines
Roanoke, Virginia
540-725-WINE
540-772-7858 (fax)
www.valhallawines.com

## WASHINGTON
Arbor Crest Winery
Spokane, Washington
509-927-9894
509-927-0574 (fax)
www.arborcrestwinery.com

Bookwalter Winery*
Richland, Washington
509-627-5000 or 877-667-8300
509-627-5010 (fax)
www.bookwalterwines.com

Cadence*
Seattle, Washington
206-381-9507
206-860-9906 (fax)
www.cadencewinery.com

Canoe Ridge Vineyard
Walla Walla, Washington
509-527-0885
509-527-0886 (fax)
www.canoeridgevineyard.com

Cayuse Vineyards*
Walla Walla, Washington
509-526-0686
509-526-4686 (fax)
www.cayusevineyards.com

Chateau Ste. Michelle
Woodinville, Washington
425-488-1133
425-415-3657 (fax)
www.ste-michelle.com

Chinook Wines*
Prosser, Washington
509-786-2725
509-786-2777 (fax)

Covey Run Vintners
Zillah, Washington
509-829-6235
509-829-6895 (fax)
www.coveyrun.com

DeLille Cellars/Chaleur Estate*
Woodinville, Washington
425-489-0544
425-402-9295 (fax)
www.delillecellars.com

Domaine Ste. Michelle of Stimson
Lane Vineyards and Estates
Woodinville, Washington
425-488-1133 or 866-701-3187
425-415-3657 (fax)
www.domaine-ste-michelle.com

Dunham Cellars
Walla Walla, Washington
509-529-4685
509-529-1219 (fax)
www.dunhamcellars.com

Glen Fiona
Walla Walla, Washington
509-522-2566
509-526-5299 (fax)
www.glenfiona.com

Hedges Cellars*
Issaquah, Washington
425-391-6056 or 800-859-9463
425-391-3827 (fax)
www.hedgescellars.com

Hogue Cellars
Prosser, Washington
509-786-4557
509-786-4580 (fax)
www.hogue-cellars.com

Kiona Vineyards Winery
Benton City, Washington
509-588-6716
509-588-3219 (fax)

L'Ecole N° 41*
Lowden, Washington
509-525-0940
509-525-2775 (fax)
www.lecole.com

McCrea Cellars
Rainier, Washington
Rainier, WA 98576
360-458-9463
360-458-8559 (fax)
www.mccreacellars.com

Pepper Bridge Winery
Walla Walla, Washington
509-525-6502
509-525-9227 (fax)
www.pepperbridge.com

Terra Blanca Vintners
Benton City, Washington
509-588-6082
509-588-2634 (fax)
www.terrablanca.com

Washington Hills Cellars
Sunnyside, Washington
509-839-WINE or 800-814-7004
509-839-6155 (fax)
www.washingtonhills.com

Waterbrook Winery *
Walla Walla, Washington
509-522-1262 or 509-526-4343
509-529-4770 (fax)
www.waterbrook.com

Woodward Canyon Winery
Lowden, Washington
509-525-4129
509-522-0927 (fax)
www.woodwardcanyon.com

**WISCONSIN**
Wollersheim Wines
Sauk City, Wisconsin
1-800-VIP-WINE
608-643-6515
608-643-8049 (fax)
www.wollersheim.com

# RESOURCES

*information and organizations*

## CHEESE RESOURCES

*American Cheese Society*
FSA Group
304 West Liberty Street, Suite 201
Louisville, Kentucky 40202
502-583-3783
502-589-3602 (fax)
www.cheesesociety.org
The American Cheese Society is a
nonprofit organization that
encourages the understanding,
appreciation, and promotion of
America's farmstead and natural
specialty cheeses.

*American Dairy Association (Dairy
Management Incorporated)*
10255 West Higgins Road
Rosemont, Illinois 60018
847-803-2000
847-803-2077 (fax)
www.ilovecheese.com

*California Milk Advisory Board*
400 Oyster Point Boulevard
Suite 214
South San Francisco, California
94080
650-871-6459
650-583-7328 (fax)
www.realcaliforniacheese.com

*Great Cheeses of New England*
(New England Dairy Promotion
Board)
156 Worcester/Providence Rd.
Suite 26
Sutton, Massachusetts 01590
508-865-6336
508-865-6222 (fax)
www.newenglandcheese.com

*New England Cheesemaking Supply*
P.O. Box 85
Ashfield, Massachusetts 01330
413-628-3808
413-628-4061 (fax)
www.cheesemaking.com
One-stop shopping for cheesemaking supplies for the home and
professional cheesemaker

*Oldways Preservation &
Exchange Trust*
266 Beacon Street
Boston, Massachusetts 02116
617-421-5500
617-421-5511 (fax)
www.oldwayspt.org

*Slow Food USA*
434 Broadway, 7th floor
New York, New York 10013
212-965-5640
212-226-0672 (fax)
www.slowfood.com

*Vermont Cheese Council*
116 State Street
Montpelier, Vermont 05620
888-523-7484
www.vtcheese.com

*Wisconsin Milk Marketing Board*
8418 Excelsior Drive
Madison, Wisconsin 53717
608-836-8820 or 800-373-9662
608-836-5822 (fax)
www.wisdairy.com

*Wisconsin Specialty Cheese
Institute*
P.O. Box 233
Monroe, Wisconsin 53566
608-329-3922
608-328-2120 (fax)
www.wisspecialcheese.org

## CHEESE WEBSITES
*www.cheese.com*
Resource and information about
cheese

*www.cheesenet.wgx.com*
Information about cheeses around
the world

*www.projecttruffle.com*
Sells American and other artisan
cheeses

*entertaining.about.com/es/
cheeseinformation*

## WINE RESOURCES

### ARIZONA
*Arizona Wine Growers Association*
P.O. Box 181
Vail, Arizona 85641
520-762-8585
520-762-8586 (fax)
www.arizonawine.org

## CALIFORNIA

*Amador Vintner's Association*
P.O. Box 667
Plymouth, California 95669
209-267-2297 or 888-655-8614
209-267-2298 (fax)
www.amadorwine.com

*Calavaras Wine Association*
P.O. Box 2492
Murphys, California 95247
800-225-3764
209-728-3418 (fax)
www.calaveraswines.org

*California Association of Winegrape Growers*
555 University Avenue, Suite 250
Sacramento, California 95825
916-924-5370 or 800-241-1800
916-924-5374 (fax)
www.cawg.org

*COPIA*
*The American Center for Wine, Food & the Arts*
500 First Street
Napa, California 94559
707-259-1600 or 888-51-COPIA
www.copia.org

*El Dorado Winery Association*
P.O. Box 1614
Placerville, California 95667
800-306-3956
530-295-2009 (fax)
www.eldoradowines.org

*Mendocino County Alliance*
525 S. Main Street, Suite E
Ukiah, California 95482
707-462-7417 or 866-goMendo
707-468-9887 (fax)
www.gomendo.com

*Monterey County Vintners & Growers Association*
P.O. Box 1793
Monterey, California 93942-1793
831-375-9400
831-375-1116 (fax)
www.montereywines.org

*Napa Vintner's Association*
P.O. Box 141
St. Helena, California 94574
707-963-3388
707-963-3488 (fax)
www.napavintners.com

*Santa Barbara County Vintners' Association*
Post Office Box 1558
Santa Ynez, California 93460-1558
805-688-0881 or 800-218-0881
805-686-5881 (fax)
www.sbcountywines.com

*Santa Cruz Mountains Winegrowers Association*
7605-A Old Dominion Court
Aptos, California 95003
831-479-9463
831-688-6961 (fax)
www.scmwa.com

*Sonoma County Wineries Association*
5000 Roberts Lake Road
Rohnert Park, California 94928
707-586-3795
www.sonomawine.com

## COLORADO

*Colorado Wine Industry*
Development Board
4550 Sioux Drive
Boulder, Colorado 80303
720-304-3406
720-304-3405 (fax)
www.coloradowine.com

## ILLINOIS

*The Illinois Grape & Wine Resources Council*
14931 State Highway 37
Whittington, Illinois 62897
www.illinoiswine.org

## MICHIGAN

*Michigan Grape and Wine Industry Council*
P.O. Box 30017
Lansing, Michigan 48909
517-373-1104
517-335-7071 (fax)
www.michiganwines.com

## MISSOURI

*Missouri Department of Agriculture & Market Development Division Grape & Wine Program*
P.O. Box 630
Jefferson City, Missouri 65102
800-392-WINE
www.missouriwine.org

## NEW JERSEY

*Garden State Wine Growers Association*
www.newjerseywines.com

## NEW YORK

*Long Island Wine Council*
P.O. Box 74
Peconic, New York 11958
631-369-5887 or 631-765-9528
631-765-6237 (fax)
www.liwines.com

*New York Wine Cork*
55 Baker Road
Granville, New York 12832
518-632-9260 or 877-302-WINE
www.nywinecork.com

New York Wine & Grape Foundation
Penn Yan, New York 14527
315-536-7442
315-536-0719 (fax)
www.nywine.com

## NORTH CAROLINA

North Carolina Grape Council
P.O. Box 27647
Raleigh, North Carolina 27611
919-733-7125
919-715-0155 (fax)
www.ncwine.org

## OHIO

The Ohio Wine Producers
Association
P.O. Box 157
822 North Tote Road
Austinburg, Ohio 44010
440-466-4417 or 800-227-6972
440-466-4427 (fax)
www.ohiowines.org

## OREGON

Oregon Wine Advisory Board
1200 NW Naito Parkway,
Suite 400
Portland, Oregon 97209
503-228-8336
503-228-8337 (fax)
www.oregonwine.org

## PENNSYLVANIA

Pennsylvania Wine Association
411 Walnut Street
Harrisburg, Pennsylvania 17101
1-877-472-9463
610-379-9480 (fax)
www.pennsylvaniawine.com

## TEXAS

Texas Wine and Grapegrowers
Association (TWGGA)
701 S. Main Street
Grapevine, Texas 76051
817-424-0570
817-251-4329 (fax)
www.twgga.org

The Wine Society of Texas
2318 Huldy Street
Houston, Texas 77019
1-877-WST-WINE
www.winesocietyoftexas.org

## VIRGINIA

Virginia Wine Marketing Program
P.O. Box 1163
Richmond, Virginia 23218
800-828-4637
www.virginiawine.org

## WASHINGTON

Washington Wine Commission
93 Pike Street, Suite 315
Seattle, Washington 98101
206-667-9463
206-583-0573 (fax)
www.washingtonwine.org

## WISCONSIN

Wisconsin Winery Association
7600 Terrace Avenue, Suite 203
Middleton, Wisconsin 53562
866-947-9463 (toll free)
608-831-1152
608-831-5122 (fax)
www.wiswine.com

## NATIONAL
## ORGANIZATIONS

American Institute of Wine and
Food
304 West Liberty Street, Suite 201
Louisville, Kentucky 40202
502-992-1022 or 800-274-AIWF
(2493)
502-589-3602 (fax)
www.aiwf.org

Free the Grapes!
3316 Jefferson Street
Napa, CA 94558
707-254-9292
707-254-2433 (fax)
www.freethegrapes.org
An organization dedicated to
streamlining the wine distribution
and shipping system in the United
States to make wine more readily
available to all consumers, regardless of where they live.

University of California Davis
One Shields Avenue
Davis, California 95616-8749
530-752-0380
530-752-0382 (fax)
wineserver.ucdavis.edu
Viticulture and Enology

Wine Institute
425 Market Street, Suite 1000
San Francisco, California 94105
415-512-0151
415-442-0742 (fax)
www.wineinstitute.org

WineAmerica
1200 G Street NW, Suite 360
Washington, DC 20005
800-879-4637
202-347-6341 (fax)
www.americanwineries.org

Wine Market Council
www.winemarketcouncil.com
A nonprofit association of grape
growers, wine producers,
importers, wholesalers, and other
affiliated businesses and organizations devoted to consumer wine
education.

## WINE WEBSITES

www.bluewine.com
A wine spirits portal

www.ewine.com
Gives online web sites for all
wine-related companies

www.hiddenwineries.com
A guide to small wineries around
the United States

www.travelenvoy.com/wine.htm
A guide to wineries, wines, and
wine destinations around the
world

www.vine2wine.com
A wine directory

www.wineaccess.com

www.wineanswers.com
Part of the Wine Market Council,
this site gives loads of information
about almost every aspect of wine.

www.winecountry.com
A guide to the wine regions of
California

## SELECTED CHEESE RETAILERS ACROSS THE COUNTRY

### ARIZONA
AJ's Fine Foods
Phoenix, Arizona
602-230-7015
602-230-2910 (fax)
www.ajsfinefoods.com

Chez Eynard Ltd
Phoenix, Arizona
602-260-2433

Duck & Decanter (2 locations)
Phoenix, Arizona
602-274-5429
602-274-5672 (fax)
www.duckanddecanter.com
(cheese and wine)

Two Sisters Gourmet Foods
Phoenix, Arizona
602-955-5369

### CALIFORNIA
Andronico's Market
510-524-2696
Locations throughout Northern
California
www.andronicos.com

Artisan Cheese Shop
San Francisco, California
415-929-8610
415-929-8619 (fax)

Bristol Farms
(several locations throughout
Southern California)
El Segundo, California (corporate
office)
310-726-1300
310-726-1339 (fax)
www.bristolfarms.com

The Cheese Board Co-Op
Berkeley, California
510-549-3183

The Cheese Course
Healdsburg, California
707-433-4998
707-433-4896 (fax)

The Cheese Shop in the Carmel
Plaza
Carmel, California
831-625-2272
831-625-2272 (fax)
(cheese and wine)

The Cheese Store of Beverly Hills
Beverly Hills, California
310-278-2855 or 800-547-1515
310-278-3429 (fax)
www.cheesestorebh.com

Coopers Gourmet
San Francisco, California
415-934-9463
415-934-6644 (fax)
www.coopersgourmet.com

Dean & Deluca
St. Helena, CA
707-967-9980
www.deandeluca.com
(cheese and wine)

Full of Life (Whole Foods)
Claremont, California
909-624-3420
909-624-2620 (fax)

Oakville Grocery
(several locations throughout
Northern California)
Oakville, California
707-944-8802 or 800-736-6602
707-944-1844 (fax)
www.oakvillegrocery.com
(cheese and wine)

Pasta Shop (2 locations)
Oakland, California
510-547-4005
510-652-4669 (fax)
www.rockridgemarkethall.com

Rainbow Grocery
San Francisco, California
415-863-0620
415-863-8955
www.rainbowgrocery.org

Tomales Bay Foods
Point Reyes Station, California
415-663-9335
415-633-5418 (fax)
www.cowgirlcreamery.com

*Wally's*
Los Angeles, California
310-475-0606 or 888-992-5597
310-474-1450 (fax)
www.wallyswine.com
(cheese and wine)

*The Wine House*
Los Angeles, California
310-479-3731 or 800-626- 9463
310-478-5609 (fax)
www.winehouse.com
(cheese and wine)

## COLORADO
*Marczyk Fine Foods*
Denver, Colorado
303-894-9499
303-894-9491 (fax)
www.marczyk.com

*The Truffle, Inc.*
Denver, Colorado
303-322-7363
303-322-7363 (fax)
www.denvertruffle.com

*Wild Oats Corporate Headquarters*
(several locations around the
country)
Boulder, Colorado
303-440-5220 or 800-494- 9453
303-928-0022 (fax)
www.wildoats.com

## CONNECTICUT
*Darien Cheese and Fine Foods*
Darien, Connecticut
203-655-4344

*The Good Food Store*
Darien, Connecticut
203-655-7355 or 888-343-1113
203-662-9249 (fax)
www.thegoodfoodstore.com

*Say Cheese Too!* (2 locations)
West Hartford, Connecticut
860-233-7309 or 888-243-3373
860-233-7342 (fax)
www.saycheese-lgp.com

## FLORIDA
*Miami Epicure Market*
Miami Beach, Florida
305-672-1861 or 800-232-3218
305-672-0479 (fax)
www.epicuremarket.com

## GEORGIA
*Star Provisions*
Atlanta, Georgia
404-365-0410
404-365-8020 (fax)
www.starprovisions.com

## ILLINOIS
*Chalet on the Gold Coast*
Chicago, Illinois
312-787-8555
312-787-92669 (fax)

*Dominick's Finer Foods &
Dominick's Fresh Stores*
Several locations throughout
Illinois; 1 location in Indiana
708-492-5443
www.dominicks.com

*Don's Finest Foods*
Lake Forest, Illinois
847-234-2700
847-234-7038
www.donsfinestfoods.com

*Fox and Obel*
Chicago, Illinois
312-410-7301
312-410-7305 (fax)
www.fox-obel.com

*Sam's Wine and Spirits*
Marcey Street Market inside Sam's
Wine and Spirits
Chicago, Illinois
312-664-4394
312-867-3237 (fax)
www.sams-wine.com
(cheese and wine)

## INDIANA
*The Cheese Shop*
8702 Keystone Crossing
Indianapolis, Indiana 46240
317-846-6885
317-846-6932 (fax)
www.thecheeseshop.com

## KENTUCKY
*Party Source* (5 other stores in
Kentucky)
Bellevue, Kentucky
859-291-4007
859-291-4147 (fax)
www.thepartysource.com
(cheese and wine)

## LOUISIANA
*Lakeview Fine Foods*
New Orleans, Louisiana
504-482-7333
504-488-0510 (fax)

*Spice, Inc.*
1051 Annunciation Street
New Orleans, Louisiana 70130
504-558-9992
www.spiceinc.com

*The Wine & Cheese Shop*
Baton Rouge, Louisiana
225-926-8847
225-926-8848 (fax)
www.thewineandcheeseshop.com

## MAINE

*Horton's Naturally Smoked*
Seafoods at the Portland Market
(yes, they sell cheese!)
Portland, Maine
207-228-2056
www.portlandmarket.com or
www.hortons.com

## MARYLAND

*Sutton Place Gourmet*
Bethesda, Maryland
301-564-6006 or 800-346-7863
301-493-5947 (fax)
www.suttongourmet.com
(Other locations include Balducci's
in New York and Hay Day Country
Farm Markets in New York and
Connecticut)

## MASSACHUSETTS

*Fine Wine Cellars of Chestnut Hill*
Boston, Massachusetts
617-232-1020
617-739-2520 (fax)
(cheese and wine)

*Formaggio Kitchen, Inc.*
(2 locations)
Cambridge, Massachusetts
617-354-4750 or 888-212-3224
617-547-5680 (fax)
www.formaggiokitchen.com

*The Richmond Store Grocers*
Richmond, Massachusetts
413-698-8698
413-698-8688 (fax)

*Savenor's Market*
Boston, Massachusetts
617-723-6328
617-367-0753 (fax)

*The Seasonal Table*
Boston, Massachusetts
617-236-7979
617-247-6556 (fax)
www.seasonaltable.com
(cheese and wine)

*University Wine Shop* (2 locations)
Cambridge, Massachusetts
617-547-4258
617-576-0135 (fax)
sites.netscape.net/university-
wine/home
(cheese and wine)

*Wasik's Cheese Shop*
Wellesley, Massachusetts
781-237-0916

## MICHIGAN

*R Hirt Jr. Company*
Detroit, Michigan
877-840-2327
313-567-8123 (fax)
www.rhirt.com

*Royal Oak*
Holiday Market
Royal Oak, Michigan
248-541-1414
248-541-5829 (fax)
www.holiday-market.com

*Zingerman's*
Ann Arbor, Michigan
734-663-3354 or 888-636-8162
734-930-1942 (fax)
www.zingermans.com

## MINNESOTA

*Kowalski's Market*
(several locations)
Woodbury, Minnesota
651-578-8800
651-578-0600 (fax)
www.kowalskis.com

*Lund's and Byerly's*
(several locations)
Minneapolis, Minnesota
612-825-2440 or 952-927-3663
(corporate number)
612-825-7812 (fax)
www.lundsmarket.com
www.byerlys.com

*Surdyk's*
Minneapolis, Minnesota
612-379-3232 or 612-379-9757
612-379-7511 (fax)
www.surdyks.com
(cheese and wine)

## MISSOURI

*The Better Cheddar* (2 locations)
Kansas City, Missouri
816-561-8204 or 888-561-8204
(toll-free)
816-561-5793 (fax)

*Provisions Gourmet Market*
St Louis, Missouri
314-989-0020
314-989-0021 (fax)
(cheese and wine)

*The Wine & Cheese Place*
(3 locations)
St. Louis, Missouri
314-962-8150
314-962-4291 (fax)
www.wineandcheeseplace.com
(cheese and wine)

*The Wine Merchant, Ltd.*
St. Louis, Missouri
314-863-6282 or 800-770-8466
314-863-5670 (fax)
www.winemerchantltd.com
(cheese and wine)

## NEBRASKA

*Broadmoor Market*
Omaha, Nebraska
402-391-0312
402-343-3634 (fax)

## NEW JERSEY

*Gary's Wine & Market Place*
(3 locations)
Madison, New Jersey
973-822-0200
973-822-3536 (fax)
www.garysmarket.com
www.garyswine.com
(cheese and wine)

## NEW MEXICO

*Juan Tabo Wild Oats Natural
Marketplace*
Albuquerque, New Mexico
505-275-6660
505-275-7102 (fax)

*Tesuque Village Market*
Tesuque, New Mexico
505-988-8848
505-986-0921 (fax)
(cheese and wine)

## NEW YORK

*Artisanal*
New York, New York
212-725-8585 or 212-532-4033

*Balducci's*
New York, New York
212-673-2600
212-982-4591 (fax)

*Citarella* (several locations)
New York, New York
212-874-0383 x 5535 or 718-
830-6366
212-595-3738 (fax)
www.citarella.com

*D'Amico Foods*
Brooklyn, New York
718-875-5403
718-875-0998
www.damicofoods.com

*Dean & Deluca*
New York, New York
212-226-6800 or 800-999-0306
www.deandeluca.com

*Fairway Market* (several locations)
New York, New York
212-595-1888
212-595-9843 (fax)

*Ideal Cheese Shop*
New York, New York
212-688-7579 or 800-382-0109
212-223-1245 (fax)
www.idealcheese.com

*Ithaca Bakery*
Ithaca, New York
607-273-7110
607-273-4253 (fax)

*Murray's Cheese Shop*
New York, New York
212-243-3289
212-243-5001 or
888-642-4339 (fax)
www.murrayscheese.com

*Price Chopper* (many locations
throughout the Northeast)
Schenectady, New York
(headquarters)
518-356-9445
518-357-0968 (fax)
www.pricechopper.com

*Tuller Premium Food*
Brooklyn, New York
718-222-9933
718-222-9939 (fax)

*Wegmans Food Markets (several
locations)*
Rochester, New York
585-328-2550
www.wegmans.com

*Zabar's*
New York, New York
212-787-2000 or 800-697-6301
212-580-4477 (fax)
www.zabars.com

## NORTH CAROLINA

*City Beverage*
Winston-Salem, North Carolina
336-722-2774
336-725-1481 (fax)
www.citybeverage.com
(cheese and wine)

*Dean & Deluca*
Charlotte, North Carolina
704-643-6868
www.dean-deluca.com

*Fowler's Gourmet*
Durham, North Carolina
919-683-2555 or 800-722-8403
919-956-8403 (fax)
www.fowlersfoodandwine.com
(cheese and wine)

*The Fresh Market*
(several locations)
Raleigh, North Carolina
919-828-7888
919-664-8255 (fax)

## OHIO

*Annemarie's Dairy at the West Side
Market*
Cleveland, Ohio
216-344-9333
www.westsidemarket.com/ven-
dors/Annemarie/

The Cheese Shop at the West Side
Market
Cleveland, Ohio
216-771-6349
www.westsidemarket.com

Dorothy Lane Market (2 locations)
Dayton, Ohio
937-434-1294
937-434-1299 (fax)
www.dorothylane.com

Jungle Jim's
Cincinnati, Ohio
513-829-1919
513-674-6001 (fax)
www.junglejims.com
(cheese and wine)

The Kroger Company
(numerous locations)
Cincinnati, Ohio
513-762-4877 or 513-697-8141
513-762-4372 (fax)
www.kroger.com

West Point Market
Akron, Ohio
330-864-2151 or 800-838-2156
330-869-8666 (fax)
www.westpointmarket.com
(cheese and wine)

OREGON

Cheshire Cat
Portland, Oregon
503-284-5226
503-284-7499 (fax)

Elephants Delicatessen
Portland, Oregon
503-224-3955
503-224-4097 (fax)
www.elephantsdeli.com
(cheese and wine)

Food Front Cooperative Grocery
Portland, Oregon
503-222-5658
503-227-5140 (fax)
www.foodfrontco-op.com

Pastaworks
Portland, Oregon
503-232-1010
503 221-3028 (fax)
www.pastaworks.com

Zupan's Market
(several locations)
Portland, Oregon
503-203-5962
www.zupans.com

PENNSYLVANIA

DiBruno Brothers
Philadelphia, Pennsylvania
215-922-2876 or 888-322-4337
215-922-2080 (fax)
www.dibruno.com

Downtown Cheese
Philadelphia, Pennsylvania
215-351-7412
215-351-6689 (fax)

McGinnis Sisters
Pittsburgh, Pennsylvania
412-884-2323
412-884-0331 (fax)
www.mcginnis-sisters.com

North Star Market
Bakerstown, Pennsylvania
(724) 443-7240

Pennsylvania Macaroni Company
Pittsburgh, Pennsylvania
412-471-8330
412-471-8318
www.pennmac.com

Pittsburgh Cheese Terminal
Pittsburgh, Pennsylvania
412-434-5800

SOUTH CAROLINA

O'Hara & Flynn Wine & Cheese
Merchants
(2 locations)
Charleston, South Carolina
843-534-1916
843-534-1778 (fax)
www.cris.com/~Maguire/
ohara&flynn
(cheese and wine)

TENNESSEE

Corner Market
Nashville, Tennessee
615-352-6772
615-352-3800 (fax)

TEXAS

Central Market (H-E-B)
(2 locations in Austin; 1 in San
Antonio)
Austin, Texas
512-206-1000 or 800-360-2552
www.centralmarket.com or
www.heb.com

EatZi's Market and Bakery
(locations also in Houston,
Atlanta, and Rockville, MD)
Dallas, Texas
214-526-1515
214-526-1540 (fax)
www.eatzis.com

Marty's
Dallas, Texas
214-526-7796
214-520-9576 (fax)
www.martysdfw.com
(cheese and wine)

Village Gourmet Market
San Antonio, Texas
210-402-4053
210-491-4446 (fax)

Whole Foods Market
Austin, Texas
512-477-4455 or 888-945-3637
www.wholefoods.com
Nearly 100 locations throughout
the United States
(Depending on location, also
operates under the name Fresh
Fields, Bread and Circus, Nature's
Heartland, Bread of Life, Merchant
of Vino, and Wellspring Grocery)

## UTAH
Tony Caputo's Market & Deli
Salt Lake City, Utah
801-531-8669
www.tonycaputos.com

Juhl Haus Market and Deli
Salt Lake City, Utah
801-582-7758
801-583-7836 (fax)
www.juhlhaus.com

Liberty Heights Fresh
Salt Lake City, Utah
801-467-2434
801-466-2491 (fax)
www.libertyheightsfresh.com

## VERMONT
Brattleboro Food Co-op
Brattleboro, Vermont
802-257-0183 or 802-257-0236
x 115
802-254-5360 (fax)
www.brattleborofoodcoop.org

Cheese Outlet/Fresh Market
Burlington, Vermont
802-863-3968 or 800-447-1205
802-865-1705 (fax)
www.cheeseoutlet.com
(cheese and wine)
Cheese Traders and Wine Sellers
South Burlington, Vermont
802-863-0143 or 800-540-4261
802-863-1928 (fax)
www.cheesetraders.com
(cheese and wine)

## VIRGINIA
The Cheese Shop
Williamsburg, Virginia
757-220-0298 or 800-468-4049
757-564-3927 (fax)

The Pottery Wine & Cheese Shop
(2 locations)
Williamsburg, Virginia
757-229-6754
757-229-6503 (fax)

River City Cellars, Inc.
Richmond, Virginia
804-355-1375
804-355-1381(fax)
www.rcc-wines.com
(cheese and wine)

Warwick Cheese Shoppe
Newport News, Virginia
757-599-3985
www.warwickcheese.com
(cheese and wine)

## WASHINGTON
De Laurenti Specialty Food Market
Seattle, Washington
206-622-0141
206-622-3262 (fax)
(cheese and wine)

Larry's Market
Seattle, Washington
206-527-5333
206-244-9663 (fax)
5 other locations in Washington

## WASHINGTON, DC
Dean and Deluca
Washington, DC
202-342-2500
202-342-2525 (fax)
www.dean-deluca.com

Sutton Place Gourmet
Washington, DC
202-363-5800
202-363-7060 (fax)
www.suttongourmet.com

## WISCONSIN
Brennan's Country Farm Market
(4 locations)
Madison, Wisconsin
608-233-2777
608-328-2719 (fax)

House of Wisconsin Cheese
Madison, Wisconsin
608-255-5204 or 800-955-0238
608-255-5321 or 800-458-8947
(fax)
www.houseofwisconsincheese.com

Larry's Market
Milwaukee, Wisconsin
414-355-9650 or 800-236-1307
414-357-4629 (fax)
www.larrysmarket.com

# SELECTED WINE RETAILERS ACROSS THE COUNTRY

## ALABAMA

*Classic Wine Company*
Homewood, Alabama
205-871-9463
205-871-9482

## ARIZONA

*AZ Wine Company*
Scottsdale, Arizona
480-423-9305
Phoenix, Arizona
www.azwineco.com

*Duck and Decanter* (2 locations)
Phoenix, Arizona
602-274-5429
602-274-5672 (fax)
www.duckanddecanter.com

*Epicurean Wine Service*
Scottsdale, Arizona
480-998-7800
480-367-8325 (fax)
www.epicureanwine.com

*The Rum Runner*
Tucson, Arizona
520-326-0121
www.rumrunnertucson.com

*Sportsman's Wines Spirits*
Phoenix, Arizona
602-955-7730
602-955-7739 (fax)
www.sportsmans4wine.com

*Wine Merchant*
Phoenix, Arizona
480-706-9885
480-706-9865 (fax)
www.onlinewinemerchant.com

## ARKANSAS

*Liquor World*
Fayetteville, Arkansas
501-587-0480
501-973-9448 (fax)

## CALIFORNIA

*All Seasons Wine Shop*
Calistoga, California
707-942-6828 or 800-804- 9463
707-942-9420 (fax)
www.allseasonswineshop.com

*Amphora Wine Merchants*
San Francisco, California
415-863-1104
415-863-0926 (fax)
www.amphorawine.com

*Arlington Wine and Spirits*
Kensington, California
510-524-0841
510-524-2308 (fax)

*Back Room Wines*
Napa, California
877-322-2576
707-226-3560 (fax)
www.backroomwines.com

*Beltramos Wines and Spirits*
650-325-2806 or 888-710-WINE
650-323-8450 (fax)
www.beltramos.com

*David Berkley Fine Wine and Specialty Foods*
Sacramento, California
916-929-4422
916-929-0066 (fax)
www.davidberkley.com

*Beverages & More!*
(various locations throughout California)
888-77-BevMo
www.bevmo.com

*Cannery Wine Cellar*
San Francisco, California
415-673-0400 x23/x12 or 800-756-9463 x23/x12
415-673-0461 (fax)
www.cannerywine.com

*Capitol Cellars*
Gold River, CA
916-853-3030
916-853-3031 (fax)
www.capitolcellars.com

*Coopers Gourmet*
San Francisco, California
415-934-9463
415-934-6644
www.coopersgourmet.com

*Dean & Deluca*
St. Helena, CA
707-967-9980
707-967-9983 (fax)
www.deandeluca.com
(cheese and wine)

*D & M Wines and Liquors*
San Francisco, California
415-346-1325 or 800-637-0292
415-346-1812 (fax)
www.dandm.com

*Draeger's Market* (3 locations)
San Mateo, California
650-685-3725 or 800-642-9463
650-685-3749 (fax)
www.draegers.com
(cheese and wine)

*Enoteca Wine Shop*
Calistoga, California
707-942-1117
707-942-1118 (fax)

Hi-Time Wine Cellars
Costa Mesa, California
949-650-8463 or 800-331-3005
949-631-6863
www.hitimewine.com

The Jug Shop
San Francisco, California
415-885-2922 or 800-404-9548
www.jugshop.com

K&L Wine Merchants
San Francisco, California
415-896-1734
415-896-1739 (fax)
www.klwines.com

Oakville Grocery
(several locations throughout
northern California)
Oakville, California
707-944-8802 or 800-736-6602
707-944-1844 (fax)
www.oakvillegrocery.com
(cheese and wine)

Pacific Wine Merchants
Upland, California
909-946-6782 or 800-871-6077
909-946-7004 (fax)
www.pacific-wine.com

Palisades Market
Calistoga, California
707-942-9549
707-942-6476
(cheese and wine)

Pasadena Wine Merchants
Pasadena, California
626-396-9234
626-396-0910 (fax)
www.pasadenawine.com

Rancho Cellars
Carmel, California
831-625-5646
831-625-5866 (fax)
www.ranchocellars.com

Red Carpet Wine
Glendale, California
800-339-0609
818-247-6151 (fax)
www.redcarpetwine.com

St. Helena Wine Center
St. Helena, California
707-963-1313 or 800-331-1311
707-963-8069 (fax)
www.shwc.com

Taylor's Market
Sacramento, California
916-443-6881
916-443-3663 (fax)
www.taylorsmarket.com

Terranova Fine Wines
Monterey, California
831-333-1313
831-649-4124 (fax)
www.terranovafinewines.com

Tra Vigne
St. Helena, California
707-963-4444
707-963-1233 (fax)
www.travignerestaurant.com

Vintage Wine and Spirits
Mill Valley, California
415-388-1626
415-388-4249 (fax)

Vintage Wines Ltd.
San Diego, California
858-549-2112
858-549-0557 (fax)
www.vintagewinessd.com

Wally's
Los Angeles, California
310-475-0606 or 888-992-5597
310-474-1450 (fax)
www.wallyswine.com

Wine Cask
Santa Barbara, California
805-966-9463 or 800-436-9463
805-568-0664 (fax)
www.winecask.com

The Wine Club (3 locations)
Santa Ana: 800-966-5432
San Francisco: 800-966-7835
Santa Clara: 800-678-5044
www.thewineclub.com

The Wine House
Los Angeles, California
310-479-3731 x260
310-478-5609 (fax)
www.wineaccess.com/
store/winehouse

The Wine Merchant
Beverly Hills, California
310-278-7322 or 800-621-8092
310-278-6158 (fax)
www.winemerchantbh.com

The Wine Rack
San Jose, California
408-253-3050
408-252-0223 (fax)
www.wineracksanjose.com

The WineSellar and Brasserie
San Diego, California
858-450-9557 or 888-774-WINE
858-558-0928 (fax)
www.winesellar.com

The Wine Shop
Healdsburg, California
707-433-0433
707-433-2389 (fax)

*Wine Vault*
Paso Robles, California
805-239-WINE
805-237-8455 (fax)
www.prwines.com

*The Wine House*
San Francisco, California
415-355-9463
415-355-1050 (fax)
www.winesf.com

## COLORADO

*Applejack Wine & Spirits*
Wheat Ridge, Colorado
303-233-3331or 800-879-5525
303-233-7542 (fax)

*The Boulder Wine Merchant*
Boulder, Colorado
303-443-6761
303-443-5938 (fax)
www.boulderwine.com

*City Wine Denver, Colorado*
303-393-7576
303-393-1725 (fax)
www.citywine.com

*Mondo Vino*
Denver, Colorado
303-458-3858
303-458-3857 (fax)
www.mondo-vino.com

*The Vineyard Wine Shop*
Denver, Colorado
303-355-8324
303-355-1413 (fax)
www.vineyardwineshop.com

## CONNECTICUT

*Amity Wine & Spirit Co., Inc.*
New Haven, Connecticut
203-387-6725
203-397-1414 (fax)
www.amitywine.com

*BevMax Bridgeport*
Bridgeport, Connecticut
203-333-5401
203-333-8124 (fax)
www.discountwinesct.com

*Cost Less Wines & Liquors*
Stamford, Connecticut
203-329-2900
www.costlesswl.com

*New Milford Spirit Shoppe*
New Milford, Connecticut
860-354-7712
860-355-5407 (fax)
www.newmilfordspirits.com

*Spiritus Wines*
Hartford, Connecticut
860-247-5431 or 800-499-9463
860-728-6920 (fax)
www.spiritus.com

*Surrey Wine Shop*
Farmington, Connecticut
860-677-0381
860-677-9044 (fax)
www.surreywine.com

*Warehouse Wines & Liquors*
Stamford, Connecticut
203-357-9151
203-359-9967 (fax)
www.warehousewinesct.com

*West Side Wines*
West Hartford, Connecticut
860-233-1241
860-233-1243 (fax)
www.westsidewines.com

## FLORIDA

*ABC Fine Wine & Spirits*
(150 locations)
Pembroke Pines, Florida
954-450-6632
www.abcfinewineandspirits.com

*Sunset Corners Fine Wines & Spirits*
Miami, Florida
305-271-8492
305-271-5390 (fax)

*Great Spirits Fine Wine*
Vero Beach, Florida
561-567-WINE
561-569-2977 (fax)

*Wine Watch*
Fort Lauderdale, Florida
800-329-WINE
954-523-9213 (fax)
www.winewatch.com

## GEORGIA

*The Grape Escape Wine Shoppe*
Atlanta, Georgia
404-843-9099
404-843-9778 (fax)
www.thegrapeescape.net

*Green's Discount Beverage Stores*
(2 other location in Georgia; 3 locations in South Carolina)
Atlanta, Georgia
404-321-6232
404-633-0232 (fax)
www.greensbeverages.com

*Happy Herman's*
Atlanta, Georgia
404-321-3012 1-866-271-3814 (outside of Atlanta)
404-633-5012 (fax)
www.happyhermans.com

Sherlock and Sanders Purveyors of
Fine Wines, Spirits & Beers
Atlanta, Georgia
404-233-1514
404-233-1678 (fax)
www.sherlocks.com

## IDAHO
Wine Sellers on the Mountain
(2 locations)
Sandpoint, Idaho
208-265-6300
www.winoworld.com

## ILLINOIS
Binny's on Grand
Chicago, Illinois
312-332-0012
312-329-9820 (fax)
www.binnys.com

Knightsbridge Wine Shoppe
Northbrook, Illinois
Phone: 847-498-9300
Fax: 847-498-4263
www.knightsbridgewine.com

Sam's Wine and Spirits
Chicago, Illinois
312-664-4394
866-SAMSWINES or
866-726-7946
312-664-7037 (fax)
www.samswine.com

## KENTUCKY
Liquor Outlet (several locations)
Louisville, Kentucky
502-447-6590
502-447-1194 (fax)
www.partysource-louisville.com

Old Town Liquors
Louisville, Kentucky
502-451-8591
502-451-7356 (fax)

Party Mart
Louisville, Kentucky
502-895-4446
502-893-9847 (fax)
www.partymartlouisville.com

The Party Source
Bellevue, Kentucky
859-291-4007
859-291-4147 (fax)
www.thepartysource.com

## LOUISIANA
Cellars of River Ridge
New Orleans, Louisiana
504-734-8455
504-734-7225

Martin Wine Cellar
New Orleans, Louisiana
504-899-7411 or 800-298-4274
504-896-7340
www.martinwine.com

The Wine & Cheese Shop
Baton Rouge, Louisiana
225-926-8847
225-926-8848 (fax)
www.thewineandcheeseshop.com

Wine Seller
New Orleans, Louisiana
504-895-3828
504-899-7619
www.wine-seller.net

## MAINE
Market Wines
Portland, Maine
207-828-0900
207-772-1743 (fax)
www.marketwines.com

Miranda's Vineyard
Portland, Maine
207-228-2016
207-228-2017 (fax)
www.portlandmarket.com

## MARYLAND
Roland Park Wines and Liquors
Baltimore, Maryland
410-366-1676
410-366-1706
www.rolandpark.com

The Wine Merchant
Lutherville, Maryland
410-321-6500
410-321-8951
www.thewinemerchant.org

## MASSACHUSETTS
Back Bay Wine & Spirits Inc.
Boston, Massachusetts
617-262-6571
617-262-1134 (fax)

Bauer Wines & Spirits
Boston, Massachusetts
617-262-0363
617-266-0871 (fax)
www.bauerwines.com

Beacon Hill Wine & Spirits
Boston, Massachusetts
617-742-8571
617-742-2224 (fax)

Federal Wine & Spirits
Boston, Massachusetts
617-367-8605
617-367-0451 (fax)
(cheese and wine)

Fine Wine Cellars of Chestnut Hill
Boston, Massachusetts
617-232-1020
617-739-2520 (fax)

Gary's Liquor
Chestnut Hill, Massachusetts
617-323-1122
617-323-6024 (fax)
www.garyswinesandspirits.com

*Nejaime's Lenox Wine Cellar*
(3 locations)
Lenox, Massachusetts
413-637-2221 or 800-946-3978
413-637-1941 (fax)
www.nejaimeswine.com

*State Road Liquor Mart* (dba Busa
Brothers Wine and Spirits; several
locations)
Burlington, Massachusetts
781-272-1050
781-272-0603 (fax)
www.busastateroad.com

*University Wine Shop* (2 locations)
Cambridge, Massachusetts
617-547-4258
617-576-0135 (fax)
sites.netscape.net/university-
wine/home

*Walpole Wine & Spirits*
Walpole, Massachusetts
508-668-3338
508-668-8650
www.walpolewine.com

## MICHIGAN
*Alban's Bottle & Basket of
Birmingham*
Birmingham, Michigan
248-258-5555
248-258-3262 (fax)
www.albans.com

*Gibb's World Wide Wines*
(2 locations in Detroit)
Detroit, Michigan
313-886-0670
313-886-0821 (fax)

*Merchant's Fine Wine*
Dearborn, Michigan
313-563-8700
313-563-1219 (fax)
www.merchantsfinewine.com

*Village Corner*
Ann Arbor, Michigan
734-995-1818
734-995-1826 (fax)
www.villagecorner.com

*Merchant's Fine Wine* (3 locations)
Grosse Point Woods, Michigan
313-417-0400
313-417-7274 (fax)
www.merchantsfinewine.com

## MINNESOTA
*Haskell's*
(5 other locations in Minnesota;
1 location in Naples, Florida)
Minneapolis, Minnesota
612-333-2434
612-342-2440 (fax)
www.haskells.com

*Liquor Depot*
Minneapolis, Minnesota
612-339-4040
612-339-2132 (fax)
www.liquordepot.com

*Surdyk's*
Minneapolis, Minnesota
612-379-3232
612-379-7511 (fax)
www.surdyks.com

*Sutler's Wines & Spirits*
Stillwater, Minnesota
651-439-3399
651-439-3400 (fax)
www.sutlers.com

## MISSOURI
*Berbiglia Wine & Spirits*
(several locations)
Kansas City, Missouri
816-942-0070
816-942-1777 (fax)
www.berbiglia.com

*The Vintage Room*
St. Louis, Missouri
314-FOR-WINE
314-533-4369 (fax)
www.corkdork.com

*The Wine & Cheese Place*
(3 locations)
St. Louis, Missouri
314-962-8150
314-962-4291 (fax)
www.wineandcheeseplace.com

## NEBRASKA
*The Spirit World*
Omaha, Nebraska
402-391-8680
402-391-4363 (fax)

*The Winery*
Omaha, Nebraska
402-391-3535
402-391-2713 (fax)

## NEVADA
*Las Vegas Wine Co.*
(2 locations)
Las Vegas, Nevada
702-434-2675

*Nevada Wine Cellar & Spirits*
Las Vegas, Nevada
702-222-9463
707-222-9763 (fax)
www.nvwinecellar.com

## NEW JERSEY

*Gary's Wine & Market Place*
(3 locations)
Madison, New Jersey
973-822-0200
973-822-3536 (fax)
www.garyswine.com

## NEW MEXICO

*Tesuque Village Market*
Tesuque, New Mexico
505-988-8848
505-986-0921 (fax)
(cheese and wine)

## NEW YORK

*Astor Wine & Spirits*
New York, New York
212-674-7500
212-673-1218 (fax)
www.astoruncorked.com

*Best Cellars*
(2 locations in Boston; 2 in
Washington state; and 1 in
Washington DC)
New York, New York
212-426-4200 or 800-624-6250
212-989-8530 (fax)
www.bestcellars.com

*Century Liquor Store*
Rochester, New York
585-621-4210
585-621-6227 (fax)

*Is-Wine*
New York, New York
212-254-7800
212-254-9357 (fax)
www.is-wine.com

*Morrell & Company*
New York, New York
212-262-7700
212-262-6547 (fax)
www.morrellwine.com

*Park Avenue Liquor*
New York, New York
212-685-2442
212-689-6247 (fax)
www.parkaveliquor.com

*Prime Wines*
Buffalo, New York
716-873-6688 or 800-666-6560
716-877-6589 (fax)

*Union Square Wines & Spirits*
New York City, New York
212-675-8100 or 877-675-8100
212-675-8663 (fax)
www.unionsquarewines.com

*Vintage New York*
New York City, New York
212-226-9463
212-226-8812 (fax)
www.vintagenewyork.com

## NORTH CAROLINA

*A Southern Season*
Chapel Hill, North Carolina
919-929-7133 or 800-253-3663
919-942-9274 (fax)
www.www.southernseason.com

*Carolina Wine Company*
Raleigh, North Carolina
919-852-0236 or 888-317-4499
919-852-0237 (fax)
www.carolinawine.com

*Fowler's Gourmet*
Durham, North Carolina
919-683-2555 or 800-722-8403
919-956-8403 (fax)
www.fowlersfoodandwine.com
(cheese and wine)

*Seaboard Wine Warehouse*
Raleigh, North Carolina
919-831-0850
919-831-2836 (fax)
www.seaboardwine.com

*The Wine Guy*
Ashville, North Carolina
828-254-6500
828-254-6500 (fax)
www.theashevillewineguy.com

*Wine N Things*
Raleigh, North Carolina
919-847-4986 or 877-571-5953
919-847-4673 (fax)
www.winenthings.com

## OHIO

*Chateau Pomije Wine Store*
Cincinnati, Ohio
513-871-8788
513-871-4735 (fax)
www.chatpom.com

*Dorothy Lane Market*
(2 locations)
Dayton, Ohio
937-434-1294 or 800-824-1294
937-434-1299 (fax)
www.dorothylane.com

*Hyde Park Gourmet Food & Wine*
Cincinnati, Ohio
513-533-4329
513-533-4328 (fax)
www.cincywine.com/
merchants/hpgfw
(cheese and wine)

*Jungle Jim's*
Cincinnati, Ohio
513-829-1919 or 877-770-4438
513-674-6001 (fax)
www.junglejims.com

Rozi's Wine House Inc.
Cleveland, Ohio
216-221-1119
216-221-1112 (fax)
www.rozis.com

The Wine Barrel
Cleveland, Ohio
440-442-8150
440-442-6646 (fax)
www.the-wine-barrel.com

## OREGON
Burlingame Market
Portland, Oregon
503-246-0711
503-246-0723 (fax)
www.burlingamemarket.com

Elephants Delicatessen
Portland, Oregon
503-224-3955
503-224-4097 (fax)
www.elephantsdeli.com
(cheese and wine)

750ml
Portland, Oregon
503-224-1432
503-224-1355 (fax)
www.750-ml.com

Vino
Portland, Oregon
503-235-8545 or 888-922-8545
www.vinobuys.com

## SOUTH CAROLINA
Gervais & Vine
Columbia, South Carolina
803-799-8463
803-799-8442 (fax)
www.gervine.com

O'Hara & Flynn Wine & Cheese
Merchants
(2 locations)
Charleston, South Carolina
843-534-1916
843-534-1778 (fax)
(cheese and wine)

Wine & Pine
Charleston, South Carolina
843-723-0447
843-723-0448 (fax)

The Wine Shop (2 locations)
Charleston, South Carolina
843-577-3881
843-577-2054 (fax)

## TENNESSEE
Buster's Liquors & Wines
Memphis, Tennessee
901-458-0929
901-324-3983 (fax)
www.bustersliquors.com

## TEXAS
The Austin Wine Merchant
Austin, Texas
512-499-0512
512-499-0558 (fax)
www.theaustinwinemerchant.com

The Cellar
Austin, Texas
512-328-6464
512-327-8333 (fax)
thecellar.ausinfo.com

Central Market (H-E-B)
(3 locations)
Austin, Texas
512-206-1000 or 800-360-2552
www.centralmarket.com or
www.heb.com
(cheese and wine)

Grape Vine Market
Austin, Texas
512-323-5900
512-374-1473 (fax)
www.grapevinemarket.com

Marty's
Dallas, Texas
214-526-7796
214-526-1140 (fax)
www.martysdfw.com

Sigel's Fine Wines & Great Spirits
(10 locations)
Dallas, Texas
214-739-4012
www.sigels.com
(cheese and wine)

Spec's Liquor Warehouse
(several other locations throughout the greater Houston area)
Houston, Texas
713-526-8787 or 888-526-8787
713-526-6129 (fax)
www.specsonline.com

Stoney's Wine & Gifts
Dallas, Texas
214-953-3067
www.stoneys.com

Whole Foods Market
(Approximately 100 locations
throughout the United States)
Austin, Texas
512-477-4455 or 888-945-3637
www.wholefoods.com
(cheese and wine)

WineSource
San Antonio, Texas
210-492-6634
www.winesourceonline.com

## VERMONT

*Cheese Outlet/Fresh Market*
Burlington, Vermont
802-863-3968 or 800-447-1205
802-865-1705 (fax)
www.cheeseoutlet.com
(cheese and wine)

*Cheese Traders and Wine Sellers*
South Burlington, Vermont
802-863-0413 or 800-540-4261
802-863-1928 (fax)
(cheese and wine)

*Wine Works*
Burlington, VT
802-951-WINE
802-865-9435
www.wineworks.net

## VIRGINIA

*The Curious Grape*
Arlington, Virginia
703-671-8700
703-671-0100 (fax)
www.curiousgrape.com

*Fine Wine.com* (2 locations)
McLean, Virginia
703-356-6500
703-356-6502 (fax)
www.finewine.com

*Market Street Wine Shop*
(2 locations)
Charlottesville, Virginia
804-979-WINE or 800-377-VINE
434-296-2432 (fax)
www.marketstreetwine.com

*The Pottery Wine & Cheese Shop*
Williamsburg, Virginia
757-229-6754
757-229-6503 (fax)
(cheese and wine)

*River City Cellars, Inc.*
Richmond, Virginia
804-355-1375
804-355-1381 (fax)
www.rcc-wines.com
(cheese and wine)

*Washington Street Purveyors*
Lexington, Virginia
540-464-9463 or 888-678-9463
www.gopherwine.com

*The Wine Seller*
757-564-4400
757-564-4402 (fax)
www.grapesbythecrate.com
(cheese and wine)

## WASHINGTON

*Arista Wine Cellars*
Edmonds, Washington
425-771-7009
425-778-6809 (fax)

*Champion Wine Cellars*
Seattle, Washington
206-284-8306
425-483-6534 (fax)
www.championwinecellars.com

*City Cellars Fine Wines*
Seattle, Washington
206-632-7238
206-632-5680 (fax)
www.citycellar.com

*De Laurenti Specialty Food Market*
Seattle, Washington
206-622-0141
206-622-3262 (fax)
(cheese and wine)

*Esquin Wine Merchants*
Seattle, Washington
206-682-7374 or 888-682-WINE
206-682-1545 (fax)
www.esquin.com

*Fine Wines, Ltd.*
Redmond, Washington
425-869-0869
425-861-0107 (fax)
www.finewinesltd.com

*The Grape Choice*
Kirkland, Washington
425-827-7551
425-803-6875 (fax)
www.thegrapechoice.com

*Madison Park Cellars*
Seattle, Washington
206-323-9333

*McCarthy & Schiering Wine*
Merchants
Seattle, Washington
206-524-9500
206-524-0310 (fax)

*Pete's of Bellevue*
Bellevue, Washington
425-454-1100
425-454-1392 (fax)
www.petes.cc

*Pike & Western Wine Shop*
Seattle, Washington
206-441-1307
206-441-1308 (fax)
www.pikeandwestern.com

*Seattle Cellars Limited*
Seattle, Washington
206-256-0850
206-256-0849 (fax)

*West Seattle Wine Cellars*
Seattle, Washington
206-937-2868
www.wscellars.com

## WASHINGTON, DC

*Addy Bassins MacArthur Beverages*
Washington, DC
202-338-1433
202-333-0806 (fax)
www.bassins.com

*Calvert Woodley*
Washington, DC
202-966-4400
202-537-5086
www.calvertwoodley.com

*Circle Wine & Liquor Inc.*
Washington, DC
202-966-0600
202-966-7680 (fax)
www.circlewinelist.com

## WISCONSIN

*Larry's Market*
Milwaukee, Wisconsin
414-355-9650 or 800-236-1307
414-357-4629 (fax)
www.larrysmarket.com

*Otto's Wine Cask*
Milwaukee, Wisconsin
414-354-5831
414-354-5971 (fax)

*Ray's Liquor*
Wauwatosa, Wisconsin
414-258-9821
414-258-5802 (fax)
www.raysliquor.com

*Star Liquor*
Madison, Wisconsin
608-255-8041
608-255-8051 (fax)
www.starliquor.com

# BIBLIOGRAPHY

Adams, Leon D. *The Wines of America*. 3d ed. New York: McGraw-Hill Book Company, 1985.

Apps, Jerry. *Cheese: The Making of a Wisconsin Tradition*. Amherst, Wis.: Amherst Press, 1998.

Cass, Bruce, (ed.). *The Oxford Companion to North American Wine*. Oxford, England: Oxford University Press, 2000.

Ewing-Mulligan, Mary, MW, and McCarthy, ed. *Wine for Dummies*, 2d ed. Foster City, Calif.: IDG Books Worldwide, 1998.

Lukacs, Paul. *American Vintage: The Rise of American Wine*. New York: Houghton Mifflin Company, 2000.

Mondavi, Robert, with Paul Chutkow. *Harvests of Joy: My Passion for Excellence How the Good Life Became Great Business*. Orlando, Fl.: Harcourt Brace & Company, 1998.

Robinson, Jancis, (ed.). *The Oxford Companion to Wine*. 2d ed. Oxford, England: Oxford University Press, 1999.

Stamm, Eunice R. *This History of Cheese Making in New York State*. New York: The Lewis Group Ltd., 1991.

Studd, Will. *Chalk and Cheese*. South Melbourne, Victoria, Australia: Purple Egg, 1999.

# METRIC CONVERSION CHART

## WEIGHT EQUIVALENTS

The metric weights given in this chart are not exact equivalents, but have been rounded up or down slightly to make measuring easier.

| Avoirdupois | Metric |
|---|---|
| ¼ oz | 7 g |
| ½ oz | 15 g |
| 1 oz | 30 g |
| 2 oz | 60 g |
| 3 oz | 90 g |
| 4 oz | 115 g |
| 5 oz | 150 g |
| 6 oz | 175 g |
| 7 oz | 200 g |
| 8 oz (½ lb) | 225 g |
| 9 oz | 250 g |
| 10 oz | 300 g |
| 11 oz | 325 g |
| 12 oz | 350 g |
| 13 oz | 375 g |
| 14 oz | 400 g |
| 15 oz | 425 g |
| 16 oz (1 lb) | 450 g |
| 1 ½ lb | 750 g |
| 2 lb | 900 g |
| 2 ¼ lb | 1 kg |
| 3 lb | 1.4 kg |
| 4 lb | 1.8 kg |

## VOLUME EQUIVALENTS

These are not exact equivalents for American cups and spoons, but have been rounded up or down slightly to make measuring easier.

| American | Metric | Imperial |
|---|---|---|
| ¼ t | 1.2 ml | |
| ½ t | 2.5 ml | |
| 1 t | 5.0 ml | |
| ½ T (1.5 t) | 7.5 ml | |
| 1 T (3 t) | 15 ml | |
| ¼ cup (4 T) | 60 ml | 2 fl oz |
| ⅓ cup (5 T) | 75 ml | 2 ½ fl oz |
| ½ cup (8 T) | 125 ml | 4 fl oz |
| ⅔ cup (10 T) | 150 ml | 5 fl oz |
| ¾ cup (12 T) | 175 ml | 6 fl oz |
| 1 cup (16 T) | 250 ml | 8 fl oz |
| 1 ¼ cups | 300 ml | 10 fl oz (½ pt) |
| 1 ½ cups | 350 ml | 12 fl oz |
| 2 cups (1 pint) | 500 ml | 16 fl oz |
| 2 ½ cups | 625 ml | 20 fl oz (1 pint) |
| 1 quart | 1 liter | 32 fl oz |

## OVEN TEMPERATURE EQUIVALENTS

| Oven Mark | F | C | Gas |
|---|---|---|---|
| Very cool | 250-275 | 130-140 | ½-1 |
| Cool | 300 | 150 | 2 |
| Warm | 325 | 170 | 3 |
| Moderate | 350 | 180 | 4 |
| Moderately hot | 375 | 190 | 5 |
| | 400 | 200 | 6 |
| Hot | 425 | 220 | 7 |
| | 450 | 230 | 8 |
| Very hot | 475 | 250 | 9 |

Riesling, late-harvest, 71
    pairing cheese with, 64, 71, 73, 79, 81
    profile of maker of, 86–87
Rinds:
    bloomy, 27, 42
    tending to, during aging, 15–16
Roche, La (Lazy Lady Farm), 262
Rollingstone Chèvre, 250–51
Romaine lettuce, in Caesar Fingers with
    Cheese Crisps, 101
Romano, 40
Rondo (Andante Dairy), 27, 170
Roquefort, 71
Roquefort-style cheeses, 34, 40, 81
Rouge et Noir label (Marin French Cheese
    Company), 232, 233
Rustic Blue (Bingham Hill Cheese
    Company), 62, 67, 141, 141–42

## S

Salad dressings:
    Caesar, 101
    Vinaigrette, 218
Salads:
    Caesar Fingers with Cheese Crisps, 101
    Caprese, on a Stick, 204, 205
    Chicken "Waldorf" Pitas, 212
    Cranberry Bean–Goat Cheese, Grilled
        Shrimp and, 218–19
    Watermelon-Feta, 225
Salsa, Plum, Pork and Cheddar Sandwiches
    with, 228, 229
Salt:
    in cheesemaking, 14
    in hard cheeses, 31–32, 80
    pairing cheese and wine and, 32, 65,
        67, 68, 70, 71, 80
Sandwiches:
    Camembert with Honey-Rhubarb
        Compote on French Rolls, 196, 214, 215
    Chicken "Waldorf" Pitas, 212
    Chile, Roasted, and Cream Cheese, 222
    Pork and Cheddar, with Plum Salsa,
        228, 229
    Two-Cheese Panini, 201
Sangiovese, 57
    pairing cheese with, 64, 65, 68, 70, 74,
        76, 77, 79, 80, 83
San Joaquin Gold (Fiscalini), 31, 226
Sauternes, 71
Sauvignon Blanc, 56, 71
    pairing cheese with, 65, 70, 74, 76, 77,
        82
    profiles of makers of, 93–94, 135–36,
        147, 165–66, 182–83, 223–24
Sauvignon Blanc, late-harvest, 71
    pairing cheese with, 71, 72, 73
Scamorza, 36
Schad, Judy, 28–30

Schloss (Marin French Cheese Company),
    232
Secondary fermentation, 49–50
Sediment, filtering and, 50
Semi-hard cheeses, 30–31
    list of, 39
    making, 13, 30
    pairing wine with, 63–64, 68, 78–79
    storing, 42–43
    what to look for, 39
    see also specific cheeses
Sémillon, 56
    pairing cheese with, 74, 82
    profiles of makers of, 182–83, 186–87
Semi-soft cheeses, 17, 26–27
    list of, 36
    pairing wine with, 63, 64–65, 68, 75
    storing, 41
    what to look for, 36
    see also specific cheeses
Serena (Three Sisters Farmstead Cheese),
    62, 189, 189–90
Serving:
    cheese, 45
    wine, 60
Seyval Blanc, 10, 56
    pairing cheese with, 82
    profiles of makers of, 192–94, 223–24
Sheepish Blue (Bingham Hill Cheese
    Company), 142
Sheeps' milk cheeses, 30, 34
    Garlic, and Green Olive Pizza, 131
    hard, 32
    Kumquat-Peppercorn Compote with,
        152, 167, 167
    pairing wine with, 67, 70, 71, 74, 77,
        79, 80, 82–83
    profile of producer of, 235–36
    ricotta, 26, 74, 236
    Ricotta, Wine-Soaked Melon with Herbs
        and, 240
    semi-hard, 79
    semi-soft, 26–27
    soft-ripened, 27, 28, 77
    Two-Cheese Panini, 201
Shepherd's Wheel (Old Chatham
    Sheepherding Company), 28, 77
Sherry, 54, 57
    pairing cheese with, 70, 71, 73, 78, 79,
        80, 81, 83
    profiles of makers of, 192–94
Shipping wine, 61
Shrimp, 53
    Cherry Tomatoes with Herbed Goat
        Cheese and, 95
    Grilled, and Cranberry Bean–Goat
        Cheese Salad, 218–19
Smell:
    flavor and, 51–53
    see also Aroma

Smokey Mountain Round (Goat Lady
    Dairy), 180
Snow Rose (Sweetwoods Dairy), 236
Soft cheeses. See Fresh or soft cheeses
Soft-ripened cheeses, 27–28, 38
    making, 15, 17
    pairing wine with, 63, 65, 68, 76–77
    storing, 42
    what to look for, 38
    see also specific cheeses
Sorbet, Crème Fraîche, 257
Soup, Cucumber, with Mint Pesto and Feta
    Cheese, 208, 209
South Mountain Products (Berkshire
    Blue), 34, 176–77
Spanish:
    Almonds, 158
    Pizza, Spicy, 146
Sparkling wines, 56, 59
    pairing cheese with, 64, 67, 76, 77, 80,
        81, 82
    profiles of makers of, 109–10
Spiced Eggplant with Baked Feta, 122
Spicy:
    Pecans, 157
    Spanish Pizza, 146
Spinach-Ricotta Filling, Artichoke Leaves
    with, 115
Spring Cheese (Port Madison Farm),
    258–59
Starter cultures, 13
Steel tanks, 48, 51
Stilton, 71
Stilton-type cheeses, 34, 40
Stirred-curd cheeses, 13–14
Storing:
    cheese, 40–45
    wine, 59–60
Strawberries, Balsamic-Drizzled, with
    Washed-Rind Cheese, 181
Stretched-curd cheeses (pasta filata), 14, 24
String cheese, 14
Sugar, 53
    level of, in grapes (Brix level), 47
    residual, 53, 71
Sweet Grass Dairy, 20, 26, 62, 113–14
Sweet wines, 53
    see also Dessert wines; specific wines
Sweetwoods Dairy, 32, 235–36
Swiss chard, in Swiss Pizza, 140
Swiss cheese, 30, 39, 42
    baby, 31, 39, 82–83
    pairing wine with, 78, 82–83
    Swiss Pizza, 140
Swiss Pizza, 140
Syrah, 54, 57
    pairing cheese with, 64, 67, 68, 70, 73,
        83
    profiles of makers of, 109–10, 123–24,
        128–29, 132–33, 165–66, 198–200